(continued from front flap)

States. By May of 1942, however, the British cabinet, determined to improve relations with Moscow, became convinced that recognition of Soviet sovereignty over these states would win Stalin's confidence and lead to closer wartime and postwar collaboration between the Soviet Union and the Western Allies. But, as Miner shows, this act of accommodation, along with London's other ill-advised attempts to win Moscow's trust, only encouraged the Soviets to demand further territorial concessions later in the war.

Drawing on British and American archival and published sources as well as newly available Soviet documents, Miner challenges the traditional view of Anglo-Soviet wartime relations, which holds that serious conflict between the two countries did not begin until 1943. He shows how disagreement over the Baltic States foreshadowed many of the later, better-known inter-Allied clashes—such as those over Poland and the Balkans—and argues that the origins of the Cold War are to be found in the earlier, not the later, disputes.

Steven Merritt Miner is assistant professor of history at Ohio University in Athens.

BETWEEN
CHURCHILL
AND STALIN

BETWEEN

CHURCHILL

AND STALIN

THE SOVIET UNION,

GREAT BRITAIN,

AND THE ORIGINS

OF THE GRAND

ALLIANCE

STEVEN MERRITT MINER

The University of North Carolina Press

Chapel Hill and London

© 1988 The University of North Carolina Press

Manufactured in the United States of America
The paper in this book meets the guidelines for
permanence and durability of the Committee on
Production Guidelines for Book Longevity of the
Council on Library Resources.

92 91 90 89 88   5 4 3 2 1

Library of Congress Cataloging-in-Publication Data

Miner, Steven Merritt, 1956–

   Between Churchill and Stalin.

   Bibliography: p.

   Includes index.

   1. World War, 1939–1945—Diplomatic history.

2. Great Britain—Foreign relations—Soviet Union.

3. Soviet Union—Foreign relations—Great Britain.

I. Title.

D750.M56   1988   940.53′2   88-4828

ISBN 0-8078-1796-1 (alk. paper)

To My Families

CONTENTS

ACKNOWLEDGMENTS

As is always the case with a first book, there are a great number of people to thank for their help, assistance, and encouragement during the research and writing of this work. In the first place, I would like to thank Professor F. L. Loewenheim, whose remark over dinner one evening led me to embark on this project and who gave invaluable advice and help at every stage of research and writing; I am deeply in his debt both for his kindness and for sharing some of his erudition with me. I must also thank Professor Gale Stokes, who showed enough faith to unleash me on this project; he, too, gave invaluable encouragement and support.

There are a great many people who read and commented on early versions of this work. Most notable among them are Professor Barbara Jelavich and Professor Robert F. Byrnes, both of whom read and suggested many alterations to the earlier, very rough drafts. Professor Charles Jelavich and Professor Yuri Bregel also read a portion of the manuscript and imparted many useful pieces of advice. My friends Hal Kosiba, James Felak, Sara Birtles, and Parris Hawkins also assisted me in many more ways than they know. To all of these people I am very grateful, and, though I owe to each of them many useful insights, all errors of omission or commission are of course entirely my own.

Most of all I should like to thank my families, to whom this book is dedicated. Both my own parents gave me unflinching support, even during the most difficult periods when my obsession must have been very tiring. I am particularly grateful to my mother, who not only typed two early drafts but also showed an almost inexplicable interest in the work itself. My in-laws also helped in countless ways, and I am especially grateful to James McMillan, my father-in-law, for the opportunity to draw on his deep knowledge of wartime Britain, which he shared with me in many memorable conversations.

Finally, I would like to thank my wife, Doreen, who endured a great deal of difficulty and uncertainty on my behalf. Without her support, I could not have achieved what little I have done. My daughter Emily, too, though fortunately for her still too young to be pressed into copyediting, has enriched both our lives and supported us without even knowing.

BETWEEN CHURCHILL AND STALIN

INTRODUCTION

Since the end of World War II, scholars have combed the history of wartime relations between the partners of the Grand Alliance, searching for the origins of the cold war. Historians seeking the causes of this conflict have returned again and again to the inter-Allied disputes, especially over Poland, that led directly to the breakup of the wartime alliance between Great Britain, the United States, and the Soviet Union. [1]

But looking backward in history to find the causes of later conflicts can distort the relative importance of events and issues. All the attention lavished on the Polish imbroglio and the other diplomatic quarrels regarding Eastern Europe and the Balkans has partially obscured the fact that many of the issues over which the Allies clashed in the final years of the war—Soviet territorial demands, the right of smaller nations to self-determination, and the balance of power in Europe, for example—had already arisen between 1940 and 1942 because of Stalin's earlier territorial claims, to the Baltic States, Bessarabia, and Bukovina. Most histories of the Cold War only treat this vital, formative period of the Grand Alliance as a prologue to the events of 1943 and after. [2]

Stalin's claim to the Baltic States may merely have been a "pawn," or an "opening gambit," heralding much wider demands, but for that reason alone the history of this dispute is worth examining. The diplomatic, political, and moral issues that eventually sundered Britain's wartime alliance with the USSR were all present and appeared in miniature during the Anglo-Soviet negotiations over Stalin's first wartime territorial claims, between 1940 and the spring of 1942. A study of this period sheds light on the reasons why the alliance between the USSR and the West did not, and could not, outlast the war.

This book examines Anglo-Soviet relations during two critical years, 1940–42, from the early days of the Nazi-Soviet Pact to the signing of the Anglo-Soviet Treaty. During these years the two nations were transformed from virtual enemies into allies, albeit not terribly close ones. The transformation was not smooth, and this is a history both of Stalinist diplomacy and of British attempts to develop a viable Soviet policy. It is, above all else, a story of how British leaders chased a diplomatic mirage, trying to gain Stalin's confidence by acceding to his early territorial demands, only to discover that by doing so they had undermined their ability to resist Soviet expansion later in the war.

Stalin's first territorial demands had a lengthy gestation; they sprang from the years immediately following World War I and from the humiliating territorial losses suffered by the Soviets at that time.[3] The victorious Allies excluded the Soviets from the Versailles Peace Conference and recognized the secession from the new Bolshevik state of many of the former Russian Empire's western dominions: Poland, the Baltic States, and other provinces, such as Bessarabia, which was seized by the Romanians, and parts of Belorussia, which the Poles acquired through the Treaty of Riga in 1921, at the end of the brief Russo-Polish War. Finland also established its independence. Most of the peoples in question took advantage of the Soviet state's temporary weakness to rid themselves of Soviet control, and the Western Allies, hostile as they were to Bolshevism, were happy to sanction Soviet losses.

As one historian notes, exclusion of the Soviets from the peace conference backfired, since it "allowed the Soviet statesmen to denounce freely what was indeed a very bad settlement."[4] And denounce it they did; the USSR's refusal to accept the postwar status quo provided a strong bond with other dissatisfied powers, primarily Germany, easing the diplomatic isolation of the revolutionary state. Cooperation between Weimar Germany and the Soviet Union, though not warm, bore fruit; although both nations were too weak to gain lost territory through joint efforts, they greatly assisted one another, especially in military matters.[5]

The USSR's relations with Britain were substantially colder than its ties with Germany. Stalin told the Fourteenth Congress of the Communist Party of the Soviet Union in December 1925 that "an Anglo-American union" dominated the world, and that the Soviet Union, which stood "at the head of the dissatisfied countries," should "work for rapprochement with the countries defeated in the imperialist war" to destroy this hegemony.[6] Throughout the 1920s and early 1930s, the Soviet press portrayed Britain, not without some justice, as unremittingly hostile to Bolshevism. As one former German diplomat stationed in Moscow for many years recalled, "England was . . . regarded as the chief representative of the capitalist world. . . . London, not Wall Street, was the one symbol which . . . epitomised the capitalist system."[7]

Hitler's accession to power started a "diplomatic revolution" in Europe. Detesting Bolshevism, the Führer cut short the German-Soviet partnership despite Moscow's determined efforts during 1933 and early 1934 to prolong it. The USSR turned in an unaccustomed direction—to the Western democracies—in an ultimately vain search for "collective security" and allies.[8] In September 1934, the USSR joined the League of Nations, having previously denounced that body as a tool of the satisfied powers. And in May 1935, the USSR signed with France a mutual assistance pact that fell far short of a full military alliance. In spite of these moves, however, the West and Moscow remained suspicious of each other. The Soviets found themselves diplomatically isolated, spurned by the Nazis yet not fully accepted by the Western democracies.

Collective security never took firm root, in part because Britain and France remained wary of Soviet intentions and almost as distrustful of Stalin as of Hitler. The all-too-rapid shift of the Comintern away from a policy of promoting revolution to one of cooperation with the West likewise did little to clear the path for East-West rapprochement.[9] At any rate, as bulwarks of the old order, Britain and France were unnatural allies for the Communist state. Only a common distrust of Hitler bound the three states uneasily together.

In 1938–39, Hitler once again transformed European diplomacy and severed the frail Soviet-Western partnership. On March 15, 1939, he invaded the rump of Czechoslovakia in violation of the Munich Agreement. Chamberlain's government, shocked by the invasion, abandoned its efforts to appease Hitler. It made what Churchill called a "right-about-turn," to draw the line against further German aggression by hastily guaranteeing Poland's frontiers against German attack, hoping that this gesture would deter Hitler.[10]

Chamberlain's abrupt reversal of policy was, in Churchill's words, "taken at the worst possible moment and on the least satisfactory ground."[11] By all accounts, Chamberlain was affronted by Hitler's invasion of Czechoslovakia, but anger is seldom a prudent counsel. The prime minister's fury is perhaps understandable, but the guarantee of Poland prior to the conclusion of an Anglo-Soviet agreement was a rash act.

Had the British better understood Joseph Stalin, they might have waited until they had reached an understanding with the Soviet Union before extending their guarantee to Poland. Leon Helfand, who defected from Russia's embassy in Rome in the summer of 1940, suggested to Neville Butler that "Stalin had been nibbling for an agreement with Hitler since

1933," but Hitler had not responded to Soviet overtures. For this reason, Helfand said, Stalin had been prepared to negotiate with the Western democracies. But Britain's "refusal to swallow the indirect aggression formula as regards the Baltic States" during the Anglo-Franco-Soviet talks of spring and summer 1939 had, Helfand claimed, caused Stalin to hold back, hoping that the Germans would offer a better deal.[12] This finally happened: the Nazi-Soviet pact was the result.

The indirect aggression formula to which Helfand referred was a demand made by the Soviets in 1939 that Britain and France should recognize the Soviets' right to defend themselves from any "indirect threat" emanating from the Baltic States. In effect, Moscow was claiming the right to occupy these states at any time it chose. The Allies felt themselves unable to accept such a formula, and therefore, as Helfand pointed out, the Allied-Soviet talks foundered.

Other equally important differences had prevented the USSR and the Western democracies from reaching an agreement: most important among these was the attitude of the Eastern European nations toward the two great powers that dominated the region, Nazi Germany and Soviet Russia. A rearmed Germany under the leadership of Hitler was clearly a threat to states such as Poland and Romania. But East European leaders were equally concerned about the intentions of the Communist giant, worried enough to forbid transit to Soviet troops in the event of a German invasion. London was sensitive to the concerns of these states, although Britain's military leaders were dubious about the strength of the recently purged Red Army. Chamberlain's government was unwilling to offer Stalin what he demanded in exchange for an alliance—territory.

Helfand's assertions contradicted the official Soviet explanation of the Nazi-Soviet Pact, which claimed, then as now, that the Munich Agreement "had shown the whole world that the official bourgeois democratic West was united in shutting its eyes to Hitler's aggression and channeling it to the East, in the direction of the USSR." Faced with such perfidy, the Soviets claimed, Stalin came to terms with Hitler, "having no better alternative for getting out of the situation that had arisen."[13]

Helfand told a different story. According to Neville Butler's account:

I asked [Helfand] whether the exclusion of Stalin from the Munich conversations had been a prime obstacle to an Anglo-Soviet agreement in 1939. He did not think so. He said that our great fault had been to give Poland the guarantee before we had got an agreement with Russia signed and delivered. He insisted that Stalin and Molotov believed that we should keep our word to Poland and therefore that the

Western Powers would embroil themselves without the Soviet needing to give any undertakings.

In the summer of 1939, Hitler ceased to ignore Soviet overtures. He wanted to settle his score with Poland, but the Western powers' guarantee of that country blocked his path. He needed a separate agreement with the USSR to avoid a two-front war. Thus, Stalin was thrust suddenly into a formidable bargaining position. He had two alternatives: either to conclude an alliance with the Western powers in an attempt to avert a war—and to win should war break out anyway—or to extract a high price from Hitler merely to stay out of a war that the Führer seemed intent on launching, preserving Soviet strength to act as arbiter once the warring parties had exhausted themselves. Both options were attractive when contrasted with the diplomatic isolation the USSR had endured during the 1930s. But allying with the West involved some risk: in the event of war, the Soviets might be left to fight Germany while Britain and France sheltered behind the Maginot Line. Nor could Moscow ignore the threatening situation in the Far East, where the Red Army and Japanese forces skirmished several times during 1938–39.[14]

As early as January 1925, in a speech to the Central Committee, Stalin had indicated what choice he would make in such a situation: "If war breaks out," he said, "we shall not be able to sit with folded arms. We shall take action, but we shall be the last to do so in order to throw the decisive weight into the scales, the weight that can turn the scales."[15]

The sudden Anglo-French guarantee of Poland blocked the only viable route for a German invasion of the USSR. The Allies provided the Soviet Union with a defensive buffer at no cost to Stalin, who could now afford to stall Britain and France diplomatically while waiting for a better German offer. When it finally came in August 1939, the price Hitler was willing to pay for Soviet quiescence was very high.

Stalin opted for the German proposal for at least two reasons. First, Hitler had no scruples of the sort which prevented the Western Allies from sanctioning Soviet territorial gains in exchange for an agreement, so Stalin was able to extract far more in concrete terms from a German connection. Second, Stalin did not share the view, common in the West, that a major war would be an unmitigated disaster. In fact, Bolshevik experience had taught that war, far from being calamitous, provided opportunities to expand Soviet power and influence.[16] From the Marxist perspective, war between rival imperialist powers was inevitable; if war was unavoidable, at least the Soviet Union could attempt to profit from the turmoil.

Stalin was not anxious to join the Western powers in defense of what he saw as an unsatisfactory status quo. As Soviet statesmen said repeatedly during the period of the Nazi-Soviet Pact, German and Soviet aims did indeed coincide. Stalin was remarkably frank about this when he spoke to the British ambassador, Sir Stafford Cripps, in July 1940: "During the pre-war negotiations with England and France," he said, "the USSR had wanted to change the old equilibrium, for which these countries stood, but . . . England and France had wanted to preserve it. Germany had also wanted to make a change in the equilibrium, and this common desire to get rid of the old equilibrium had created the basis for the rapprochement with Germany."[17]

In cooperation with Hitler, Stalin was able to shift the European balance of power better to suit his goals. As a result of the Nazi-Soviet Pact, the Soviet Union eventually annexed the three Baltic States, Bukovina, Bessarabia, parts of Finland, and much of what had been eastern Poland. Abundant evidence suggests that Stalin hoped to extend the scope of the pact beyond the confines of Europe.[18] This was certainly the opinion of Helfand, who told Neville Butler that Stalin aspired to expand Soviet influence toward the Dardanelles and the Persian Gulf.

Soviet behavior presented the British with a problem: nobody in Britain knew just how closely Moscow and Berlin were cooperating. After the successive shocks of the Nazi-Soviet Pact, the USSR's role in the dismemberment of Poland, and finally the Soviet invasion of Finland, it seemed to many in Britain that Nazi Germany and Soviet Russia were tarred with the same brush and should both be treated as enemies. At this time, as two historians of Anglo-Soviet relations have noted, "Stalin and Hitler were depicted by British cartoonists as virtually the same person."[19]

To other Britons, such as Sir Stafford Cripps, former solicitor general in the second Labour government and left-wing gadfly of British politics, the USSR represented the last real hope of defeating Nazi Germany and Fascism in general. Cripps's attitude, held by many others as well, demonstrated that the unity the British nation manifested in the face of the German threat might be considerably weakened should the government decide to include the Soviet Union among its enemies.

During the winter and spring of 1940, British policy toward the Soviet Union vascillated between treating the USSR as an ally of Germany—thus making her the object of Allied military action—and attempting diplomatically to entice Stalin away from Germany. Facing this difficult choice—neither option offered a clear hope of success—Chamberlain's cabinet adopted a characteristic attitude: they dithered. Eventually, the limitations of Allied resources compelled a choice. Churchill's government, which replaced Chamberlain's in May 1940, resolved to attempt a diplomatic solution of the Soviet problem, dispatching Sir Stafford Cripps, long-time advocate of a pro-Soviet British foreign policy, to Moscow as ambassador.

The history of British efforts, through the medium of Cripps, to disrupt Russo-German cooperation forms the subject of the first half of this study (Chapters 1–4). That these efforts were ultimately fruitless does not detract from the importance of the attempt. Britain's diplomats taxed their ingenuity to find some modus vivendi with Moscow, only to meet repeatedly with Soviet indifference. Cripps journeyed to the Soviet Union confident that years of misguided British policy had driven the Kremlin reluctantly into the arms of the Germans. Once in Moscow, however, Cripps found that winning Stalin's confidence was a far more difficult task than he had previously imagined. Despite his best efforts, he was unable to drive a wedge into the Nazi-Soviet partnership.

Cripps was only the first of many Western wartime representatives to feel that he knew the secret of winning the trust of what he believed to be a paranoiac Kremlin and for transforming Stalin into a friend of the Western democracies: Lord Beaverbrook, Anthony Eden, Winston Churchill, Franklin D. Roosevelt, and others followed him. Each thought he alone understood Stalin and knew the secret of winning his trust; each, in turn, failed. Cripps's experience is especially interesting: as he bent all his energies to forge Anglo-Soviet friendship, his colleagues on the British Left continued to believe—as Cripps had before going to Moscow—that ill-advised British policy was the sole impediment to Anglo-Soviet cooperation. But each of Cripps's approaches were met with Soviet unresponsiveness.

Hitler's invasion of the USSR created the rapprochement between London and Moscow so long desired by the British Left; but the new Anglo-Soviet partnership was not all the British had hoped for. Stalin was transformed overnight into an ally of Britain, not a friend, and the transformation had not come as the result of any British act or gesture. Stalin had clung to his profitable Nazi connection until the moment of the German invasion; clearly he had done so for his own reasons.

The British could not fathom their new ally. There was none of the free communication between London and Moscow that characterized Britain's alliances with France and, later, with the United States. London's efforts to construct a closer military alliance with the USSR form the subject for the second half of this work (Chapters 5–7). Ultimately, of course, these further efforts to win Soviet trust also failed: although the Western Allies provided the Soviets with badly needed supplies, and although the Red

Army broke the back of the Wehrmacht, Western military cooperation and coordination with the Soviet Union remained rudimentary throughout the war.

The common element in this otherwise split subject is the question of the Baltic States. Britain's refusal to approve a Soviet takeover of these states and of Finland had been one of the principal reasons for Chamberlain's inability to secure a defensive alliance with Moscow in 1939; Stalin confirmed this on the second day of his talks with Anthony Eden in December 1941.[20] In 1939 the British had refused to sanction the USSR's claim to these states; by 1942, however, the pressures of war and the perceived need for closer cooperation with Moscow caused the British government to abandon its earlier resolve. London—odd as it may seem—came to believe that Stalin was demanding a sacrifice of principle over the Baltic States as the price of Soviet trust, and for a multitude of reasons the British decided to accede. In the end, only a new factor, American intervention, prevented the British from recognizing by treaty Soviet sovereignty over the Baltic States.

It may be argued that this history assigns too prominent a role to the question of the Baltic States. Yet in February 1942 Sumner Welles, the American under secretary of state, wrote that this was "the most important issue of a political character which had come up for discussion . . . since the United States had entered the war or, for that matter, since Great Britain herself had entered the war."[21] As Welles pointed out, the way the Allies resolved this dispute would affect, and perhaps mold, later inter-Allied conflicts.

By 1944 Anthony Eden realized that British flexibility over the Baltic States and Bessarabia had weakened Britain's ability to curb further Soviet territorial demands. He wrote in that year, "Our powers of leverage are, I am afraid, much weakened by the fact that we have, either in public or in private, already acquiesced in the strength of their claims to the Baltic States and Bessarabia."[22] Welles had foreseen this eventuality in April 1942, when he wrote that British willingness to recognize Soviet sovereignty over the Baltic States was "not only indefensible from every moral standpoint, but likewise extraordinarily stupid," since it would only lead to "new additional demands," such as "eastern Poland."[23] Poland may have been the rock upon which the Grand Alliance finally foundered, but, as Welles had warned, it loomed in the Allies' path only after the matter of the Baltic States, Bessarabia, and Bukovina had been settled.

A study of the three-cornered discussions between London, Moscow, and Washington over the fate of Eastern Europe during the spring of 1942 can contribute to a fuller understanding of inter-Allied diplomacy during World War II in other ways as well. One of the most resilient beliefs about Western relations with the USSR during the war holds that the British in general, and Churchill in particular, identified the emerging Soviet threat to Europe long before Roosevelt and the Americans, and that the British struggled, in the face of American incomprehension, to restrict Soviet gains in Eastern Europe. This view, most ably propounded by Churchill himself, might be accurate if one looks only at the years 1943–45. It is therefore all the more interesting to examine the negotiations of spring 1942, when the Americans, opposed by the British, tried to resist Soviet expansion.[24] Britain's leaders later felt uncomfortable with their role in these negotiations. Churchill chose to deal very lightly with this period in his otherwise detailed memoirs, and at one point he shielded his colleague Anthony Eden by editing a quoted document without informing his readers that he had done so. Eden's revision of history is more blatant. In his memoirs, he distorted the meaning of a crucial memorandum he had written in early 1942.

One of the most important aspects of this story concerns Stalin's motives. Kremlin archives are inaccessible, and, therefore, it is difficult to speak about Soviet aims with the same assurance with which we discuss questions of Western diplomacy. The relative scarcity of reliable Soviet documentary material should not, however, discourage the effort to understand Soviet foreign policy. After all, the student of Stalin's diplomacy is in no way worse off than a historian of Byzantium, or of the Ottoman Empire. In fact, we are probably in a better position as regards documentary material than most historians of periods prior to, say, 1800. Although Soviet archives are closed to Western scholars for the foreseeable future, Western documents—particularly British, American, and German—fill many of the yawning gaps. The capture of Nazi archives in 1945 in particular has shed light on negotiations that might otherwise have remained secret forever. This study also uses newly published Soviet documents, which go some way toward illuminating Soviet diplomacy.

Based on these sources we can attempt a form of historical navigation: by fixing three points—that is, the Soviet position vis-à-vis the Americans, British, and Germans as revealed in these countries' documents—we can guess the location of the missing fourth point, Stalin's overall goals. That said, the process still involves some conjecture, and the conclusions drawn below doubtless will not suit everyone's taste.

Stalin's decision to cooperate with Hitler in 1939 and to carry that cooperation on into 1941 had an enormous impact on the history of Europe and of the world. The old European equilibrium, which Stalin told Cripps he wanted to "get rid of," was dealt a blow from which it has never recovered. The Soviet dictator's judgment in deciding to work with Hitler was vindicated—if only barely. He came within a hair's breadth of losing everything after the German invasion and was forced to work with his old enemies, the British, to rid the world of his erstwhile ally, Hitler. Stalin's reasons for cooperating first with Hitler, then with the Western democracies, are certainly worth examining, since many of the aftereffects of his policies, in the form of Europe's retreat from the world and the Cold War, are still with us today.

In one respect, at least, the story is optimistic: Anglo-Soviet relations ascended from a nadir during the Russo-Finnish War, where this history begins, to the signing of the Anglo-Soviet Treaty of May 1942, where it ends. Genuine "peaceful coexistence" for the first time characterized Anglo-Soviet relations. The West is unlikely to cooperate with Moscow in a similar venture in the near future, but perhaps something may be learned of the Soviets by studying what it was like to be their allies. At the very least, it is useful to remember that, however small the common ground, the USSR and the West were able to work together when it was in both sides' interest to do so, even though cooperation was invariably laced with distrust.

During the Russian Civil War, Churchill, then secretary of state for war, was the leading advocate of British aid for the White forces, who were trying to crush the Bolshevik regime. On March 24, 1920, he wrote Lloyd George: "I do not of course believe that any real harmony is possible between Bolshevism and present civilisation."[25] Stalin, for his part, fully reciprocated Churchill's hostility in the years before 1941. It is one of the curious ironies of modern history that in 1942, as prime minister, Churchill would sign a treaty with Soviet foreign commissar Viacheslav Molotov pledging their nations to twenty years of friendship and cooperation.

CHAPTER ONE

A QUICK QUARREL

WITH THE SOVIET

JANUARY–JUNE 1940

In late August 1939 the British man in the street might well have thought that relations between London and Moscow could scarcely get worse. Stalin and his foreign commissar, Viacheslav Molotov, had hosted Joachim von Ribbentrop, Hitler's foreign minister, in the Kremlin, where the Soviet dictator had actually toasted the health of the Führer—though this last fact would not be known to the world until the capture of German archives at the end of the war. What the British knew in 1939 was, for them, ominous enough: Stalin had rejected the Western democracies' offer of a defensive alliance in favor of a non-aggression pact with the Nazis; an Anglo-French military mission had been in Moscow ironing out the details of a military protocol when the news of the Nazi-Soviet Pact broke.

Our average Briton would have been wrong had he thought Anglo-Soviet relations could deteriorate no futher than they had by August: they quickly did just that. In a secret protocol attached to the Nazi-Soviet Pact, Stalin and Hitler partitioned much of Eastern Europe between themselves. Though the existence of this protocol was also revealed only after the war, its outward manifestations were soon evident. Once war had broken out and the German Army was on the verge of crushing Polish resistance, on September 17 the Red Army moved into eastern Poland—ostensibly to restore order, in fact to enforce prearranged Soviet territorial claims. Fuzzy black and white photographs portray smiling Nazi officers side by side with grinning Red Army men as they made adjustments to the new border between the German and Soviet empires. After the Polish state was safely crushed, Molotov exulted to the Supreme Soviet:

> The ruling circles of Poland boasted quite a lot about the "stability" of their State and the "might" of their army. However, one swift blow to

Poland, first by the German Army and then by the Red Army, and nothing was left of this ugly offspring of the Versailles treaty which had existed by oppressing non-Polish nationalities. The "traditional policy" of unprincipled manoeuvering between Germany and the USSR and the playing off of one against the other, has proven unsound and suffered complete bankruptcy.

The collapse of Poland did not lead immediately to fighting between Germany and the Western democracies. Instead, the two sides quietly faced each other throughout the winter of 1939–40 in what became known derisively as the "Sitzkrieg," or "Phony War." And the war did indeed have a distinctly unreal air about it; for months, for example, the British and French high commands debated whether sowing mines in German rivers and canals would provoke Hitler to retaliation.[1]

But the war could not long remain in suspended animation. Once again acting on the basis of his secret protocol with Hitler, on November 30 Stalin declared war on Finland in order to create a territorial buffer zone north of Leningrad and to extend further the Soviet sphere of influence, possibly even to annex all of Finland. It is one of the paradoxes of the period of World War II between September 1939 and April 1940 that, as world attention was riveted on the German-French border, the Red Army, not the Wehrmacht, was the most active force.

We now know that Nazi-Soviet friendship was short-lived, but from August 1939 to June 1941 Western leaders could not be so sure. Seen from the outside, relations between Moscow and Berlin seemed at times to be quite close, and nobody in the West knew for certain whether the Soviet Union had in fact joined the Axis powers in formal alliance. In the spring of 1940, the British government sought to devise a Soviet policy suited to this ambiguous situation.

Searching for a Policy

The Soviet attack on Finland evoked widespread outrage in the West, the virulence of which surprised the Soviets. As Molotov later pointed out, up to 1939 Western opinion had been far more passive in the face of German expansionism. The Soviets must have assumed that with world attention fixed on the Franco-German border the Finnish operation could be carried out quickly and quietly. The Western reaction, combined with evidence of Red Army inefficiency, must have come as a rude shock in Moscow. On January 1, 1940, in a final meeting with the departing British Ambassador, Sir William Seeds, who was being withdrawn because of the Finnish War, Molotov dropped his customarily icy facade, revealing the extent of Soviet fears, when he told Seeds that "Finland would never have been so openly hostile to the Soviet Union even during the negotiations [preceding the war] had she not been instigated by us [Great Britain]. Nobody in their senses would instigate a people of three millions against one of one hundred and eighty millions."[2] Molotov might not have been so irate had Finnish resistance not proven so stubbornly effective.

In Britain reaction to the Russo-Finnish war ranged from concern that the USSR must now be considered an enemy in the German camp to jubilation and more than a bit of smugness when Finnish resistance and Soviet military ineptitude proved greater than expected. According to Churchill, "In British circles many people congratulated themselves that we had not gone out of our way to bring the Soviets in on our side, and preened themselves on their foresight. The conclusion was drawn too hastily that the Russian Army had been ruined by the purge, and that the inherent rottenness and degradation of their system of government and society was now proved."[3] One of Ambassador Seeds's last telegrams from Moscow on January 2 reflected this attitude. Reporting the sudden departure of the Italian ambassador, Seeds wrote: "This is very satisfactory from every point of view . . . the French Ambassador has also been recalled. Thus the British, French, and Italian Ambassadors will all have left Moscow for an indefinite period within a week of each other. It is a pity that Mr. [Laurence] Steinhardt [the American ambassador] didn't go too."[4] Moscow seemed for the moment to be a diplomatic leper, but British optimism was premature. Finland's defensive resources, though stronger than most had foreseen, were finite. The USSR would not long remain bogged down in the Finnish quagmire.

To comprehend British diplomatic thinking at the beginning of 1940, it is necessary first to understand British military reasoning. The central point in British strategic thought around which all else revolved was the war against Germany; operations in theaters other than France were subsidiary. The worth of such operations was judged solely by their probable impact upon the German war effort. In prosecuting the war against the Germans, the British not unnaturally drew upon what they felt to be the lessons of World War I. The first such lesson was that a repetition of trench warfare and attrition in the style of 1914–18, with its enormous casualty lists, should be avoided at all costs. Consequently, the idea grew that naval blockade might prove once again to be the decisive strategic factor. The War Cabinet therefore rather optimistically hoped to duplicate the successes of World War I without the costs: the Maginot Line would be held with the fewest possible casualties while at the same time the Germans would be starved into submission as in an enormous medieval siege.[5]

For such a siege to be successful, the naval blockade would have to be nearly watertight, but on this point the analogy to World War I broke down. In 1939–40, as in the Great War, the British Navy was more than a match for its German adversary, but the situation on the Continent differed in one crucial respect from 1914–18: there was no Eastern Front as yet, and the neutrals, especially the USSR, leaked contraband like a sieve.

The Germans fully realized the importance of the Soviet Union as a chink in the British blockade. As the German author of a memorandum on the Russo-German Commercial Agreement of February 11, 1940, noted: "If we succeed in extending and expanding exports to the East in the required volume, the effects of the English blockade will be decisively weakened by the incoming raw materials."[6] Ivan Maiskii, the well-informed, sometimes perceptive, but always slippery, Soviet ambassador to Britain, summed up the situation succinctly in a conversation with the Yugoslav ambassador. "It seems to me," he said, "and this is the view of a great number of people in leading English circles, that neither the Maginot line, nor the Siegfried line can be broken. The war must be decided by three factors, the economic factor, . . . the naval factor, . . . and the political factor. This last means that that side will win which succeeds, at the [right] psychological moment, in finding new and powerful allies or in preventing the other side from doing so." It hardly needs to be pointed out that the "new and powerful" ally of which Maiskii spoke was none other than the Soviet Union. Nor was Moscow oblivious to the value Berlin placed on trade with the USSR. Stalin himself told the German ambassador in Moscow, Count von der Schulenburg, that "the Soviet Union rendered a very great service to Germany" by selling the Nazis raw materials that would otherwise have been denied them by the British blockade.[7]

Until June 22, 1941, an analysis very much like Maiskii's underlay British policy toward Russia. The USSR, the British reasoned, must either be divided from the Germans by means of an Anglo-Soviet agreement, or at the very least closed off as a conduit for contraband supplies to Germany. In the early part of 1940, however, London saw precious little chance of splitting Germany and Russia by a deal with the latter. Soviet-German collaboration looked far too cozy for that. This drove British planners reluctantly to consider the second option, some sort of military action against the USSR.

Apart from extending the naval blockade to Soviet shipping, there were only two points of contact where the British could inflict serious damage on the Soviets, Scandinavia and the Caucasus. In the War Cabinet Churchill, as first lord of the admiralty, was the strongest advocate of extending aid to the Finns. British military aid to Finland, he argued, would have the added benefit of disrupting supplies of Swedish iron ore to Germany. On January 9, the War Cabinet considered such a Scandinavian operation as well as possible moves against the Soviets in the Middle East. On the tenth, they discussed an eighteen-page "Review of Military Policy in the Middle East," prepared by the General Staff. This report concluded that any attack on the Soviet Union would enmesh Britain in a far greater struggle than her slender and already overextended resources would warrant.[8]

The Cabinet did not, however, firmly reject military action against Russia in the Middle East, in part because the aforementioned military policy review was somewhat out of date. Fitzroy Maclean, the hawkish Russian expert at the Foreign Office, commented in a minute on the review that, "in my opinion there are several new aspects of the situation which it does not take sufficiently into account, notably the repercussions of the Finnish War, the evidence of close Soviet-German collaboration and our decision to regard the Soviet Union as an actual rather than a potential enemy."[9]

For the time being, aid to Finland appeared to be the most effective means of striking a blow at the Soviet Union, and through her at Germany. On January 17, a Foreign Office memorandum concluded "that in assisting Finland, His Majesty's Government are best serving their own interests." The fundamental consideration regarding any British move, it was stressed time and again, must be the probable effect of such a move on the war against Germany. The author of the memorandum felt that aid to Finland would be unlikely to push Germany and the Soviet Union closer together and might in fact disrupt their cooperation by tying the Soviets down and forcing them to divert resources that might otherwise be channeled to Germany.[10] On February 2 Fitzroy Maclean further developed this line of thinking in another memorandum: "The obvious conclusion is that it is to our interest to continue to afford all possible support to Finland, regardless of the consequences, and do everything in our power to damage Soviet interests on the grounds that the prolongation of the war in Finland must necessarily make it difficult for the Soviet Union either to afford any help to Germany or to embark on any further military adventures in regions where British interests are more directly concerned."[11]

The problem with aiding Finland militarily was the attitude of the Scandinavian neutrals, without whose help or at least acquiescence any British assistance would be impossible. Norway and Sweden were markedly cool to the idea of a British force crossing their territory en route to Finland. The Swedes even balked at the idea of British naval forces operating in Norwegian territorial waters in retaliation against German sinkings there, as Oslo felt this might provoke the Germans into occupying Denmark or even all of Scandinavia. On January 7, Erik Boheman, secretary general of the Swedish Ministry of Foreign Affairs, rather acidly told a British diplomat: "I should have thought that the British Government had the fate of a sufficient number of smaller States on their consciences as it is."[12] Clearly, no help could be expected from that quarter.

In mid-January, the British hoped that the Italians, who at this stage of the war had not yet irrevocably cast their lot with the Nazis, might send some aid to the Finns, perhaps, for example, aircraft and pilots with experience from the Spanish Civil War.[13] The Foreign Office even heard from the French ambassador that the Pope might favor such a course: "He himself was naturally opposed to war as such, but he felt that if the Italians were going to fight there was no better cause than a crusade against the Bolshevik abomination of desolation."[14] Although eventually the Italians did send some equipment to Finland, the aid was minimal and made no impact on the course of the war.

In the Middle East, British policy was also checkmated by frightened and hesitant neutrals. The Soviet invasion of Finland had understandably sent a shock wave through the Soviet Union's smaller neutral neighbors. The Iranians adopted the rather curious attitude that Finland had somehow brought her troubles on herself and "had acted precipitately in breaking off their conversations here [in Moscow] and that with a little more patience and forebearance they might have reached an agreement more satisfactory both to the Soviets and to themselves."[15]

The position of Turkey was more ambivalent, since the Turks regarded the USSR as a very real threat; but, like the Iranians, they were reluctant to take steps that might anger Moscow. The British ambassador in Ankara, Sir Hughe Knatchbull-Hugessen, consistently warned London of the Soviet threat to the British position in the Middle East and relayed Turkish fears to London.[16] Responding to one of these dispatches, Deputy Under Secretary of State Sir Orme Sargent wrote to Knatchbull-Hugessen, "It is extremely satisfactory that the Turkish Government should not only be taking active measures to strengthen their defence against the Soviet Union, but should also be willing to discuss these measures with us." It would be best, Sargent reasoned, for Turkish-British cooperation to receive the widest possible publicity in the hopes of "deterring [the Soviets] strongly from embarking on any such adventures." Then, if deterrence failed, and if the Soviets should attack Afghanistan or Iran, "we could with the support of Turkey, if the need arose, make a counter attack against the Caucasus, and in particular against the oil wells of Baku and the Batum-Baku pipe line. With Turkey as our active ally we should be able to send a force into the Black Sea; and we should also stand a much better chance of stirring up a rebellion in the Caucasus. With the Caucasus in a state of turmoil and the oil supplies cut off, we should have little to fear from the Russians anywhere else." "The weakness of the Red Army, about which we never had any illusions," Sargent wrote, "has been abundantly demonstrated in Finland." In conclusion, he pointed out that "the success of any action we decide to take against the Soviet Union depends in the ultimate analysis upon Turkey."[17]

With these considerations in mind, Turkey became one of the focal points of British foreign policy. British diplomats expended considerable effort trying to contact anti-Soviet elements in those areas of the USSR bordering Turkey in the hopes that should the occasion arise, these groups might cooperate with any British move against the Soviet Union. On February 2, Knatchbull-Hugessen informed the Foreign Office that the Afghan ambassador believed that "the whole Moslem element in Russia was ready for revolt if Russia's present difficulties lasted long."[18]

During a visit to Romania, R. M. A. Hankey, minister without portfolio, discussed the Caucasus with two experts on the USSR from Poland's embassy in Bucharest. They told Hankey that "the Achilles heel of European Russia was the Caucasus and the Caucasus was a fertile field for subversive propaganda, if only we [the British] would take a hand." The Poles also noted an Italian interest in the Caucasus but regretted that, since the Turks coveted the area, Ankara would by no means wish to see the Italians become involved there. In Hankey's opinion, cooperation with Mussolini in this matter was impractical.[19] Such considerations evidently did not restrain the British ambassador to Romania who addressed Lord

Halifax in a telegram commenting on this talk: "Your Lordship will observe that the Poles assert that the Italian Government is taking a considerable interest in the Caucasus. One is therefore almost tempted that some importance should be attached to Monsieur Gafencu's [Romania's foreign minister] suggestion regarding the possibilities of interesting Italy in that area."[20]

On the basis of such information about instability in the Caucasus, the British made contact with a Georgian separatist movement based in Paris under the leadership of an M. Gugushvili. In the end, nothing came of such links. Nevertheless, Foreign Office records indicate that they were maintained at least until October 1940, by which time the German occupation of Paris meant, as one Foreign Office official wrote, "we must exercise, if possible, even greater reserve in our dealings with him [Gugushvili] than we have up to the present."[21]

On February 20, William Strang, assistant under secretary at the Foreign Office, met with another dissident group called "Young Russia." From the British point of view, this group was less satisfactory than the Georgian separatists for an interesting reason: it was composed of ethnic Russians. Strang had suggested to the "Young Russians" that they might volunteer for service in Finland, but they had declined saying that they could not fight against their own countrymen. A memorandum by Maclean highlighted the difficulties of dealing with Russians: "Whatever part H.M. Government may take in overthrowing the present regime in Moscow, the less they have to do with the establishment of a new one the better. . . . There is something to be said for the theory that, so long as Transcaucasia and Turkestan are under the sway of Moscow, there is likely to be trouble between the governments of Moscow and London."[22] Far better, it would seem, for the rulers of India to detach bits of Russia's empire than simply to overturn the Communist government in Moscow.

Maclean was simply airing the traditional Foreign Office fear of Russian designs on India. And indeed, much of the pressure for improved relations with the Turks came from those persons most closely associated with the administration and defense of India, who hoped to use Turkey as a counterweight to the Soviet Union. The secretary of state for India, for example, wrote Halifax on February 21, "it is most desirable to secure the cooperation of Turkey in our endeavours to improve our intelligence with regard to matters within Soviet Russia and particularly along the frontiers of Iraq, Iran and Afghanistan."[23]

But the Foreign Office was receiving contradictory signals from the

Turks. Plans for stirring up trouble in the Caucasus were seemingly dampened by the Turkish foreign minister, who told the British ambassador that "the Turkish Government were reluctant to engage in anything which involved sending agents into Russia, also he thought that many local chiefs . . . were too well known to be of any use."[24] But three days later, on February 29, the same British ambassador telegraphed that the deputy chief of the Turkish General Staff seemed most helpful and that he was "willing to place all information at our disposal."[25]

In addition to inciting the Caucasus to rebel against the Moscow regime, British planning ran along a second track, consideration of direct military action. One area where the British felt that they could inflict a serious and possibly decisive blow against the Soviets was Baku, where Soviet oil supplies were judged to be vulnerable to air attack. The origin of the idea to consider bombing the Caucasian oil fields remains obscure, but the official Foreign Office historian strongly implies that it was a French idea that arose sometime in late February 1940.[26] A telegram from John Le Rougetel, the British chargé d'affaires in Moscow, suggests that the idea must have emerged earlier. On January 11 Le Rougetel told Laurence Collier at the Foreign Office that he believed any military action against the USSR would be highly unlikely to provoke retaliation against the British position in the Middle East. He reasoned that the Finnish fiasco proved "the palpable inability of the present Russian regime to organise difficult operations of this kind and on this scale, [and] they are more exposed to attack by us than vice-versa." Le Rougetel then suggested that British bombers stationed in Egypt and Iraq might be used to destroy the Caucasian oil fields, and, with what seems in hindsight to be astounding optimism, he concluded that "the effective and continuous bombardment of Baku should therefore present no great difficulty to us and it alone should be sufficient to bring Russia to her knees within a very short time."[27]

Even if the original suggestion to bomb the Caucasus was not their idea, the French were enthusiastic champions of any strategy that promised to shift the center of military action away from their borders. Paris pressed their allies for some sort of direct action against the USSR, either in Scandinavia in tandem with the Finns or in the Caucasus, giving little weight to the risks this might entail for the security of the British Empire. Most of the British War Cabinet took a much graver view of these risks than did Le Rougetel and, moving at a glacial pace, resisted pressure from the French, Churchill, and the hard-liners at the Foreign Office to make a definite commitment to an attack on the Soviet Union.

For a time the Cabinet's policy of waiting on events seemed to work. Since Seeds's departure from Moscow, there had been only one official contact with the Soviets, a meeting between Maiskii and Richard A. Butler, parliamentary under secretary of state for foreign affairs, on February 8. Maiskii had tried to pour oil on the troubled waters, saying with remarkable cynicism, according to Butler's account, that he "understood that we [the British] might object to what the Soviet Government were doing in Finland, and might even help the Finns; but we must not be too spectacular, and on the rest of the front, both sides must try to maintain their diplomatic relations."[28] Such a relationship, though hardly cozy, would at least avoid all-out war between Britain and the Soviet Union. But the pressures of war doomed such an ambivalent policy. From the end of February through March, Anglo-Soviet relations reached a crisis as the British government continued to examine various ideas for striking at the USSR, while the Soviets strove diplomatically to avert an Allied attack.

Moscow Reacts

Finnish resistance began to crack in late February 1940, and the Western Allies faced the prospect of a Red Army freed for mischief elsewhere. British inaction became less tenable, and London made a concerted effort to deliver bombers and a small contingent of troops to Finland. On March 8 the War Cabinet met to discuss a report by the Chiefs of Staff on the military implications of the French proposals to attack the USSR. They concluded that war with the Soviet Union would only be worthwhile if it "might cause the early defeat of Germany, capture of the Gallivare orefields [in Sweden] would be a case in point." As for the idea of an aerial campaign against the Soviet oil sites in the Caucasus, the memorandum continued, "assuming the cooperation of Turkey, [a] successful attack on the Caucasian oilfields might in time result in the economic and military collapse of Russia, which in turn would deprive Germany of any hope of supplies from that source."[29] The Chiefs of Staff were sufficiently optimistic about the prospects of inflicting a serious blow against Soviet oil supplies to proceed with planning along those lines.

The Soviets began to sense the harsher Allied attitude, possibly via Maiskii in London. In his memoirs, Maiskii claims that on February 25, "I learned that the British refusal to mediate [in the Russo-Finnish War] was partly to be explained by strong pressure from Paris, where the wave of anti-Soviet fury still stood very high."[30] Whatever the source of information—and most probably the Soviets were receiving such hints from many different quarters—during late February and early March Moscow became inordinately polite and conciliatory. The Foreign Office began to receive information from neutral countries that the Soviets were worried about Allied military activity in the Middle East, especially the army being assembled in Syria.[31] In Moscow, the American ambassador, Laurence Steinhardt, told Le Rougetel on March 3 that, when they had last met, Molotov had "oozed niceness" and that "Stalin [was] now hypnotized by [the] bogey of Allied intervention in the Caucasus while he is still entangled in Finland." Molotov had also seemed quite impressed when an American told him that the ground around Baku was so soaked in oil that bombing would start a fire the like of which the world had never seen.[32] The Turkish ambassador told Le Rougetel that he had also spoken to Molotov on the fifth, when he "was particularly struck by M. Molotov's tone, which was far calmer and more conciliatory than at any of their recent meetings, although he was still extremely nervous about Allied activities in the Middle East."[33]

It is not difficult to account for Molotov's civility when one considers Turkey's strategic position in relation to any conceivable Allied attack upon the Caucasus; nor is it difficult to understand Soviet worries about Allied military intentions. Further convincing evidence that the Soviets knew the Allies were up to something was provided in a telegram from Knatchbull-Hugessen of February 29, in which the ambassador said he had learned that the Soviets were mining their Black Sea ports, in all likelihood in preparation to repel an Allied attack.[34]

It is in the context of these Soviet worries that Sir Stafford Cripps's first trip to Moscow must be seen. Cripps, whose political background will be examined in the next chapter, was on what American Congressmen call a "fact-finding tour," traveling around the world. When Cripps spoke to the Soviet ambassador in China, the proposition was made—the British record does not indicate by whom—that Sir Stafford should journey to Moscow to hear from Molotov himself why British policy had allegedly brought Anglo-Soviet relations to an impasse. Cripps decided to make the trip and after a grueling journey arrived in Moscow on February 16. It is interesting to contrast the Soviets' eager greeting of Sir Stafford in February with their marked coolness to Cripps's suggestion the previous September that he should visit Moscow. At that time the Soviets had refused to grant him a visa. Moscow's changing attitude can be explained only in terms of their concerns about Allied military activity and their vulnerable position owing to the Finnish War.

Cripps reported on his talks in a six-page telegram to Halifax sent from China on March 4. In a preliminary talk with M. Tikchomerov, of the Ministry of Foreign Affairs, Cripps "gained . . . the . . . impression of anxiety for a rapprochement with Great Britain and also for some undisclosed reason [that] they considered the matter urgent." (Cripps, unlike the Soviets evidently, was not aware of Allied military plans, so his confusion was understandable.) After his talk with Tikchomerov, Cripps had a one-and-three-quarter-hour meeting with Molotov, during which the foreign commissar treated his receptive visitor to a brief summary of the by-now-familiar Soviet arguments justifying the Nazi-Soviet Pact and the Finnish War.

Cripps pressed Molotov to explain why his government had not chosen to respond to British trade proposals of the previous October. Molotov brushed Cripps's questions aside with the assertion "that Great Britain was interfering to prevent success of Russo-Finnish negotiations. He did not therefore consider [the] political situation favourable for arriving at [a] trade agreement." "In fact," Cripps noted, "[Molotov] seemed more anxious about politics than trade relations." Molotov pointed out that the search and seizure of Russian shipping and the rough handling of the Soviet Trade Delegation in Paris proved that "both Great Britain and France were bent on antagonising Russia."[35] But Cripps completely missed the point and continued to talk about trade. Molotov "made it quite clear," Cripps wrote, "in answer to a specific question that Russia was quite prepared to make a trade or political agreement with Great Britain provided that Great Britain was prepared to act in a friendly and not hostile way to Russia." Molotov then said that such a deal must come soon if it were to come at all: "He indicated very clearly that any long delay might lead Russia to commit herself elsewhere."[36] Convinced of the urgency of the matter, Cripps closed his telegram with a plea to Halifax for a speedy response to the Soviet offer.[37] In addition to this long telegram, he sent two smaller ones in which he offered to return to Moscow as His Majesty's representative if this would help speed negotiations along and, in the second, asked Butler to use his influence to prod Halifax.[38]

Back in London, Maclean was unimpressed with the meeting, seeing nothing new in Soviet protestations and noting that "They appear to have found a willing tool in Sir Stafford Cripps." The Foreign Office thought little of Molotov's threat about pulling closer to the Germans: "We know by experience that the fact that they were negotiating with us would not be likely to deter the Soviet Government from drawing still closer to the Germans, or still less cause them to dissolve a profitable connexion on our account."[39] The reason for Molotov's offer, the memorandum concluded, was Stalin's "blunder" of embarking upon a protracted war with Finland while his southern flank was vulnerable. Soviet discomfiture in Finland, the Foreign Office reasoned, meant that London could afford to respond coolly, if at all, to Soviet overtures.

But Stalin's Finnish nightmare was rapidly approaching an end, and late on March 12 a Soviet-Finnish peace treaty was signed. Allied efforts to help the Finns had been too little too late. As Alexander Cadogan, the permanent under secretary at the Foreign Office, noted the next day in his diary: "So the Finns have capitulated. I don't blame them, as we could only (honestly) offer them 13,000 men by the second half of April. And I don't blame us, as we couldn't (honestly) promise more. A black day, but there it is."[40]

The War Cabinet met on the day the peace treaty was signed but before they knew its specific terms, again to discuss possible action against Russia and to consider yet another report by the Chiefs of Staff on the question. Once again, the authors of the report "had reached the conclusion that there was no action we could take against Russia which would bring about the early defeat of Germany." This was, of course, the fundamental consideration, even though the Chiefs took a rather sanguine view of the possible effects of bombing Soviet oil fields. "We had no experience of such an operation," the report stated, "but the air staff estimated that three bomber squadrons, operating for a period of from six weeks to three months, would probably put the oilfields out of action altogether." The Cabinet discussion then revolved around possible countermeasures the Soviets might be likely to adopt should the decision be made to bomb the Caucasus, and the conclusion was drawn that these would be "more in the nature of embarrassing diversions than vital blows." "It was generally agreed," the conclusion stated, "that if war with Russia did break out, it would probably be limited to certain theatres and would not amount to a formal declaration of war." Regarding any Soviet move toward India, Churchill thought that air forces alone would be enough to "delay their advance for a very long time." The lord privy seal injected a note of realism into the discussion when he reminded Churchill "that air forces were not at present available for such an operation."[41]

The official British Foreign Office historian claims that the War Cabinet concluded at this session "that it was not in our interest to declare war on Russia."[42] It would seem from the record, however, that the question was left up in the air—a common enough practice during Chamberlain's years as prime minister. Chamberlain himself seemed reluctant finally to dismiss the option of military action against the USSR, though he was by no means enthusiastic about leaping into the unknown. He told his Cabinet colleagues that "it might be as well to wait the outcome of present developments in Finland before embarking on an exhaustive enquiry into the possibility of an expedition into Afghanistan." In conclusion, the Cabinet agreed that "a decision [about war with Russia] should be deferred for a few days."[43]

The Russo-Finnish peace and the lack of any clear ministerial direction triggered a wave of speculation in the Foreign Office that lasted until the meeting of the Supreme Allied War Council on March 28. The Foreign Office did not react to the news from Finland by abandoning war planning against the USSR. On the contrary, as Maclean pointed out in a memorandum: "it is for consideration whether we ought not to seek alternative means of disabling Germany's only ally."[44]

In a remarkably cold-blooded memorandum of March 23, Cadogan weighed the arguments for and against an Allied attack on the Caucasus: "I confess," he wrote, "I am very doubtful as to the ability of 3 squadrons of bombers to knock out the Caucasian oilfields. But that is a technical question, outside my ken. If I had a sure sign that they could, I shd [sic] advocate it. We shall have to rely on air experts for an opinion on this." As we have already seen, the air experts had assured the War Cabinet on March 12 that such an operation was indeed feasible. Cadogan proceeded to assess the political aspects of the problem:

> We should have to pick a quick quarrel with the Soviet, I suppose, before we launched our bombers. This I think could be done on the blockade issue. Cannot we refer to the German-Soviet economic agreement, which we can maintain establishes the Soviet as a supplier of contraband to Germany? Then stop every shipment to Russia that we can catch. If that doesn't goad her into war, can't we then demand that she cease supplying certain articles to Germany? She certainly won't cease—or we can complain that she hasn't ceased—and we might then take action.

The most critical aspect of the problem, besides the effect on Germany's war effort, Cadogan reasoned, was the possible reaction of the neutral nations. "Turkey might wink at our flying over Turkish territory," he noted, referring to an assessment received from Ankara on March 15,[45] "but if we 'aggress' in this way, that will give her a splendid excuse (which I shd think she wd be glad of) for not coming into the war."[46]

Sir Orme Sargent further examined the problem of neutral opinion in a memorandum on March 24. Sargent argued that Japanese help would be vital in closing off Vladivostok and that such help would force the Soviets to divert forces to the East.

> I do not suggest that we should make our decision to attack Baku, thus involving ourselves in war with Russia, dependent upon either Turkish or Japanese co-operation. But I do think that we ought at once to work systematically to bring these two powers in. Turkey is evolving in the desired direction, but it would be dangerous to rush her. If, however, we set the example of a successful attack on Baku, this might go a long way to encourage her to follow suit at Batoum.

The Japanese, he felt, might also respond to such an example. But the problem with any Anglo-Japanese cooperation would be the effect on American opinion, which was decidedly anti-Japanese owing to the Sino-Japanese War. On March 26 Cadogan took note of this problem, pointing out that Britain could do very little to extract Japan from her war in China and that furthermore "any direct help that we gave in that direction would get us into trouble with the U.S."[47]

One result of the Foreign Office debate was the dispatch of a telegram to the British embassy in Ankara, asking the ambassador to ascertain the likely Turkish response to an Allied attack on the USSR. Halifax wrote: "I presume [that the] Turkish Government could not be induced to join in, or give facilities for this; but I should be glad if, without consulting them, you will telegraph your estimate of their probable reaction to an air attack on Baku over Persian territory (a) if Turkish territory were not affected or (b) if, as is unlikely, it were necessary to fly over Turkish territory as well."[48]

The Foreign Office received a reply from Knatchbull-Hugessen on March 27, but it was not all they might have wished. The Turks, it seemed, were preparing against a Soviet invasion, but they were equally concerned about Italian designs. Knatchbull-Hugessen drew the conclusion that if the Allies were to attack the Caucasus, "They would not have Turkey with them if war started now but if [the] attack took place later when Turkey was more prepared and had previously [been] taken into [the Allies'] confidence and also satisfied as regards Italy they would probably obtain Turkish participation."[49]

This is how the matter stood on the eve of the Supreme Allied War

Council meeting, a meeting where the British must have known the French would continue their agitation for an attack on the Soviet Union. Chamberlain and Halifax faced the prospect of an extremely risky attack on the USSR that might well be a mere pin-prick but that could lead to unspecified Soviet countermoves against the British Empire in South Asia. On top of all this there was little encouragement from the neutrals concerned. No wonder the War Cabinet was "doubtful" about the Baku project when it met on March 27, as Cadogan recorded in his diary.[50]

Therefore, the Soviets chose a critical psychological moment to submit to the British an offer of trade talks. Maiskii met with Halifax later on the twenty-seventh and told him that the Soviets were now willing to negotiate along the lines of the British proposals of October, to which, he told the foreign secretary, his government had not replied "for various reasons." Halifax pressed the ambassador to explain just what these various reasons were, but without success. Maiskii ducked the question by complaining about the British seizure in February of the *Selenga* and *Mayakovsky,* two Soviet vessels bound for Vladivostok.

Halifax pointed out that it would be difficult for the British government to deal with a power that was apparently in such close alliance with Nazi Germany. Maiskii took exception to this, asserting that, "Many people, both in this country and others, seemed to be under a misapprehension as to the extent and the nature of Soviet trade with Germany, which was merely a business proposition undertaken because it was of advantage to the Soviet Union, who, incidentally, was doing far less for Germany in the economic sphere than the United States, for example, were doing for the Allies." This was cold comfort for the British, and Halifax told the ambassador that any improvement in relations would hinge on "the attitude of [the USSR] towards German attempts to break the Allied blockade."

At this point Maiskii revealed his lure: the Soviets, he said, might be willing to assure the British government that any goods received from the empire as a result of an Anglo-Soviet trade agreement would not be reshipped to Germany.[51] This was not much to go on, perhaps; the Soviet ambassador had been very opaque in his comments. But Maiskii's vague offer was enough to reinforce the doubts that had hitherto prevented Chamberlain's Cabinet from reaching a definite conclusion about whether to take military action against the USSR.

The timing of the Soviet offer was masterful. The day before the Allies were to meet and discuss military measures to close off Germany's pipeline to the East, the Soviets were apparently offering at least partial achievement of the same end by trade agreement. The Soviets had evidently sensed that the British attitude was less firm than the French and had for this reason chosen to strike the Allied chain at its weakest link.

In characteristic Soviet fashion, once the offer was made, the Soviets agitated for negotiations at all levels, from the ambassador to contacts with sympathetic newspapermen. Only two days after the Maiskii-Halifax meeting, a Mr. Peake of the Foreign Office met with the editor of the *Daily Herald* and M. Korj of the Soviet embassy. Korj said that if the British "would release the two detained Soviet ships, almost anything might be possible." But he also set the tone for future talks, showing that his "anything" might have very real limits when, in answer to a question about possible Soviet restraint in reshipment of imported goods to Germany, he testily declared that "Russia is an independent great power and cannot be dictated to in connection with its relations with other countries."[52]

In the meantime the Supreme Allied War Council, which met on March 28, came to no definite conclusion about what measures to take regarding the Soviet Union. Reynaud, who had replaced the more cautious Daladier as French prime minister, pressed Chamberlain to agree to active steps to close the Soviet gap in the blockade. His assessment of the likely effect of a successful attack on Baku was quite extraordinary, believing that it would dislocate Soviet agriculture "and might even help in bringing Russia to the side of the Allies."[53]

Chamberlain stalled, saying that the Allies must be patient in order to allow the blockade of Germany to take effect and arguing that Maiskii's approach the day before might offer an alternative solution to the Soviet problem. As a sop to the French he did, however, agree that the details of an aerial campaign against the USSR's oil fields should be further studied.[54]

The War Cabinet met the day after the Council and reviewed the situation. The Foreign Office, which had submitted its thoughts on Maiskii's approach, was less inclined than the prime minister to take the Soviets at their word. Former Ambassador Seeds wrote a memorandum on the Halifax-Maiskii talk and concluded that the Soviet approach "does not indicate a change of heart but only an attempt to secure free passage for Soviet ships." He also thought the Soviets were likely to grab military concessions in the Baltic States "*if conditions are favourable*," (Seeds's emphasis) but that they would "not go to war with us if they can possibly help."[55] In the Cabinet discussion, Halifax said that in his opinion Maiskii had been ordered to approach the British government because, as the ambassador had told the foreign secretary in their talk, the Soviets were concerned about "the intentions of the Allies 'in certain quarters of the globe.'"

After Halifax had recapitulated the essence of his conversation with Maiskii, Churchill "stressed the importance of using the threat of bombing Baku as a weapon in any negotiations of this character," if the Cabinet decided to proceed with talks. The prime minister, speaking from bitter experience gained the previous year during the failed Anglo-Soviet talks that preceded the announcement of the Nazi-Soviet Pact, declared that future talks should not "be drawn out . . . as part of a scheme to use the interval in improving the defences of Baku."[56]

On the same day, March 29, Molotov delivered a major speech on foreign policy to the Supreme Soviet in which he took a very hard line on relations with the Allies, whom he accused of standing aside while the Fascist powers attacked Czechoslovakia and Albania only to spring into action when the Soviets invaded Finland. He charged Chamberlain with prolonging the Finnish War, "thus turning his 'peace loving' imperialist soul inside out for all the world to see." Why, he asked rhetorically, did the democracies draw the line against aggression by aiding Finland? (He apparently had forgotten Poland.) "This assistance," Molotov said, answering his own question, "is to be explained by the fact that in Finland they had a *place d'armes* ready for an attack upon the Soviet Union." But Allied scheming, he said, had come to naught. "These plans were thwarted by the brilliant successes of the Red Army." Toward the end of the speech, Molotov delivered an ominous warning about Bessarabia, "whose seizure by Rumania the Soviet Union had never recognised."[57] At no point in the speech did Molotov refer to the possibility of an improvement in relations with the Allies.

The British were not sure what to make of such a negative speech delivered so soon after Maiskii's demarche. Le Rougetel, in reporting the content of the speech, included an assessment of its import: "The main impression which I have derived from the speech is that it was intended primarily for internal consumption and that the Soviet Government intend to pursue a policy of prickly negativity, at any rate until the considerable wastage of the Finnish War has been made good." Although Le Rougetel felt that Molotov's description of the origins of the war between Germany and the Allies "might have been taken from a speech by the German Führer," he also pointed out that "little positive light was shed upon the question of German-Soviet relations."[58] Another possible reason for Molotov's uncompromising tone toward the Allies, which Le Rougetel did not suggest, might have been a Soviet desire to convey a message of trustworthiness to Berlin.

In London the search continued for a coherent Soviet policy. On March 30, Cadogan's private secretary, Gladwyn Jebb, wrote that since the primary British concern in the matter was to deny an energy-starved Germany access to Soviet oil, the best course might be for the British to buy the oil themselves. Then, he continued, "unless they [the Soviets] can guarantee us at least half-a-million tons a year, there will not only be no trade agreement with us, but we shall be quite unable to answer for the consequences." In other words, why not blackmail them? He continued, "It is possible (I do not think that it is very likely) that the Russians may react to such treatment as this, and if they did we should get most of the advantages which would accrue from the bombing of Baku without its very considerable disadvantages."[59]

This seemingly common-sense approach formed the basis of British thinking until the middle of April. British planning proceeded along two tracks, detailed consideration of the Baku operation and efforts to conclude a trade deal that would limit Soviet raw materials exports to Germany. Faced with two unpalatable alternatives, however, Chamberlain continued to vacillate, hoping something would come along to rescue him from his dilemma. In truth, the British still had no Soviet policy at all.

On April 2, the Joint Intelligence Committee started to draw up extensive plans for an attack on Baku,[60] and on the next day Sir Frederick Leith-Ross, director-general of the Ministry of Economic Warfare, submitted some thoughts on Soviet oil supplies. He claimed that, with "slight internal rationing [the Soviet Union] could make additional quantities available for export," but that British purchases "would undoubtedly reduce the quantities available to Germany and *pro tanto* embarrass her." Nevertheless, if the British were to trade raw materials from the Empire—for example, jute, nickel, and rubber—he concluded that it must be as part of a comprehensive war trade agreement in which the Soviets would agree to cease transshipment of these critical items to Germany. Otherwise little was to be gained from a trade deal with the USSR. Unfortunately, he felt the Soviets were unlikely to agree to any conditions circumscribing their trade with Germany.[61] Sir A. Faulkner, of the Mines Department, agreed with Leith-Ross that oil was the Achilles heel of Germany and saw nothing wrong with a large purchase of Soviet oil.[62]

But the Foreign Office was wary of the Soviets and thought that Maiskii's approach might have had the full blessing of Berlin. The author of one memorandum argued that Germany "is able to derive far greater benefits from a neutral than from a belligerent Soviet Union." The author then considered the problem of transshipment to Germany.

Of the two methods of preventing this that are open to us, viz. by diplomacy or by force, the latter would seem infinitely more likely to prove effective. If, however, in order that it may not be said that H.M.G. have not explored every possibility of achieving their object by peaceful means, it is decided to attempt the former, it would seem essential to set a strict time limit to any negotiations, and meanwhile to tighten the blockade of Soviet ports such as Vladivostok and to continue active preparations for action of a more drastic kind should the need arise.[63]

Domestic political considerations would, as the memorandum suggested, play a part in the ultimate decision by any British government. In this matter Chamberlain was acutely sensitive to the accusation of doing too little to secure Soviet assistance in view of the pounding he had sustained when the Nazi-Soviet Pact was signed, and on April 8, only four days after the memorandum above, the prime minister received fresh evidence of what lay in store for him should he decide to bomb before talking had been exhausted. Sir Stafford Cripps, who by this time had reached Washington, renewed his suggestions by telegram that Britain should accept the Soviet offer of talks. He argued that the Soviets would like to see the war end before they could be dragged in and "that the Soviet and Germany are fundamentally antagonistic." He also claimed that "the present imports via Vladivostok are mainly merely replacing goods normally imported through European ports," though where he got his information and how he felt able to contradict the Ministry of Economic Warfare must remain a mystery.[64] Cripps again stressed the urgency of the matter, claiming that time was short if the Allies wished to prevent an outright alliance between Germany and the USSR.

The tide was beginning to turn against the idea of bombing. Cripps had gained one valuable ally, "Rab" Butler, the man responsible for defending the government's foreign policy in the House of Commons. In a handwritten minute referring to Cripps's Washington telegram, Butler wrote: "I think, tho overstated, there is a lot in what Sir S. Cripps . . . say[s]. I am prepared to tell Maisky that we accept in principle the idea of exploring what we can get out of trade talks."[65]

Narrowing Options

Far more important in crystalizing British policy than any telegram from Cripps was the German invasion of Denmark and Norway, which began on April 9. This understandably threw British plans into confusion and made any diversion of force appear less attractive. Though the German attack was not the decisive factor in the British decision to postpone an attack on the Soviet Union indefinitely, it was simply the final, most convincing justification for the rejection of a course for which the temperament of the government and the already overstretched Allied resources were entirely unsuited.

If the rapid success of the German invasion was an unwelcome shock for the British, the Soviets viewed the situation quite differently. Count von der Schulenburg, the German ambassador to the Soviet Union, noticed a marked change in his hosts' behavior after the attack. Before, they had been sullen and uncooperative, but when Schulenburg met Molotov on April 9, after news of the invasion had been received in Moscow, "Herr Molotov was affability itself." Schulenburg guessed the reasons for this:

> In my opinion there is only one explanation for this about-face: our Scandinavian operations must have relieved the Soviet Government enormously—removed a great burden of anxiety so to speak. What their apprehension consisted of, can again not be determined with certainty. I suspect the following: the Soviet Government is always extraordinarily well-informed. If the English and French intended to occupy Norway and Sweden it may be assumed with certainty that the Soviet Government knew of these plans and was apparently terrified by them.[66]

The Allies had indeed intended to invade Scandinavia and were only preempted by the German attack. If the Soviets had got wind of this, as Schulenburg thought, they must have feared a reopening of the Finnish ulcer in tandem with an attack on the Caucasus.

As Molotov's brightened mood indicated, there was little likelihood of that now. On April 15 in London, the War Cabinet discussed the Scandinavian problem and the French fear of a Soviet move on Narvik. The decision was made, with which the French later agreed, that any further plans to attack the Soviet Union must wait until "some hostile act had been committed by the Soviet Government."[67]

The War Cabinet returned to the matter four days later, April 19, and by this time the emphasis was on negotiating rather than on military action. Referring to Cripps and those who shared his views, Halifax noted: "The matter had its political aspects in our own country; an attempt to negotiate a trade agreement with Russia might act as a lubricant, to ensure a better reception in certain Parliamentary quarters for our recent trade agreement with Spain and for the trade agreement which we hoped to negotiate with Italy." Chamberlain reiterated that the Soviets should not be allowed to string the talks along, but Halifax assured him that "this danger could be averted by giving the Russians at the appropriate stage of negotiations, a time limit of, say, a month." For this reason the Cabinet agreed to continue the vetting of ships bound for Vladivostok and other Soviet ports during the negotiations to keep pressure on Moscow. British options were rapidly shrinking; at this meeting there was no talk of bombing.[68]

Acting on instructions from the Cabinet, Halifax summoned the Soviet ambassador later the same day to tell him that the British government was interested in his suggestions of March 27 and handed him a memorandum to that effect. After scanning the piece of paper, Maiskii quickly picked out the key phrase stating that "His Majesty's Government would wish to be reassured as to the amount of Soviet goods going to Germany, and as to the destination of goods imported into the Soviet Union from abroad." He pointed out that this might well be difficult for his government to accept, since it implied an infringement of their sovereignty. Halifax assured the ambassador that this was not His Majesty's Government's last word and that he expected the Soviet reply to suggest changes. "I had little doubt," he told Maiskii, "that the Soviet leaders would make criticisms of any formula, since I had already found them adept at this art."[69]

The British did not receive an official reply immediately, but, in an ominous return to the Soviet negotiating tactics of the previous spring, they did get a clear indication of what such a reply might be when, three days later, the *Daily Worker*, the British Communist newspaper, referred to the "shiftiness and insolence" of the British note. A Foreign Office minute noted wearily that "in the absence of any comment in the Soviet press the present article may be taken to represent the Soviet reaction to our reply."[70] In an informal meeting with Maiskii the next day, April 23, Butler received confirmation of this when the ambassador told him that "any request by us to limit the Russian exports to Germany of her own produce would be doomed to failure." In a rather interesting subsequent discussion of the European situation, Maiskii "remarked with a leer that Italian policy was very simple. They had only to choose a winner and then place their bet."

Presumably, Soviet policy was not similarly opportunistic, since which-
ever side Moscow might eventually choose would, perforce, have the
sanction of history.[71]

Maiskii delivered the official Soviet response on April 29, and, as
expected, it gave the British very little to hope for regarding the possibility
of shutting down the Soviet conduit. The memorandum declared uncompromisingly that "the Soviet Government has a trade agreement with
Germany which it is carrying out, and intends to carry out in the future.
The Soviet Government considers this agreement its internal affair, which
cannot be made the subject of negotiations with third countries." The
memorandum hinted that the Soviets might agree not to reexport any goods
received from the British Empire but added the proviso that "the best
possible condition enabling trade negotiations to be commenced" would be
the release of the *Selenga* and the *Mayakovsky*, the two Soviet ships seized
by the British blockade.

After Halifax and Maiskii discussed this memorandum, the conversation turned to the situation in Scandinavia, and the foreign secretary
warned Maiskii that Sweden was in danger from a possible German attack.
The ambassador "implied that Swedish neutrality was threatened by the
Allies as much as by Germany." If further evidence were needed, it was
clear from this conversation that an Anglo-Soviet agreement would be very
difficult to engineer.[72]

Particularly annoying to the British was the Soviet habit of leaking
distorted accounts of the negotiations to the neutral press in London,
especially U.P.I. Censorship was incomplete in Britain, and such leaks
made it look as though the British were making unreasonable demands of
the Soviets and consequently increased the pressure on the government to
be more accommodating.[73] On April 30, the War Cabinet discussed the
problem but decided to continue the talks since Maiskii, though abrasive,
gave the impression that his government was serious about improving ties
with the British.[74]

The Foreign Office was, as usual, less optimistic, and in one memorandum Maclean even suggested that "in the circumstances it is hard to see
what use there would be in pressing the matter further or, if it were decided
to do so, what our next step should be." Nor was the opinion of other
British diplomats more optimistic. The only hope of closing Vladivostok, one departmental memorandum argued, would be to secure Japanese
help—but this would annoy the Americans, whose support was absolutely
vital to Britain. In short, the matter was complex, and British freedom of

maneuver was shrinking daily. The memorandum continued: "If we close with the Russian offer we shall not only not be able to use the failure of our negotiations with them as an excuse with the U.S. for dealing with the Japanese, but having ourselves compounded with the Soviet devil we shall be in no position to ask the United States to re-enforce the moral embargo if that were ever to become possible. We shall also have to desist from stopping Russian ships."[75]

But the Cabinet was unwilling to make the leap into the unknown by courting the Japanese wholeheartedly and preferred to respond to the Soviets, yet again hoping that something might turn up. The war in Norway was going badly for the Allies, with the evacuation from central Norway being made on May 1 and 2; so for the time being it seemed better to wait. At what Cadogan called a "Long Cabinet and a very bad and gloomy one" on May 6,[76] Halifax was authorized to draft a response to the Soviets.[77]

Two days later, the foreign secretary delivered it to Maiskii. Halifax reported Maiskii's unfavorable response, that the "present note simply repeated in a more elaborate form the arguments put forward in the memorandum which I [Halifax] had handed him on the 19th April." Furthermore, the USSR would tolerate no interference in its internal affairs, but "if the Soviet government had made a proposal for trade negotiations, we [the British] might assume that possibilities of trade existed." Maiskii laid the blame for bad relations squarely on His Majesty's Government and had asserted that "if there was to be any improvement in relations it would certainly not be achieved by such exchanges as these."[78]

To Robert Vansittart, Halifax's chief diplomatic advisor, such talks with the Soviets were distasteful, as he made clear in a letter to his chief: "M. Maisky's attitude is most impertinent. I hope you will give him no encouragement. Personally I regret to see that these conversations are being started at all, and, had I been consulted, I would not have encouraged them, because they seem to me to be both undignified and unlikely to lead to any real result."[79]

By the beginning of the second week of May, time had run out for Chamberlain's policy of watching and waiting. The House of Commons and the public were in an uproar over the Norwegian fiasco, for which Churchill shared a great deal of responsibility, though the fury was directed at the prime minister. In a Commons debate on the issue on May 7 and 8, it became clear that even though the government was still able to win a vote of confidence, the prime minister's support had slipped. Chamberlain decided to step down and allow Churchill to form a coalition Cabinet. The new government was born at a dramatic moment: as Churchill replaced Chamberlain on May 10, the Germans launched their offensive in the West.

Decision to Send Cripps

The pressure to accommodate the Soviets, far from easing, increased after the change in government. On May 11, an article in the *New Statesman and Nation* blasted the government for even thinking of selling out China in order to gain Japan's help against the Soviet Union. Showing signs of influence from Maiskii, the article announced tendentiously that, "While Downing Street asks for an undertaking, which it can get for the asking, that nothing imported from the British Empire shall reach Germany, it still pursues the alternative plan of a blockade of Vladivostok."[80] The Soviets had never offered any such guarantee, and, even if they had done so, there would have been no reliable means of verification. Besides that, agreement with the Soviet Union was, in and of itself, valueless unless it would lead to a reduction of Soviet raw materials exported to Germany, and the Soviets had explicitly stated that they would continue to trade with the Nazis at the current level, trade deal or no. Nevertheless, this would have been difficult to explain to the British public, especially the political Left, since the German offensive in France made it seem imperative to grab at any straw.[81]

The new War Cabinet, including as it did men from the Labour and Liberal parties, was even more receptive to such pressures than Chamberlain's government had been. Although both these parties included men who were long-time opponents of domestic Communism, both major opposition parties had believed that Chamberlain's anti-Soviet sympathies had been a major factor in Britain's failure to gain a defensive pact with Moscow before the war. In the new Cabinet's discussions of May 14–15, there was a greater sense of urgency to make some gesture toward the Soviets, even though it was still felt that the only likely result would be a limited barter deal. Clement Attlee, the new lord privy seal, suggested that in order to avoid Soviet obfuscation it might be wise to send an important British political figure to Moscow to tackle the problem directly.[82]

Attlee's idea was given impetus when, on May 16, Butler met with Maiskii, who came to protest the seizure of another Soviet ship. The ambassador said that he thought his government unlikely to respond to the British note of the eighth and agreed that the only way forward would seem to be by direct high-level contacts in Moscow.[83]

After his visit to Moscow and his years of advocating cooperation with the USSR, Cripps seemed the obvious man for the job, though some who had worked with him doubted his suitability. Nevertheless, many M.P.s felt that Cripps's consistent record of sympathy for the USSR might make him an appropriate representative of Great Britain in Moscow. After his talk with Maiskii, Butler, who was more in touch with the mood of the House than Halifax, wrote to the foreign minister advocating Cripps's appointment: "There is a fairly strong urge in this new Govt. both on right and left for a rapprochement and you will only be pressed if Cripps doesn't go."[84]

On May 18 the War Cabinet met again and held a long discusson of the Soviet problem. Halifax thought that the Soviets "were uneasy at the German advance" and that this might prove to be the opening for which the government had long hoped. Acting on Maiskii's suggestion to Butler about sending a British representative to Moscow, Halifax told the Cabinet that he had talked with Sir Stafford Cripps. Cripps still felt that the British government was at fault for the poor relations between the two countries but indicated that he was willing to go to Moscow to try and clear things up if asked—though he did not request the duty. The Cabinet agreed that Cripps should go, though it must be made clear to him that his purpose in going was merely to explore the ground and not to sign any agreement. Clearly, there were still some doubts about Cripps's political judgment, and, though the Cabinet records do not tell us who raised the idea that Cripps should be accompanied by a "watchdog," the diary of Hugh Dalton, the new minister of economic warfare, sheds some light on the matter. He recorded a conversation with Halifax the day before:

> H[ali]fax wants to send Cripps to Moscow. I throw some doubts on his suitability. Hfax thinks he might seem new and *persona grata* to them. I say that I have had an uncomfortable experience of him, and that it fell to me when the Labour Party finally despaired of training him in the House, to put him outside. Hfax asks what my relations with him are now. I say "rather sketchy." It is between us that, if he goes he must have a policeman from my Ministry and must have very close instructions and no power to make a settlement on his own.[85]

This was curious indeed. The suggestion to send Cripps came from the Conservatives, and the strongest caution came from the new Labour ministers.

Evidently then, it was on Dalton's suggestion that the Cabinet agreed "that at least one experienced advisor should be attached to Sir Stafford Cripps on a 'special mission' " and that Cripps should not be appointed full ambassador. The reason for this is unclear, but perhaps Churchill did not want the dispatch of an ambassador to the USSR, and a left-wing one at that, to be one of his first acts as prime minister. More to the point, he may also have felt that if Cripps's mission were to fail—as most expected it would—it would be much more embarrassing if Sir Stafford were a full ambassador rather than a messenger. At any rate, Halifax was authorized to approach Maiskii with the suggestion that Cripps be sent.[86]

During the next few days, Cripps was briefed on the policy of his government in various parts of the world and told just what should and should not be revealed to his future hosts. On May 21 he met with Butler, who discussed travel details, briefed Cripps some more, and subtly let it be known that the mission was purely exploratory and that no agreement should be signed.

The briefings show just how little hope the British government held for successful cooperation with the Soviets, even in the unlikely event of Cripps's success. In fact, it was believed that too close an identification with the Soviets in the Far East might be counterproductive, inducing the Japanese to turn southward against Hong Kong and Singapore. Hugh Dalton, the author of the Far East briefing, concluded, moreover, that if the British and Soviets were seen to be working together, this "would be likely to have the effect of throwing Chiang Kai-shek into Russia's arms with a consequent spread of communist influence in unoccupied China and the possibility of a civil war on an ideological basis as in Spain."[87] Regarding the Balkans, Cripps was told that it was in the British interest for the nations there to form a "united front" to resist aggression not only from Germany but also from the Soviet Union. Cripps was told quite clearly that "we should not welcome any Soviet expansion or increase of Soviet influence in the Balkans."[88] Later, in his first meeting with Stalin, Cripps forgot this last bit of advice, much to the chagrin of the Foreign Office.

In order to prevent an increase of Soviet influence in the Balkans, and in case the Baku project were ever to be revived, Cripps was informed that Turkey was to be wooed patiently to the Allied side. "Generally speaking our policy towards Turkey in regards to the Soviet Union is to put Turkey in a state of willingness . . . to help us against the Soviet Union in the event of our needing such help."[89]

Fitzroy Maclean wrote the main brief, which drew a rather gloomy and, as it turned out, remarkably accurate picture of the chances for drawing the Soviets away from their Nazi partners. He argued that the frequently repeated claim (one which Cripps himself espoused) that the Soviets were yearning for an opportunity to reverse their policy and aid the Allies was unfounded. In his opinion, "M. Stalin is concerned, first, to avoid hostilities with any great Power, and, secondly, to prolong the war between the Allies and Germany in the hope of weakening both sides." Maclean felt that Stalin had decided to help the Nazis for two reasons. First, in the Soviet estimation Berlin was the weaker side strategically so long as the British navy could keep the German fleet bottled up. By aiding the Germans, Maclean reasoned, Stalin hoped to prolong the war and thus weaken both sides, increasing the relative might of the USSR. Second, the Germans, if vexed, could more easily strike against the USSR than the Allies, so Stalin was trying to appease them. Maclean questioned the reasoning of those who felt that the German breakthrough in France might scare the Soviets into changing sides.[90] Militarily, the Soviets would be poorly advised to attack the Germans, he argued, and any economic pressures they might exert would take effect too slowly to alter the situation in France. "In other words," Maclean wrote, "the stoppage of supplies to Germany from Russia and even Soviet intervention would not materially affect the prospects of an *early* German victory, while a last minute change of attitude on the part of the Soviet Government would be likely to have unpleasant consequences for the Soviet Union should Germany achieve such a victory."

Indeed, the assumption that Stalin was afraid of an Allied defeat, Maclean thought, might be fundamentally mistaken, since such a defeat could lead to a revolutionary world situation, providing opportunities for Communist expansion: "It would involve the collapse of the British Empire, which has always stood for everything that the rulers of Russia, whether Imperial or Bolshevik, have most detested, and would in particular remove the limits which we have set to Russian expansion in Asia."[91] In Maclean's view, the chances of a reconciliation between Britain and the USSR were slim.

The next day, May 22, Maiskii seemed to confirm Maclean's pessimistic analysis when he delivered the Soviet response to the British proposals of

May 8. The reply, which as Halifax sharply pointed out had already been leaked to the press, claimed that the British had made the first approach in the current round of negotiations but that the retention of Soviet ships and British insistence upon a restriction of Russo-German trade made agreement unlikely. Still, Maiskii claimed that face-to-face talks in Moscow might iron out these problems. Maclean, who was present at the meeting, spoke privately, in Russian, with Maiskii before the latter returned to the Soviet embassy. The ambassador said, surprisingly frankly, that the most the British could hope for was "a simple barter agreement," and, as Maclean recorded, Maiskii said "that if we insisted on a war trade agreement, there was no prospect whatever of coming to terms." He did hold out one shred of hope, however, when he did not flatly deny that a political agreement might follow a trade pact.[92]

It may be, as Maiskii claims in his memoirs, that he was "delighted" with the appointment of Cripps, but from these conversations it is difficult to see how any real improvement could have been made in Anglo-Soviet relations in light of the two countries' differing aims.[93] A much more plausible explanation of the sudden Soviet frigidness is that Moscow, no longer feeling directly threatened by the Allies, did not care much one way or the other about the progress of the negotiations. The Soviet aim in talking was now limited to gaining free passage for their ships through the British blockade.

Also on May 22, TASS published an article that closely followed the official Soviet response. As in the earlier Soviet note to the British government, the article claimed that the British had set the current round of trade talks in motion after approaching the Soviets in February and that Maiskii's meeting with Halifax on March 27 had merely been a response to the British offer. Nor did the Soviets accept the British assertion that the *Selenga* and *Mayakovsky* were in French hands and therefore beyond the control of the British. The article ended with a blast at the British request for a restriction of Soviet trade with Germany: "The Soviet Government points out that the very fact that the English Government brought forward for discussion questions which fall exclusively within the competence of the Soviet Government shows that the English Government has no desire to conduct trade negotiations with the USSR."[94] This article provided further evidence that Soviet ardor for an agreement with Great Britain had waned after the German conquest of Norway. It looked as though Cripps would have his work cut out for him in Moscow.

When Butler met with Maiskii the day after the TASS article appeared, the ambassador again seemed more encouraging than his government. In what was surely an unusual event, he admitted that the TASS article had been mistaken in claiming that the British had initiated the trade talks— an admission he indirectly adhered to in his memoirs by not mentioning the article at all.[95] Butler recorded his impression that "the Ambassador seemed to attach considerable importance to Sir Stafford Cripps' visit and said that if a barter trade agreement could be reached, other more important decisions could follow."[96]

It is difficult to tell at this distance whether this is just another example of Butler's perennial optimism or if Maiskii was serious. Certainly, Maiskii was unprepared to be so forthcoming in public; but, as Cripps believed, this may have been owing to a fear of German retaliation. A more convincing explanation is that Maiskii, who from the tone of his memoirs appears to have developed a small degree of sympathy for the British, may have privately disagreed with his government's line. This would explain the consistent disparity in signals the British were receiving from the Soviets. The true test of Soviet intent would be the tone of negotiations in Moscow.[97]

In a very interesting conversation the next day, Hugh Dalton tried to convince Maiskii that the British Cabinet change had been like a new broom. Dalton gave the Foreign Office minutes of this conversation: "I strove to persuade him that there was now a new spirit here, a firmer will and a much stronger drive to win the war, and a keen desire to get rid of all the stale old misunderstandings on both sides between his country and ours. I said I thought that the recent exchange of notes between the two Governments was worse than useless, causing irritation and leading to no progress. What were wanted now, I said, were frank talks aiming at practical results." The Foreign Office was understandably a bit skeptical of such sweeping optimism—one is tempted to say naiveté—and Sargent noted next to this passage, "How frank and plausible it all sounds!" Dalton, and many others new to the problem of dealing diplomatically with the Soviets, would have to learn through experience that Anglo-Soviet distrust and conflict sprang not so much from personalities of those in charge, nor from "stale old misunderstandings," as from fundamentally different state interests and world views.

The two touched upon other matters in their talk. As he recorded in his diary, Dalton "gave Maisky foreknowledge of our attitude about the two Russian ships detained at Saigon."[98] He told the ambassador that Cripps was empowered to release the ships "as a gesture of good will." By tipping his hand in this dubious effort to win Maiskii's confidence, Dalton had in a stroke undercut any concessions that might have been extracted in return for the release of the ships.

Dalton also inquired about the Soviet government's attitude to the two advisors accompanying Cripps. One, Professor Postan from the Ministry of Economic Warfare, had been born in Bessarabia but was a naturalized British citizen. Maiskii assured him that there would be no protocol problems. Nevertheless, problems emerged immediately. The day after his talk with Dalton, Maiskii, presumably acting on orders received from Moscow, met Halifax and told him "that the Soviet Government had no objection to receiving Sir Stafford Cripps or anyone else in whom His Majesty's Government had confidence, but were anxious that whoever was sent should proceed to Moscow, not as special envoy, but as a regular Ambassador."[99] The War Cabinet had already debated whether to send Cripps to Moscow as ambassador and had rejected the idea for reasons discussed above. Soviet motives are the most interesting in this matter: it has been claimed that the request for Cripps's appointment as ambassador stemmed from the Soviet desire to talk with a more official figure than a mere "messenger boy."[100] But Soviet considerations may well have been quite the opposite. The day on which Maiskii delivered his government's message, May 26, the British began their final withdrawal from the continent at Dunkirk, and the Soviets may have thought that Cripps, coming as he was on "special mission," would send the wrong signal to the Germans. Hitler might think that the USSR had been frightened by German military successes and that Stalin was running into the arms of the British. If Cripps were simply an ambassador, the Soviets perhaps reasoned, then the event would seem less out of the ordinary and consequently less likely to provoke the Nazis.

As for the British, one member of the government had no objections to naming Cripps ambassador. Dalton wrote in his diary on May 27 that the Soviets "want a proper Ambassador. They are very touchy and troublesome. . . . I tell Butler that I am quite prepared for Cripps to be given any title or status that they like . . . it might as well be worth considering whether we should not leave him in Moscow as a permanent Ambassador. (This would have advantages from another angle.)"[101] Cripps had been a headache for the Labour party, and, as Dalton's last line suggests, Moscow was a suitably distant spot for exile.

The British government took some time to decide what title to give Cripps, as their attention was riveted on the evacuation from France. But rather than recall him (he had left England on his roundabout journey to

Moscow on the twenty-seventh) the Cabinet decided on May 31 to appoint Sir Stafford Cripps ambassador to the Soviet Union.[102]

As soon as the decision was made, the news was leaked to the press in Moscow, as Le Rougetel informed the Foreign Office on June 1: "Some hours before I could possibly have seen M. Molotov, [the] Moscow correspondent of the United Press had heard that agrément for Sir S. Cripps had been asked for."[103] Maclean blamed Moscow for the leak, though he presented no hypothesis explaining why the Soviets were being so prickly. They continued to be difficult when, on June 5, they refused to admit the same Professor Postan about whom Maiskii had assured Dalton. Perhaps the rulers in Moscow felt that the admission of a Bessarabian-born diplomat, only days before they intended to seize that province, was not the best idea.

As Cripps proceeded slowly toward Moscow via the Balkans, several Foreign Office officials debated the wisdom of sending Sir Stafford on his mission. Some British diplomats were skeptical about sending a man with such pronounced left-wing views as Sir Stafford's to Moscow as His Majesty's representative. Sir Orme Sargent wrote a long analysis of the matter, which deserves to be quoted at some length: "The Soviet Government do not trust Sir Stafford Cripps whom they no doubt look upon as a renegade inasmuch as he is serving His Majesty's Government. At the same time they know perfectly well that he is not in the confidence of H.M. Government. I suspect therefore that Stalin, who probably has a keen sense of humour, is going to make the most of the false position into which he has now manoeuvered us." Sargent believed the Soviets would claim that the Cripps mission was a replay of the ill-starred Strang mission of the previous summer, when the head of the mission also had no real authority to conclude a deal. "I fear therefore," Sargent continued, "that in the immediate future we must face the fact that we may have to give Sir Stafford Cripps full authority to negotiate a settlement and trust to luck that he will not commit us beyond a harmless barter agreement, since this is all the Russians want to obtain from us, i.e. just enough to annoy the Germans without provoking any unpleasant measures of retaliation from them." In Sargent's opinion, Stalin's only motive for inviting a British representative to Moscow was to frighten Berlin with the prospect of an Anglo-Soviet rapprochement and thus to pressure the Germans to accept Soviet occupation of "either Lithuania or Bessarabia or both." He worried that if Cripps were given more authority he might agree to such a Soviet move "for the sake of Russian 'goodwill.' "

Alexander Cadogan was even less enthusiastic about giving Sir Stafford Cripps free rein than his colleague: "I shd be very apprehensive of what Sir S. Cripps might sign," Cadogan wrote. "He is an excellent lawyer & a very nimble debater in Parliament, but he has not yet won his spurs in diplomacy." Cadogan was less concerned than Sargent about offending the Soviets: "I personally attach no importance whatever to Russia. Russia is in no event going to do us any good: and I am optimistic enough to think that she won't do us much harm. Enthusiastic individuals like Sir S. Cripps . . . think they can 'swing' a country. I'm afraid I don't share their enthusiasm." Halifax had the last word in this amusing exchange, and, characteristically, he advised patience: "We must see how the affair develops," he wrote, "and hope that all Sir O. Sargent's forebodings will not be realised!"[104]

So, with profound misgivings in the Foreign Office back in London, Sir Stafford Cripps arrived in Moscow on June 12, only one week after the completion of the evacuation from Dunkirk. He would face a formidable task trying to vindicate his belief that the Soviets' genuine desire was to aid the Western Allies and that they had only been prevented from doing so by the ineptitude of British diplomacy.

At least Cripps himself remained optimistic. En route to Moscow he told the American representative in Bulgaria that "there has been a tremendous change in the last two weeks in the attitude of Russia toward France and Great Britain," and that he had "real hope of something 'very constructive' being arranged." He claimed that "Russia at last realizes that Germany's war-machine in the event of conquest of France and Great Britain will not be abandoned until Russia is crushed."[105] Evidently, Cripps did not entertain the notion that the Soviets believed in Britain's capacity to resist.

The British government's decision to dispatch Sir Stafford Cripps to Moscow was a watershed in Anglo-Soviet relations. It requires little imagination to envision that the history of the war would have been quite different had the Western Allies decided as part of their war with Germany to launch an attack on the Soviet Union. One can easily understand the Cabinet's reluctance to make such a decision precipitately. In the end, the new British government under Churchill decided to try negotiation once more. Cripps's mission might not produce much, they reasoned, but the imponderables of an attack on the USSR were daunting indeed.

Curiously, the British decision to talk with Moscow rather than fight has received little attention. Historians discuss this incident parenthetically, if at all. One recent, detailed history of this period, for example, devotes only one paragraph to the Cabinet's decision to send Cripps and ascribes the decision to two causes: London's perception that the Soviets were frightened by the rapidity of Hitler's advance into France, and the hope that Moscow would thus welcome closer ties with London.[106] Another historian correctly pinpoints as the origin of Cripps's mission the February meeting between Molotov and Cripps, during which the former dangled the carrot of an Anglo-Soviet trade agreement before his guest's eyes.[107] This second historian does not, however, show how Soviet enthusiasm for an agreement waned rapidly after the successful German invasion of Norway and does not discuss the critical Allied debate over whether to bomb or talk with the Soviets.

Neither of these explanations is entirely wrong, but they neglect important British considerations. Churchill's Cabinet certainly hoped that German military successes might provide an opening for an Anglo-Soviet rapprochement, and Molotov's approach to Sir Stafford Cripps indisputably planted the seed of the Cripps mission. The Cabinet's decision to send an ambassador to Moscow five months after the recall of Sir William Seeds was, however, the culmination of a lengthy and complex process. If there was one central cause it was that the British government hoped, by means of a trade agreement with the Kremlin, to disrupt or restrict the transport of strategic commodities to Nazi Germany through the Soviet Union.

Between January and April, London decided that the risks of trying to shut the Soviet conduit by air attack were far too great to hazard; and in May the German offensive in France destroyed any lingering Allied notions that the USSR could be safely attacked. So Sir Stafford was sent to Moscow to try his hand at negotiating with the Kremlin. For the British government, an improvement in Anglo-Soviet relations would be a welcome by-product of a trade agreement. But such an improvement was not, as the historians cited above suggest, the primary purpose of Cripps's mission.

The inter-Allied debate over whether to bomb the Soviet Union was not as lunatic as it might seem at first sight. To be sure, an air of unreality pervades the predictions by some British leaders that the Soviet Union could be brought to her knees in a very short time by air assaults on the Baku oil fields. But in 1940 experience had not yet taught governments the strengths and weaknesses of aerial bombardment. Wild overestimations of the efficacy of bombing were current during the interwar period, as the following from Giulio Douhet, the Italian aerial theorist, shows: "A complete breakdown of the social structure cannot but take place in a country subjected to this kind of merciless pounding from the air. The time would soon come when, to put an end to horror and suffering, the people themselves, driven by the instinct of self-preservation, would rise up and demand an end to the war—this before their army and navy had time to mobilize at all!"[108] Given the actual performance of air forces during the war, as opposed to such hair-raising predictions, it was perhaps just as well that the British Cabinet decided to give the arts of diplomacy one more chance rather than launching an air offensive against the USSR.

An important and perhaps decisive factor leading the British toward a diplomatic solution of the Soviet problem was the Cabinet change of May. Churchill's coalition government included Labour members, almost all of whom were more inclined to view the USSR sympathetically than had the ministers of Chamberlain's government. For example, Hugh Dalton, the new minister of economic warfare, believed that the British should have handed over the Baltic States to the USSR in the Spring of 1939 as the price of an alliance with Moscow.[109] He was prepared to go even further in 1940: "I would gladly let them have India," he wrote in his diary, "if they would change over to our side. This has been a favorite idea of mine for years!"[110]

By late May 1940, the Allies no longer had the military power to deal the Soviet Union a serious blow while simultaneously fighting the Germans. The Cripps mission—the success of which few British diplomats expected—was the result. As Lord Kitchener said in 1915, "One makes war, not as one would like to, but as one must."[111]

Soviet thinking during the period January–May 1940 is, of course, more difficult to reconstruct with certainty than British. Certain points are clear, however: the Soviets sensed Allied preparations for an attack, either via Scandinavia or in the Black Sea region. Molotov's conversation with Sir Stafford Cripps and Maiskii's follow-up meeting with Lord Halifax were certainly related to these Allied military preparations. As Schulenburg noted, Stalin was quite well informed, and it is hard to believe that the astute Soviet diplomacy of spring 1940 was not supported by an excellent intelligence network.

Soviet intelligence efforts were bolstered by a slipshod attitude to military security in the Allied camp, and to ineffective press censorship. On January 19 in Paris, for example, *Le Temps* printed a story about Allied military plans to aid the Finns, to land a force near Murmansk, and to create a diversion in the Black Sea region. Naturally, the Soviets reacted, and *Pravda* denounced Allied scheming the very next day.[112] John Colville, Churchill's private secretary, despaired of preserving military security when allied with the French, who, in his opinion, "cannot keep a secret."[113] But the British themselves may not have been entirely blameless for damaging leaks. In particular, a string of poor appointments in the British Embassy in Moscow may have compromised security, as the following from a Foreign Office memorandum shows:

> I think that we should lose no time in drawing the attention of the Air Ministry to the folly of sending to Moscow as confidential clerk to the Air Attaché, a man whose parents are in the power of the Soviet authorities. This it may be observed is not the first unfortunate appointment to this post; Wing Commander Hallawell's first clerk, Hubbard, made no attempt to disguise tastes which soon caused him to fall an easy victim to the wiles of the Peoples Commissariat for Internal Affairs, whom he appears to have supplied with confidential documents extracted from the Air Attaché's safe. His successor, who arrived in response to an urgent request for a completely normal man, was improbable as it may seem, a Mohammedan, a drunkard and a Communist.[114]

Such carelessness, if indeed it was not more than that, made Soviet intelligence gathering a relatively easy task. But the Soviets were also quick to react to the information they gleaned from Allied leaks. Each Soviet move can be traced to some specific aspect of the European military situation. When they were worried about a possible Allied attack, they became conciliatory and proposed negotiations. As soon as the threat vanished, so did Soviet conciliation, and Moscow began to dig in its heels over details which, had it been truly interested in an agreement, could have been dispensed with in hours. Then, as the French front collapsed, the Soviets sent an appropriate signal to Berlin by demanding that Cripps be made ambassador. As Cripps once wrote, "The Russians have always been realists in their foreign policy."[115]

The Soviets were more sensitive to the shifting military balance than were the Allies, whose policy debates seemed to lack a sense of urgency. Colville lamented that "dilatoriness is inseparable from democracy, it appears."[116] As the events of the next few weeks would show, the Soviets could quickly alter their foreign policy to suit a fluid situation: after the French capitulation left Germany the dominant continental power, the Soviets would pull closer to Germany, not to Britain; the British could not harm them, Germany could. By the same token, London could offer nothing to entice Moscow away from the Germans. So, paradoxically, even though the crisis in Anglo-Soviet relations had passed, and the threat of an Allied attack had disappeared, the two countries were even further from an understanding than before.

CHAPTER TWO

FROM THE FALL

OF FRANCE TO

ORAN—MOSCOW

REASSURED

JUNE–AUGUST 1940

When Sir Stafford Cripps was appointed British ambassador to the Soviet Union on May 31, 1940, he had not held a governmental post since the collapse of the second Labour government in August 1931. This hiatus in practical governmental experience was important, accentuating as it did certain extreme aspects of Cripps's character. Since he was one of the central figures involved in Anglo-Soviet affairs from 1940–42, it is worth examining his background in order to understand his occasionally curious behavior as ambassador.

Cripps came from a family with a long tradition of political activity in reformist causes. On his mother's side one of his ancestors had supported the colonies during the American War of Independence, and a later relative had been an M.P. siding with John Bright. Cripps's father, Lord Parmoor, was himself a politician who defied the laws of political gravity by moving leftward as he became older. He was an M.P. in a Tory government, received a peerage from the Liberals, and gained ministerial rank from Labour.

Religion was as important in Cripps's upbringing as was the family tradition of politics. His parents were devout Christians, but they practised an ecumenical Christianity—an important factor in Cripps's future world view. His mother, a sister of Beatrice Potter Webb, died when Stafford was only four, but in a letter she wrote before her death she described how she wished her children to be raised: "I should like them to be trained to be undogmatic and unsectarian Christians, charitable to all churches and sects, studying the precepts and actions of Christ as their example, taking their religious inspiration directly from the spirit of the New Testament."[1] His parents' universalism would leave its mark on Cripps.

Young Stafford received his education at Winchester, where he developed a close relationship with the headmaster, Dr. Burge, whose religious views were akin to those of Cripps's parents. On leaving Winchester, Cripps took the unusual step of turning down a place at Oxford, choosing instead to study chemistry at University College, London. He was adept at his work, but there was little likelihood of putting his training to use in industry. Instead, social and family pressures pushed him in the direction of law and public service, as an extract from a letter written to Cripps's father from his future father-in-law illustrates: "We have to look further ahead than they at their time of life are likely to do, and the day will probably come when the necessity of amassing money in business will no longer exist."[2] So, with the characteristic public-school bias against a career in industry firmly implanted, Cripps turned to law and was called to the Bar in 1913. He eventually became one of Britain's most highly paid barristers.

As with many of his generation, the World War was a shattering experience for Cripps. Though unable to serve at the front because of poor health, he drove an ambulance in France until the government became aware of his experience in chemistry and called him back to Britain to help in the operation of a munitions factory. There he worked so hard that within a short time he suffered a physical collapse.

Until 1916 Cripps had been a whole-hearted supporter of the war, but during his recuperation he came under the influence of his father, who had opposed the war from its early days.[3] Later in his life, Cripps's resentment against the war and its leaders became quite intense. He believed that the "German threat" had been a capitalist-imperialist hoax, and he referred to the war itself as an "orgy of capitalist profiteering."[4] In his opinion, the high ideals of the generation of 1914 had been deliberately manipulated for wicked, selfish purposes. As he put it in a 1935 speech: "I cannot rid my mind of the sordid history of capitalist deception. The empty and hollow excuses of 1914 which I was then fool enough to believe."[5]

During the 1920s, Cripps, working again with Dr. Burge, participated in an attempt to prevent future wars by promoting international Christian cooperation through the "World Alliance for Promoting International Friendship through the Churches." This episode sheds light on the dominant strain in Cripps's personality: his idealism and his belief, derived from his ecumenical upbringing, that men of Christian goodwill are all aiming at essentially the same ends.

Unfortunately, the World Alliance failed because of doctrinal differences and even more because the bitterness generated by the war marred cooperation between the various national churches. But Cripps, undaunted, refused to abandon his belief that such heterogeneity could eventually be fused into a common effort, if only the obstacles could be removed.

The Labour movement seemed to offer the means to root out the secular impediments blocking mankind's reconciliation. Cripps had been impressed by the MacDonald-Henderson foreign policy of the first Labour government, and he was consequently upset by Conservative moves to reverse it, such as the severing of diplomatic relations with the Soviet Union in 1927. The seemingly uncompromising idealism of the young party fired Cripps's imagination as well. As one of his biographers notes, Labour "had no history of the compromises that make up so much of practical politics."[6]

Herbert Morrison, who was on the lookout for the kind of badly needed legal and technical expertise Cripps possessed, was largely responsible for drawing him into the party.[7] Because his legal skills were so valuable, Cripps, unlike most Labour leaders, bypassed service in the party's lower echelons. Instead, he entered at the top as solicitor general of the second Labour government, before he had even gained a seat in the House of Commons. After one unsuccessful attempt to secure a seat, Cripps found a constituency in East Bristol and became an M.P. on January 16, 1931. Judged by the standards of his later career, his platform was fairly low key, being limited to calls for improved social services and disarmament.[8]

The collapse of the Labour government in August 1931 was a seminal event in Cripps's life, on a par with the Great War. Believing that the financial crisis had been artificially engineered by the capitalists to destroy the Labour party, Cripps agreed with Clement Attlee, who called Ramsay MacDonald's creation of a "National Government" "the greatest betrayal in the political history of this country."[9] If the capitalists were going to use extraconstitutional methods to thwart the verdict of the electorate, Cripps reasoned, then this was nothing less than a declaration of class war. His politics veered sharply to the Left, far outpacing the bulk of the party.

Most of the Labour party refused to join MacDonald in the National Government and were martyred for their beliefs in a massive electoral reverse. Suddenly, Cripps, who with George Lansbury and Clement Attlee was one of the few prominent Labour men to retain his seat in the House, became a major leader of the opposition after less than a year in Parliament. Deprived of governmental office, and hence of responsibility, during the 1930s Cripps was able to spin out his theories about a sweeping reconstruction of society, having had in his extremely short political career almost no experience of the practical constraints on political effectiveness. And as luck would have it, his new-found prominence gave his theories an unusually wide audience.

It is difficult to describe Cripps's political views, since he never did so himself in a comprehensive manner. He wrote a number of books and articles dealing with the broad goals of Socialism as he saw them, especially concentrating on the mechanics by which a future Socialist government could speed up legislation.[10] But he never examined the bases of his belief in the Socialist paradise, which he felt was destined to prevail. Faith was the root of his vision, and his Christianity mingled with his Socialism until the two became completely indistinguishable. Political opponents appeared not as men with alternative views of the world but as evil men barring the road to humanity's progress for their own selfish purposes. A messianic tone pervaded his writing: "At the end of the road," he once wrote, "we shall . . . discern our goal, the Kingdom of Heaven here on earth, the social salvation of our people and of the world."[11] He rejected the idea that men acting in their own interests are guided by an "unseen hand," unconsciously benefiting all mankind. What was needed to eradicate war, poverty, and scarcity in the world, Cripps felt, was "to pull down the building [of state] and start its erection upon more secure foundations."[12] The ultimate goal, as the Socialist League constitution stated, was the creation of the "Socialist Commonwealth." "The purpose of this Commonwealth is to create an environment ·within which all its citizens may achieve self-expression and happiness as cooperating members of a society animated by a common purpose."[13] "That purpose," Cripps later wrote, "is not [for individuals] to enrich themselves, but to serve the community."[14] Such a common motivation was impossible, he argued, within a capitalist system, which by its nature required inequality: "A prosperous and privileged ruling economic class necessarily means an exploited working class and a world of comparative scarcity. The very structure of capitalism demands it, however much it may be regulated."[15] Only nationalization of the means of production could guarantee that goods and services would be provided for the benefit of the entire population rather than for the profit of a small group of capitalists.

Conservative efforts to rescue capitalism from its historically, scientifically, and divinely ordained collapse meant that Britain was being "steadily driven . . . towards more and more totalitarian conceptions."[16] The choice was stark: either a slow drift toward Fascism in a vain effort to save capitalism and to cling to "outworn democratic forms,"[17] or else the adoption of Socialism. "So long as we are ruled by those who regard capitalism as their real religion," he wrote, "it must mean the abandonment of all true democracy and Christianity in favor of capitalism, just as it has done in Fascist countries."[18] The Conservatives may pay homage to democracy, but "inevitably the Fascist tendencies must win in the long run because of their far greater efficiency in preserving capitalism."[19]

It is quite true, as one of Cripps's laudatory biographers claims, that Sir Stafford eschewed violence and repeatedly affirmed his belief that Socialism could be created by peaceful means—in Britain at least. Nevertheless, Cripps felt that extraconstitutional opposition by the capitalists was inevitable. He stated uncompromisingly that a Socialist government would brook no such behavior and that "those who use unconstitutional means must not complain if they are met with force."[20] Although this comment seems reasonable, and is in fact no more than any government would maintain, Cripps's definition of unconstitutional tactics was disturbingly broad. For example, he wrote: "The coming to power of a Labour Government would be the immediate signal for an attempt by the capitalists to precipitate a crisis."[21] Cripps never seems to have given a thought to the possibility that such a crisis might be the result of a spontaneous fear of expropriation, fueled in part by his own extremism, rather than by conscious design or deliberate sabotage by a capitalist cabal.

And if capitalist opposition in the opening stages of a Labour government was inevitable, what was to happen to these opponents after the Great Transition? Would they be imprisoned? (After all, Cripps wrote of the "class war.") Or would they be converted by the self-evident success of Socialism? One can search Cripps's writings in vain for an answer. His unwillingness to address the more unpleasant implications of his ideas frequently landed him in trouble with the press. Although he undeniably believed in the democratic process—as he interpreted it—some of his frank theorizing scared the less adventurous public.

Cripps's principal biographer attempts to explain away the extraordinary string of political gaffes his subject made when speaking about the tactics a future Socialist government would have to adopt: "It must be said . . . that Stafford Cripps' passion for honesty in politics led him into statements which did not represent his mind."[22] This biographer contends that Cripps was too frank about the means by which a Socialist government should deal with potential extraconstitutional threats, whereas the accepted practice in British politics was not to anticipate or discuss publicly problems that might never arise, thereby reducing political friction. Cripps's habit of thrashing everything out in public did him no great service, his biographer writes, since "it is foreign to the peculiar political genius of this island to consider anything but ends."[23]

This explanation is, however, fundamentally faulty, since it assumes that Cripps saw clearly all the ramifications of his political beliefs. He did not. Cripps was a very busy person, pursuing an active and hugely successful legal practice as well as maintaining a hectic political schedule. Such frenetic activity gave him little time to reflect on the logical consequences of his ideas, ideas that were, as his aunt Beatrice Webb noted in her diary, often "immature" and "slapdash."[24] Cripps's political indiscretions were not lapses from some unwritten political code but were, rather, the consequences of what was a fundamentally undemocratic political philosophy— even though Cripps argued and genuinely believed that he stood for a higher form of democracy.

Like many Utopians, Cripps concentrated on two points, vague descriptions of the coming Socialist society and detailed discussions of the mechanics necessary to overcome the transition crisis. In a phrase that probably caused him more political headaches than any other he ever wrote—but which, significantly, he never retracted—Cripps explained in 1933 how a Socialist government would have to deal with such a crisis: "It is unlikely that a Socialist Party will be able to maintain its position of control without adopting some exceptional means such as the prolongation of the life of Parliament for a further term without an election."[25] Four years later, in 1937, the controversy over this comment was still very much alive. Cripps attempted to explain this phrase to one inquirer: "The implication [of the passage]," he wrote, "is that the Labour Government which failed in the first five years to carry through a real program of change would find itslef [*sic*] in the impossible position of having to try and prolong Parliament as the only way out, and that this was put forward to prove the necessity for a drastic program of action in the first five years."[26] Because of his implicit faith in the desirability and viability of his vision of Socialism, Cripps never seems to have asked himself several obvious questions. What if the Socialist experiment failed? What were the criteria for failure, or what should be done if the electorate found the sacrifices on the road to the

Socialist Utopia too great to bear? For Cripps, anything short of complete success (which was itself never defined precisely) could be explained as the result of illegal capitalist machinations, justifying the indefinite continuance of a Labour government. And from his writings it is clear that Cripps believed capitalist plots, like streetcars, would trundle along at regular intervals during the creation of Socialism in Britain. "If a policy of real Socialism is to be followed out," he once wrote, "then we anticipate the most active opposition of every capitalist in the country."[27]

Cripps was holistic in his thinking; he believed that one enormous change—state acquisition of the means of production—would eliminate the divisions that have plagued mankind since the dawn of history. This made his views not so much a political philosophy as a quasi-religious faith. Consistent with his ecumenical upbringing and his attempts to unify the Christian church in the 1920s, Cripps tolerated all who proclaimed Socialism as their goal. If belief in the Ultimate Utopia was genuine then all methodological divergences could be dismissed as mere tactical vicissitudes on the road to Socialism. This explains why, of all the major leaders of the Labour party, Cripps was most inclined to cooperate with the Communists. At their 1933 Conference, Labour had declared uncompromisingly: "Fascism and Communism alike are a challenge to our democratic institutions and to the system of society based on political, social and economic equality which we seek to establish."[28]

Cripps rejected this view, and in the same year he wrote: "There is an essential difference between dictatorships of the right and of the left, not so much in their form as in the class objective which underlies them."[29] Comparing Nazi Germany with Soviet Russia, he felt: "The two types of government are essentially different, though in some matters of detail the means adopted to seize or maintain power are similar [since with] Communism the objective is to destroy privilege and to put the economic power effectively into the hands of the common people."[30]

The terrain of Cripps's political perception comprised a great continental divide: the precipitation on one side flowed toward the great Socialist sea, on the other toward the Fascist pit. Parties of the Left, whether Britain's Labour party or Soviet Communists, were, Cripps felt, all groping toward the same end. If Stalin seemed a bit brutal to British Socialists, that was simply because the Bolsheviks had faced such tremendous obstacles dragging their country into the twentieth century. In a rambling sentence, Cripps explained this to a doubting friend in February 1939:

I myself do not think that there is any other method by which [the Russians] could make the advances they have made during the recent years, and the Tsarist regime had completely prevented any possibility of a real democracy in the early stages, and I am convinced that by no other way could the Russian people have made the advances in standards which they are now undoubtedly enjoying in spite of the enormous sacrifices they have had to make for armaments in view of the hostility of their neighbors.[31]

This passage reveals a great deal about Cripps's world view. He could dismiss suffering in the USSR, since he saw it as a temporary phenomenon, to be endured only during the creation of Socialism. In Britain, however, Cripps remained a vocal opponent of rearmament right up until the outbreak of war in September 1939. He saw Chamberlain's efforts to rearm as a step calculated both to impoverish the workers, thereby increasing capitalist profits, and to prepare for an aggressive imperialist war. Such behavior was in the very nature of capitalist governments, he believed. In the only major work he ever wrote dealing with international politics, *The Struggle for Peace*, he argued that as long as there are capitalist governments there will be rivalry and war, "because war is inherent in a system which is based on economic competition."[32] Therefore, capitalist control of Britain's government made it a greater threat to world peace than the USSR. "Had we a Worker's Government in this country," he wrote, "as they do in Russia, the whole situation would be completely different. Then, with a Socialist Government, there would be no risk of capitalist or imperialist wars being pursued."[33]

Such an outlook made Cripps a bitter opponent of the Chamberlain-Halifax foreign policy. He was able to see the faults of Nazi Germany more clearly than many of his Conservative counterparts, but his equation of British Conservatism with Nazism meant, paradoxically, that he opposed the British government's measures to prepare for possible war against Hitler. Of the drive to rearm, Cripps wrote: "The armaments which are being now so busily prepared will not be used to crush fascism. Indeed it is clear now that, as some of us have always insisted, they will be used in all probability to crush democracy and the workers and to uphold fascism and capitalism."[34]

Cripps eventually went too far for the more conservative Transport House leadership of the Labour party. His proposals for a United Front of the Left, which would include the Communists, and his funding of a private campaign contrary to the decisions of previous party conferences and decisions of the party's national executive committee, led to his expulsion from the Labour party in 1939.[35] Cripps's increasing extremism alienated potential supporters, many of whom rejected Sir Stafford's portrayal of British politics as a struggle between the forces of good and evil. Even Cripps's son Richard was disturbed by the stridency of the Unity Campaign. In March 1939, he wrote his father:

> I was at your meeting at the Empress Hall last Sunday night. I was interested in hearing the speeches, but rather "put off" by the very vulgar doggerel rhymes about Neville Chamberlain. Whether one agrees with him or not, there is no reason to think that he is politically less sincere in his views than are his opponents. I should have thought that poetry of this nature would have the opposite effect of that intended, and I was interested to note the very feeble response to the community singing.[36]

Because of his extremism, Cripps had become a political liability for the Labour party, and few were surprised by his expulsion.

Although out of the party, he continued to flail away at Conservative foreign policy, and, though at first troubled by the Nazi-Soviet Pact and the Soviet invasions first of Poland and then Finland, he suspended his considerable critical faculties when dealing with the Soviet Union. In frequent meetings with Cripps, Ivan Maiskii was easily able to persuade him of the essential justice of Soviet policy.[37] In a draft article written for the "Tribune" on September 19, 1939, Cripps wrote a justification of the Soviets' participation in the conquest of Poland. Conceding that "from the Polish point of view this looks like a fresh aggression," Cripps was able, from his safe vantage point in London, to rise above such subjectivity. Russia, he wrote,

> will remain in Poland until the war is over, for her own protection and to encourage the Polish people in their struggle against the landlord class that has—up till this moment—misgoverned and exploited them.
>
>   To rush hastily into diatribes against Russia is to do nothing but join in the "Red Scare" which has already done enough damage in the world since 1917. There are of course large bodies of people in this country and in other countries who will delight in the opportunity to misrepresent the actions of their hatred [*sic*] enemies the Soviet Union. All the Anti-Communist feeling will be stirred up in all

political parties and will present this country with a distorted picture that will bring with it the imminent danger of adding Russia to our enemies.[38]

It can be seen how far the British government was prepared to bend to conciliate the Soviets, sending such a man to Moscow as ambassador. But the plan backfired, as Churchill noted after the war: "We did not at that time realise sufficiently that Soviet Communists hate extreme left-wing politicians even more than they do Tories or Liberals. The nearer a man is in sentiment, the more obnoxious he is to the Soviets unless he joins the Party."[39]

Cripps might as well have been a Nazi for all the good his pro-Soviet sympathies did him in working with the Kremlin. The man who likened Chamberlain to the Führer soon found himself the uncomfortable object of a similarly unjust comparison.

First Disappointments

Upon arriving in Moscow, Cripps was slow to realize that he had been mistaken about the USSR; it would take several months of bitter ambassadorial experience to convince him that Soviet Communists did not share completely the world view of Western Socialists. In a rather harsh judgment, Hugh Dalton wrote in his diary that Cripps had "the political judgement of a flea," and that this explained his behavior, which at times seemed divorced from reality.[40] But Cripps's political ineptitude owed more to the effect of strongly held and inflexible ideas on political actions than to personal shortcomings.

Cripps believed that the USSR, by virtue of her economic organization, must by definition be a peaceful power. It followed, he felt, that if given the chance, the Soviets must be more inclined to ally with the Western democracies than with Nazi Germany. In the past, Moscow had been prevented from doing so by what Cripps considered the Conservatives' pro-Fascist sympathies. This experience had "taught the Soviet Government to look upon [the British] as fundamentally hostile to the Soviet Union." Now in need, His Majesty's Government was scrambling to secure Soviet assistance. Using an extraordinary simile in a letter he wrote to Halifax, Cripps likened British policy to "the attitude of a Nazi to a Jewish shopkeeper. The Nazi has no desire to have any really friendly relations with the shopkeeper but if there is some commodity he needs badly and he cannot get it elsewhere, then he demeans himself by entering into relations with the shopkeeper and may even pose as his friend for the moment in order to get the advantage that he desires for himself."[41]

Nevertheless, during his visit to Moscow in February 1940, Cripps had wholeheartedly accepted Molotov's claim that the Soviets were willing and eager to reach an agreement with Britain, and moreover that they would do so quickly if given the proper inducements by Britain. Why then did the Kremlin not desert the Germans upon Cripps's arrival in Moscow as the new British ambassador in June 1940? In a review of British policy after his first six months as ambassador, Cripps offered one explanation:

> Ever since the collapse of France, Soviet policy, despite minor varia-
> tions dictated by external events and actuated by bargaining needs,
> has been founded on (a) the conviction that the USSR will ultimately
> be confronted with a German attack, (b) determination to remain
> neutral until these dangers can be faced with prospects of success.
> Thus while the Soviet Government are seizing every opportunity to
> strengthen their position further (c) they cannot afford, until Ger-
> many's position becomes much weaker, to endanger Soviet-German
> relations by any overt political agreement conjointly [with Britain]
> and in the light of past experience they are convinced that no agree-
> ment with us could be kept secret.[42]

Cripps did not entertain the idea that the Soviets might be cooperating with the Germans because Berlin and Moscow shared certain vital inter-ests. To admit this would have struck at the base of his entire political faith—the belief that nationalization of the means of production guaran-teed a nonaggressive foreign policy. Also, since he himself, a Socialist, was the representative of His Majesty's government, British policy could no longer be entirely at fault, though he would soon have many differences with the Foreign Office approach. Cripps was forced to explain the reluc-tance of the Soviet government to come to terms with Britain by the vulnerable position in which the fall of France had left the USSR.

Cripps is not alone in identifying the French collapse as a watershed in Soviet policy. In a book on Soviet foreign policy written a short time after the war, one historian agrees, believing the collapse of France "put a new complexion upon Soviet-German relations." But he draws different con-clusions from the event: "Although Soviet economic aid for Germany was still forthcoming, the acute hostility earlier shown towards Great Brit-ain was slightly moderated in favor of a more genuine neutrality."[43] A more contemporary account claims much the same: "The Russians [went] through an agonizing reappraisal—to use an anachronistic term—of their policies."[44]

The theory that all Stalin's plans were upset by German successes gained some credence from Nikita Khrushchev's account, written over twenty years after the war: "I remember we were all together in the Kremlin when we heard the news over the radio that the French Army had capitulated and that the Germans were in Paris. Stalin's nerves cracked when he learned about the fall of France. He cursed the Governments of England and France: 'Couldn't they put up any resistance at all?' he asked despairingly."[45]

This sounds plausible, but there are some problems with Khrushchev's story. It is hard to credit that French capitulation came as a sudden shock after the Allied defeats in the Ardennes and at Dunkirk, and because the French did not sue for peace until several days after the fall of Paris, it is unlikely that the two events would have been announced simultaneously on the radio. (One might also doubt that Stalin depended on such a dubious source as Moscow radio for such important news.)

But there is a more important question here than the accuracy of Khrushchev's memory: Did the French disaster really trigger a change in Soviet policy? Certainly, the Soviets did not suddenly become more accommodating toward the British—far from it. They eventually became less accessible, as Cripps discovered to his chagrin. Instead, the events in France seem to have triggered a comparatively brief period of uncertainty in Moscow as Stalin fretted over British staying power. As soon as he received assurances that London was in the war to the end, Soviet policy slipped back into its old track being a loyal, if somewhat demanding, partner of the Nazis. Indeed, Soviet worries, such as they were, passed completely unnoticed by the Germans. Schulenburg told the German Foreign Office: "There is no reason for apprehension concerning Cripps' mission, since there is no reason to doubt the loyal attitude of the Soviet Union toward us and since the unchanged direction of Soviet policy toward England precludes damage to Germany or German vital interests. There are no indications of any kind here for belief that the latest German successes caused alarm or fear of Germany in the Soviet Government."[46]

At any rate, when Cripps arrived in Moscow, he had no inkling of how difficult the Soviets would be and plunged immediately into vigorous efforts to persuade Moscow to declare for the Allies. On the day of his arrival, June 12, he met with M. Labonne, the French ambassador, to coordinate their approaches to the Kremlin. Unused as yet to the delicate wording of the Foreign Office telegrams—indeed, he never seems to have learned the art—Cripps reported the conversation back to London:

> In view of the extreme gravity of the present situation in France [M. Labonne] intends to remind the Soviet Government of the fact that German successes in the West are imperilling [the] military equilibrium in Europe. His purpose will be to compel the Soviet Union to decide once and for all whether they are prepared to take, or threaten to take, action which would result in a diversion of German military forces to their eastern frontier.[47]

Halifax was more accustomed to the snail's pace at which talks with Moscow generally moved and sent a word of warning to his enthusiastic representative: "I do not think you can expect to compel the Soviet Union to decide once for all a possible turn of policy the implications of which they have always dreaded."[48]

Two days after his arrival, on June 14, Cripps had an hour-long meeting with Molotov, who was no doubt interested to see if Cripps had brought any useful new information. After saying that he hoped there would be no delays in the trade talks, Molotov aimed a string of questions at his visitor. From his own account it appears as though Cripps did most of the talking; he claimed that he believed a French collapse to be unlikely, but if that were to occur "the British would continue the struggle whatever happened in France." Cripps showed how little he understood Soviet motives when he raised the issue of the Balkans: "Our policy . . . was to maintain independence of the Balkan States against German and Italian aggression[49] and that in this I believe that we had common cause with the Union of Soviet Socialist Republics who might assist in bringing the Balkan countries together for this purpose. I said that we were glad that the Union of Soviet Socialist Republics had appointed a minister at Bucharest." At this point, Molotov undoubtedly suspected greater guile than Cripps was capable of, for he answered sharply: "On this subject he said the Soviet policy in the Balkans was well known and that they had special interest in certain areas such as Rumania and that it was to guard these, that they had sent a minister to Bucharest."[50]

There is no mystery in Molotov's quick reaction when the subject of the Balkans and Eastern Europe was raised. On the same day as his interview with Cripps, the Soviets began to gather their compensation for not opening a second front against the Germans. That very evening the USSR presented an ultimatum to the Lithuanian government followed by Soviet occupation the next day. Estonia and Latvia suffered the same fate on June 17. As the Soviets no doubt expected, the British government was far too preoccupied with events in France to press effectively their objections to these new Soviet moves. But after London had recovered its balance, the question of the Baltic States would become the central bone of contention in Anglo-Soviet relations right up until May 1942.[51]

Those who contend that France's travail had a cathartic effect on Soviet policy point to an incident at this time as evidence.[52] The Germans discovered on June 14 that Mme. Alexandra Kollontai, Soviet ambassador to Sweden, had told the Belgian foreign minister "that it was to the common interest of the European Powers to place themselves in opposition to German imperialism."[53] This, it is claimed, proves that the Soviets had begun to doubt the desirability of continued German successes. But an exhortatory remark by the eccentric Kollontai did not necessarily signal a sea change in Soviet policy. There is no compelling evidence to suggest that Moscow either pulled closer to the British after France fell or that the Soviets tried to limit German gains. At any rate, Schulenburg thought the matter so unimportant that he did not even raise it when he met with Molotov. Soviet policy remained essentially unchanged.

Cripps, whose enthusiasm had been sustained by meeting Molotov, still felt that he could "swing" the Soviets over to the British side. As he told the Foreign Office on June 15: "I am having a preliminary meeting with [Anastas] Mikoyan this afternoon and it is evident to me that [the] Soviet Government are extremely anxious to get down to business at the first possible moment."[54] Be that as it may, the Soviets became more reticent with Cripps, who, after the meeting, described Mikoian as "entirely non-committal."[55] But Cripps was as yet undaunted, believing that assurances of American cooperation were all that were needed to bring the Soviets to the Allied side.[56]

The Soviets were stalling, waiting to see what would happen in France. On June 15, only one day before the French asked for an armistice and one day after the capitulation of Paris, Labonne met with Molotov in a vain effort to "compel" the Soviets to open a second front before it was too late. The latter coldly asked what price the French were willing to pay. "M. Molotov [asked] whether the French Government had modified their attitude with regard to Bessarabia and whether they were ready to accept the Soviet point of view." Labonne equivocated, saying he would have to ask his government before he could answer. Molotov, who had a better deal in hand from the Germans, was not interested. "M. Molotov next observed that the French Government's change of attitude towards the Soviet Government was very sudden. . . . In conclusion M. Molotov recalled that Soviet policy was based on neutrality, in accordance with the declaration made by the Soviet Government at the beginning of the war and with their international obligations."[57] In retrospect, perhaps it is surprising that the French ambassador was not immediately willing to promise the moon, though by this time the battle in France had been decided; a surrender of principle, therefore, would have been worse than wrong, it would have been useless.

Seeing that there was apparently very little the Western powers were prepared or able to give them, the Soviets once again raised procedural obstacles. In their meeting Molotov had assured Cripps that there would be no problem regarding credentials,[58] but on June 17 the Soviet foreign minister wrote to Halifax, saying that Cripps's credentials must be sent soon if he were to continue as ambassador.[59] In normal times, the British could have complied readily with this request, but Italy's declaration of war and the closure of the Mediterranean as well as the German occupation of Denmark and Norway made communications between the USSR and Britain circuitous and dangerous. In his memoirs, Maiskii makes light of this incident and suggests that the delay was caused by British stuffiness and a reluctance to break tradition by wiring Cripps's credentials.[60] From the British records, however, it appears that the Soviets were being purposefully difficult. Having heard that Cripps brought no momentous offer with him, the Kremlin had decided to stall, waiting to see what the Germans would do next.

But if the Soviets hoped for limited results from talking with Cripps, it was clearly in their interests to see that the British should continue the war against Germany. The prospect that Britain might seek terms could hardly have been a pleasant one. What was needed was both a little stiffening of resistance in London and some notice of that stiffening in Berlin. This would require a concrete demonstration. On June 17 Andrew Rothstein, chief London correspondent of TASS, approached the Foreign Office with a proposal that Churchill should publicly summon Maiskii for consultations. When Mr. Ridsdale of the Foreign Office suggested that Halifax, rather than the prime minister, should speak to the ambassador, Rothstein revealed the Soviet motive: "There is really no novelty in Monsieur Maisky and Lord Halifax seeing each other. If the Prime Minister sent for the Ambassador it would be an interesting gesture." In other words, the meeting was to be purely cosmetic, designed as a demonstration for Berlin. This explains why the Soviets were being so prickly with Cripps, with whom it would have been necessary to negotiate anything of substance, while at the same time hinting to the Foreign Office in London that they were ready to change sides. Rothstein told the British what they wanted to hear: "Let us look at it frankly. It is no more in the Soviet's interest than it is in the interests of Britain and France that Germany should be all-powerful in Europe. Russia knows that some day she must have a settlement with Hitler; she has known it all along. It is for that reason that she has taken her present line about Lithuania—a development that certainly will not be popular in Berlin."[61]

This remark was clearly designed to encourage British resistance by holding out the carrot of eventual Soviet intervention against Nazi Germany. Rothstein, however, was being less than candid—or, equally probable, he was kept only partially informed. Hitler could hardly have been surprised by the Soviet invasion of the Baltic States, since back in September 1939 he had agreed "that the territory of the Lithuanian State falls to the sphere of influence of the USSR."[62] Another thing Rothstein did not reveal to the British was the timing of the blow that he said Moscow was planning to deliver to Hitler. Had he done so, the London government would not have been pleased. In December 1940 Maiskii told the Turkish ambassador in London "that each day he reckoned up the military damage [in the war between Great Britain and Germany] not in two columns but in one column showing the total loss to the non-Russian belligerents."[63] If ever it were to intervene, an uncertain prospect at best, the USSR would do so only after both sides had been sufficiently weakened to enable Soviet power to act as arbiter. And there was, of course, no concrete guarantee that Moscow would ultimately side with London. In the meantime, comments such as those by Rothstein and Kollontai were aimed at keeping the two warring sides battering away at each other.

As for Rothstein's request that Churchill summon Maiskii for the "novelty" of it, such a meeting would certainly remind the Germans that continued Soviet quiescence was worth paying a diplomatic price. The Soviets perhaps expected nothing more from talking with Churchill than to send a message to Berlin. Had the Kremlin wanted to conclude anything of substance with the British, they could have done so in secret talks with Sir Stafford Cripps in Moscow rather than shunning the ambassador as they continued to do. But a request from Churchill to see Maiskii would be safe from the Soviet point of view, since it would not appear in Berlin that the

Soviets were courting the British, while at the same time it would remind Hitler not to take Moscow's friendship for granted.

For the next few days the Kremlin held Cripps at arms length. He had still not overcome his reflexive habit of blaming delays on London and believed, mistakenly, that his difficulties in arranging a meeting with Molotov stemmed from his as yet undelivered credentials. On June 21 he telegraphed the Foreign Office: "Uncertainty regarding the present position which cuts me off from all normal official contact is becoming increasingly embarrassing and may even lead to adverse comment in diplomatic circles here."[64]

Maiskii faced no such problem of access, meeting Butler on the same day in London to examine Cripps's credentials. Maiskii's tone was hardly that of a worried man; rather, it seems he enjoyed watching the British squirm. According to Butler's account: "[Maiskii] said that the leaders of the Soviet Union examined the international chessboard with much more attention than the leaders of any other country, to whom they were superior in their power of assessing the rival worth of the different nations. He, M. Maisky, had never been under any illusion as to the real state of France. Now that France had collapsed, he agreed with me that European equilibrium had been considerably upset." Maiskii then justified Russia's invasion of the Baltic States. "He said that his country had observed the manner in which the Albert Canal had been crossed, and did not intend Germany to do the same with the bridgehead of Lithuania." This was all well and good, and Butler seems to have been convinced, but the Germans had not yet crossed the Albert Canal back in September when the Soviets had laid their claim to Lithuania.

Maiskii said that he felt the Germans still intended to move east—sufficient reason to keep the British in the war. Therefore, "M. Maisky considered that there was distinct value in Turkish-Russian friendship, but he did not leave me with a clear impression as to whether the Soviet would 'sell' Turkey, and keep themselves out, or whether they would stand with Turkey and Iran against an eastward German drive, themselves taking payment by increased Soviet influence in Iran, and a possible reward from the Mosul oilfield."[65] Molotov's visit to Berlin in November would shed more light on how the Soviets intended to deal with Turkey and Iran.

In Moscow, Cripps was frustrated after nearly a week of being ignored by the Soviets. On June 22 he had asked Molotov for another audience, only to be told that "owing to unusual pressure of work Monsieur Molotov will have great difficulty in receiving me for another 2 or 3 days." Cripps had been shaken by a Soviet broadcast on that day, which denied allegations that Soviet troops were massing on the German border and which concluded that "the good neighborly relations, resulting from the conclusion of the Nonaggression Pact between the USSR and Germany, cannot be shaken by any rumours or petty poisonous propaganda, because their relations are not based on motives of opportunism but on the fundamental interests of the USSR and Germany."[66] The next day Cripps told the Foreign Office that in his opinion the Soviets had, from fear, finally cast their lot with the Germans.[67] The Foreign Office, which had long experience in dealing with Soviet stalling tactics, was amused that Cripps should have been, in Maclean's words, "so easily discouraged." Laurence Collier wrote: "What has happened is only that it has now become obvious that the Soviet Government are not going to allow their relations with Germany to deteriorate, for the time being. We have never had any illusions about that in the Foreign Office; but to Sir S. Cripps it comes as more of a surprise, no doubt." Sir Orme Sargent was even more pointed:

> Sir S. Cripps, in his capacity as an ordinary Ambassador and not as a Special Envoy, has no means of protecting himself against these Soviet methods of procrastination and boycott. Stalin has, meanwhile, got Sir S. Cripps exactly where he wants him, that is to say, as a suppliant on his doormat holding his pathetic little peace offerings of tin in one hand and rubber in the other. Stalin hopes to be able to counter any German browbeating and nagging by pointing to Sir S. Cripps on the doormat, and by threatening to have him in and start talking with him instead of with the German Ambassador.

Butler, who had gambled on a favorable Soviet response, was less inclined to levity, telling his sardonic civil servants, "I am not despondent nor do I think that Sir S. Cripps will throw up the sponge." He felt that poking fun at Cripps was in poor taste—especially since he had shared Cripps's enthusiasm: "We must be very careful about comments on such Envoys who with complete disregard for their own private convenience undertake duties such as this which might at times be odious."[68] Butler did not mention that the political benefits of a successful mission would have been anything but "odious."

If the Soviets were, as Cripps felt, trembling from fear that a talk with the British ambassador would trigger a German invasion of the Soviet Union, then it is difficult, if not impossible, to explain the rounding out of Soviet territorial acquisitions. Adopting Hitlerian phrasing, Molotov told

Schulenburg on June 23: "The solution of the Bessarabia question brooked no further delay. The Soviet Government was still striving for a peaceful solution, but it was determined to use force, should the Rumanian Government decline a peaceful agreement."[69] Even the Germans were astonished by the Soviet demands, especially their claim to Bukovina, "which," as Schulenburg noted, "never belonged even to Tsarist Russia."[70] Again taking a page from Hitler's book, Molotov "countered by saying that Bucovina [*sic*] is the last missing part of a unified Ukraine."[71] Eventually, German pressure made the Soviets limit their demands to the northern part of Bukovina and all of Bessarabia.

In London, there were varying interpretations of the Soviet agitation for Bessarabia. As Sargent told Halifax:

> [Dalton] would like us to be more forthcoming about Bessarabia, on the grounds that it is in our interests to encourage Russia to occupy Bessarabia in present circumstance, presumably on the ground that if they do so they will equally occupy the Roumanian oilfields. I cannot believe that the Russians in any circumstances would do anything as foolish as this. If they occupy Bessarabia it is not in order to push westwards and come into contact with the Germans, but to push southwards in order to threaten the Straits.[72]

As it turned out, it did not matter a great deal what the British did. Two days later, on June 26, the Soviets presented an ultimatum to the Romanians, who, lacking German support, accepted Soviet demands. On the twenty-eighth Bucharest ceded Bessarabia and North Bukovina to the USSR.

Meeting Stalin

In the meantime, the British came to the conclusion that the only way to break the impasse in Anglo-Soviet relations was to go directly to the top. Sargent telegraphed to Cripps on June 24: "As Stalin alone controls Soviet policy, I feel that our one chance of securing change in Soviet policy is [a] personal approach to him. I presume he would not refuse you an audience if you asked for one as bearer of [a] special message from [the] Prime Minister." Sargent also gave Cripps some advice regarding the touchy situation in the Baltic: "Should the question of the Baltic States be raised you may affect to believe that the Soviet Government's recent action was dictated by the imminence and magnitude of the German threat now threatening Russia."[73] Cripps would not have to "affect" such an attitude because he was already a true believer. As with the Soviet invasion of Poland, he would have no trouble explaining the destruction of the Baltic States as a purely defensive move. In fact, Cripps later became obsessed with arguing the Soviet case in the Baltic States dispute. But, for the British government, avoiding conflict with the USSR over these states for the time being was merely a tactical move. Until the German offensive had spent itself there was little to be gained in alienating the Soviets by being prickly. Besides, there was still a chance that Cripps might be more successful than expected.

The best way of effecting an audience with Stalin, the British felt, was for Cripps to deliver a personal message from Churchill. In the message, sent to Cripps on June 25, the prime minister stressed the German danger to all of Europe and Britain's determination to fight on: "The fact that both our countries lie not in Europe but on her extremities puts them in a special position. We are better enabled than those less fortunately placed to resist Germany's hegemony, and as you know the British Government certainly intend to use their geographical position and great resources to this end."[74] Paradoxically, Churchill's efforts to assure Stalin of Britain's will to resist would make cooperation less, not more, likely, because the Soviets were interested in seeing the Germans distracted, not in entering the war themselves.

One thing that Cripps was not authorized to mention to Stalin was the Soviet claim to Bessarabia, about which Molotov had spoken on March 29.[75] The Cabinet rejected Dalton's reasoning in favor of Sargent's, that is, any Soviet move into Romania would be viewed in London as offensive, not as directed against German oil supplies. There were other reasons militating against recognition of Soviet claims, as Halifax wrote to Dalton on June 26: "If we were to show ourselves more forthcoming, the Russians would immediately suspect (and in this they wouldn't be too far wrong) that we were trying to bring about a clash between them and the Germans, or between them and the Turks. Finally, there is always the danger that particulars of our approach may become known, and the fact that we had egged on the Russians to invade Roumania would take a good deal of explaining away."[76] Cripps was told to avoid the issue if possible.

The situation in the Far East was another touchy subject. The French surrender had left the British even more vulnerable there than they had already been, and the Foreign Office reasoned that any word reaching the

Japanese of Anglo-Soviet collusion might precipitate an attack on British Far Eastern possessions.[77] Cripps was instructed to limit his discussions of the matter to vague generalities about the British desire for peace in China.

When Cripps met Molotov on the next day, June 27, he informed the foreign minister that he wished to deliver Churchill's message directly to Stalin. Although the Soviets had delivered the long-expected ultimatum to Romania the previous day, the record of this conversation suggests that, true to his instructions, Cripps did not mention the Bessarabian situation.[78]

On July 1 Cripps finally got his interview with Stalin. If the course of the conversation can hardly be judged satisfactory for the British, for Cripps the mere fact of meeting the general secretary was in itself encouraging after having been ignored for so long. His six telegrams sent immediately after the talk convey his ebullience and his feeling that, at long last, relations were moving in the right direction.

Cripps had given Molotov a copy of Churchill's message an hour and a half before the meeting so the Soviets would be able to examine it. Part of Stalin's reaction to the prime minister's message has already been cited above.[79] Stalin responded to Churchill's warning about the destruction of the European balance of power by Germany with the chilling comment: "If the Prime Minister wishes to restore the old equilibrium we cannot agree with him." The Soviets had signed the Nazi-Soviet Pact, Stalin told Cripps, "to get rid of the old equilibrium."

The rest of the conversation was no warmer. In one of his short telegrams Cripps assured the Foreign Office: "I did not, of course, touch upon the question of territories occupied by the Union of Soviet Socialist Republics since the war."[80] This was strictly true, since the actual names of the occupied territories never came up. But in a broader sense Cripps managed to convey an unfortunate message to the Soviets. Speaking of the Balkans, Cripps told Stalin that what he had suggested to Molotov in a previous conversation was that "without a lead in this part of the world by some major and neighbouring power who desired to bring these countries together, it would be difficult to insure any stabilization in the Balkans. M. Stalin here interjected that this was easier said than done." In what in retrospect seems an improbable scenario, the British ambassador was encouraging a reluctant Stalin to pursue a more aggressive Balkan policy. Stalin told Cripps: "In general it seems to me that anyone who gets into the Balkans with the idea of acting as a super-arbitrator has every chance of getting embroiled." Showing his historical ignorance, Cripps "said that in this matter it would seem that Russia and Turkey, with their traditional friendship and extensive interests in the Balkans, might be able to assist in bringing about more stable conditions." Stalin replied that "the Turks are too fond of the political game" to be reliable partners. (The man who said that "Sincere diplomacy is no more possible than dry water or iron wood"[81] was presumably not "fond of the political game.") Turkey, he said, might launch an offensive against the Near East: "It is difficult to say in what direction [Turkey] will make a spring. The Soviet Union has no wish to assume the role of super-arbitrator or to get embroiled in the Balkans." Stalin made it appear as though Turkey were a greater threat to the stability of the Balkans than Germany, which, he felt sure, would not "disperse her forces by sending troops to the Balkans." The general secretary appears to have been laying the groundwork for future claims against Turkey for which, we know, Molotov would press the Germans in November. Cripps reported that: "M. Stalin went on to say that it was wrong for the control of the Straits to be under the control of one power, which might abuse it; the other Black Sea Powers ought to have a say in the matter." The Soviets had evidently changed their minds since July 1936 when, at the end of the Montreux Conference on the Straits, Litvinov, then foreign commissar, had said: "It seems to me that all those who have taken part in the conference will leave it satisfied, and there will be none dissatisfied."[82] This ominous reversal in the Soviet attitude seemed to confirm Foreign Office fears that Soviet expansion into the Balkans was aimed at the Straits rather than at German oil supplies. Stalin, according to his own account, felt no need to take active steps to curb German designs.

In fact, Stalin explicitly played down the German threat. When Cripps, quite naturally stressing German weaknesses and British strengths, pointed out that Britain's control of the seas would prevent rapid German domination of Europe, Stalin agreed, going even further: "M. Stalin said that he was not so simple-minded as to believe what individual German leaders said as to their not wanting to dominate Europe or the world. He was however aware of the physical impossibility of their dominating Europe or the world, which was the same thing, and it was this that convinced him, rather than their assurances that they did not desire to do so." "Germany could not establish a hegemony over Europe without the domination of the seas," Stalin declared. The events of the near future would show how much importance the Soviets attached to the balance of seapower.

Since Stalin felt the German threat was as yet remote, he was unreceptive to Cripps's talk of a trade agreement. Regarding the issue of transshipment, he told the ambassador that some of the raw materials the USSR might import from the British Empire would be sent to Germany in order to fulfill Soviet orders for German manufactured goods.[83] If the Soviets were unprepared to accept restrictions on the use of British imports, they surely were not yearning to double-cross Germany by allying with Great Britain.

But Cripps refused to face the obvious meaning of Stalin's words. Since he could not bring himself to believe that Stalin was committed to a restructuring of Europe in collusion with the Germans, he was forced to reinterpret Stalin's arguments. He told the Foreign Office:

> My general impression gained from [the] interview was that Stalin is at the moment professing to accept German protestations at their face value to excuse himself (?from) acting in concert with us against Germany. He probably feels that [the] Union of Soviet Socialist Republics is not ready and that anyway he can stall off a German attack until it is too far on in the year to make such an attack likely before the frost breaks next spring.[84]

Cripps's impression was completely inaccurate, even if understandable when his political perspective is taken into account. Stalin certainly did not disregard the possibility of a German attack, but it is clear from his remarks that, unlike Cripps, he did not believe such an invasion to be inevitable or even likely in the near term. On the contrary, Hitler had repeatedly stressed the fact that Germany's mistake in World War I had been to fight on two fronts simultaneously, and Stalin apparently took him at his word. This is one reason he would be so surprised after the German invasion in June 1941. According to his daughter, Svetlana, "He had not guessed or foreseen that the pact of 1939, which he had considered the outcome of his own great cunning, would be broken by an enemy more cunning than himself. This was the real reason for his deep depression at the start of the war. It was his immense political miscalculation. Even after the war he was in the habit of repeating, 'Ech, together with the Germans we would have been invincible!' "[85]

Stalin projected his own caution in foreign policy upon Hitler. As he told Cripps, he felt that the domination of Europe by a single power was highly unlikely and the Ribbentrop-Molotov Pact had shown that Hitler was flexible about his ideological crusade against Bolshevism. In truth, so long as Germany was faced with a defiant Great Britain led by the inflexible Churchill, the Soviets would mine the German vein, taking advantage of the coincidence of "the basic national interests of both countries," even though they might be temporary.[86]

The Soviets Are Reassured

Cripps's meeting with Stalin had undermined British interests. One recent historian claims that "British documentation does not permit definite conclusions about how far Sir Stafford Cripps exceeded his instructions by offering specific inducements."[87] But in his May briefings Cripps was told that the Soviets were as great a threat to the Balkans as were the Germans and that the Turks should be patiently coaxed to resist pressure from both powers.[88]

Instead of obeying his instructions, Cripps had struck out on his own quite early in his conversation with Stalin. He had singlehandedly reversed British policy by raising the question of creating a Balkan bloc under a Soviet aegis and by suggesting that the British government might help by extracting concessions from the Turks as payment for a more cooperative Soviet attitude toward Britain. It was Stalin who downplayed the practicability of this line, odd as that may seem in retrospect. Stalin must have reasoned that the Germans were more likely to deliver on such promises than the British.

Cripps's first telegram to London after his talk with Stalin gave a fragmented account of the conversation and conveyed the incorrect impression that Stalin had broached the idea of pressuring the Turks. The Foreign Office was unimpressed:

In the circumstances M. Stalin's proposal, even as presented by Sir Stafford Cripps, does not seem to offer a very satisfactory basis for Anglo-Soviet co-operation. On the contrary, it very much looks like an attempt on the part of M. Stalin to make us spike one of our most valuable guns. It must be remembered that in the event of a long war Soviet economic support to Germany, which M. Stalin shows no inclination to withold, may become a decisive factor. There are also signs that Russian ambitions in the Middle East are reviving so that before long we may find the Soviet Union cooperating with Germany in the West and attacking our interests in the East. In such circumstances we might feel obligated to retaliate and this we could only do if Turkey were on our side.[89]

Only two days after Cripps's meeting with Stalin, the Soviets received confirmation that the British were going to be in the war for some time yet and that a German invasion, if one were attempted, would not have the benefit of adequate seapower. Responding to the fear that the French fleet would fall intact into the hands of the Germans, on July 3 the British attacked and sank most of the French navy stationed at Oran in Algeria.

The attack impressed the Soviets as it encouraged the British. Maiskii gives great weight to the event in his memoirs, noting the immense relief of members of Parliament of all parties when Churchill spoke in the House of Commons the next day. "It was obvious," Maiskii wrote, "that . . . a mountain had fallen from their shoulders." "For me as Ambassador of the USSR," Maiskii continued, "the events of 3–4 July were also of great significance. They demonstrated convincingly that Britain really would continue to fight on," thus, he might have added, freeing Soviet soldiers from the necessity of doing so for another year.[90] Current Soviet historians also place a good deal of emphasis on Oran. One prominent Soviet scholar points out that the British had an ulterior motive for the attack—to cripple an already weakened imperial rival. But, he writes, "Apart from the clash of purely imperial interests, [Oran] also had great significance from the point of view of the future correlation of forces in the theaters of military activity and in the entire strategy of the war."[91] Another Soviet scholar, who subsequently emigrated to the West, writes that Oran was Britain's "answer" to Hitler's so-called "peace offensive"—a welcome answer from the Soviet perspective.[92]

Stalin was now reassured that Britain would continue to fight, regardless of anything the Soviets might do. Consequently, he showed how little he cared for improved relations with London by relaying an astonishingly accurate account of his talk with Cripps to the Germans. The only point not included was Stalin's assertion that German domination of Europe was a physical impossibility. He doubtless felt it unwise to tempt fate.[93]

As for the British, they faced the daunting prospect of resisting Germany unaided, at least for the time being, and the Foreign Office saw in Stalin's words no flicker of hope for a change. In a meeting held to discuss the Cripps-Stalin conversation, the decision was taken that there was very little common ground for improving relations, in spite of Sir Stafford

Cripps's optimism. In fact, having failed to bring about a rapid rapprochement, Cripps became more of a hindrance than a help. The longer he remained in Moscow, the more likely he was to surrender various points of principle and to relay confused signals to and from the Kremlin.

After Oran the Soviets felt safe enough to continue their risky partnership with Hitler. For the price of a little oil and wheat Stalin had been able to reclaim the losses Russia had suffered at and after the Paris Peace Conference. The British could offer nothing comparable, and the Foreign Office realized it, even if Sir Stafford Cripps as yet did not.

CHAPTER THREE

THE EDUCATION OF

SIR STAFFORD

AUGUST–NOVEMBER 1940

The tenor of Sir Stafford Cripps's audience with Stalin convinced all those privy to his account that Anglo-Soviet rapprochement would be difficult, if not impossible, to create. But Sir Stafford and the London government differed over what could or ought to be done to break the impasse. Cripps, on the one hand, believed that the British must prove to Stalin their reliability as a potential ally. He argued that a sweeping British gesture, the recognition by London of Soviet sovereignty over the Baltic States, would overcome the suspicion that the Soviet leaders held in their hearts about British intentions. Soviet distrust, Cripps believed, dated from British intervention against the Bolsheviks during the Russian Civil War and could only be overcome by a large British concession toward the needs of Soviet security.

The Foreign Office was considerably less optimistic than the ambassador about the prospects of quickly gaining Soviet trust. British diplomats believed, however, that, given enough patient effort and some luck, Britain could still exert some influence on the nature, if not the extent, of Soviet trade with Germany. The idea of using military measures to close the Soviet gap in the blockade of Germany had died with the fall of France. And Stalin had told Cripps quite clearly that he did not intend to stray from the conditions of the German-Soviet Trade Agreement of February. Therefore, the only option open to the British—and it offered only a slim chance of success—was to attempt to conclude their own trade deal with Moscow, buying those commodities most needed by the Germans.

In the meantime, the British continued to enforce their navicert system, searching Russian shipping for contraband goods that the Soviets were importing for transshipment to Nazi Germany. This policy had already led to the seizure of two Soviet ships in the early part of 1940 and, predictably, to diplomatic protests.

In a review of Soviet policy referred to above,[1] the Foreign Office had identified Soviet trade with Germany as a possibly decisive factor in a protracted war. But, in the summer of 1940 the British were by no means certain that the war would last much longer. The Germans threatened Britain with a massive aerial assault—the destructiveness of which nobody could predict—followed by an invasion, for which the British were ill prepared. London was transfixed by the German threat, and everything else, especially long-term planning for a protracted war, was subordinate to the military needs of the moment. For this reason, and because of an understandable reluctance to appear as suppliants to Stalin, the British were hesitant to approach the Kremlin anew.

Nor were the Soviets, for their part, particularly interested in what the British had to offer, though they followed the course of the Battle of Britain intently. Having given Cripps his hearing, the Soviets once again refused him access. Cripps, who was an extraordinarily active man, champed at the bit, as Dalton noted wryly in his diary. "Cripps from Moscow is grumbling that no-one will receive him. He has been kept waiting twelve days for an interview with Molotov, for which he has asked on three occasions. He is refusing to see subordinates. If this goes on, he says, he thinks he should be recalled. This is both amusing and troublesome."[2] The government decided it would be inappropriate to recall Cripps, since doing so would simply broadcast British failure. There may have been another motive as well, judging from Cadogan's comment in his diary that Cripps's unrewarding experiences dealing with the Soviets would be "damned good for him!"[3]

Cripps had still not abandoned his inclination to blame London for his predicament, since he remained ignorant of what the Soviets were doing behind his back. For example, in mid-July he was outraged by a leak to the London press of an account of his talk with Stalin. On July 17 Halifax telegraphed Cripps that the Foreign Office had been unable to forestall publication of the leak, since it was difficult to control the activities of neutral correspondents in London. But, he assured Cripps, "Every effort is being made however to prevent it from receiving undue prominence."[4] From the Foreign Office records, it appears that the British government learned that a Mr. Kuh of U.P.I. had somehow acquired an account of the conversation. The British believed that Maiskii had leaked the information and so authorized two BBC broadcasts to preempt what they felt would surely be a biased version.

This explanation did not mollify Cripps. On July 18 he telegraphed London: "A leakage in the British press would have been bad enough. But I cannot expect [the] Soviet authorities to believe what I find it hard to believe—that after a year of "total war" His Majesty's Government are still unable to prevent a thoroughly pernicious piece of political news, in the circumstance where secrecy was known to be essential, from being broadcast."[5] Cripps's righteous indignation was, however, misdirected. His Soviet hosts had given the Nazis a detailed account of his talk with Stalin on July 13, three days before the leak in London. The Soviets were, one may assume, using the bourgeois press in London to confirm the veracity of their reporting to Berlin.[6]

At the end of one month in Moscow barren of positive results, Cripps was subjected to pressure from a new and, for him, surprising quarter. The British Left was not convinced that the Foreign Office was doing everything possible to secure Soviet friendship. Willie Gallagher, the Communist M.P., contacted R. A. Butler with a proposal that a delegation of British Communists should be sent to the Soviet Union to give the talks some much-needed impetus. The War Cabinet was cool toward the idea but was concerned that turning the offer down outright would look bad.[7] In a memorandum on the subject, Butler revealed the attitude that had in the past made him amenable to appeasement:

> If we are going to improve our relations with Russia, we have to take a scientific interest in the Communist Party in Great Britain, and not regard them as pariah dogs. Perhaps the degree of improvement in our relations with Russia will depend upon our attitude to the Communist Party. We may never be able to embrace Russia to the extent she desires, since we shall always have a distaste for Communists. All therefore we can do at the present is to stop them being Fifth Column, and not offend them by positive action.[8]

Cripps, concerned by this possible diminution of his own authority, did not feel the need for any aid from the British Communist party, though he had no objection to a visit from Harry Pollit, with whom he had established friendly relations during the Unity Campaign.[9] Conveniently forgetting his own foray into Anglo-Soviet relations in February, he argued that the Soviets would listen only to official representatives of His Majesty's Government.

If Cripps felt he could forgo British Communist help, he did not feel the same about Foreign Office assistance. At the end of July he sent a series of telegrams asking London to persuade the Soviets to grant him an audience.[10] His difficulties in obtaining a hearing from Molotov, however, did not yet incline him to be any less tolerant than previously of Soviet policy. On July 27 he gave the Foreign Office his interpretation of the motives behind Stalin's territorial acquisitions accompanied by his own political prognostications. The Soviets, he argued, were "inclined to work with Turkey and Iran against [the] German danger which has become more immediate." But, he continued, the Soviets would only cooperate with Turkey and Iran "so long as [the] two latter countries keep together." If they did not, then, "it is not by any means outside possibility that [the] Soviet Government may come to [the] conclusion that Germany is too strong to antagonise and that consequently it must at all cost work with Germany even to [the] extent of agreed joint pressure upon Turkey and Iran with contemplation that in case of need a new bribe treaty will be made with Germany, with Russia yielding a part of [the] Ukraine and obtaining compensation in the South."[11] Cripps was wildly misinterpreting Soviet considerations. During Molotov's visit to Berlin in November, the Soviets would prove eager to expand in the direction of the Straits and the Persian Gulf. Their eagerness to do so would not be the result of German strength but, rather, the result of Stalin's perception that Hitler was in a tight spot and in need of continuing Soviet cooperation.

A few days later, on August 1, Molotov delivered a more authoritative exposition of Soviet policy than that offered by Cripps, when the foreign commissar addressed the Supreme Soviet. His reference to Anglo-Soviet relations, in what was a major review of Soviet foreign policy, was both brief and grim. Molotov mentioned the publication by the Germans of captured French documents revealing Allied plans for an attack on the Caucasus. Molotov proffered no olive branch to London. He did concede that "the appointment of Sir Stafford Cripps as ambassador to the USSR does, possibly, reflect a desire on the part of Britain to improve relations with the Soviet Union," but he gave no indication that this desire would be satisfied. Instead, after referring to the manner in which the peoples of the Baltic States, Bessarabia, and Bukovina had clamored to join the USSR, he berated both the United States and Great Britain for their refusal to recognize the USSR's gains and its seizure of the Baltic States' assets. Molotov warned: "We can only remind both the Government of the United States and the Government of Great Britain . . . of their responsibility for these illegal acts." He proceeded to point out that the collapse of France and the weakening of Britain had made "the question of the redivision of the colonies . . . ever more acute." The USSR was, he said, taking steps to prepare for "a world imperialist war" over the spoils. The Soviet Union's territorial gains, which had, Molotov boasted, added twenty-three million souls to the Soviet empire, was not, of course, imperialism.[12]

Molotov's speech indicates how wrong Cripps had been in his analysis of Soviet conduct. The Kremlin was clearly expecting the war between Britain and Germany to develop into a worldwide scramble for spheres of influence and colonies. The vulnerable British Empire would present the Nazis with a more tempting target than the meager pickings to be had in the Soviet Union. Surely Hitler would continue his drive westwards, and for that opportunity the Führer would be willing to pay a price for continued quiet in the East.

It is enlightening to contrast Molotov's indignant reaction to the Anglo-American seizure of the Baltic States' assets with the Soviets' own handling of an analogous situation. Back in late June, when the Soviets were pressing the Germans over the Bessarabian question, Schulenburg had suggested that a little moderation might oil the wheels of diplomacy. Schulenburg informed the Foreign Office in Berlin: "To my statement that a peaceful solution might more easily be reached if the Soviet Government would return the Rumanian National Bank's gold reserve, which had been transferred for safekeeping during World War I, Molotov declared that this was absolutely out of the question, since Rumania had exploited Bessarabia long enough."[13] The Soviet position on seized assets was evidently flexible.

War Cabinet decisions of July 26 and August 12 set British policy against recognizing the Soviets' gains in the Baltic.[14] Opinion in Britain, especially religious opinion, opposed the extension of Soviet sovereignty to the three Baltic nations, and the Cabinet felt the liabilities of recognition would outweigh its dubious advantages.

A Logically Defensible Principle

On August 7 Cripps finally gained his interview with Molotov, after Halifax had pressured Maiskii to arrange an invitation. Cripps opened the conversation by scolding Molotov for Soviet unreceptiveness and said that the Kremlin's behavior "did not show a strict neutrality or an encouragement to Great Britain to cultivate better relationships." According to Cripps's account, he then

> sketched the history [of his mission] and emphasized the eight weeks
> delay without [a Soviet] reply, excuse or indication of their attitude
> and asked for a statement as to whether the Soviet Government
> desired to proceed with these negotiations. I stated that we did not
> want to negotiate for the sake of having negotiations but only if they,
> as we, intended to arrive at a satisfactory agreement as soon as
> possible. If they did not want to proceed or if they wanted for any
> reason to delay negotiations, I asked that they would frankly say so.

Molotov replied with the most detailed explication of Soviet policy to date. He said there were eight reasons why the Soviet Union was closer to Germany than to Great Britain: (1) The Soviets had a nonaggression treaty with Germany; (2) the Germans had acquiesced to Soviet territorial gains, or, as Molotov delicately phrased it, "we were able to secure our interests in the Western Ukraine and in White Russia"; (3) "agreements with Germany have thus been of real value; Soviet interests are protected by these pacts and agreements"; (4) Soviet-German cooperation facilitated "the adjustment of our relations with the Baltic States"; (5) it also produced a favorable trade agreement; (6) the talks failed with Great Britain in the summer of 1939; (7) Britain had not fulfilled past trade agreements; (8) "geographical situation" drew the Soviets and Germans into partnership.[15]

Such frankness was refreshing indeed, though Molotov had seen fit to distort certain aspects. Britain had offered to meet Soviet demands on all points except two, three, and four. Point eight was, of course, irremediable. Indeed, the British had gone further than Germany in one respect at least, by offering a full defensive alliance, as opposed to a mere nonaggression pact, as early as May 1939.[16] One sticking point then, as in 1940, had been the British refusal to hand over the Baltic States to the Soviet Union (as well as the attitude of Poland and Romania in 1939 toward the transit of Soviet troops). Molotov's arguments were a clear admission of Soviet motives: they had coolly stood back in 1939 waiting for the best offer, which had come finally from Germany. Now they were committed, and the British could not offer them anything sufficiently tempting to induce a change of course.

The Soviet foreign minister tried out a new line on Sir Stafford, claiming that the Soviets were, for their part, willing to let bygones be bygones, "though it could hardly be expected that the Soviet Government would make [the] first gesture towards better relations as they were the injured party in the matter of the [Baltic States'] gold." This tactic might have worked back in February, but Cripps, who was after all an excellent lawyer, was now learning the ropes as a diplomat as well and would not allow such a spurious argument to pass unanswered. He fired back at Molotov: "I . . . emphasised that there had been a six weeks delay by the Soviet Government as regards trade negotiations before any question of the Baltic gold arose, of which delay there had so far been no explanation. Monsieur Molotov did not give me any, though he clearly realized the force of the point."[17]

For a moment it seemed that Sir Stafford had finally understood Soviet disingenuousness in their claims to be interested in a deal with Britain, the hopelessness of his own position, and the need henceforth to be more circumspect in his dealings with the Kremlin. But, unfortunately, he continued to display that curious divorce between his extraordinarily impressive grasp of detail and a simple ability to draw obvious conclusions. Having just refuted Molotov's use of the assets gambit, Cripps turned around and told the Foreign Office that only a more forthcoming policy on the Baltic question would move the Soviets. He telegraphed London that the situation "demands some sacrifice and a thoroughness equal to that of Germany. Soviet Government are not yet convinced of genuineness of His Majesty's Government's professed desire for better relations and in particular it is evident that the action of His Majesty's Government in respect of Baltic assets and Baltic shipping in [the] United Kingdom is a stumbling block to any real improvement."[18] The only answer, he felt, would be to bow to Soviet demands—this alone would show British "genuineness."

Sir Stafford Cripps, the passionate proponent of "Christian Socialism," was advocating a restructuring of British policy along lines akin to those of Nazi Germany. It was very easy to speak of "sacrifice" when Baltic citizens, not Britons, were to pay the price. Having bitterly denounced Chamberlain for Munich, Cripps was willing to adopt a similar policy toward the Soviet Union.

The Foreign Office remained immune to Cripps's reasoning. As Robert Vansittart wrote to Halifax, "No amount of sacrifice will avail unless and until we both become and remain stronger." The Soviets, Vansittart felt, had opted for the Germans because "we were simply not a tempting proposition." Fitzroy Maclean recommended the line that the British government was to adopt: simply "to let Anglo-Soviet relations go on as best they can, while standing up resolutely for our own interests."[19]

There was a distinct air of resignation about Halifax's reply to Cripps's proposals. The foreign secretary wrote Cripps on August 13th: "As regards recognition, I have given full weight to considerations you advance, but I see great difficulties in advancing de jure recognition . . . it is important that we should not be driven into a position where we shall find it difficult to refuse recognition of every fait accompli achieved by countries like Russia and Japan, who are taking advantage of the war situation, and that we should not provide precedents for the recognition of German faits accomplis by other countries."

The problems with which Halifax was wrestling in this telegram went right to the heart of the British war effort. While the British were distracted by their war against Germany, Japan and the Soviet Union were making the most of the upheaval to redraw the world map. The British government could not afford to oppose the latter two countries militarily, but they could refuse to recognize any wartime territorial changes in the hopes that at the peace conference (assuming Britain emerged from the war on the victorious side) something could be done to limit the gains of the aggressive powers. Such, at least, was the reasoning of the Cabinet. Therefore, Halifax told Cripps: "In these circumstances [the] only safe course is to adhere to [the] logically defensible principle that political changes produced during this war ought not to be recognised de jure pending a general peace settlement." On September 5 Churchill committed his government publicly to this line when he told Parliament that "we do not propose to recognize any territorial changes which take place during the war unless they take place with the free consent and goodwill of the parties concerned."[20] This was a momentous decision, and it reflected Britain's weakened condition. Given the fact that the British had their hands full in 1940, such a course was perhaps the only one open to London, short of accepting Japanese and Soviet claims. Deciding what not to defend is always one of the most difficult tasks for leaders in wartime. But once the British government had made the decision to defer territorial questions until the end of the war, it was not so easy to backtrack. Britain's strength relative to her allies would peak during the war—around 1942, before the United States had mobilized to its full potential, and while the Red Army was still inferior to the Wehrmacht—only to slip back by the end of the war. The decision to leave important political and territorial questions until the end of the war, though understandable in the circumstances of 1940, meant, as it turned out, postponing important decisions until after British power had waned relative to that of her larger allies.

The full import of these questions would not be revealed until well after Hitler's invasion of the USSR. In the meantime, Cripps was told that for the time being, considering the unpromising Soviet attitude, any formal negotiations with the Soviets might best be conducted in London, while he was to concentrate upon a "psychological improvement in [the] atmosphere."

Another reason for curbing Cripps was continuing doubt about his judgment. On August 17 Cadogan confided in his diary: "Cripps argues that we must give everything—recognition, gold, ships and trust to the Russians loving us. This is simply silly. Agreed to tell him to sit tight. We will see what we can do here with Maisky. Exactly nil, I should say."[21]

Three days later, Cripps was told that he "need not, for the time being at least, attempt any negotiation with the Soviet Government."[22] But, just as the British had seemingly halted their attempts to persuade Moscow, and for the first time since Cripps's arrival in Moscow, the Soviets approached the ambassador with trade proposals of their own. On August 22 he was called in to see Mikoian, who said the Soviet government wanted a barter agreement trading Soviet flax for rubber from the British Empire. As one can well imagine, Cripps was taken aback. The Soviets seemed quite well prepared, having already arranged for "this transaction to be handled by an Iranian firm and to be effected at [the] Iranian rail head on the Caspian."

Having recovered from his initial shock, Cripps became cagey: "I replied that the circumstances had probably altered during the ten weeks delay and I doubted whether His Majesty's Government would be attracted by a limited deal of this kind as they wished for an all-in barter agreement."[23] But Mikoian would have none of this, as his instructions had evidently been to limit the deal to a simple barter arrangement. He referred to grievances "too numerous to specify" that stood in the way of a comprehensive agreement. But after Cripps applied his best courtroom technique, Mikoian "grudgingly admitted that the only real obstacle was the dispute regarding the Baltic gold and shipping." This was what the ambassador was waiting to hear, and he ended his account with a renewed plea to the Foreign Office for recognition of the Soviet seizures.

What were the British to make of this sudden Soviet demarche? Cripps believed that the Soviets simply wanted the rubber, but what he could not have known then was that two days later, at Soviet request, trade talks began in Moscow between the USSR and Germany, in which the former traded raw materials for manufactured goods. What better commodity to trade than rubber, which Germany needed acutely?

If that was the Soviet aim—as it almost certainly was—the glacial pace of British policy-making foiled the attempt. The Foreign Office did not reply until September 19, and even then the answer was not an unqualified affirmative. Cripps was told that he should protest Mikoian's August 23 article in *Izvestia*, in which the latter flaunted the importance of the USSR as a gap in the British blockade of Germany. Halifax wrote: "Such boasts that [the] Soviet Union is helping Germany to defeat our blockade do not increase our anxiety to supply [the] Soviet Government with rubber, of which Germans stand in great need."[24] Mikoian's behavior had been tactless. It showed with what scorn the Soviets viewed the British, who were at this time very much alone in the war. So far as the Soviets were concerned, the British ambassador was simply waiting on the doormat to be summoned when convenient, as Sir Orme Sargent had warned in June.[25]

After this brief, discouraging interval, Anglo-Soviet relations slipped back into their former routine. On September 4 Butler met Maiskii in a fruitless exchange of views on the Baltic problem. The Soviet ambassador attempted, unconvincingly, to explain why his government was prepared to conclude a trade deal with the United States while still refusing to do so with Britain. After all, the United States had seized the Baltic States' assets, as had the British. Butler, no doubt believing that he was delivering a sharp riposte to Maiskii's complaints, told the ambassador—in a poorly judged, though remarkably revealing phrase—that Maiskii's "country had done pretty well out of the acquisition of the three new States, part of Poland and a large province of Bessarabia [*sic*]. . . . [The British government] were not adopting an unreasonable or lachrymose attitude about the passing of the States, but a decent attitude at the funeral was surely what he would expect from this country."[26] Butler was never at his best when dealing with Maiskii, but this was a bit much. He made it appear as though the British stance on the Baltic issue was so much sound and fury. One can hardly imagine Molotov surrendering such a point for nothing; it tells us a great deal about the difference between British and Soviet negotiating tactics.

The October Proposals

On the surface, Anglo-Soviet relations appeared becalmed, but just below things were beginning to churn, making untenable the British policy of benign neglect of the Soviet Union. In an ironic twist of fate, after less than half a year in Moscow, Cripps, who owed his present post as ambassador to his constant, vitriolic charges that the Conservatives had incompetently handled relations with the USSR, was the subject of criticism from his old friends on the Left of British politics. On September 14 in an open letter printed in the *New Statesman and Nation*, D. N. Pritt, like Cripps a Socialist, a barrister, a long-time political ally, and chairman of the fellow-traveling Society for Cultural Relations with the U.S.S.R., gently accused Sir Stafford of being a cat's-paw for Halifax's supposedly pro-Fascist policies. "Dear Stafford," he wrote, "many of your innumerable friends here in Britain are very worried. We suspect that Halifax is using you as a screen to blind public opinion while he destroys the chances of better relations with the Soviet Union." Pritt then related an account of the Anglo-Soviet talks that could only have come from Maiskii: "It was sinister enough that, although the Soviet Government had proposed negotiations as early as March 27th, Halifax had blocked and parried the proposal for eight weeks before you were appointed. But today it is worse; nearly three months have gone since Stalin received you, and there is not the slighest [*sic*] sign of an agreement." Of course, the situation was by no means so one-sided. It was true that Halifax held out no great hope for the Anglo-Soviet talks, but even Cripps, whose patience with the Soviets verged on indulgence, had been upset by Soviet disinterest in better relations.

Pritt put his finger on what he felt was now blocking an Anglo-Soviet agreement:

> without any legal justification, [the British government] seized or arrested the gold of the Baltic Banks, which had been lawfully transferred to the USSR before the change in the status of the Baltic States. And then they openly paraded their affection for the Baltic Fascist regimes by refusing to recognise the decision of those States to enter the Soviet Union. Surely it is sheer hypocrisy to send you along to offer a trade agreement in the atmosphere they have created by this conduct.

Pritt had swallowed the Soviet line in its entirety, using an argument to justify the Soviet invasions strikingly like that with which Cripps had excused Moscow's actions in Poland the previous year. Pritt objected to Halifax acting as though the Baltic States were still independent, since they "beyond doubt have effectively entered into the Soviet Union." He accused Halifax of "publicly asserting that the real will of the peoples of these countries is expressed by the groups of bankers, landowners and manufacturers which recently ceased to hold power."[27] Evidently, inequitable distribution of wealth was now in the opinion of the British Left a legitimate casus belli.

Pritt's article, and arguments of a similar nature, had a damaging effect on British diplomacy, since they reinforced Cripps's inclination to believe that inept British policies, rather than his own inflated hopes, were at fault for his disappointment in Moscow so far. For Cripps to fault the Soviets for his slow progress, he would first have to shed the political habits and prejudices of a lifetime.

Problems could not be as easily disposed of in Moscow as they could in the pages of the *New Statesman*. Had the British been anxious to give in on the Baltic issue, which they certainly were not, they could not easily have done so on their own. One major difference in approach to foreign policy between the Chamberlain and Churchill governments—arguably the greatest difference—was the extent to which Britain under Churchill attempted to dovetail its policies with those of the United States. In September, an exchange of telegrams with Washington was enough to show the British that recognition of the Soviet Union's Baltic conquests would be very unpopular in the United States and might lead to an alienation of public opinion there, which the British had been trying patiently to nurture.[28]

The only way around the problem, the British believed, was to agree with the Soviets on some form of postponement of a permanent solution. Cripps met Vyshinskii on September 14, the same day Pritt's article appeared in London, and suggested that the two sides might agree to lay aside their differences for six months in order to remove this stumbling block to better relations. Vyshinskii said that he would convey the proposal to his government. He probably did so; it is hard to tell, since the Soviets did not deign to respond.[29] But Cripps was nothing if not determined, and when he spoke to Vyshinskii again on September 20, he pressed for an answer. What he got was the runaround. Cripps asked why the Baltic dispute should interrupt trade talks. According to Cripps's account, Vyshinskii

suggested that trade matters were for Mikoyan and said he knew nothing of them. I said Mikoyan disclaimed knowledge on [the] political side: could not someone come to a decision, taking [?trade] and political situation together? . . . He expressed the view that [the] Soviet Government were ready and anxious to talk trade and suggested that I should see Mikoyan again. I replied that that was of no use if Mikoyan was again to say that [the] political situation made trade talks inopportune. He promised that either he or Mikoyan would see me again in a day or two and let me know definitely about continuing trade talks. I pointed out that we were still awaiting [an] answer to our proposals of June 15th.[30]

Cripps must have felt like a tennis ball. Still, he seemed to see a glimmer of hope. He told the Foreign Office that Britain's air victories were beginning to impress Moscow and might soon convince the Soviets to talk in earnest. He dispensed a good piece of advice, saying he thought it best not to make piecemeal barter deals with the Soviet Union but rather to hold out for a full agreement. In his words, "something more valuable may be achieved by waiting a little longer." There is quite a contrast, to say the least, between this account of the trials of dealing with the Kremlin and the breezy optimism of Pritt's "Open Letter."

With a unity of purpose that is one of the more striking aspects of Soviet diplomacy, Maiskii added his efforts to his government's attempts to hoodwink the British into surrendering on the Baltic issue. In a meeting with A. V. Alexander, first lord of the admiralty, Maiskii rather bald-facedly argued that the British should give in in order to cultivate Soviet goodwill. But Alexander was not fooled by airy promises. In his account: "The implication behind [Maiskii's suggestions] is, of course, that we must do what his Government wants in questions such as that of the Baltic States because we shall need their help against Germany; but . . . he always avoids producing any evidence to show that we shall ever get that help . . . he now gives the peace conference as the earliest date at which we might expect advantage from cultivating Soviet friendship." Maiskii was wasting his breath with Alexander, who branded the Soviet justification for the Baltic seizures "an 'imperialist' argument if ever there was one."[31]

Like water running down a hill, the Soviets continued to seek out and erode weak spots in the British position. On October 7 Maiskii met with Butler, asking the under secretary if the British would put any obstacles in the way of supplies being sent from the Soviet Union to China. The question was such an odd one that it immediately put even the credulous Butler on his guard, for the British were unlikely, even unable, to stop transport between the USSR and China. Then Maiskii dropped the other shoe: "The Ambassador said that the part of the world in which his Government were particularly interested was the route via the Caspian Sea, Iran and Basra; would we impose any restrictions on goods passing by this route?" Butler ended his account of the talk he sent to Cripps with a request of the Foreign Office: "I should be obliged for the Office comments as to whether they think there is, in their view, anything behind this request [by Maiskii], since this would seem to be not unlikely."[32]

The most plausible explanation of Soviet motives came from Professor M. M. Postan of the Ministry of Economic Warfare: "I suggest that the Soviet Government are anxious lest Russian goods, if exported via the Trans-Persian Railway, should have difficulties from British naval controls in the Persian Gulf."[33] Maiskii's talk about supplies for China was simply a smokescreen. He presented a scenario to which he knew the British were unlikely to object in order to extract information about the extent of the British blockade.

In the meantime, Cripps barraged the Foreign Office with telegrams advocating recognition of the Baltic seizures. On October 8 he wrote Halifax: "As you are aware, I consider it hopeless to play our present hand with small stakes grudgingly advanced. [The] other side have always played fantastically high, and although so far [the] Soviet Government have repaid them by taking most of the pool for themselves, this state of things cannot be expected to continue indefinitely."[34] This time Cripps's arguments made some impact, as Cadogan wrote in his diary on October 10: "Had a talk with H.[alifax] about Cripps' telegram from Moscow proposing fresh approach to Soviets. Might be a good way of drawing Molotov."[35]

Why the sudden change? Had Cripps's eloquence finally won the day? The answer is provided by a telegram sent to Cripps on October 12, in which the Foreign Office informed the ambassador that they had received military information about German strategic intentions. According to an unnamed source, the Germans were about to coordinate an assault on Suez with a "drive through the Balkans."[36] The Foreign Office believed corroboration for the theory that the Germans were preparing a move in Eastern Europe came from the way in which Berlin had distributed Romanian provinces to Bulgaria and Hungary, suggesting an attempt to turn the Balkan States against each other. Perhaps most important of all was the defeat the Germans had suffered in the Battle of Britain. Unable to assault the British mainland effectively, the Germans were casting about for ways to loosen Britain's grip on the Mediterranean. As with Napoleon before him, this would lead Hitler to attack Egypt.[37]

In his response the next day, Cripps once again warned that this was "almost the last opportunity of moving Russian policy in our direction."

But, he cautioned, it would not be enough simply to warn the Soviets of the German danger. What was needed was recognition of Moscow's territorial gains and especially guarantees of postwar cooperation: "They . . . fear that after the war if we are victorious (?we will) form an anti-Soviet alliance out of the rest of the world which will be more dangerous for them than a victorious and war-weakened Germany." In a key paragraph, Cripps outlined his suggestions:

> Is it not possible in order to make a real effort to change [Soviet] policies for us to inform them that in the event of their behaving to us in as friendly a way as they behave to Germany and substituting a benevolent neutrality at least towards Turkey and Iran in event of either of them being attacked, we would (a) guarantee in the event of our being victorious to consult with them fully on post-war settlement of Europe and Asia in association with other victorious powers. (b) Not to form or enter any anti-Soviet alliance after the war. (c) for the time being till after the war [?recognize] their *de facto* sovereignty of the Baltic States and part of Poland Bessarabia and Bukovina which they have occupied. (d) Arrange to supply them with articles they require and we can spare for arming themselves against Axis should they be attacked. (e) Guarantee that they will not be attacked from the south from Iran or Turkey and especially that Baku will not be attacked from these countries by us or any of our allies.

Cripps was arguing that all these points should be surrendered in return for what the Soviets already claimed they were pursuing, namely genuine neutrality. In closing he emphasized that, for fear of German reprisals against the USSR, the matter must be kept secret. (The leaks after his talks with Stalin had made Cripps doubly aware of the need for secrecy.)[38]

On October 15 the War Cabinet considered Cripps's proposals and a draft response. Halifax said that he had at first thought that prior agreement with the United States would be necessary, but now he felt it would be adequate simply to inform the American government of the British position on the Baltic States. He felt that position should be that His Majesty's Government should recognize de facto Soviet control, "which," he said, "we should be unable to alter, at any rate until the end of the war." Halifax made it clear, if any still doubted, that this new approach to the Soviets was unlikely to yield results. "It would be imprudent," he told his Cabinet colleagues, "to build any hopes on the outcome of a new approach to Russia, which was mainly influenced by fear of Germany. Nevertheless, it was right that at the present juncture one more approach to Russia should be made, and that it should be on record that we had made it."[39] This time, unlike August 1939, the British government would not leave itself open to the accusation that it had not done enough to court the Soviets.

That same day, Halifax sent a telegram authorizing Cripps to approach the Soviets "on [the] lines you suggest." But some of his points were softened. For example, he was told that the Soviets must promise to aid Turkey if she were attacked by the Germans "by all steps consistent with technical neutrality, as the United States have done for us, and as the Soviet themselves have done for China." As for the guarantee of postwar cooperation, Halifax was not prepared to give Stalin the carte blanche Cripps had proposed. "Guarantee of post-war consultation," Halifax told the ambassador, "would not of course imply readiness to accept Soviet views on [the] future of Europe or Asia, and [an] undertaking not to form anti-Soviet alliance must necessarily be conditional on Soviet Government undertaking nothing against our interests either directly, or indirectly through revolutionary agitation." As for the central issue, the territories occupied by the Soviet Union, the British were prepared to go as far as possible short of de jure recognition—which would have been extremely unpopular in both Britain and the United States. Halifax said the Cabinet had "no objection" to de facto recognition, but "*de jure* recognition would gravely compromise [Britain's] post-war position; and I fear this is what [Moscow] want[s]." As for the assets problem, the foreign secretary said the government was prepared to return the Baltic ships seized in Britain but would retain some of the gold in British banks "to set off British claims to confiscated property." Halifax closed his telegram with a rebuttal of Cripps's analysis of Soviet fears: "Ready as I am to give you all the support I can in your efforts, I confess that I find it difficult to think that [the] Soviet Government are really more afraid of our post-war attitude than of a victorious Germany."[40]

In a separate telegram, Cripps was told that it might be impossible to keep negotiations a secret, since censorship in Britain was still incomplete, and, as Halifax pointed out, "It is particularly those organs of [the] press who are most sympathetic to [the] Soviet Union and in closest touch with [the] Soviet Embassy here who are the worst offenders."[41]

Because of this British decision to try once again to accommodate the Soviets, made by the War Cabinet on October 15, this was the crucial month in Anglo-Soviet relations between the abandonment of Allied plans to bomb the Caucasus in April and the German invasion of the USSR in

June 1941. The proposals outlined above represent the high-water mark of British efforts to conciliate the Soviets during this period. Politically and, as they saw it, morally, the War Cabinet believed they could offer no more. The British offer would prove insufficiently compelling to tempt Moscow to sever its Nazi connection; but the crucial question is whether anything the British might have offered could have done so. Halifax did not think so, as the resigned tone of his dispatches to Cripps testifies. Even with the benefit of hindsight, it is difficult to question the foreign secretary's judgment.

German defeat in the Battle of Britain, though of course adding immeasurably to British security, had actually lessened Britain's chances of converting the USSR into an ally. As long as a defiant Britain, backed by the industrial might of the United States, confronted Germany in the West, the Soviet Union could successfully cooperate with Hitler. The Soviets meant what they said when they repeatedly told Cripps that political conditions were not favorable for a full rapprochement between Great Britain and the USSR. According to standard Soviet procedure, Moscow never slammed the door in Cripps's face, since doing so would have deprived them of bargaining strength with the Germans. Also, if an outright break with London were avoided, the British might be forced in desperation to make unilateral concessions in an effort to bribe Moscow. Therefore, with each British offer of compromise, the Soviets taxed their ingenuity to find plausible objections so that, like a juggler, they could keep the maximum number of balls in the air at one time.

The problem with the British offers, as Cripps rightly pointed out, was that London only promised to recognize gains already made by the Soviet Union—and only de facto recognition at that. They could do no more without undermining their diplomatic and political position. The Germans, by contrast, were prepared to pay for Soviet cooperation in concrete ways.

As Stalin had told Cripps in July—and as Molotov had essentially repeated a month later—the Soviets believed that Germany was strategically weaker than Britain so long as the latter controlled the seas and maintained its links with the U.S. There is no reason to believe that the two Soviet leaders were not telling the truth on these occasions. Paradoxically, however, Germany was a greater threat to the USSR, since it was the dominant continental military power. If by siding with Hitler the Soviets could keep the two sides warring and exhaust their strength, they might build up their own military might for eventual intervention, should a tempting opportunity present itself. Once the two sides were weakened, the

European balance of power would be altered in the USSR's favor. As Molotov stated in a memorandum he gave to Schulenburg summing up Stalin's meeting with Cripps: "The so-called European balance of power had hitherto oppressed not only Germany, but also the Soviet Union. Therefore the Soviet Union would take all measures to prevent the re-establishment of the old balance of power in Europe."[42] The whole analysis was seductive, but unfortunately for Stalin it rested on a fundamental overestimation of the extent to which Britain could interdict German military strength. Not until the rapid collapse of both Yugoslavia and Greece in the spring of 1941 would Stalin show signs of realizing how much German power lay untapped, but by then Soviet options had shrunk.

On the evening of October 16 Cripps met with Mikoian, though probably because of slowness in translation Sir Stafford did not present his government's offers. Mikoian was not encouraging about the prospects of a comprehensive agreement, preferring a "group barter" deal. The Soviet sounded one rather ominous note when he discussed the route the bartered goods might take: "His proposal was that [the] Soviet Government supply commodities via [the] Trans-Iranian railway . . . and he stated that they were prepared to use that railway to the fullest capacity."[43] Acting on this, Cripps asked the Foreign Office for particulars about the Iranian rail route.[44]

The Soviets were showing an increasing and, for the British, disquieting interest in Iran. Maiskii had mentioned the Iranian route in his strange meeting with Butler on October 7, and, more to the point, the Foreign Office learned from the Aga Khan that the Soviets had approached the Iranians "with a friendly proposal that they be allowed to lease air bases on [the] Persian Gulf."[45] Clearly, something was up, but the British did not know what as yet.

Cripps presented the British proposals on October 22, but the initial omens were unfavorable: Molotov refused to see the ambassador, fobbing him off on Vyshinskii instead. Cripps began the discussion with a warning about the ever-growing German threat and the statement that "the fate of countries still neutral is largely bound up with the success or failure of the British defence, though some may not at present be able to acknowledge this openly." All the British wanted of the USSR, Cripps said, was "benevolent neutrality." This, he said in a phrase that sounded as though it came from one of his sermons, "may be nearly as valuable as armed resistance in shortening the war and bringing nearer the creation of that sane and constructive atmosphere in which we hope that a new and sounder international order may be worked out by the victorious powers and their associates." Cripps gave Vyshinskii a text of the British proposals he himself had drafted that included what London hoped for from the Soviet government in return. There were four British desiderata: (a) benevolent Soviet neutrality toward Britain; (b) the same toward Turkey and Iran, "especially in the event of either or both of them becoming involved in war with either or both of [the] Axis Powers"; (c) continued assistance to China "in undiminished volume"; and (d) conclusion of a nonaggression pact with Britain "in the event of [a] trade or barter arrangement."

In return the British text promised five points: (a) a "guarantee that the opinions of the Soviet Government shall be taken fully into account in any peace settlement"; (b) a promise "not to form or enter into any alliance directed against [the] USSR," with the provisos to which Halifax referred; (c) recognition of the "*de facto* sovereignty of the USSR" over the territories it had occupied since the outbreak of war, including "those parts of [the] former Polish State now under Soviet control"; (d) agreement to supply the Soviet Union with war material not required by Britain, as part of a barter or trade deal; and (e) a promise not to attack the USSR "by way of Turkey or Iran."[46] Cripps did not describe Vyshinskii's reaction, but the impression from the documents is that the latter merely promised to convey these offers to his government.

Cripps dispatched another telegram to the Foreign Office, recounting a conversation he had with the Turkish ambassador shortly after meeting Vyshinskii. What the ambassador told him convinced Sir Stafford of the urgency of winning the Soviets over as quickly as possible. According to the Turk, the German ambassador had returned to Moscow with a sheaf of offers for the Soviets, including a "free hand in Iran." Cripps told the Foreign Office that "both [the Turkish ambassador] and [the] Iranian Ambassador have noticed a slight but sudden worsening of Russo-Iranian relations since [the] German Ambassador's return."[47]

Foreign Office reaction to Cripps's presentation to Vyshinskii was not one of uniform joy. Two instances of Sir Stafford's wording were objectionable in London's view, as one Foreign Office memorandum explained: "[Sir Stafford] was authorised to say that we shall continue to act on the assumption that the Soviet Government are in *de facto control* of the Baltic States and the occupied parts of Poland and Roumania; but what he has said is that we are prepared to recognise their *de facto sovereignty*, which goes rather further and which they may interpret in such a way as to cause trouble with the Polish and U.S. Governments."[48] The second Foreign

Office objection was to their ambassador's use of the phrase "former Polish State," since the British had gone to war, nominally at least, to defend that state.

Cripps's deviance from his instructions presented the British with a knotty problem, as Halifax told Churchill: "we shall have to try, if the negotiations proceed, to get this phraseology altered. This will clearly not be easy, as if the Soviet reply is at all satisfactory and we then go back on Cripps, they will accuse us of watering down our original offer."[49] Once again, the foreign secretary must have wished that his ambassador in Moscow was more attuned to the wishes of the London government and that Cripps would follow his instructions to the letter.

Seven days after Cripps's meeting with Vyshinskii, Butler saw Ivan Maiskii, who did not even allude to the British proposals. Instead, the Soviet ambassador harangued his host about the ships seized by Britain, ignoring the fact that the British had promised to return them as part of a general settlement. Indulging in a bit of theater, Maiskii said that "the requisitioning of the ships had been a great personal shock to him; his moral sense had been offended."[50] If Maiskii's attitude was indicative of the Soviet stance in general, then Halifax's worries about repairing the damage done by Cripps's wording were unnecessary.

Nevertheless, the Foreign Office objections had been sent to Cripps, who dispatched a testy reply on Halloween. The ambassador argued that the document that he had given Vyshinskii was imprecise and not intended as a text, though anybody familiar with Soviet negotiating techniques would immediately see that Cripps's arguments were not to the point; the Soviets would seize on any favorable wording, official or not. As for the flap over his use of the word "sovereignty," Cripps argued correctly that the term used in the Russian translation, *vlast'*, could be translated as either control or sovereignty.[51] In explanation of having referred to "the Former Polish State," Cripps delivered a crabbed and didactic lesson on international law, as he understood it:

> I was not aware that His Majesty's Government desired to maintain [the] fiction that [the] former Polish State (as distinct from the Government) still exists de facto. Existence or non-existence of a state at a given moment seems to me a question of ascertainable fact (see e.g. *Hall's International Law*, p. 17 lines 5 to 9 + p. 22 lines 23 to 27) and to maintain this de facto fiction is quite inconsistant with any de facto recognition of Soviet control. . . . I appreciate however that it is

undesirable psychologically to use the term "former Polish State" in a definite text when it comes to be drawn up.[52]

Cripps had ducked responsibility for his blunder, though it is hard to believe that he had Hall's book in mind when he composed his note to Vyshinskii. In London, Maclean was unimpressed; in a memo he wrote: "With all due deference to the Ambassador's knowledge of international law, I find it hard to accept his justification of the term 'former Polish State.' "[53]

Cripps Rebuffed

Foreign Office objections to Cripps's presentation were largely pro forma, since they did not expect the Soviets to respond favorably. Indeed, in a memo, Halifax sounded as though he would have turned down the British offer had he been in charge of Soviet policy: "All this hardly seems to me very attractive from the Soviet point of view, but their reply should give a useful indication of the main lines of their immediate policy." So it should have, had the Soviets bothered to respond. But they did not.

Like a huge oil tanker, British diplomatic planning had tremendous inertial force. Even though those on the bridge saw no compelling reason to proceed, the vessel continued moving long after the engines had been cut. The lower echelons busied themselves with planning the route by which goods traded with the USSR might be delivered and were especially worried by Soviet designs on the Iran route. So were the Iranians, as Cripps discovered in discussion with that country's ambassador to Moscow. On November 1 Cripps cabled the Foreign Office that the Iranian "has noticed a definite deterioration in Perso-Soviet relations, and he considers that [the] Germans, who are undoubtedly instigating Russian pressure on Iran, are quite capable of arranging for 'loss' or sabotage of consignments on [the Iranian] railway thus providing a share in the administration of control of line." Amazingly, Cripps felt the Soviets were being duped by the Germans and that they had no aggressive designs of their own on the route to the Persian Gulf. He told the Foreign Office that such German moves should be countered, "because [the] USSR would thereby be distracted from countering German advancement in the Balkans."[54]

Others, perhaps remembering the role railways played in the Japanese conquest of Manchuria, were less inclined to give Moscow the benefit of the doubt. Professor Postan of the Ministry of Economic Warfare, for example, felt that the Soviets might deliberately clutter up the Basra railway "with more cargo than it can move," and then "they might . . . turn to the Shah and demand physical control of the route in order to ensure greater efficiency."[55] This was quite likely, Postan reasoned, since the Persian railroads were ramshackle and most probably unable to handle even modest traffic. The next day, November 8, Hugh Dalton developed Postan's argument in a letter to the foreign secretary, stating that "in the view of [the Soviets'] ancient ambitions in Iran, it is most likely that they would seize the first opportunity" to take control of the railway.[56]

Intelligence reports of Soviet designs on both Iran and Turkey were being received regularly in London. One such report is enlightening about both Soviet aims and the ways by which the Foreign Office gathered information. Mr. Rendel, British ambassador to Bulgaria, relayed a bit of gossip received from the Archbishop of Sofia, who had spoken to the Soviet ambassador's Bulgarian teacher, "to whom," the Archbishop said, "he speaks freely though he says little to anyone else." The Soviet had said that his country was not yet ready for involvement in the war and was busily repairing the Red Army's defects revealed during the Finnish War. "Moreover," Rendel's account continued, "both Germany and [the] British Empire were still too strong and it was desirable that the war should continue till they were both further enfeebled but Russia would keep her hands free. Germany had offered her access to the Persian Gulf but this was no substitute for control of the Straits."[57] In early November this line gained further credibility when the British learned from a source in Belgrade that Vyshinskii had told the Yugoslav ambassador that, in order to protect their interests in the Straits, the Soviets were prepared to join the Germans if the latter were to attack Turkey. The author of a Foreign Office memorandum thought this information might well be accurate, noting that "in the case of Turkey, as in that of Poland, [the Soviets] would no doubt feel that unless they staked out their claim immediately there would be no claim left to stake."[58]

The Soviets were busy doing just that, that is, staking out their claims. And in the process they were giving Sir Stafford a rude shock. While the British were hard at work preparing and delivering their trade offers, on the other side of the hill Moscow had accepted an invitation for Molotov to visit Berlin. In fact, the Germans had beaten their enemy to the punch, since Ribbentrop's invitation had been extended on October 13, nine days before delivery of the British proposals. The wording of Ribbentrop's note to Stalin, doubtless written in a style calculated to please the general secretary, is worth quoting. In a phrase that echoed Stalin's remarks to Cripps on July 1, Ribbentrop stated that Nazi Germany and Soviet Russia "were animated in the same degree by the desire for a New Order in the world as against the congealed plutocratic democracies." The foreign minister continued: "In summing up, I should like to state that, in the opinion of the Führer, also, it appears to be the historical mission of the Four Powers—the Soviet Union, Italy, Japan, and Germany—to adopt a long-range policy and to direct the future development of their peoples into the right channels by delimitation of their interests on a world-wide scale."[59] On October 21 the Soviets had accepted the German invitation, and while Cripps delivered the British proposals and waited patiently—even optimistically—for an answer Stalin and Molotov had been preparing their Berlin shopping list.

Upon learning of Molotov's departure for Berlin, Cripps confronted Vyshinskii in what must have been a rather unpleasant meeting. The ambassador delivered what he called "a strong statement" accusing the Soviets of bad faith: "Vyshinsky's previous assurance to me that Molotov's refusal to receive me had no political significance was now conclusively disproved by [the latter's] Berlin visit. Molotov's treatment of myself and my non-Axis colleagues was unprecedented and shewed [*sic*] unmistakeably his completely un-neutral attitude. I presumed that the Berlin visit must be taken as [the] Soviet Government's reply to my proposals, but if so [the] form of reply was most discourteous."[60] Cripps asked Vyshinskii two questions: "(a) Have the Soviet Government decided not to proceed with the very important proposals put forward by His Majesty's Government? (b) Am I to impress on my Government that Molotov's visit to Berlin indicates the Soviet Government's unwillingness to improve relations with His Majesty's Government?" Vyshinskii reverted to tried and true Soviet stalling tactics, but this time Cripps was not put off. The Soviet claimed that Molotov's visit was merely in return for Ribbentrop's trip to Moscow, but Cripps fired back: "I said I was not quite so simple as he seemed to think and that we should see [the visit's] purpose when we heard the results."[61] Sir Stafford threatened to withdraw the British proposals, since "twice already we had put forward proposals for such an agreement without receiving even the courtesy of an answer." The interview concluded in this unpleasant atmosphere with Vyshinskii groundlessly accusing Great Britain of forming an anti-Soviet alliance.[62]

The episode left something of a mark on Cripps. In Maclean's words, "Sir S. Cripps seems to have lost his temper."[63] Henceforward, the ambassador was to take a much harsher line in dealing with the Soviets, though as time would show, he was unable or unwilling to be uniformly firm. On November 20 he telegraphed the Foreign Office for permission to withdraw the British proposals in retaliation for Soviet actions. With iron-clad logic, Cripps employed an argument that only six months ago the Foreign Office might well have used on Cripps himself: "However undesirable it may be to invite accusation that we do not desire an improvement of Anglo-Soviet relations," he wrote, "the one fatal error of tacticians is to show that whatever line [the] Soviet Government may take in major political questions our attitude towards them will remain unchanged."[64] Sir Orme Sargent could only agree with the ambassador's new-found skepticism, writing in a minute that, "this little homily is particularly noteworthy as coming from Sir S. Cripps. I wish he would address it to some of his friends in this country."[65] Maclean could also not rise above a little gloating over Sir Stafford's abrupt conversion. In a memorandum he wrote, "It is amusing that after only six months in the Soviet Union the Ambassador should have become so strong an advocate of a firm line with the Russians."[66]

Sir Stafford Cripps's vanity had been wounded. For many years, he had sat comfortably in the wings of international relations, condemning the British players for their incompetence, only to fall flat on his face in his debut as diplomat. Cripps was not the first, and sadly not the last, Western politician who felt he could singlehandedly manage the Soviets if only given the chance. Confronting his failure, Cripps momentarily lost his equilibrium and his temper. Earlier in November, an exasperated American diplomat had told Dalton that "in his opinion Sir Stafford Cripps did not really understand what he was up against; the Russians were not people you could, or should expect to behave in a reasonable fashion. If you did you were exploited; immediately and thoroughly." The Soviets, he moaned, "were not reasonable people." Next to the passage claiming that Cripps misunderstood the Soviets, Maclean penned, "He is beginning to now."[67] He certainly was, though after recovering his balance, Sir Stafford forgot much of what he had learned.

CHAPTER FOUR

THE RUSSIAN

DANGER IS

OUR DANGER

DECEMBER 1940 – JUNE 1941

Molotov in Berlin

Sir Stafford Cripps's disillusionment with the Soviets would have been even greater had he known the details of the Berlin talks. Far from being bullied by the Germans, Molotov eagerly entered into the spirit of the occasion. The Germans were anxious to direct Soviet attention toward the vulnerable British Empire, which was, Hitler assured his guest, "a gigantic world-wide estate in bankruptcy."[1] "The Russian Empire," Hitler told Molotov, who voiced no objection to the Soviet Union being referred to in terms normally used for the defunct tsarist regime, "could develop without in the least prejudicing German interests. (Molotov said this was quite correct.)"[2]

The Soviet-German talks appeared to contemporaries to be the apex of cooperation between the two dictators, but the veneer of mutual friendship masked a deepening rift. One American historian has, with understandable exaggeration, called Molotov's forty-eight hours in Berlin "the real turning point of World War II."[3] This point of view, which probably results from too close a focus on Soviet motives, holds that Stalin, feeling that Hitler was in an embarrassed position with an unfinished war on his hands, pressed the Führer too closely for concessions in exchange for continued Soviet good will. Hitler, arrogant and enraged, this version claims, turned on his erstwhile ally and ordered the planning of "Case Barbarossa," the invasion of the Soviet Union.

Hitler was, most probably, angered by Soviet intransigence, though after Molotov's visit he remarked that he "hadn't expected anything of it anyway." In fact, the November conference was not the catalyst of Barbarossa; as long before as the previous July, Hitler had decided that an invasion of the USSR should be launched in spring 1941, and he thus treated the meetings with Molotov as camouflage. His Directive Number 18, issued on the date of the Soviet foreign commissar's arrival in Berlin, decreed that regardless of the visit's outcome, "all preparations for the East already verbally ordered are to be continued."[4] Hitler's long-range strategy, so far as that can be reconstructed, dictated an eventual offensive against "Jewish Bolshevism" in pursuit of *Lebensraum*, and it is highly doubtful whether anything the Soviets might have offered could have permanently dissuaded him.[5]

Be that as it may, if November 1940 gave the Soviets a last opportunity to at least postpone—if not prevent—a German invasion, they lost the chance of doing so by overplaying their hand. Molotov harangued Hitler and Ribbentrop about the presence of German troops in Finland and brushed aside the Führer's attempts to distract him with promises of territorial aggrandisement at Britain's expense by replying curtly that Germany and the USSR "should only contemplate a continuation of what had been begun."[6] Molotov shunned generalities, declaring that "Stalin had given him exact instructions."[7] He pursued these instructions with characteristic single-mindedness, criticizing the Germans for their activities in Romania and demanding Soviet spheres of influence in Bulgaria, the Dardanelles, and Finland. Molotov revealed what lay in store for the latter country, asserting that his government desired a settlement there "on the same scale as in Bessarabia," that is, annexation.[8] Molotov extracted a promise from the German dictator that he "would be prepared at any time to help effect an improvement for Russia in the regime of the Straits." In his final meeting with the Germans on November 13, the Soviet foreign commissar made it quite clear to Ribbentrop that a simple revision of the Montreux Convention, which governed the use of the Straits, would not satisfy his boss, since "paper agreements would not suffice for the Soviet Union; rather, she would have to insist on effective guarantees of her security."[9] That could, of course, only mean Soviet bases in Turkey.

Twelve days later, on November 25, showing how wrongly he had interpreted Hitler's intentions, Stalin offered to join the Tripartite Pact if certain conditions he specified were met. One historian has rightly pointed out that Stalin's offer of alliance with Nazi Germany has been "too often overlooked."[10] Stalin, one must surmise, continued to view Hitler through the Marxist prism, overestimating Nazism's economic and underestimating its racial component. Much of the Western world lay at Germany's feet, and the defeat of Britain would remove a much greater economic competitor than would destruction of the Soviet Union. Molotov said repeatedly that the USSR must prepare itself for a worldwide scramble for the redistribution of colonies. From the Soviet perspective, it would make greater economic sense for Hitler to turn West and grab the crumbling British Empire rather than drive against the impoverished USSR. But Hitler aimed to destroy Soviet Communism and to subject the Slavs to German rule; the Soviets also had at least one asset Hitler coveted—land contiguous to the new German Empire.

The four Soviet conditions for joining the Axis cast serious doubt on the contention that Stalin was actuated purely by defensive motives during the period of the Nazi-Soviet Pact. Only the first condition was defensive, calling on the Germans to withdraw from Finland; but, as Molotov had shown in Berlin, Moscow wanted the removal of German forces from Finland only to replace them with Soviet troops. The other three demands were, to say the least, frankly expansionist. The second condition demanded the scrapping of the Montreux Convention and "the establishment of a base for land and naval forces of the U.S.S.R. within range of the Bosporus and the Dardanelles." The third condition had been predicted as long ago as September by Leon Helfand: "That the area south of Batum and Baku in the general direction of the Persian Gulf is recognized as the center of the aspirations of the Soviet Union." The final condition demanded that Japan drop her claims to economic concessions in Northern Sakhalin.[11] Hitler, of course, ignored Stalin's demands and continued to plot his invasion of the USSR.

Cripps's Dilemma

While the Soviets were trying to extract the last possible ounce of advantage from Germany's supposed discomfiture, the British decided that, for the time being at least, they would not continue to put themselves out to obtain Soviet good will. On November 12 the War Cabinet decided that the Baltic States' ships seized in Britain should now be employed in the British merchant marine.[12]

Sir Stafford Cripps was prepared to go even further. On November 19 he cabled the Foreign Office for permission to withdraw the British proposals, "to keep pressure upon the Soviet Government in all directions."[13] But the ambassador's indignation with the Soviets did not at once draw him closer to his own government. Once again, as had been the case with his meeting with Stalin in July, Sir Stafford's proposals to the Soviets had been leaked to the press, and he was angry that the Foreign Office had not done more to prevent this. He wrote: "I fear that this publication has removed the last chance of effecting anything here and will merely make [the] Soviet Government even more convinced that it is not safe for them to try to come to any secret arrangement with us—even if they should wish to do so, which is not, of course, at all certain."[14] Cripps did not seem confident of whom he should blame for the failure of his mission, the Soviets or his own government. He accused his hosts of behaving abominably by shunning him and rushing off into the arms of the Germans, while at the same time he illogically claimed that leaks in the British press had forced Moscow to do so—even though the leaks had occurred after Molotov had already publicly announced his intention to visit Berlin. Cripps simply could not accept the fact that his own inflated hopes were responsible for his dis-illusionment.

Laurence Steinhardt, the American ambassador to Moscow, was a wit-ness to Cripps's predicament. Sir Stafford often told his troubles to Stein-hardt, who promptly relayed them, with comments, to the State Depart-ment. At one meeting, Cripps would fulminate about "sabotage" of his efforts by the Foreign Office and would blame press leaks on them alone;[15] at the next, he would tell Steinhardt that "he had finally become convinced that the Soviet authorities are more amenable to retaliatory action than to the customary diplomatic methods."[16] At times, Cripps would actually applaud the Foreign Office, which, in his words, "realizes more and more clearly that a policy of conciliation and appeasement with respect to the Soviet Government produces results diametrically opposite to those ex-pected and that the Soviet Government responds more readily to an aggres-sive policy than to a policy of concessions."[17] In one telegram, Steinhardt tried to analyze the reasons for Cripps's rapidly fluctuating moods:

I judge from the Ambassador's recent attitude and general remarks that he has not yet lost all of his illusions about the virtues of the Soviet Government, but that he has now reached the stage of obsti-nately clinging to some of his earlier beliefs while being forced to recognize that the natural intentions and conduct of the Soviet Gov-ernment are very much at variance with those beliefs which he has long championed. He is now realistic and at times even bitter, but will suddenly defend indefensible acts of the Soviet Government. His present state of mind is characteristic of that of virtually every chief of mission whose initial approach to the Soviet Government has been one of belief in its sincerity, integrity, or honesty of purpose and has invariably resulted in a deep-seated bitterness and hatred as distinguished from those individuals who have never had any illusions about the character of the Soviet Government.[18]

The Foreign Office remained unwilling to follow Cripps's advice and would not withdraw the British offers merely to satisfy the ambassador's wounded amour propre. The author of one memorandum agreed that to do so would "simply afford [the Soviets] an opportunity of declaring, not without some justification, . . . that we had never been genuinely anxious for a trade agreement or for an improvement in Anglo-Soviet relations."[19] Such a claim would strike a sympathetic chord with the British Left, not all of whom had experienced the same disappointments as Sir Stafford.

Withdrawal of the proposals was not the only way Cripps suggested to increase pressure on Moscow. On November 20 Cripps argued that a Soviet request to exchange visits of military attachés should be "held in suspense pending more definite information regarding results of [Molotov's] Berlin visit."[20] When the Foreign Office informed him that his advice had once again been disregarded and that the exchanges would proceed, Cripps fired back an angry reply: "It is of little use trying to maintain [a] firm negative attitude, which I have advocated so strongly during the last few weeks, if His Majesty's Government gives way in London to the first attempt by the Soviet Ambassador to put pressure on them, and if I am conscious that at any time decisions may be reversed without consulting me."[21] How strange this must have sounded in London. The British government, not having suffered from exaggerated hopes about Soviet good will in the first place, was less inclined than Cripps to adopt retaliatory measures now. The Foreign Office realized that, for the time being at least, they needed the Soviets more than vice versa and that furthermore it was inadvisable to appear overly disconcerted by Moscow's apparent disinterest in better relations. To do so might vent British frustration, but it would be unlikely to convince Stalin that his own interests were bound up in the defeat of Nazi Germany, which was, after all, the object of British diplomacy. On December 2, therefore, Halifax told Cripps that withdrawal of the British proposals would be bad tactics at the moment; but if "the situation should deteriorate," Halifax continued, "I should naturally be ready in consultation with you to reconsider the question without delay in the light of the new circumstances."[22]

The Foreign Office had further reasons militating against withdrawal of their October proposals. Information reaching London suggested that Molotov's visit to Berlin had been a failure and that "any attempt that Herr Hitler may have made to enlist Soviet co-operation and support in a German move against Allied interests in the Near and Middle East encountered an unresponsive attitude on the part of the Soviet Government. Indeed, there have been clear indications that the Soviet Government are not only not prepared to further German designs in the Balkans and elsewhere, but that their policy tends to run counter to German interests there." This was, as we now know, only partly true. German and Soviet designs were indeed on a collision course, and the Balkans—especially Romania and Bulgaria—might have been points of impact, but the Soviets had not been entirely uncooperative with the Germans. Instead, they merely tried to drive a hard bargain in exchange for their continued services. Be that as it may, anyone trying to understand the past should have it engraved on their consciousness that what is believed to be true is often as important, or more important, than what is true in fact. The British Foreign Office believed that the Soviets were drifting away from the Germans and decided to act on this belief—even though their information was, in this instance, partially faulty. Halifax continued:

> My own impression is that the Soviet Government are genuinely anxious to preserve their independence of action and to avoid involving themselves too deeply with the Axis powers. If so, I feel that in the circumstances our attitude towards the Soviet Government should continue wherever possible to be forthcoming and helpful, and that while leaving the Soviet Government to make the next move we for our part should abstain from any action which might suggest impatience, suspicion or irritation.[23]

But Cripps's pique was not so easily dispelled. In his reply to Halifax the next day, the ambassador said that he agreed with Foreign Office analysis of Soviet policy but rejected the conclusions drawn. He still believed that the British offers should be withdrawn. "A firm and dignified attitude of reserve," he wrote, "is more likely to succeed than any attempt to court the Soviet Government. . . . Having received no encouragement whatever as regards our political or our commercial proposals, we should at all costs avoid the appearance of running after the Soviet Government (which would only be interpreted as weakness) and should await advances from them." Cripps argued that the British should use those commodities from the Empire most needed by the Soviets—rubber and tin for example—to exert influence. He proposed to deliver a letter to Mikoian, "recounting in moderate language" the dismal history of his mission and arguing that the British proposals must be withdrawn to allow for disposal of Britain's "surplus commodities." He proposed to add that "it naturally remains open to the Soviet Government to put forward counter-proposals if they wish." Cripps did not believe that such a note would work a miraculous transformation in Soviet policy, "but it would, I am sure, go a long way towards convincing them that we are not to be trifled with," he wrote.[24]

On December 8 Cripps sent the Foreign Office a draft of his proposed note to Mikoian, which was not notable for its "moderate language." After a recapitulation of the previous six months' talks, stressing what he saw as Soviet rudeness and deceit, Cripps wrote: "The only interpretation which I am able to give to the facts set forth above is that the Soviet Government have never had any serious intentions of coming to any arrangement with His Majesty's Government on (?questions of) trade." Cripps felt he had been deceived by the Soviets and was clearly resentful. The Foreign Office thought that such frankness, though perhaps good for the morale of British diplomats, would be counterproductive. Fitzroy Maclean wrote:

> It has always been maintained by one school of thought (which evidently now includes Sir Stafford Cripps) that the best way of dealing with the Soviet Government is to take a strong line with them. If it is our intention to give this policy a trial, the letter which Sir Stafford Cripps proposes would seem to answer the purposes very well. If, on the other hand, it is intended that we should continue our policy of uniform amiability, the note will clearly have to be redrafted completely.

In considering the two options open, Maclean could not resist a barbed comment on the dejected Cripps: "his well-known sympathy for and personal contacts with the Soviet regime should enable him to judge how best to approach the Soviet Government in matters of this kind."

Cripps's draft letter was handed around the British government for comment and suggestion. It was agreed that his frankness must be toned down if an outright break with Moscow were to be avoided. But those like Dalton who knew Cripps felt that the ambassador might resign if his advice was not followed.[25]

While London was pondering Cripps's letter, the ambassador continued to press for a positive response. On December 16 he told the Foreign Office that he had even reversed his opinion—which had bordered on obsession—about recognition of the USSR's territorial gains. "Although I was strongly in favour of giving way at the very beginning of the difficulty," he told the Foreign Office, "I do not now think any value would be obtained from such action unless [the] Soviet Government were to make some direct and specific proposal for a settlement."[26] He now argued that "we had a legal right to requisition [the Baltic States'] ships" and that there was no compelling reason to surrender this point so long as the Soviets remained obstinate.

On December 18 the Foreign Office sent Sir Stafford a watered-down redraft of his letter to Mikoian, which Cripps derided as "feeble." The British government decided that, as much for domestic political reasons as for anything else, it would be best not to risk a break in relations with the USSR. Although Cripps surprisingly did not threaten to resign, he complained that the proposed text "definitely burkes the question as to who is responsible for the failure" of negotiations—oblivious to the fact that this was precisely the Foreign Office's intention. Speaking now from experience, the ambassador dispensed a bit of sage advice: "It is absolutely essential to appreciate the mentality of the Soviet Government in these matters. They will take every advantage of apparent weakness and are more likely to respond to a firm and dignified line."[27] Cripps's worries might well have been partly political. It would be difficult to return to Britain empty-handed to face inevitable accusations from his erstwhile left-wing colleagues that he had been duped by the Conservatives. He had staked his political reputation—or, rather, he hoped to revive it—on his ability to persuade the USSR to adopt a pro-British foreign policy, and if he were to return to Parliament without even a shred of an agreement at the very least he would want to explain why he had not been personally at fault.

Two days before Christmas Cripps sent London an analysis of Soviet policy based on his first six months' experience in the USSR. He was, understandably, not hopeful. He believed that the best way to move forward, however, would be to attempt to separate Stalin from his supposedly pro-German advisors: "The Red Army and popular sentiment . . . is more anti-German than that of the political leaders. Hence the wrangle while Stalin's principal advisers remain Molotov and Mikoyan, who are both pro-Axis and the latter of whom, as an Armenian, is anti-Turk and anti-

Iranian as well." Cripps then continued his series of lectures to the Foreign Office about Soviet guile, with an exposition that sounds remarkably contemporary:

> It is essential to realise the following characteristics of Soviet diplomacy: (1) Soviet Government are definitely un-sentimental, realist and nationalist; (2) They attribute "gentlemanly" diplomatic methods to weakness; (3) they will use all kinds of indirect methods of approach to create an atmosphere without actually doing anything [Cripps must have felt a twinge as he wrote this]; (4) they are very touchy where their national pride is concerned and desire quite naturally to be treated as a power of first-rate importance.[28]

Cripps's attribution of Soviet-German cooperation to personal intervention by Molotov and Mikoian vividly illustrates both how far his own ideas had changed and how practical experience in diplomacy is likely to temper theoretical notions. In 1936 Cripps had written that "policies are not made or carried through by individuals; they are the reflection of the economic interests that control Governments."[29] Now the USSR was pursuing a course that, according to all Cripps's long-cherished beliefs, should have been impossible. In theory, the Soviet Union, having eliminated the economic causes of a belligerent foreign policy by nationalizing the means of production, should by its very nature have been resisting Nazi aggression. In fact, they were abetting Hitler. This caused Cripps to abandon his talk of impersonal "economic forces" and to attribute Soviet behavior to misguided, or evil, individuals. Reading Cripps's wrestling match with his convictions, as revealed in his didactic telegrams, is an insight into the sobering effect of responsibility upon a theoretician. Cripps's telegrams seem as much an effort to persuade himself as to convince the Foreign Office.

The Advent of Eden

Sir Stafford's efforts to compel the Foreign Office to withdraw their trade proposals were disrupted by an act of God. Lord Lothian, the British ambassador to the United States, died on December 12, leaving Britain's most important ambassadorial post vacant. The position was so crucial to Britain's war effort that it required a person of obvious national prominence. Churchill briefly considered the octogenarian Lloyd George for the job; John Colville, Churchill's private secretary, even suggested Cripps, whom he believed "was being wasted in Russia." But Churchill would have none of that, saying that Cripps "was a lunatic in a country of lunatics and it would be a pity to move him."[30] Eventually, the prime minister decided to ask Lord Halifax to accept a demotion and move to Washington. There were more reasons for sending Halifax than his obvious prominence: he was a political liability. Churchill is quite frank about this in his memoirs: "[Halifax's] high character was everywhere respected, yet at the same time his record in the years before the war [when he had supported appeasement of Hitler] and the way in which events had moved left him exposed to much disapprobation and even hostility from the Labour side of our National Coalition."[31]

Halifax was replaced by Anthony Eden, who enjoyed a largely undeserved reputation for having opposed appeasement in the spring of 1938 and who was therefore more acceptable to the Labour partners in the coalition government. The newcomer to the Foreign Office was in some respects not unlike Sir Stafford Cripps; indeed, the similarities between the two would become more apparent during the next year and a half. Like Cripps, Eden believed that the personalities and personal political convictions of British diplomats could have an important impact on Soviet policy, and, again like Cripps, Eden was susceptible to a little flattery. Because of his matinee idol appearance and vanity, around the Foreign Office Eden was at times nicknamed "Ronald Coleman." Eden would bring a new style to the Foreign Office, which would affect the way the British dealt with Moscow, particularly after the German invasion of the USSR in June 1941.

After taking over the reins at the Foreign Office, Eden wrote to Cripps, telling him that, should he give Mikoian the harsh note the ambassador had drafted, it might give the Soviets an incorrect impression. They might conclude that Eden himself opposed Anglo-Soviet rapprochement. On December 28 the new foreign minister telegraphed Cripps: "If such a communication is made at this juncture to the Soviet Government the latter may well conclude that it represents a new policy in Anglo-Soviet relations which I have personally introduced on becoming Foreign Secretary. M. Maisky has been to see me and appealed for my help to try to better Anglo-Soviet relations and he has frequently stated that I sought to do this when I was Foreign Secretary before."[32] (One can only admire Maiskii's touch and his astute reading of Eden's character.) Later, in his formal greetings on becoming foreign secretary, Eden returned to this theme, telling Cripps that he felt it "an advantage that the Russians profess to regard me as one who has no prejudice against them."[33]

Cripps reluctantly accepted Eden's logic but said that he would retain the second draft of his letter to Mikoian "so that if at a later date it is decided to send such a letter the draft will have been settled."[34] Cripps clearly disagreed with Eden's reservations regarding the introduction of a "new" attitude toward the USSR; after all, Sir Stafford was a recent convert to a hard line with Moscow and as such was still fired by enthusiasm.

In his conversation with Maiskii on December 27, Eden discussed Germany, and, predictably, the Soviet ambassador treated him to a monologue about the outstanding Baltic States dispute. There were three points of conflict: the Baltic States' gold, seized by Britain in compensation for nationalization of British subjects' property; Baltic ships seized in Britain, which the British were now using while paying rent for usage into a blocked fund until ownership could be determined (they of course did not yet recognize Soviet ownership); and the fate of sailors who had been aboard the ships when seized. After his talk with the Soviet ambassador, Eden believed that some progress could be made, at least on the third point, without rekindling the dispute over sovereignty. The foreign secretary therefore informed Cripps that, since the mechanics of repatriation could best be handled from Moscow, he was authorized to negotiate this matter with the Kremlin.[35]

Cripps's reply, sent on December 29, was rambling, confused, and contradictory. He misinterpreted Eden's request to negotiate repatriation of the crews to be an order to negotiate a full settlement of all outstanding problems concerning the Baltic States. Always quick to take offense, Cripps replied that he had tried repeatedly in the past to reach an agreement with the Soviets on these questions: "They were turned down [by the Foreign Office] and His Majesty's Government have never come to a firm decision as to what their final offer is to be or how far they are prepared to go to get a settlement on these questions."

This was just not so. To be sure, the British position remained short of the full recognition desired by the Soviets, but Britain's October proposals had certainly constituted a "firm decision"; even Cripps had thought so at the time. Indeed, the British proposals had been drafted largely by Cripps himself, with mere semantic alteration by the Foreign Office—and these changes were made privately, after Cripps had submitted the proposals to the Soviets. The Kremlin had not even bothered to respond negatively.

Nevertheless, Cripps now argued that the British should go a step further: "Necessity is in my opinion to acknowledge the de facto sovereignty [again that term] of the Soviet Government in the Baltic States from which you must not follow that [sic] His Majesty's Government would acknowledge the Soviet Government as entitled to negotiate about questions as to gold and ships." Did this mean that Cripps now felt that such action by Britain would incline the Soviets toward more genuine neutrality? Cripps wrote: "Even if we were to get the Baltic questions settled, . . . other forces [that is, fear of German attack and the influence of allegedly pro-German advisors such as Molotov] would be the determining factor as regards any improvement in relations."

Cripps suggested that his government should offer to settle the three outstanding Baltic questions by agreeing to "acknowledge *de facto* the right of the Soviet Government to the gold" in exchange for the Soviets agreeing to compensate British citizens for nationalized property. "So far as the ships are concerned," Cripps continued, "it could be repeated that we had a legal right of the necessity [sic] to seize them and that we cannot give [them] up," but London could agree to charter the ships from the Soviets. The crews should be repatriated, Cripps felt.[36]

The Foreign Office was nonplussed by the ambassador's attitude. Since November his telegrams had stressed the need to bargain in the toughest possible manner with the Kremlin, and now he was suggesting that the British should make a unilateral gesture. But even Cripps seemed uncertain as to what purpose this would serve, writing that "the making of a fresh offer would no doubt encourage [the Soviets] to press for more." Even more extraordinary, however, was that each of the points Cripps made had already been discussed with the Soviets as part of a general trade agreement back in October. The Kremlin had not responded, and Cripps himself had advocated withdrawal of the offers. In a long memorandum analyzing Cripps's latest proposals, Maclean admitted to being confused. "I cannot help feeling that Sir Stafford Cripps tends to put the wrong emphasis on our attitude in these matters," he wrote. "In point of fact, we have proposed to the Soviet Government quite reasonable solutions of each of the Baltic problems, which, however, they have failed to take up. Sir Stafford Cripps, through whom these offers were made, must be well aware of this." Laurence Collier, head of the Northern Department in the Foreign Office, was equally surprised, taking Cripps to task for proposing a solution "in which, as is shown by the last paragraphs of [his] telegram, Sir Stafford Cripps himself does not believe. Sir Stafford Cripps, in short, has got the whole matter in the wrong perspective." Noting the discrepancy between the ambassador's repeated requests for a firm line with the Soviets and his strange proposals about the Baltic States, Collier guessed at a reason: "I find it difficult to understand . . . why he should take up a different attitude on Baltic questions alone, except on the assumption that he has a paternal weakness for the idea of recognising Soviet ownership of the Baltic ships, which was originally his own. Logically it stultifies his whole position."[37]

Collier was partly right; Cripps was indeed loath to admit a mistake. But there was more behind Cripps's extraordinary behavior than Collier's analysis would suggest. Sir Stafford's continued advocacy of British surrender on the Baltic States issue was so consistent, and apparently at such odds with his changing attitude toward the Soviet Union, that it can only be explained in terms of his rapidly fluctuating views about the USSR, which Laurence Steinhardt had noted. Many of Cripps's political friends and associates during the previous ten years were either Communists or fellow-travelers. Among such people, criticism of the USSR amounted to the sin of apostasy. As Eugene Lyons, an American fellow traveler who broke with the Soviets in the late 1930s, wrote: "The desire to 'belong,' not to be a political dog in the manger," was a powerful inducement to quell one's private doubts.[38]

Although Cripps found the obtuseness of Soviet foreign policy frustrating, and even felt that the Soviets were harming their own long-term interests, he nevertheless attributed their suspicions to a legacy of distrust caused by twenty-four years of anti-Soviet excesses by Britain's Conservatives. As he wrote Lord Halifax in October 1940, the experience of the previous two decades "has taught the Soviet Government to look upon [the British government] as fundamentally hostile to the Soviet Union."[39] The Conservatives argued that their hostility to Bolshevism had simply been a reaction to Soviet advocacy of violent world revolution, but Cripps dismissed this excuse with the assertion that "Russian policy had turned from the idea of international revolution with the disappearance of Trotsky."[40] For Cripps, the Soviets had to be blameless for the sorry state of Anglo-Soviet relations. After all, the Communists were a party of the Left, of progress, and they were aiming to build the common dream: worldwide Socialism. To admit otherwise would have meant breaking with his past, with his beliefs, and with his friends.

Since Cripps attributed the blame for Soviet hostility to Britain's misguided policies in the past, it naturally followed in his view that, given the proper leadership, a solution for this unfortunate state of affairs lay within Britain's powers. He argued that a surrender on the Baltic dispute might be a sufficiently grand gesture to demonstrate to Moscow that the British had mended their ways. As Steinhardt pointed out, Cripps clung to this fiction rather than face the collapse of his beliefs. That Cripps should persuade himself in this manner is, however, less surprising than is the fact that within a year he would be able to convert the foreign minister and a sizable portion of the British government to his way of thinking.

Back in London, it was clear from the tone of his telegrams that Cripps was distraught, and Eden tried to soothe his ambassador. He suggested that, rather than accept the entire Soviet position regarding their new conquests, he might attempt to place Anglo-Soviet relations on a better footing by means of a personal note from himself to Stalin. As he told Cripps: "While I do not expect any very sensational results, I cannot help feeling that such a move on my part might help to dispel doubts that M. Stalin, who is of a notoriously suspicious nature, may feel as to the sincerity of our desire for co-operation."[41] Sir Stafford might have thought this tactic a good one during the previous summer, but now he believed that the foreign secretary's personal intervention would be ineffective. In answering Eden's telegram, the ambassador reverted to one of his favorite themes, that the press leaks of their conversation in July had made Stalin chary about direct talks with the British. It would not be possible, Cripps wrote, for him to get an audience with the dictator, and the two options open—either a letter or a meeting with Molotov—would not yield any useful new information. A simple letter would be undignified, and Molotov, should he even deign to meet the ambassador, would only rant about Britain's supposedly lawless behavior.

Taking Cripps's arguments into account, Eden decided, for the time being, against a personal note to Stalin.[42] In view of the poor prospects for success, the Foreign Office decided that in this instance it might be better not to try any new moves with the Soviets. Perhaps remembering their inability the previous September to play down relations with the Soviet Union, the author of one Foreign Office memorandum argued that this time steps should be taken to muzzle press speculation about the USSR.[43]

For these reasons, January 1941 was a quiet month in Anglo-Soviet relations. Britain's diplomats could think of no further approaches to Moscow. And the Soviets, for their part, did not court the British, in spite of the fact that their relations with Germany were beginning to deteriorate. Stalin had not received a response to his November 25 offer to join the

Tripartite Pact, and, furthermore, German moves in Romania and Bulgaria caused some concern in the Kremlin. Molotov had explicitly stated that Bulgaria was within the USSR's sphere of influence when he had spoken to Hitler, and German troops in Romania posed a direct threat to the Soviet Union. On January 17, 1941, therefore, Molotov summoned Schulenburg and questioned him on these matters.[44] The Germans replied that their activity in the Balkans was aimed at countering British moves in Greece, an explanation that provided little comfort to Stalin, since German behavior fell far short of the full cooperation he had proposed in November.

In mid-January, back in London, Maiskii began to hint that he wanted to meet Eden again. It would be reading far too much into his efforts to regard them as somehow linked with the worsening relations between the USSR and Germany, since, in Moscow, the Soviets continued to ignore Cripps. One Foreign Office official suggested that the British should retaliate against Sir Stafford's poor treatment by refusing to admit Maiskii. He argued that, in light of the decision to deemphasize relations with Moscow, "there is nothing that we particularly want to say to M. Maisky, and, to judge by past experience, it is unlikely that he has anything of interest to say to us."[45]

Eden ignored the advice of his subordinates and chose to meet Maiskii on January 29. The foreign secretary used the occasion to complain that Molotov, who was after all foreign commissar and should therefore be accessible to resident ambassadors, had not seen Cripps in three and one-half months, even though he had met repeatedly with the German and Italian ambassadors. Maiskii argued unconvincingly that Molotov was a very busy man, since he was prime minister in addition to being the executor of Soviet foreign policy. But Eden replied that if Cripps continued to receive such cold treatment, Maiskii could expect the same.[46]

Eden's arguments had immediate effect, showing how unnecessary Cripps's isolation had been and how much the Soviet government valued Maiskii's access to the portals of power in London. Three days after Eden met the Soviet ambassador, Cripps was invited to visit the Kremlin, but, judging from the result of Sir Stafford's subsequent conversation with Molotov, the foreign secretary might well have saved himself the effort. Molotov displayed the curt, slick qualities that made him such an effective diplomat. In response to Cripps's obvious agitation about his cool treatment, Molotov responded calmly, assuring the ambassador that the only problem was "an accumulation of unfriendly measures on the part of His Majesty's Government," which, Molotov claimed, had created a situation that was "quite sad." Molotov even became personal, telling Cripps that "he wished . . . to put on record that the expectations which the Soviet Government had entertained on the Ambassador's appointment to Moscow had not been realised." This was too much for Cripps, who could tolerate to a certain degree Soviet criticism of British policy but would not leave personal slights unanswered. In his account sent later to the Foreign Office, Cripps wrote of Molotov's personal snub: "I presume [from Molotov's remark] that he wished, somewhat stupidly as far as I am concerned, to create a sense of my personal failure, in order to stimulate my efforts to settle [the] Baltic questions." The foreign commissar had clearly struck a nerve; such a remark must have wounded Cripps deeply, since he regarded himself, with some justice, as the best friend of the Soviet Union in the Foreign Office.

Molotov's rudeness spurred Cripps to press Molotov, claiming that the latter "was wrong in his analysis of the situation," and "that the offers which [the British] had made in 1940 showed quite clearly that they were genuinely anxious for better relations with the Soviet Union." Cripps continued, asking whether the Soviets might agree to a wider political settlement if the "present difficulties" could be disposed of. Molotov's reaction is informative. According to Cripps, "M. Molotov (who by this time was showing signs of boredom and impatience) replied that of course if the existing problems were disposed of there would be a better basis for an improvement in relations. To this he had nothing to add." Molotov must have thought Cripps a bit slow. The foreign commissar had promised nothing, saying that, should the British be entirely forthcoming, there would merely "be a better basis for an improvement in relations."[47]

The tone of Cripps's analytical telegrams back to the Foreign Office reflected dejection itself; the Soviets offered no way forward. As Cripps wrote: "[Molotov] made no reference of any kind to any method by which the existing difficulties might be solved." One can only agree with Cripps's summation: "[The] whole interview was quite unproductive though Molotov was polite. His only objects appeared to be to disprove the contention that he is inaccessible and to give some semblance of a reply regarding [our] political proposals while pretending that it had already been given."[48] In other words, Molotov was not oblivious to the importance of British public opinion. Above all, his purpose was apparently to appear open, while making the British look unreasonable.

Cripps ended his account with a familiar plea: "I am still in favor of attempting a settlement on the Baltic questions, though my repeated suggestions to this effect have not been accepted."[49] Cripps's persistence in this matter is truly remarkable. Molotov had told him, and Cripps had seemingly understood, that should Britain accept completely the Soviet position in the Baltic States, this would not lead automatically to a general agreement—or, indeed, to any concrete improvement in relations. Collier once again ascribed Cripps's obtuseness to "paternal weakness," and Eden minuted: "It certainly seems that Sir S. Cripps' advice is contradictory." But why Sir Stafford should be so passionate about abandoning the peoples of Latvia, Lithuania, and Estonia to their fate remained a mystery to the Foreign Office.

Molotov's clear lack of enthusiasm did not incline the British toward compromise, and Cripps, true to his post-November form, continued to press for tough measures against the Soviets on every issue—excepting always the Baltic imbroglio. Sir Stafford argued against admission to Britain of a Soviet air attaché,[50] and he urged a tighter application of the British blockade, a suggestion on which the British government acted by persuading the Americans to tighten exports to the USSR. Speaking to the Foreign Office about certain Soviet contraband, Cripps telegraphed: "You are in a position to intercept any or all of these cargoes. I think it would be far better to act first and talk afterwards. [The] Soviet Government responds more favourably to deeds than threats."[51]

In the meantime, Maiskii again suggested to Butler that unilateral British concessions might incline his government toward negotiations with the British.[52] Learning of this, Cripps returned to the attack:

> All Maisky's promises, hints and suggestions as to what the Soviet Government might do if this or that concession is made must henceforth be wholly disregarded by all departments of His Majesty's Government. [The] Soviet Government should be made to understand that we attach no importance whatever to them and will not meet their requirements in any way—however apparently unimportant—until they are prepared to negotiate some general agreement, rather than to be vague about it.

Just to confuse the issue, Cripps added: "This telegram represents my considered view at this stage of our relations. If at any point it gives the impression of varying what I have said before, what is said here should prevail."[53] Did this mean that Cripps had changed his mind about the Baltic impasse? He gave no clue beyond stressing the need for firmness with the Soviets, and it is impossible to guess, since at this point his views could, as his accumulated telegrams show, change from dispatch to dispatch, indeed even vascillating within the same telegram. The intriguing question is: To whom was Cripps addressing these scattered gems of advice? Nobody on the British side, with the exception of Cripps himself and, to a lesser extent, Eden, advocated a conciliatory line with Moscow. Perhaps the ambassador was simply venting the frustrations of his isolated and vexing post, as he did when speaking with Steinhardt.

On February 21, pursuant to the Foreign Office decision to deemphasize relations with the Soviet Union, Cripps was finally authorized to withdraw the British proposals of October 22, 1940. He did so in a note to Mikoian that left the door open should the Soviets change their minds. The proposals could be kept on the table no longer, the note said, but His Majesty's Government would "be willing to consider" any new Soviet offer.[54]

Upon learning the next day that Eden intended to journey to the Middle East, Cripps wired the foreign secretary, asking him to visit Moscow and assuring him that "Stalin agreed to see you."[55] But Eden was not prepared to show up on the Kremlin's doorstep solely on the invitation of the British ambassador. He gently rejected Cripps's advice, wiring: "I have always shared your view that it is bad policy for us . . . to run after the Soviet Government," though he was, he stated, prepared to come to the Crimea or Odessa if invited by the Soviet leadership.[56] That Cripps should ask the foreign secretary to Moscow without a Soviet invitation while at the same time rejecting exchanges of air attachés on the grounds that the Soviets should first agree to serious negotiations was curious indeed.

Although Eden did not wish to visit the Soviet Union uninvited, he did ask Cripps to meet him in Ankara. So Cripps left Moscow on February 27, arriving the next day in Turkey.[57] While there, he argued the case for a settlement of the Baltic questions with some success. Eden was inclined to accept the USSR as, in his biographer's words, "a genuine ally of liberal democracy and an agent of 'progress.'"[58] To be sure, Eden was more inclined to this view after June 22, and he changed his mind later in the war, but the tendency was evident earlier in his willingness to accommodate the Soviets and in his fatuous belief that his personal assurances of good will might somehow lessen Stalin's "suspiciousness."

War in the Balkans

While Eden and Cripps were conferring in Turkey, Soviet-German relations continued to deteriorate. Schulenburg explained to Molotov the accession of Bulgaria to the Three Power Pact, assuring the commissar for foreign affairs that this "was in no way prejudicial to the interests of the Soviet Union." Molotov was not convinced, stating that "it was unfortunately not evident to him that events were unfolding within the framework of the Soviet Government's *démarche* of November 25."[59] Indeed they were not; the indications began to multiply that Germany's aims and those of Soviet Russia were no longer as historically congruent as Stalin had once claimed—or hoped.

German refusal to accept the Soviet Union into the ranks of its allies led Stalin to take measures in the Balkans to counter German influence, in hopes of creating a defensive glacis. On March 1, the same day as Schulenburg's talk with Molotov, the Bulgarians announced that they had signed the Tripartite Pact, and German troops entered the country. Two days later, in a statement broadcast on Soviet radio, the Kremlin aired its displeasure: "The Soviet Government cannot share the view of the Bulgarian Government as to the correctness of its attitude in this question: as this attitude, independently of whether the Bulgarian Government wished it, leads not to the consolidation of peace, but to an extension of the sphere of war and the involving of Bulgaria in war."[60]

One might assume that in a logical world the evidently increasing Soviet suspicions about Hitler's aims might have induced the Kremlin to pull closer to the British. But this would have to wait until after the German invasion of the USSR in June. Stalin was prepared to conclude nonaggression pacts with neutrals that the Germans might attack; to negotiate with Britain, a power already at war with the Nazis, was a far more momentous, and riskier, step. The Soviets must have feared that Anglo-Soviet talks—if Berlin were to learn of them—would rule out the possibility of further fruitful collaboration with Germany, should relations take a turn for the better. For once, Cripps's warnings that the Soviets were chary of talking with the British for fear of leaks may have had some validity—even though the Soviets themselves had done the overwhelming share of leaking to this point.

On March 5 Cripps returned from Turkey determined to bring about closer cooperation between the Turks and Moscow, in hopes of countering German influence in Southeastern Europe. Reflecting the changing Soviet mood, on March 10 Vyshinskii told the ambassador that the Kremlin would welcome such cooperation, and that the Soviet government had told the Turks that Turkey could count on "full understanding and neutrality of the USSR" in case of German attack.[61] As seen from Moscow, German moves in the Balkans were beginning to assume a pattern. A Nazi foothold in Turkey would open yet another invasion route for German troops. Cripps thought Vyshinskii's statement reflected a new spirit in the Kremlin and relayed his enthusiasm to London.

Eden also began to feel that a new age in Anglo-Soviet relations may have dawned. On March 21 he told Cripps that, if possible, he should press the Soviets to move further and faster in countering German influence in Eastern Europe.[62] But when Cripps met Vyshinskii the next day and suggested that the Soviets should move to reassure Yugoslavia as well as Turkey, Vyshinskii once again fended off the ambassador's attempts to discuss wide-ranging strategic questions with the remark that "conditions did not exist for discussion of such general political questions as that of Yugoslavia between our two Governments." Evidently, the Soviets were willing to inform the British of decisions already made but not to discuss future policy. In explaining his government's unwillingness to discuss strategic problems, Vyshinskii for once did not harp on the Baltic dispute, instead claiming that the British blockade and pressure on the U.S. to curb exports to the Soviet Union revealed a "general policy of hostility to [the] USSR" on the part of the British government. Belaboring a hopeless issue, Cripps pointed out that Soviet behavior had done nothing to ease agreement, and that, as for the blockade, the British government had a legitimate interest in materials being shipped through the Soviet Union to Nazi Germany.

Writing to the Foreign Office after this meeting, Sir Stafford was unaccountably optimistic. Putting the rosiest possible coloration on the conversation, he described Vyshinskii's recriminations as "a milder attack than I had anticipated" and claimed that the Soviet argument "shows they still attach importance to Baltic questions, but these are beginning to take second place to the blockade." He also claimed that the Soviets "desire to prepare the ground for [the] possibility of a rapprochement with us." Cripps concluded that, for the time being, the British should continue to enforce the blockade, since this might compel the Soviets to talk—at last.[63]

In considering whether the Soviets were indeed preparing the ground for a future rapprochement with Britain, several contradictory factors must be taken into account. The first is that Cripps—who was after all the best to judge the tone of the interview—sensed a softening of the Soviet attitude. This, combined with the harsher Soviet stance toward the Germans after the rejection of their November proposals, might suggest that Cripps was finally correct in reading the Soviet mood. The evidence militating against Cripps's argument is, however, in balance more persuasive. Sir Stafford Cripps's judgment had proven too optimistic in the past, and, unless he omitted something from his account of his talk with Vyshinskii, there is nothing in the written record to suggest that the Soviets had abandoned their customary obduracy and coolness toward the British. Indeed, what evidence we have from Soviet sources indicates that the Kremlin's suspicions of Britain remained as strong as ever, as would soon become clear.

When Maiskii met with Butler on March 26, the ambassador's comments suggested that the Soviets' aims remained unchanged, in spite of their growing disapproval of German activity. Maiskii expressed his opinion that "it would . . . be a good thing if one great nation, namely the Soviet Union, remained neutral and was available at the end of the war to act as a makeweight."[64] One could hardly hope for a clearer statement of Soviet aims than this remarkable comment, which is quite consistent with Stalin's remark that the USSR would be the last to enter the war so as to throw the decisive weight into the scales. To be sure, Stalin was afraid of possible German moves, especially since Hitler had rejected the Soviet offer of November, but Stalin was only prepared to make small, veiled steps against Germany. The Soviets were not ready for, nor did they desire, closer relations with the British, whom they explicitly regarded as the primary bulwark of the old order. The Germans were by far the preferable partner, if only Hitler would continue to see reason.

It was perhaps to rein in the erratic Hitler that Stalin concluded the toothless nonaggression pact with Yugoslavia after that country's military coup on the night of March 26–27. The Soviet move was so hastily conceived and inept that in late April Hitler actually asked Schulenburg "what the devil had posessed the Russians to conclude the Friendship Pact with Yugoslavia?"[65] Perhaps Stalin hoped that the pact would goad the Germans into invading Yugoslavia, embroiling them in a further campaign that would buy time for the Soviet Union. Indeed, the Germans received information through leaks in Turkey suggesting that it was Stalin's fond hope that Yugoslavia would hold out long enough (say two months) to enable the British to intervene. This would squander the most suitable season for the Germans to begin an invasion of the USSR and would perhaps delay such an attack for at least a year.[66] The Soviets may not in fact have hoped to deter Hitler from invading Yugoslavia; on the contrary, such an invasion might be to their advantage. Without access to Soviet materials, one can only speculate about Stalin's motives in this curious incident.

The general secretary's failure to anticipate the eventual German attack on the USSR was almost certainly not the fault of his intelligence services (his information network might well have been the best in Europe, bolstered as it was by a net of communists and fellow travelers abroad), nor was he ill-informed from other sources; his was a failure of interpretation. The British, for their part, were receiving frequent, reliable reports of Hitler's intentions, such as the Nazi dictator's comment to Prince Paul of Yugoslavia that he intended to invade the USSR in late June—a comment that reached American ears before being relayed to London and Moscow.[67]

One British attempt to warn the Soviets of the impending attack led to tragicomic results. In late March Churchill became convinced that the intelligence reports being received from Eastern Europe conclusively pointed to German offensive preparations, and he decided to act upon this information by warning Stalin in a personal message to be delivered through Sir Stafford Cripps. Churchill wrote: "I have information from a trusted agent that when the Germans thought they had got Yugoslavia in the net, that is to say after March 20th, they began to move 3 of the 5 panzer divisions from Roumania to Southern Poland. The moment they heard of the Serbian revolution this movement was countermanded. Your excellency will readily appreciate the significance of these facts." Churchill ordered Cripps to convey this note to Stalin as soon as possible, with the following points stressed:

> You [Cripps] would of course not imply that we ourselves required any assistance from the Soviet Government or that they would be acting in any interests but their own. What we want them to realise, however, is that Hitler intends to attack them sooner or later, if he can; that the fact that he is in conflict with us is not in itself sufficient to prevent him from doing so if he is not also involved in some embarrassment, such as now confronts him in the Balkans, and that consequently it is in the Soviet interests to take every possible step to ensure that he does not settle his Balkan problem in the way that he wants.[68]

This simple request by the prime minister triggered a minor controversy that has only recently been laid to rest. Cripps did not feel it would be wise to deliver such a message to Stalin and told Churchill so two days later, on April 5. He wrote, apparently persuasively, that the general secretary would only consider the message an attempt by perfidious Albion to embroil the USSR with the Germans and that furthermore, "it is quite out of the question in the present circumstances to try to deliver personally any message to Stalin," since he would probably not receive the ambassador. But Churchill was not so easily dissuaded and answered that if an audience with Stalin was impossible, the warning was of such importance that it should be delivered at any rate through Molotov.[69]

Cripps could be as stubborn as Churchill, and he dug his heels in over the matter, refusing once again on April 6 to deliver the message. He commented tersely that the Soviet government "are fully aware" of the German danger.[70] Two days later Cripps repeated his arguments, stressing his belief that the proposed warning "might very well diminish seriously the strong effect of Prince Paul's [information]." This time Cripps's arguments convinced one important person, Sir Alexander Cadogan, who agreed that it might be unwise to appear to be too anxious to convince Stalin.[71] But the prime minister persisted, writing in his own hand: "It is my duty to have the facts conveyed to the head of the Russian State. It makes no difference to the importance of the facts that they or their channel is [sic] unwelcome. Make sure that M. Stalin gets my message."[72]

The reason for the prime minister's obstinacy has puzzled historians ever since the war, especially since Churchill's own explanation in his memoirs is so unconvincing. He claimed that, though British intelligence had been receiving regular hints of German plans to invade the USSR, up to this point they had been fragmentary. But the transfer of the three panzer divisions was different. "To me," he wrote, "it illuminated the whole eastern scene like a lightning flash. The sudden movement to Cracow of so much armour needed in the Balkan sphere could only mean Hitler's intention to invade Russia in May."[73]

But could it only mean this? One recent historian has concluded that "Churchill's deductions do not appear to have been entirely logical," since the Germans could have attacked the Soviet Union from Romania as easily as from Poland. In fact, the transfer of the panzers might just as well have signalled a German intention to move the armor closer to Western Europe for a projected cross-channel invasion.[74]

This puzzle was only solved after the revelation in the early 1970s that before the war the British had broken the German military code, the enigma cipher, and continued to read German radio traffic throughout the war. As one historian of "Ultra," the British codebreaking effort, has written: "The Cripps episode is only explicable in terms of the precisely detailed picture that Ultra and other sources had been establishing about the Barbarossa buildup." The source of the information concerning the transfer of the panzer division may well have been, as Churchill claimed, a spy, but "the mountain of evidence about Barbarossa" came from Ultra.[75] Knowing the source of Churchill's information, his impatience to see Stalin warned is readily understandable.[76]

Having refused to deliver Churchill's warning for more than a week, on April 11 Cripps took the extraordinary step of handing a note to Vyshinskii, composed by Cripps himself, warning of the impending German attack but omitting any reference to the prime minister's note. It was a long, rambling letter recapitulating the history of British efforts to resist German aggression and prefaced with the remark that these were Cripps's "personal views," which were "the result of continuous study of and thought upon, these problems." He suggested that the Soviets take "the most vital step" of cooperating with Turkey to insure that Germany would be faced with threats from as many directions as possible. He closed with a warning: "If . . . no action is now taken, then no doubt Germany will continue with her policy of dealing with countries one by one, in the meantime giving the fullest assurances to those she is not yet ready to attack. . . . The avoidance of war on several fronts has always played into the German hands. Now, owing to the Greek and Yugoslav resistance, there is already war on two fronts and the opening of a third or fourth might prove a decisive end to the German menace."[77]

Having acted unilaterally, Cripps told the Foreign Office that he could not now deliver the prime minister's message:

> Were I now to convey through Molotov Prime Minister's message, which expresses the same thesis in very much shorter and less emphatic form, I fear that the only effect would be probably to weaken impression already made by my letter to Vyshinsky. [The] Soviet Government would not, I feel sure, understand why so short and fragmentary a commentary, on facts of which they are certainly well aware, without any definite request for explanation of Soviet Government's attitude or suggestion for action by them, should be conveyed in so formal a manner.[78]

This was very strange. Cripps had resisted delivery of Churchill's note on the grounds that Stalin might sense an attempt to embroil him with the

Germans. Now Cripps claimed that the problem with the prime minister's note was that it contained no "suggestion for action." The Foreign Office was nonplussed, Sir Orme Sargent writing that "Sir S. Cripps is indeed incalculable." Eden wrote to Churchill saying that since Cripps had already acted on his own, "I think there may be some force in Sir S. Cripps' arguments."

But Churchill was livid and answered Eden on April 16. "I set special importance on the delivery of this personal message from me to Stalin. I cannot understand why it should be resisted. The Ambassador is not alive to the military significance of the facts. Pray oblige me."[79] The prime minister's message was finally delivered on April 19, but the whole episode left Churchill disgruntled. He was still angry in 1950, when he wrote: "If I had had any direct contact with Stalin I might perhaps have prevented him from having so much of his air force destroyed on the ground."[80]

Most historians have regarded Churchill as too hopeful about the possible impact his personal warnings could have had on the ever-suspicious Stalin, citing Zhukov's comment that the Soviet dictator ignored "information coming from imperialist circles" and Stalin's own reaction when, in August 1942, the prime minister reminded the dictator of the incident. "I remember it," Stalin said. "I did not need any warnings. I knew war would come, but I thought I might gain another six months or so."[81] Still, it is hard to disagree with Churchill's belief that a note from the prime minister, promptly delivered, would have carried greater weight with the Kremlin than a statement of "personal views" by His Majesty's ambassador. By the time Sir Stafford chose to deliver Churchill's warning, Yugoslavia had already surrendered, robbing the message of much chance of effectiveness.

It appears that Yugoslavia's rapid collapse worried Stalin, who embarked on a period of abject submission to Germany. In place of the prickly sensitivity the Soviets had shown over such matters as Finland and the Danube Commission during 1940, Stalin now prostrated himself trying to avoid the slightest hint of provocation toward the Germans. One prominent Soviet historian writing in 1962 argued that "the fundamental reason [for Soviet unpreparedness when the Germans attacked] was Stalin's error in estimation of the military-strategic situation forming on the eve of war. He supposed that Fascist Germany would not initiate war against the USSR in the near future if she was not provoked."[82] Although the tendency among Soviet historians of the Khrushchev period was to blame all the shortcomings—military, political, and social—of the Soviet system on Stalin, in this instance this explanation has much to recommend it in the way of supporting evidence.

One example of Stalin's pains to avoid riling the Nazis at this time is particularly enlightening: the Soviets counted over three hundred German violations of Soviet air space by reconnaissance aircraft, but their reaction was tepid to say the least. When Colonel General Kuznetsov, commander of the Baltic Special Military Region, tried to limit the effectiveness of these flights by instituting partial blackouts, the Kremlin countermanded his orders.[83] The Nazis, in turn, reacted to Soviet weakness with characteristic disdain. When the Soviets finally attempted unsuccessfully to force one of the German planes to land, the Germans had the nerve to lodge a protest against "wanton Soviet firing on a 'weather plane.' "[84]

That Stalin was not heedless of the growing German threat can be seen in the enthusiasm and haste that he showed in securing his nonaggression pact with the Japanese, which was signed in Moscow on April 13. In normal circumstances, this would have been a coup of the first order; Stalin had loosened the Axis vice grip on the Soviet Union in one deft stroke. In a widely reported incident, Stalin appeared on a Moscow railway platform to bid Japanese Foreign Minister Matsuoka farewell—in itself a sign of the unusual importance and urgency the Kremlin attached to relations with Japan. Then, within earshot of Western reporters, the dictator, who appeared to be drunk, told the departing foreign minister: "We will organise Europe and Asia. . . . We will organise the Americas," bursting into a "guffaw." And in a further display of false bonhomie, Stalin turned to the German representative, Colonel Krebs, saying: "We will remain friends with you—in any event."[85]

Stalin was sparing nothing to encourage his Axis partners to become further ensnared with the British and Americans, hoping that they would thereby leave the USSR alone. The willingness of the Japanese to sign a nonaggression pact with Moscow, without even demanding the cessation of Soviet supplies to China, must have suggested to the Soviets that Japan was preparing to attack the United States and British holdings in Asia. It may have seemed to the Soviets that Hitler would postpone an attack on the USSR until he could count on Japanese support. At the very least, the Russo-Japanese treaty should give the German dictator pause.

But then the Nazis were not about to be bluffed by Stalin. Far from being deterred, the Germans rightly interpreted Stalin's rush to befriend the Japanese as a conclusive manifestation of Soviet weakness. In his diary, Joseph Goebbels exulted in the fear inspired in Moscow by German strength:

> Big sensation: Russo-Japanese treaty of friendship and Non-Aggression. Mutual guarantees of Manchuria and Mongolia. Stalin and Molotov escort Matsuoka to his train. Stalin embraces the German military Attaché and declares that Russia and Germany will march together towards the goal. This is marvelous and for the moment extremely useful. We shall bring it to the notice of the English with all appropriate force. It is a fine thing to have power. It seems that Stalin has no desire to make the acquaintance of our German Panzers.[86]

The evidence pointing to a German attack mounted, but Stalin continued to rule out or at least play down the omens of invasion. On March 20 General F. I. Golikov, head of the Chief Intelligence Administration (GRU), submitted a remarkably accurate warning to Stalin, which stated that Hitler's forces would attack sometime between May 15 and June 15. Soviet Marshal Zhukov argues that this vital warning was "nullified," however, by an appended note that claimed: *"Rumours and documents to the effect that war against the USSR is inevitable this spring should be regarded as misinformation coming from the English or perhaps even the German intelligence service"* [Zhukov's italics].[87] One Western historian has speculated that Golikov's cautionary advice merely reflected Stalin's own predilections and that the intelligence chief sorted all the incoming information suggesting an attack into a "doubtful" pile to please his boss. Certainly Stalin was cautious about what he read. As he told Zhukov, "You can't believe everything intelligence says."[88] Stalin's tendency to accept only information he found palatable may also have led him to overestimate the strength of the Red Army. As the same historian of the Soviet military has written: "Locked up in the Kremlin, the master of a world which he had created by his own selective killings and which reflected back upon him only those images he had himself ordained, steeped in his own 'genius' and fed on its outpourings, Stalin could rage away dissension and doubt, from whatever quarter it came."[89]

One incident has come to light illustrating how the atmosphere of fear Stalin created around himself thwarted the smooth flow of information and caused his subordinates to withhold their doubts for fear of their lives. In addition to the telegram from Churchill and the personal memorandum from Cripps, the British tried to convey as much accurate intelligence as possible to Moscow about the German military buildup in the East. Sir Alexander Cadogan called Maiskii into the Foreign Office to convey to him detailed information about German troop movements. Stalin persisted in his belief that such warnings pointing to a German attack were misinformation manufactured by British intelligence. This denial in the face of growing evidence reached its apogee when, on June 14, TASS released a communiqué that declared rumors of an impending German invasion to be "devoid of all foundations," hinting that they were the result of British machinations.[90]

Maiskii has since claimed of the TASS communiqué: "The shaft in the direction of Britain left no room for doubt that it was the reply to the warning given by Cadogan."[91] As so often in the past, Cripps believed that the broadside TASS had loosed at the British government was a personal slight directed at him, and he resented the implication that the British in general, and he in particular, were attempting to embroil the Germans and Soviets in a war. But judging from the fragmentary accounts available it is possible to conclude that the TASS report had causes that were only tangentially related to Cripps and Great Britain.

Soviet historians have attempted to explain the TASS communiqué as part of a deep Soviet ploy designed to force the Germans' hand. V. A. Anfilov, for example, writes that the communiqué served the "dual purpose" of answering "provocative announcements in the bourgeois press" while trying to elicit "an answering response from the side of the leaders of Germany."[92] This explanation seems, however, to be contradictory; if the Germans were indeed preparing to launch an assault on the USSR, as Anfilov admits, then how could Western press reports be "provocative"?

Petro Grigorenko, an obscure army officer in June 1941 who later became a prominent dissident, recounts that at the time he believed the TASS communiqué to be a manifestation of Stalin's "Caucasian cleverness." He believed that Stalin hoped to send the following signal to Hitler: " 'We realize that you have drawn up your armies on our borders and we are ready to meet them there as they deserve to be met. But if you are smart and remove them, we are prepared to pretend we never noticed them there.' "[93] Grigorenko remembers believing that Stalin hoped thus to dissuade Hitler from attacking the USSR in favor of invading Great Britain. Grigorenko's willingness to give Stalin the benefit of the doubt may well have been representative of Soviet officers in general.

In the early 1960s, however, Grigorenko learned more about the origins of the communiqué. One of his personal acquaintances, Vasilii Novobranets, had been in the high ranks of Red Army Intelligence just before the outbreak of war and had written his memoirs during the brief Khrushchev "thaw." The memoirs, which contained information relating to Stalin's surprise in June 1941, were seized by the KGB before publication, but Grigorenko read them and has passed on an abbreviated account of the TASS incident, an account that supports such other memoirs as those of Marshal Zhukov.

According to Novobranets, in the late spring of 1941 Soviet military intelligence received an alleged German order of battle from Yugoslav sources; this so-called "Yugoslav scheme" held that Hitler's army was not concentrated in the east, that many Wehrmacht units were deployed along the Atlantic seacoast preparing for an invasion of Britain, and that those few German units arrayed along the Soviet frontier were simply resting from previous campaigns. According to Novobranets, Red Army Intelligence was unimpressed by the Yugoslav scheme for at least two reasons: first, it did not explain the presence of certain Wehrmacht units in the vicinity of the USSR that were known to be there from more reliable sources; second, if indeed the Germans were planning to invade Britain, they would almost certainly have left a larger covering force along the Soviet border than the Yugoslav scheme indicated. Grigorenko quotes Novobranets as saying: "I did not believe that there were idiots in the German general staff who would plan an offensive operation against the west without taking all measures to cover their rear against the east."

The head of Red Army Intelligence, Lieutenant General Proskurin, attempted to persuade the Politburo that the Yugoslav scheme was misleading and that the Germans were preparing to attack the USSR. According to Grigorenko, "Despite several nasty comments by Stalin and Beriya, he [Proskurin] delivered a convincing, broadly based and well-illustrated speech that tore the Yugoslav scheme to shreds and impressed the Politburo. Even Stalin seemed to waver." Evidently, however, if Stalin was impressed he did not remain so for long, since, on the following day, he ordered Proskurin arrested and shot.

Understandably, Proskurin's fate weighed heavily on the mind of his successor, Colonel General F. I. Golikov, who, as Zhukov pointed out, would neither countenance nor convey to Stalin any indications of an impending German attack. Indeed, Novobranets himself, who continued to warn of the German threat, was arrested and might have suffered Proskurin's fate had the German invasion not intervened and proven him right.[94] The entire incident provides an interesting insight into one of the weaknesses of the Stalinist system: in his ruthless efforts to compel his subordinates to do his absolute bidding, at times Stalin prevented accurate, if disquieting, information from receiving an adequate hearing. Those underlings who valued their lives soon learned to tailor their reports to suit the boss's prejudices.

Though clearly concerned by German moves, Stalin continued to believe that his hand was stronger than it was and that by refusing to give Hitler any pretext for displeasure (by signing a Tilsit- or Brest-Litovsk-style peace if necessary) he could still avoid a German attack. One thing was certain: in Soviet strategic thinking there was as yet no place for a closer relationship with the British.

The Germans noticed the increasingly emolient tone of TASS releases. Once again, Goebbels accurately divined the Soviet mood: "Stalin is obviously afraid, it seems. . . . So times change, when the cannon-mouths stand waiting and ready."[95] But Soviet deference availed little. So far as Hitler was concerned, the Nazi-Soviet partnership had been a temporary measure from the beginning, to be cast off at the first convenient opportunity. With Britain unable to establish a firm foothold on the European continent, Hitler felt free to engage in the quest for *Lebensraum* at the expense of his erstwhile ally. Stalin no longer had any hold on Hitler. As Goebbels succinctly put it, "The Russian card is no longer trumps."[96]

In the meantime, during the late spring of 1941, as Stalin's suspicions continued to cloud his strategic judgment, the British read the signs in Eastern Europe differently and far more accurately than the Soviets. The Foreign Office believed that for the first time since October conditions might be propitious for a renewed approach to the Kremlin, if only Moscow could be compelled to face facts. The impetus was provided by two telegrams from Cripps. The first, sent on April 3, contained the by now almost ritual call for a settlement of the Baltic States questions; the second, sent on April 17, reported that the German Ambassador had returned to Moscow with an entirely new set of offers for the Soviets.[97]

The decision to try once again with the Soviets reflects the influence of Anthony Eden, who was temperamentally and intellectually more attuned to the Soviets—or so he thought—than Halifax. Not having been involved in the previous negotiations and disappointments, he was consequently less jaded about the prospects of success. Eden informed Cripps that in a conversation Maiskii had hinted that his government might now be prepared to listen to the British and had invited Eden to formulate proposals.[98] Eden was more inclined to recognize Soviet territorial acquisitions than his

predecessor Lord Halifax had been, provided that the Soviets made counterconcessions. The foreign secretary telegraphed Cripps to this effect,
warning that, "Very careful timing will be necessary if we are to get full
value for our Baltic concession."[99]

This new line disturbed some Foreign Office officials who saw it as a
pointless abandonment of principle. Collier, for example, listed the disadvantages of such a course and wrote: "I personally have always been of the
opinion that they outweigh the very problematical advantages which it
might bring us. It has now been decided, however, to see if the policy will
work and to explain our change of front to the US Government."[100]

Encouraged by Eden's attitude, Cripps hastily composed a note that he
delivered to Vyshinskii on April 18, once again pointing out that continued
German successes in the Balkans posed a serious threat to the security of
the Soviet Union and calling upon the Soviets to join the war against
Hitler. The note also contained a blunt threat, which jarred, coming as it
did from Cripps:

> If the war were protracted for a long period . . . there might be a
> temptation for Great Britain (and especially for certain circles in
> Great Britain) to come to some arrangement to end the war on the sort
> of basis which has again recently been suggested in certain German
> quarters, that is, that Western Europe should be returned to its former
> status, while Germany should be unhampered in the expansion of her
> 'living space' to the east. . . . In this connexion it must be remem-
> bered that the maintenance of the integrity of the Soviet Union is not a
> direct interest of the British Government.

Having made this forceful argument, Cripps at once lessened its impact by
assuring Vyshinskii that "at the moment there is no question whatever of
the possibility of such a negotiated peace so far as His Majesty's Government are concerned."[101] Vyshinskii, who was more concerned with the
immediate German threat than with some hypothetical, distant British
action, was understandably indifferent, telling Cripps yet again that, "So
far as the Soviet Government was concerned no question of improving
relations existed, as they had done nothing to worsen them." Cripps seems
to have understood the point—for the time at least—closing his account of
the talk with the comment: "I have [the] strong impression that the Soviet
Government have not turned at all in our direction as a result of recent
events."[102]

On the very next day, however, Cripps was once again harping on the

Baltic issue, spurred on by Eden's sympathetic attitude, an attitude which Cripps described as "welcome news." Incredibly, Sir Stafford believed that the Baltic dispute remained one of, if not the single most important stumbling blocks preventing Stalin from attacking Hitler. He wrote: "I have no illusions as to the purchasing power of a Baltic concession, but negatively Baltic dispute is a heavy weight on the wrong side of the scale of Anglo-Soviet relations. *Its existence will not prevent rapprochement if the Soviet Government are convinced that one is desirable any more than its settlement will achieve one unless they are so convinced*" [italics added]. It is difficult to know what to make of such fuzzy thinking. In a passage that apparently conflicted with his long-held views about the need for open diplomacy, Cripps added that the British might once again try promises of simple de facto recognition, but: "If as is possible this proved insufficient we [should tell the Soviets that we] would be prepared before the end of the negotiations to go so far as to recognise without reservation as final and definite the absorption of the Baltic States in the USSR provided that if possible a formal declaration to this effect should be avoided." It is difficult to disagree with Laurence Collier's verdict that "This is an extraordinary telegram, and shows how far Sir S. Cripps' judgement has been warped by his obsession with the Baltic States."[103] All about him, Sir Stafford saw signs that the Germans and Soviets were on the brink of war, but he continued to believe that Stalin would not recognize the necessity of cooperation with London until the British first accepted his Baltic claims.

Churchill, convinced that a German attack on the USSR was imminent, did not believe that Stalin would long remain blind to German preparations. Referring to Cripps's message, the prime minister stated: "None of this seems to me to be worth the trouble it has taken to send. [The Soviets] know perfectly well their dangers and also that we need their aid. You will get much more out of them by letting these forces work than by frantic efforts to assure them of your love. This only looks like weakness and encourages them to believe they are stronger than they are. Now is the moment for sombre restraint on our part, and let them do the worrying."[104]

The prime minister's lack of enthusiasm quashed the British move to conciliate the Soviets, as did a conversation between Butler and Maiskii on April 26, in which Maiskii said that Ambassador Cripps's letter to Vyshinskii had made no impact at all on the Soviet government. Butler quoted Maiskii as saying that "Europe was now a jungle; what was needed was not words but deeds."[105] He did not, of course, specify just what "deeds" were needed, since it was not the Soviet intention to give the British an opportunity to redress the Soviets' alleged grievances. In light of this discouraging atmosphere, Cripps was told on April 26 that, if the Soviets desired to reach a compromise on the Baltic issue, they were aware of His Majesty's Government's position; for the moment, the British would go no further.

The Hess Interlude and the German Attack

From the end of April until June 22 the British made no further attempt to reach a comprehensive agreement with the Soviets. Instead, they concentrated on conveying warnings about German preparations in hopes that the Soviets would take timely defensive action, but Moscow continued to ignore British alarms.

Moscow was, however, very interested in one event in Britain at this time. On the night of May 10 Rudolph Hess, the deputy Führer of Germany, landed mysteriously in Scotland. Nobody has ever definitively established the origins of his odd mission; nor has anyone ever proven, or disproven, that Hitler knew beforehand that Hess intended to fly to Britain. Hess's own incoherence when interrogated contributed to the general confusion surrounding his mission. He claimed to be carrying an offer of an Anglo-German peace, which he evidently hoped to convey to a dubious group of supposedly pro-German British aristocrats. But, when asked whether this implied that Hitler intended to invade the USSR, Hess replied that it did not, although he stated that Berlin intended to press certain claims on the Soviets in the near future. Ivone Kirkpatrick, a Foreign Office German specialist who conducted one interrogation of Hess, later wrote: "I got the impression that Hess was so much out of things that he really did not know."[106]

At first the British government decided to refrain from commenting on Hess's arrival, in the hopes that this would keep the Germans guessing. What the government's silence did, however, was to encourage wild speculation among all concerned governments—not just the Nazis. For example, although Churchill sent an accurate account of Hess's comments to Roosevelt, the American president continued to believe that Churchill had not revealed the whole story.[107] Halifax also apprised the Foreign Office of "rumours circulating [in Washington] that our silence about Hess connotes peace talks through him."[108] The truth—that the deputy Führer of Germany had flown into Britain without warning and without any clear proposals—was simply too contrived to be believed.

It is difficult to assess the impact of the Hess mission on Anglo-Soviet relations. Soviet historians never tire of claiming that there was more to the story than London admitted. There is something about Hess's self-professed aim of contacting alleged aristocratic ruling circles that appeals to the official Soviet imagination. One Soviet account argues that Hitler not only knew of Hess's intention to fly to England but also that he gave Hess a "maximum program" and a "minimum program." The maximum aim was to conclude a separate peace with Britain and then to form with the British bourgeoisie a "unified crusade against the first socialist state in the world." The less ambitious goal was to persuade Britain to remain neutral during the coming German invasion of the USSR.[109]

All signs indicate that Stalin took the Hess affair very seriously. In October 1941 he questioned Lord Beaverbrook about it, and as late as 1944, when Churchill visited Moscow, the Soviet dictator asked the prime minister what offer Hess had brought with him. Despite Churchill's denials, Stalin apparently continued to believe that Hess had proposed "some deep negotiation or plot for Germany and Britain to act together in the invasion of Russia which had miscarried." And when Churchill persisted in his denials of the allegation, Stalin implied that British intelligence may not have kept the prime minister fully informed. Churchill wrote later that this question held a peculiar "fascination" for Stalin. "Remembering what a wise man he is," Churchill wrote, "I was surprised to find him silly on this point."[110]

Stalin's suspicions might have stemmed from faulty information he received from his agents abroad. Richard Sorge, the Soviet spy in Tokyo, allegedly learned from the German Embassy in Japan that, as he informed Moscow, "Hitler is striving for the conclusion of peace with England and for war with the Soviet Union. Therefore, as an ultimate measure he sent Hess to England."[111] One historian has recently argued that Hess's flight, coming as it did on the heels of Cripps's threat that "certain circles" in Britain might consider concluding a negotiated peace with Germany, "deflect[ed] the Russians towards a faulty and tragic evaluation of German intentions."[112] This explanation, however, places too much importance on a single comment by Sir Stafford, which may or may not have been read by Stalin. The Soviet dictator was ignoring warning signals of the impending German attack well before either Cripps's offhand comment or the Hess affair. The most that can be said is that these two incidents combined to reinforce inclinations already evident in Stalin's behavior, and, as war approached, the Soviet dictator continued to ignore the omens of attack.

Eden gave Maiskii one of the most graphic such warnings when he summoned the Soviet ambassador to the Foreign Office on June 2. After complaining about Soviet recognition of Rashid Ali in Iraq,[113] Eden gave the ambassador detailed information about the German buildup on the Soviet border. After asking whether Eden knew the information to be accurate, Maiskii said that "he found it very hard to believe that Germany was contemplating military action against the Soviet." He then enumerated Soviet strengths, domestic and military. But his performance was unconvincing. Eden wrote: "While M. Maisky delivered this statement with emphasis, I had a feeling that he might be trying to convince himself as he went along."[114]

Maiskii mentions another warning in his memoirs, this one from Sir Alexander Cadogan on June 10, which Maiskii felt prompted the TASS communiqué of June 14 denying any looming German danger.[115] Maiskii admits he felt at the time that the information was "exaggerated," yet it was so precise and detailed that it shook him, and he telegraphed the details to his government.[116]

Three days later, London received an answer to their warnings in the form of the TASS message, which denounced "clumsy fabrications." It continued: "According to Soviet data Germany, like the USSR, is also strictly observing the stipulations of the Soviet-German non-aggression pact, and therefore, in the opinion of Soviet circles, rumours of Germany's intention to break the pact and open an attack on the USSR are devoid of all foundations."[117] Stalin was clinging to his belief—or perhaps by this time only a hope—that the profitable German connection would last a little while longer, and to the last minute he would have nothing to do with the British.

By this time the British knew that German preparations for the invasion of the USSR were nearly complete. In view of the critical situation, Anthony Eden telegraphed Cripps on June 2, the same day the former had met Maiskii. "The development of Soviet foreign policy in the immediate future," Eden wrote, "is of such importance that I would like to see you come home for consultation as soon as possible."[118] On June 6 a healthy Cripps left Moscow "ostensibly to see a throat specialist."[119] The news of Cripps's return was leaked to the press, causing, as one Foreign Office official noted, a "considerable sensation."[120] This time nobody in the

Foreign Office seemed upset by the leak—even though speculation about Cripps's route might conceivably have endangered his life—leading one to assume that the British government itself disseminated the news in order to emphasize the seriousness of the German threat to the USSR.

The British government no longer seemed worried that the Nazi buildup in the East might merely be designed to force economic or territorial concessions on Stalin. As Cripps told Sikorski, the Polish general and leader, on June 18: "Hitler wants to dispose of the Russian military danger once and for all." Nor was the impression widely held in London that the Soviets could long resist the German onslaught. In the same conversation with Cripps, Sikorski opined, "The Red Army will probably fight, but it will not be able to stand the impact." Cripps could only agree. "It will not," he replied, "and it will surely break down."[121] Although he would one day regret having aired such an opinion, Cripps was merely echoing the received military wisdom of his day. Most observers in the West believed that the Red Army purges and Soviet inefficiency in general would guarantee a feeble and inadequate Soviet defence.

When Hitler's troops crossed the Bug River into Soviet territory at 3:30 A.M. on June 22, 1941, they did more than embark upon the bloodiest campaign of World War II; they also worked a radical transformation in Anglo-Soviet relations. Once Soviet Russia entered the war against Nazism, those who, like Sir Stafford Cripps, had championed the Soviet cause during the 1940s felt themselves vindicated, their own nagging doubts vanquished.

There had been cause enough for doubt, as when, on October 31, 1939, Molotov denounced the Allied war effort as "something in the nature of an 'ideological' war on Germany reminiscent of the religious wars of olden times." Molotov told the world: "One may accept or reject the ideology of Hitlerism as well as any other ideological system; that is a matter of political opinion. But everybody should understand that an ideology cannot be destroyed by force, that it cannot be eliminated by war."[122] This Soviet attitude shook Western fellow travelers who had believed in the intrinsic conflict between Communism and Fascism, as is clear from a letter Cripps wrote on November 7, 1939: "Although I much admire all that the Communist Party has done for the Workers in this country, I think in the last six weeks their leadership has been bad and confused."[123]

Now, less than two years after the Nazi-Soviet Pact and Molotov's speech, Great Britain and the Soviet Union found themselves on the same side in the crusade against Nazism. Churchill's famous speech of Sunday, June 22, 1941, undoubtedly reflected the feelings of many Britons: "No one has been a more consistent opponent of Communism than I have for the past twenty-five years," he said. "I will unsay no word that I have spoken about it. But all this fades away before the spectacle which is now unfolding." The USSR, Churchill argued, was now on the side of the angels. "The Russian danger . . . is our danger, and the danger of the United States, just as the cause of any Russian fighting for his hearth and home is the cause of free peoples in every quarter of the globe."[124]

Many on the British Left were prepared to go even further, seeing in Hitler's invasion the heretofore missing justification for the harshness of Soviet Communism. The screen was torn away, the grand design of history laid bare for all to see; but only Stalin had seen it in time. The man was genius personified. Here was justification aplenty for collectivization, for the brutal pace of industrialization, for the purges, for the Nazi-Soviet Pact, the Finnish War, and the seizure of a "protective belt" of territory on the USSR's western border. Some argued that all Soviet Russia's travails had been in preparation for this historically inevitable struggle to the death with Nazism. The general secretary's foresight was truly astounding, and Cripps, who had been doubtful at times, now joined the chorus paying homage to the Great Man. He told readers in Sheffield: "For [Stalin's] courage, his ceaseless labours, his leadership and consumate skill, we and the world owe the deepest debt of gratitude."[125] Similarly obsequious passages littered the pages of contemporary British newspapers.

Forty years later the myth that Stalin's cooperation with Hitler was a calculated step to buy time while building for an inevitable war is still very much alive. One recent history asserts: "The British Government claimed that the Munich agreement in September 1939 'bought time' to prepare for the coming struggle. Whatever the truth in that, we cannot deny the Russians the right to make the same claim for their time of neutrality."[126]

The riddle of Stalin's motives for working with Germany is one of the central questions of the period covered by this work. One cannot simply grant the Soviets the "right" to claim that their collusion with the Nazis was a temporary expedient designed to buy a couple of years if such a scenario is at odds with the available facts. Indeed, the evidence does not sustain such a theory. The Munich agreement, with all its faults, was intended by the British to satisfy specific German claims. When Hitler exceeded the terms of the agreement, the British eventually went to war in response to further aggression. The Nazi-Soviet Pact was, by contrast, an open-ended arrangement. When Stalin offered to ally with Hitler in November 1940, building on the base of the pact, he did so with the Führer's assurances that Nazi-Soviet collaboration would "find an ample field of activity for fifty to a hundred years."[127]

If Stalin intended to fight Hitler all the while he was working with Germany, then Soviet intentions were masterfully veiled. At no point during Cripps's mission—nor indeed from August 1939 until June 1941— did Moscow betray a genuine desire to develop closer ties with Great Britain, a nation whose assistance would be invaluable, indeed indispensable, in defeating Hitler. On the contrary, much Soviet activity was designed to impair Britain's war effort and to exploit her weakened position, and the British Communist party was, as Churchill later bitterly pointed out, as obstructive of Britain's war effort as its electoral and numerical weakness would allow. It is not sensible behavior to go about crippling one's potential allies. Each time the British tried to pull closer, the Soviets refused to specify their conditions for rapprochement, referring instead to grievances "too numerous to specify," as Mikoian had remarked to Cripps in August 1940.[128]

Soviet unwillingness to work with Great Britain is not in itself conclusive evidence to prove Soviet intention and desire to work with Nazi Germany toward a restructuring of the European balance of power. Conceivably, though doubtfully, evidence from Soviet archives could disprove such a theory. In the absence of such materials, however, the preponderance of evidence—including the Soviet leaders' own repeated comments and observations—does not incline one to give Moscow the benefit of the doubt.

To be sure, if he can be taken at his word, Stalin did not believe that Soviet cooperation with Nazi Germany could be a permanent feature of international life, but it was nevertheless an essential step, given the circumstances. Stalin's circumspection in foreign affairs has long been recognized as one of his more effective characteristics as a diplomat; one historian describes Stalin's diplomatic tactics as "his historic mix of expansion-and-accommodation, or revolutionary assertiveness-and-peaceful coexistence, which served the Soviet state so well for so long."[129] Stalin's combination of aggression and retrenchment were firmly in the Leninist tradition, as one can see from a confidential memorandum Lenin wrote in May 1918, after Brest-Litovsk: "The foreign policy of the Soviet power must not be changed in any respect [from its goal of world revolution]. Our military preparation is still not completed, and therefore our general maxim remains as before—to tack, to retreat, to wait while continuing this preparation with all our might."[130]

Consistent with such tactics, the USSR spent the 1930s in relative quiescence in the international arena as her industrial strength was being built up. Abroad, Stalin tried to divide the capitalist camp—for example, he acted to split the working-class movement in Germany, abetting Hitler's rise to power. A revanchist Germany would more likely embroil the capitalist powers with each other than a democratic or weak—and possibly Trotskyite—Communist Germany. As Stalin told the German Communist Heinz Neumann in 1931: "Don't you believe, Neumann, that if the Nationalists seize power in Germany they will be so completely preoccupied with the West that we will be able to build up socialism in peace?"[131]

Bolshevik experience had shown that war creates revolutionary opportunities, bringing in its train the conditions for aggrandizement of Soviet strength, an aspect of Soviet behavior that has been termed "catastrophism." The Soviet state itself had come into existence partly, if not wholly, as a result of the chaos of World War I. When it became clear in Moscow that Hitler wanted war, and when Stalin was presented with an opportunity in the summer of 1939 to stand aloof and pick up the pieces of a Europe weakened by conflict, the chance was too great to miss. It appeared as though the balance of forces had shifted in the USSR's favor and Communism could reverse its post–Brest-Litovsk retreat by entering into a phase of expansion. It would not, however, be an untidy, Trotskyite, spontaneous revolutionary uprising throughout Europe but, rather, what one historian has described as "imperial communism," or incremental expansion from the Soviet center outwards.[132]

Thus, Nazi-Soviet collaboration should be seen not as a manifestation of Soviet weakness, as many have believed, but rather as the exploitation by Stalin of perceived German discomfiture. In return for an unfavorable trade arrangement, and for Soviet quiescence during Hitler's war against what Ribbentrop called "the congealed plutocratic democracies," Stalin was able to expand his empire considerably.[133] The Soviet note of November 25, 1940, shows how Stalin wanted to go further down the road with Nazi Germany, if only Hitler would have stayed the course.

In June 1940 the Kremlin had a brief scare when France surrendered, leaving the USSR virtually alone on the Continent with an untamed Nazi Germany. But a determined Britain, backed by the tremendous industrial might of the United States, remained in the war, distracting Nazi Germany in the West and providing some measure of reassurance for Moscow. Not until April 1941, when the rapid German victories in the Balkans revealed Soviet vulnerability—and also the great reserves of untapped German offensive strength, despite the war with Britain—did Soviet behavior toward Germany become abject. Even then, however, Stalin did not approach Great Britain, believing instead that he might yet forestall a Nazi invasion by being prepared to surrender to German demands. The general secretary's surprise at the German invasion in June stemmed not from a dearth of warnings but from the fact that Hitler presented no ultimatum, giving the Kremlin no opportunity to negotiate and avoid war.[134]

The principal lesson of Cripps's first year in Moscow was that the Western democracies' broad goals—even if framed by Socialists—and those of the Soviet Union were vastly different and that no demonstrations of Western good will or generosity would change the situation. Amazingly, Cripps failed to learn this lesson. In August 1941 Oliver Harvey, Eden's private secretary, wrote in his diary: "Cripps has written to suggest that his task is now done with Soviet Russia in the war and should come back to England and be used as a link for coordinating post-war relations between the two countries. Poor man—he flatters himself that it was he who brought Russia into the war."[135] Cripps's belief in his powers to effect such changes in world history is unusual in a man of his age and experience, but not unique. This was, however, largely a matter of personality. Far more serious was the tendency by many in Britain—and eventually in the United States as well—to forget that the rulers of the USSR had a fundamentally different world view and had entered the war for vastly different reasons. This failure of understanding was ominous indeed.

CHAPTER FIVE

WE MUST BE

GUARDED IN

RELATIONS WITH

THE ENGLISH

JUNE–DECEMBER 1941

Not until July 3, twelve days after the German invasion, could Stalin bring himself to address the nation whose diplomatic affairs he had so badly mishandled. Thanks to the Nazi-Soviet Pact, Hitler had achieved a degree of domination over Europe unknown since the time of Napoleon. Like the French Emperor, Hitler turned against Russia to consolidate his grip on the Continent.[1] In his broadcast to the Soviet people, Stalin tried to answer the inevitable charges of ineptitude leveled at himself:

> It may be asked: how could the Soviet Government have consented to conclude a non-aggression pact with such treacherous monsters as Hitler and Ribbentrop? Was this not a mistake on the part of the Soviet Government? Of course not! A non-aggression pact is a pact of peace between two States. It was such a pact that Germany proposed to us in 1939. Could the Soviet Government have declined such a proposal? I think that not a single peace-loving State could decline a peace treaty with a neighboring Power, even though the latter was headed by such monsters and cannibals as Hitler and Ribbentrop.

Realizing, undoubtedly, that such a feeble justification would quell few doubts, Stalin offered a retrospective analysis of the Nazi-Soviet Pact that would later even convince many in the West, including Cripps: "What did we gain by concluding the non-aggression pact with Germany? We secured our country peace for a year and a half and the opportunity of preparing its forces to repulse fascist Germany should it risk an attack on our country despite the pact. This was a definite advantage for us and a disadvantage for fascist Germany." "Germany . . . ," Stalin claimed, "has lost politically by exposing itself in the eyes of the entire world as a bloodthirsty aggressor."[2]

Astute readers in the West noticed that in this last phrase Stalin was making a revealing claim: Hitler had not become a "bloodthirsty aggressor" until after the invasion of the Soviet Union. When Germany attacked the Western democracies, this had simply been a quarrel between two rival imperialist blocs. The transformation in Soviet relations with the West was, and would remain, a one-sided affair.

Stalin had not addressed his people immediately after the German invasion. He delegated this unpleasant task to Molotov, in a strange parallel with Hitler, who, as his military fortunes waned, left to Goebbels the unpleasant business of explaining state policy to the German nation. At noon on June 22 Molotov told his stunned listeners over the radio: "Today at four in the morning, without any claims having been presented to the Soviet Union, without a declaration of war, German troops attacked our country, attacked our borders at many points, and bombed our cities from the air. . . . This unheard of attack on our country is perfidy unparalleled in the history of civilised nations."[3] Molotov's speech represented the final abandonment of Soviet hopes for a mediated peace, hopes that had not died immediately after the German invasion. As one military historian has pointed out, Soviet leaders spent the eight hours between the German attack and Molotov's speech searching for some means of accommodation with the Nazis: "Soviet radio messages rained down on the *Auswärtiges Amt* in Berlin and, in one grotesque squirm, Stalin even turned to the Japanese for 'mediation' in resolving this Soviet-German 'crisis.' "[4] Little wonder that in his speech Molotov stressed the fact that the Germans had presented no demands. The Kremlin found it hard to believe that Hitler wanted a war when he could have gained so much simply by diplomatic threats.

In one interesting passage from his speech, Molotov grasped at a straw, appealing to the German people: "This war has been forced on us not by the German people, not by the German workers, peasants and intelligentsia, whose sufferings we can well understand, but by the bloodthirsty clique of Germany's fascist rulers."[5] Having consigned German Communists to the tender mercies of the Nazi party in 1933, Stalin was now clinging to the desperate hope that Hitler's attack on the Workers' State would provoke an uprising, or at least some resistance, among the German proletariat. In 1918 Lenin had doused similar wishful thinking by the "Left Communists" when the Bolsheviks had faced a far less terrible enemy. But in June 1941 Moscow would try anything.[6]

Confusion in Communist policy mirrored Stalin's personal crisis of confidence. Although accounts of the general secretary's nervous break-down may be fabrications of self-serving Soviet officials written during the brief era of "de-Stalinization," it is clear that the German attack deeply shook Stalin, who became reluctant to appear before the Soviet people. Having for years cultivated the impression of his own invincibility and unshakable control over the Soviet state, Stalin now made a desperate effort in his speeches and military orders to shelter behind "collective" leadership and to minimize his personal accountability for the disastrous rout of the Soviet armed forces. As Khrushchev has pointed out in his memoirs: "Directives continued to be issued from [Stalin] without his signature. Sometimes they appeared over his title, "Commander in Chief," but never over his name. And this was no accident. Nothing that Stalin ever did was an accident."[7]

Stalin's anxiousness to appear as simply one among many Soviet leaders reveals one of the reasons for his nervousness in June 1941. At the end of the war, speaking at a banquet in honor of the victorious Soviet leaders, he expressed his admiration for, and gratefulness to, the Russian people—not, significantly, the "Soviet" people—claiming that most other nations "would have said to the Government: 'You failed to justify our expecta-tions. Go away. We shall install another government.'"[8] In June 1941 Stalin clearly feared retribution at the hands of an outraged nation as much, if not more than, defeat by the Germans, and he was evidently surprised when the Russian people remained loyal to the Soviet state.

If the docility of the Soviet people came as a surprise to the Communist leadership, so did Britain's willingness readily to embrace the Soviet Union as an ally. On the day of the invasion, almost immediately after the news reached London, Eden met with Maiskii to extend a British offer of aid, which Moscow snapped up on June 23. Maiskii appeared nervous and anxious during his talk with Eden, referring to the Hess affair and to the German "peace campaign" in America. He suggested that, in his speech to be broadcast later that day, Churchill might wish to assure the Soviets "that England was firm in its determination to carry the war to its end." That is, the Soviets were worried that Britain might do precisely what they themselves had done almost two years earlier and come to an arrangement with Hitler. At one point during the conversation, Maiskii shed his normal diplomatic reserve and asked a "direct question": Would the British sign a separate peace with Germany?

Eden either failed to notice Soviet anxieties or, caught up in the spirit of the moment, felt that all Anglo-Soviet differences had been swept away. He stressed that not only was Britain's will firmly for continuance of the war but also "the British government will try, as much as it is in its powers, to fulfill all [Soviet supply] needs." "This is," Eden exclaimed, "the beginning of the end for Hitler." In this connection, Eden proposed to return Cripps to Moscow with a British military mission in tow, to facilitate military coordination. He said he "would consider it inexpedient at such a moment to change the ambassador, but he was ready to do so" if the Soviets wished.

It seems that Cripps was concerned lest he be persona non grata with the Soviets after the TASS communiqué of June 14, which had denied the existence of any Russo-German tensions and had accused the British of trying to embroil Moscow in the war. Maiskii "assured Eden that Cripps's suspicions are based on nothing, that our personal relations with him are good, and that if before Cripps had well-known difficulties in Moscow, that this resulted from completely different causes well-known to Eden."[9] This was an evasive way of admitting that Moscow had misunderstood German intentions. Molotov was, however, somewhat less effusive than his representative in London about Cripps's return, informing Maiskii that "the Soviet government d[id] not object" to the ambassador returning to Moscow.[10] Thus, on June 27, Cripps returned to the USSR with the military mission, and in stark contrast with his previous treatment, Molotov received him on the very day of his arrival in Moscow.[11]

The Soviet government required clarification of its relations with Britain, Molotov said, asking three questions to this end. What was the British position on: "(1) degree of cooperation which we [the British] proposed; (2) Whether it included political cooperation; (3) Whether we were prepared to conclude a political agreement to define the basis of co-operation." For the first time, Cripps, who barely concealed his relish for his new role, was in the position of being courted by the Soviets. He responded to Molotov's questioning cagily, and, acting on instructions he had received in London, he rejected for the moment any concrete political agreement. "Our new relations," Cripps said, "had only existed since last Sunday and it was better to wait 'till we had learned to trust each other over a period of military and economic cooperation before trying to put our political relations into the form of a written agreement."[12] According to the Soviet record of this conversation, Cripps said that Britain would aid the USSR economically and militarily. He rather egotistically pointed to his own presence in Moscow as evidence of the importance the British government attached to cooperation with the USSR, telling Molotov "in confidential form that Churchill wanted to bring [him] into the War Cabinet. However, the question was decided negatively, and Cripps returned to the USSR."[13]

Despite Britain's friendly attitude, Cripps said, "mistrust from the past" was still too fresh for a political agreement. "In Cripps' opinion," the Soviet account relates, "the general basis for the attainment of an agreement on military and economic relations is a common enemy. At the same time, a common enemy is an insufficient basis for political cooperation." Molotov understandably believed, however, that it was best not to dwell on the past: "The Soviet Union does not conceal," he said, "that it did not want to be drawn into war . . . [but] at the present moment the question of relations between England and the USSR stands differently."[14]

Cripps remained firm, and the conversation drifted to other matters. In a passage that does not appear in the published Soviet record, Cripps asked why the German attack had so obviously surprised the Soviets after they had received timely and accurate warnings from London. Molotov's reply supports the hypothesis that Moscow had been prepared to surrender abjectly to German demands: he told Cripps that "though Soviet military authorities had anticipated the possibility of war, they had never expected that it would come without any discussion or ultimatum."[15] Much to the Kremlin's chagrin, however, the Germans were uninterested in a negotiated peace, wanting instead the total extinction of the USSR.

On June 8 Maksim Litvinov delivered a radio address. This was important, as much for who Litvinov was as for what he said in his speech—and the curious manner of its broadcast. Litvinov was people's commissar for foreign affairs between 1930 and 1939, during which time he had gained a reputation as an advocate of Soviet alignment with the West. In May 1939 Stalin abruptly dismissed him from his post, an action widely interpreted in diplomatic circles as a signal to Berlin that Moscow desired to come to terms with Hitler. During the period of the Nazi-Soviet Pact, Litvinov was dismissed from one post after another, and many of his lieutenants and political allies were arrested, imprisoned, or shot. Although Litvinov had never been tried or even arrested, it was unusual during Stalin's time for a disgraced official to return to prominence.

Thus the very fact that the Kremlin allowed Litvinov to deliver a radio address was out of the ordinary; even more so, however, was the content of the speech. The former foreign commissar stated that Hitler had always striven to isolate his potential victims so as to destroy them one by one. He had been able to do this "by driving between them an 'ideological' wedge." But his plan "did not quite come off," Litvinov said, because "Mr. Winston Churchill, Prime Minister of Great Britain with that statesman-like acumen, which is characteristic of him, immediately informed the world that he was not taken in by Hitler's wiles, declaring that victory over the Soviet Union by Hitler would be fraught with innumerable disasters and catastrophies for the British Empire. We no less recognize the menace which Hitler's victory in the west would constitute for us."[16] Litvinov gave credit to the British, not the Soviets, for foiling Hitler's schemes. Litvinov even went so far as to appeal to those countries "which are still dragging out wretched independent existences under an illusory cover of neutrality and pacts of non-aggression and 'friendship' with Hitler" to join in the war against Nazism. This was a clear allusion to the Soviets' own failed pact with Hitler, and it should come as no surprise that Litvinov's speech was broadcast only on foreign wavelengths.[17]

This speech was clearly an appeal to those in the West who, like Churchill, opposed giving Hitler a free hand in the East. The Hess mission, Britain's refusal to negotiate a political agreement with Moscow, and, most of all, the Soviets' own conduct during the course of the previous two years—all these things must have indicated to Moscow that Britain had not finally rejected the option of a separate peace with Berlin.[18] During the first weeks of the Soviet-German war, the Soviets would show an understandable haste to secure a pledge from the British that they not leave the war.

Although the Soviets held out an olive branch to London, however, they soon showed how demanding they could be as wartime partners. On June 29 the Soviets presented Cripps with an astonishing list of demands for aid from the democracies' arsenals. The Soviets wanted 3,000 fighters, 3,000 other aircraft, including radar and night-fighting equipment, and 20,000 light antiaircraft guns.[19] The Soviet request—or demand—was couched in less than diplomatic language, prompting Cripps to telegraph the Foreign Office, saying that it might be necessary to approach Stalin directly in order to circumvent the suspicion and surliness of his subordinates. The attitude of these subordinates, Cripps wrote, "at present . . . , is that it is more blessed to receive than to give."[20]

These demands came as part of a general renewal of Soviet blustering as they recovered from the shock of invasion. This was reflected in Maiskii's changing tone. When he met Eden on June 26, he had been slightly sheepish, referring to the need to overcome British suspicions of the Soviet Union by increasing cultural ties.[21] (He suggested, among other things, printing an inexpensive edition of *War and Peace* for the purposes of propaganda and to illustrate how the Russians had in the past dealt with an invader.) By June 30, however, Maiskii's assertiveness had returned; he said that he was impressed by the rapid dispatch of the British military mission to Moscow and twitted Eden, saying that "this was in sharp contrast to his experience two years ago when [the British and French] mission had gone by slow stages by sea."[22] Eden remained tactful and did not point out that at that time speed had mattered little, since the Soviets were already on the verge of signing their pact with Hitler.

For the time being the British were content to keep cooperation with their new-found friends on a purely military basis. London reasoned that the USSR might not be in the war much longer, since Western military analysts almost universally believed that Stalin's purges had fatally weakened the Red Army, but, in the meantime, Hitler's war in the East would be a major drain on the German war effort.[23] Therefore, Britain would do all in her power to shore up Soviet resistance, short of two things: Britain's leaders would resist sending British forces to the Eastern Front; and London would not commit itself, as it had done for the French and Poles, to the restoration of the USSR's preinvasion frontiers. The Communists were still in very low regard among Britain's dominant Conservatives, and there was as yet no compelling reason for false camaraderie. The British had another reason for maintaining their distance from the Soviets. As Eden told Maiskii on June 30, London would not discuss wide-ranging political issues owing to "the position of the USA and its diehards [tverdolobykh]."[24] Only later, as the USSR's ever more impressive war effort manifested itself, would a great wave of pro-Soviet sympathy sweep over Britain, and by then the British were prepared to overlook initial American objections.

Although there was as yet no cause for a complete mending of fences between Moscow and London, Churchill felt that it would be a good idea to establish relations at the highest level. Consequently, on July 8 he ordered

Cripps to deliver the first of his many wartime personal notes to Stalin. The note heavily emphasized the military aid Britain could offer but contained no hint of a political reassessment. Churchill wrote: "We shall do everything to help you that time, geography and our growing resources allow. The longer the war lasts the more help we can give." The message closed with a typically loquacious Churchillian exhortation: "We have only got to go on fighting to beat the life out of these villains."[25]

Sir Stafford was able to speak with Stalin for an hour, in what was only their second formal meeting since Cripps's appointment as ambassador. Stalin, who was far from confident of continuing British cooperation, was unctuous, praising Churchill, rather belatedly, as an improvement on Chamberlain, since "the present Prime Minister understood the needs of the workers"; thus, Stalin said, "it had been possible to form [a] real Government of national unity."[26] Stalin did not mention the fact that this government had already been in existence for more than a year, but the Soviets had until this moment not responded favorably to its approaches, and Cripps did not remind him. Stalin told the ambassador that "some agreement between the two countries" was necessary and brushed aside Cripps's objections that an agreement should follow, not precede, a period of economic and military cooperation. "As England," Stalin said, "the Soviet Union finds itself in a war against Germany, and these facts cannot be avoided. The cooperation about which Cripps speaks, is inconceivable without an agreement."[27]

Cripps explained that during his meeting with the foreign commissar on June 27 he had "understood Molotov to mean that the Soviet government wishes to resolve the question of Anglo-Russian cooperation in the Near and Far East, and also to take part in the settlement of the question of a new order in Europe." Stalin replied that either Cripps had misunderstood or else Molotov had not expressed the Soviet position "clearly." He was "not raising the question of the establishment of spheres of influence."[28] The dictator said that he wanted an agreement "of a purely general nature" about two questions: "(1) mutual help without any precision as to quantity or quality, (2) neither country to conclude a separate peace. He [Stalin] said, that without this, Russia felt isolated in view of all the agreements which Germany had against her, and he thought that would be most valuable for the morale both of [the] USSR and of Great Britain." Stalin clearly wanted a promise at the earliest possible moment that the Soviet Union would not be cut adrift to face her own separate fate. According to the Soviet account, Stalin told Cripps that British stalling tactics reminded

him of the ill-fated Anglo-Franco-Soviet negotiations of 1939 and transparently threatened that "it is dangerous to delay agreement." Instead of
reminding Stalin that, unlike in 1939, Britain was now in a stronger
position than the USSR vis-à-vis Germany, Cripps responded almost
apologetically, saying that in 1939, "various people were in the nation's
leadership who did not want an agreement with the USSR." That had all
changed.[29]

Nevertheless, Cripps was quite firm regarding a formal pact; although
he stated that "he had always wanted the conclusion of such a pact,"[30] "it
was not necessarily easy or advisable to reduce [Anglo-Soviet cooperation]
to a formal agreement at this early stage." But the ambassador was so
surprised by the apparent moderation of Stalin's requests that he hinted the
British government would have no trouble agreeing with Stalin's two
points. In Cripps's account: "Both in Great Britain and in America there
were still elements of public opinion which needed converting to this idea
[of extensive cooperation]. I suggested [to Stalin] that there might possibly
be an exchange of notes on this basis and that I would recommend this to
my Government." The idea never seems to have dawned on Cripps that
Stalin was unsure of British support and that the British had been thrust
overnight into a formidable bargaining position. But even if such an idea
had flashed across Cripps's mind, there is little reason to believe that he
would have acted on it by pressing Stalin for political concessions.

Stalin easily persuaded Cripps, who advised the Foreign Office to agree
to the general secretary's two points. Completely misreading Stalin's position, Cripps told the Foreign Office: "My own very strong recommenda-
tion is that we should seize this opportunity without delay in order to bind
the Russians to continuing their resistance. I can see no possible drawback
to our stating our determination to do so and a very great advantage in
getting them publicly committed before their own people and the world."[31]
Cripps had taken Stalin's spurious threats to heart. In fact, the Soviets had
precious little choice about "continuing their resistance." They had not
chosen to go to war, had done everything possible up to the last minute to
avoid it, but Germany had nonetheless thrust war on them. Hitler offered
no peace terms short of the destruction of the Soviet state.[32] With his
unfailingly poor political judgment, Cripps could not see that for the first
time in at least two years Moscow needed London more than vice versa,
and he continued to act as though the Soviet war effort was a frail creature
that must be nurtured patiently by Britain.

In a Foreign Office memorandum analyzing the Cripps-Stalin meeting,

Sir Orme Sargent pointed out that Cripps had changed his position since his talk with Molotov on June 27. He had indeed, though Cripps's shift stemmed from his earlier misunderstanding of Soviet objectives. He had thought that Molotov was proposing a wide-ranging pact delineating Soviet and British spheres of influence. This may in fact have been Molotov's initial intention; he may have been floating a trial balloon about an agreement with territorial provisions like the Nazi-Soviet Pact. If so, British reserve led Stalin to suggest a more circumscribed agreement, which would include the one provision the Soviets wanted most of all, a British vow not to conclude a separate peace with Berlin.

Sargent wrote that there were four options open to His Majesty's Government: (1) they could sign nothing, as Cripps had originally told Molotov; (2) they could initiate "an exchange of notes" with the Soviets, as Cripps now suggested; (3) they could issue "a joint declaration" with the Kremlin; or (4) they could sign "a formal treaty of mutual assistance" with Moscow. Sargent felt that the government should make no definite commitment before consulting the Dominions and the United States. He also wrote: "In any agreement with the Soviet Government we shall presumably not want to pledge ourselves, either explicitly or implicitly, to go to war with Finland, Roumania or Hungary, merely because they happen to be cooperating with Germany in the attack on Russia."[33]

In considering Stalin's proposals, the British government worked with surprising speed. On July 9, Eden met with John G. Winant, the American ambassador, asking him what he thought of the Soviet request. Winant felt that it would be better, if possible, to avoid a full-blown treaty, since this might upset American opinion.[34]

On the same day Churchill, with characteristically sure diplomatic touch, discussed with Eden a draft of a personal response to Stalin's proposals. The prime minister must have felt that this was the time to press the Soviets for promises, as the last paragraph of his draft note shows:

You [Stalin] will of course understand that at the victorious Peace Conference in which the United States will certainly be a leading party, our line would be that territorial frontiers will have to be settled in accordance with the wishes of the people who live there and on general ethnographical lines, and secondly that these units, when established, must be free to choose their own form of government and system of life, so long as they do not interfere with the similar rights of neighboring peoples.[35]

Such a formula would, of course, have ruled out the Soviet absorption of the Baltic States and the other Soviet territorial gains from the Nazi-Soviet Pact. Indeed, if carried to its logical conclusion, this policy might have raised questions striking the very heart of the Soviet empire.

Eden was not so enthusiastic about the prime minister's note, since if Churchill were to take too close an interest in relations with the Soviet Union it would surely eclipse his own role as foreign secretary. He wrote Churchill:

> As regards the form, I think that it would be more appropriate if you would agree to this being handled through me to Cripps rather than by a direct message from yourself to Stalin. I think that we must keep the latter for occasions of capital importance [this was not such an occasion?] and I do not want you to become involved in the day to day details of diplomacy. Once we get down to texts, changes in wording are always called for and this is beneath Prime Ministers![36]

The emollient last line was obviously an attempt to flatter Churchill into abstaining.

Eden's intervention was not entirely effective, although in the War Cabinet discussion late that night he did manage to delete Churchill's reference to "ethnographical lines." This was done partly to assuage Soviet sensibilities and to help the Poles, since in the Cabinet discussion "it was pointed out that this might make difficulties for the Poles in their negotiations with the Russians." The prime minister was able to convince the Cabinet that the urgency of the situation warranted a personal note from the head of the government, but the original character of the communicaton was altered beyond recognition. The Cabinet decided against a full treaty with the Soviets in favor of a joint declaration, Sargent's third option.[37]

Time and again, as in this case, Churchill's initial impulses to attempt to limit Soviet gains by binding Moscow to favorable agreements were altered either by subordinates more inclined toward a favorable view of the Soviets than the prime minister or by Churchill himself when, on reflection, he realized that Britain's far-flung commitments ruled out the uniform application of seemingly laudable principles. In this instance, perhaps the most opportune moment to wring a considerable concession from the Soviets—that is, recognition of the principle of self-determination—was allowed to slip away because of Britain's prior commitment to the restoration of Poland's borders. The tragic irony of the situation was, of course, that later in the war when Britain's bargaining strength had been immeasurably weakened, Poland would be "moved" 200 miles to the West, making British fears of July 1941 seem almost optimistic in retrospect. By 1945, however, the British no longer had the strength either to restrict Soviet territorial gains or to assist the Polish cause.

Early on July 10 Cripps received a telegram from the Foreign Office containing his government's acceptance of Stalin's two points, conditional upon agreement by South Africa, Australia, and Canada.[38] Cripps communicated the British note to Stalin, who evidently suspected a trick. He had not yet learned—perhaps he never did—that political power in the so-called bourgeois democracies was genuinely decentralized, a fact that did not always facilitate rapid diplomatic action. Or perhaps he preferred to act as though he did not understand. Stalin tried, transparently, to threaten Cripps: "He stated that [the Soviet government] were most anxious to ensure the signature at the earliest possible moment as some Communist speakers in this country were speaking in a pro-German sense and this would enable him to put a stop to it."[39] It is difficult to conceive of an emptier threat. Not only were there no pro-Nazi Soviet Communists in July 1941—unless they were suicidal—but that they would actually speak in a "pro-German sense" seems highly unlikely. By resorting to such a ploy, Stalin showed yet again how eager he was to get a British commitment to remain in the war.

After approval from the Dominions, the "Agreement for Joint Action" between Great Britain and the USSR was duly signed on July 12. The agreement, which was based closely on Stalin's two proposals, was perfunctorily praised in *Pravda* as a "document of greatest historical and political significance."[40] The Soviets had scored their first wartime political success in dealing with the British, though for different reasons than were apparent. The British had neither the intention nor the political power to sign a separate peace with Germany as the Soviets evidently feared.

To be sure, there was some sentiment in the House of Commons in favor of coming to terms with Hitler and leaving the USSR to its own fate, as the Soviets had done to the Western democracies two years previously. The government might conceivably have been able to form a majority favoring a separate peace, but such a policy would certainly have destroyed the coalition government and would have violently riven British public opinion, not to mention the disastrous effect such a course would have had upon the balance of power in Europe.

Stalin's success had consisted in the abandonment by the British of an important principle—for the moment—at a time when its acceptance by

Moscow would have been highly likely. The British government had decided not to press the Soviets on the question of self-determination, and they had done so before even presenting the idea to Moscow. The debate had taken place beyond the earshot of the Soviets, and the British had bargained themselves down. There was no mention in the agreement of the right of self-determination.

The two central clauses of the joint agreement as finally signed were as follows: "(1) The two Governments mutually undertake to render each other assistance and support of all kinds in the present war against Hitlerite Germany. (2) They further undertake that during this war they will neither negotiate nor conclude an armistice or treaty of peace except by mutual agreement."[41] The most interesting facet of the two points was the last part of point one, which was included on Stalin's insistence. The war was to be against "Hitlerite Germany." If there was a coup d'etat or Communist revolt in Berlin (however unlikely the possibility), then the whole question of a separate peace would have to be reconsidered.

Supplies and a Second Front

The British now had to answer a crucial question, what military or material aid did they now feel able to send to the USSR? Stalin, for his part, had no doubt about the magnitude of British aid he desired. On July 18 he sent his first personal wartime message to Churchill, describing the position of Soviet armies as "strained." The note continued: "It seems to me, therefore, that the military situation of the Soviet Union, as well as of Great Britain, would be considerably improved if there could be established a front against Hitler in the West—Northern France, and in the North—the Arctic." Now was a good time to open such a front or fronts, Stalin argued, because Germany was tied down in the expanses of Russia. An invasion of France would be good, but: "It is still easier to establish a front in the North. Here, on the part of Great Britain, would be necessary only naval and air operations, without the landing of troops or artillery. The Soviet military, naval, and air forces would take part in such an operation. We welcome it if Great Britain could transfer to this theatre of war something like one light division or more of the Norwegian volunteers, who could be used in Northern Norway to organise rebellion against the Germans."[42]

This message was the first shot in a propaganda war over the "second front" issue that continued until the Western Allies' landing in France, June 6, 1944, and even to the present. But, as Churchill's reply of July 20 shows, each Soviet request for a second front ignored the fact that Britain simply did not have the resources Stalin attributed to her; it was a simple matter for Moscow to dispose nonexistent British forces. Churchill explained to the general secretary the "limitations imposed upon us by our resources and geographical position." The prime minister rejected the inference that Britain was not doing her part, writing: "You must remember that we have been fighting alone for more than a year" (a veiled reference to the Soviets' pact with Hitler). As for Stalin's main request, Britain would step up Arctic naval operations, Churchill vowed, but "there is no Norwegian light division in existence, and it would be impossible to land troops, either British or Russian, on German occupied territory in perpetual daylight without having first obtained reasonable fighter air cover. We had bitter experiences at Namsos last year and in Crete this year of trying such enterprises."[43] As Churchill admitted it was true that the British had dispatched their forces on risky missions in Greece and indeed in Norway itself. But they had not yet attempted a landing on a German-held coastline, which would have been a far more serious undertaking.

The British had at one time shown some interest in combined naval, air, and land operations with the Soviets, operating from around Murmansk against German forces in the north of Norway. Indeed, Lord Beaverbrook had raised the idea over dinner with Maiskii as early as June 27.[44] But when the British had tried to obtain Soviet military information regarding airfields near Murmansk, German dispositions, and Soviet supplies of aircraft oil and gasoline—information absolutely vital before the British could decide on the viability of such an operation—they ran up against what appeared to the British to be the almost manic Soviet penchant for secrecy. On June 30 Cripps and Lieutenant General Mason-MacFarlane, the head of Britain's military mission in Moscow, had tried in vain to induce Molotov to tell them about Soviet dispositions in the north. Molotov had responded coolly—and not very helpfully—that "the general situation at the front is already well known." The necessary information about the front, he continued, "has been published in Soviet newspapers" by the Informbiuro.[45] On July 2 when Cripps tried once again to elicit the requisite information from Molotov, Molotov replied that the British already knew "the basic facts" about the Murmansk and complained about this "petty detailed examination of questions."[46]

Perhaps owing to the chaos of the German invasion, the Soviets could not give the British the information they requested, since they did not possess it themselves. Their apparent reticence to share vital information with their allies may have been designed to mask the disarray within their own ranks. One can scarcely fault Churchill, however, for being hesitant to commit British forces to a dubious engagement north of the Arctic circle without any clear idea of what they would encounter there. It also rankled to hear Molotov brashly state so soon after the collapse of the Nazi-Soviet Pact that he "hope[d] that the English Government would do more than it is doing now."[47] When it came to convincing the British to open a second front, the Soviets were frequently their own worst enemies.

If the British were understandably reluctant to commit their forces to a hastily conceived second front, they were not hesitant to deliver military supplies to the Soviet Union, within their limited means. The problem was extracting the necessary logistical data from the Soviets, who showed the same reluctance to divulge this sort of information as they had regarding disposition of their forces. When asked what supplies were needed, the Soviets inevitably responded with astronomical and unrealistic requests. Judged solely on the basis of their ultimate need to defeat the Germans, the Soviet requests for equipment were perhaps realistic, yet they far exceeded Britain's capacity to deliver on short notice. What London needed, and the Soviets would not or could not provide, was some account of the nature of warfare on the eastern front, so that supply priorities could be established.

In order to get a better line on just what the Soviets needed, President Roosevelt sent his personal representative, Harry Hopkins, via London to Moscow in late July. It was hoped that Hopkins would work out a reasonable schedule for delivery of Anglo-American supplies to the USSR. On July 28 Churchill sent Stalin a telegram introducing Hopkins: "I must tell you that there is a flame in this man for democracy and to beat Hitler." Trying to deflect demands for a second front, the prime minister also wrote: "A terrible winter of bombing lies before Germany. No one has yet had what they are going to get."[48]

Hopkins was encouraged by his visit to Moscow, cabling Roosevelt from Scotland after his return: "I feel so confident about this front . . . there is unbounded determination to win."[49] Hopkins's confidence was, however, premature; only four days after this telegram, Soviet resistance within the Smolensk pocket ceased. In this titanic *Kesselschlacht*, the Germans netted over 300,000 Soviet prisoners, 3,205 destroyed or captured tanks, and roughly the same number of guns.[50] The Germans had torn a gaping hole in the front on the direct route to Moscow. In retrospect, Hopkins's mission was not terribly successful either, since he got no more military or supply data from Stalin than Sir Stafford Cripps had already been able to extract—which was not very much. The conclusion Churchill drew from Hopkins's visit was that further high-level meetings would be needed to wheedle more information out of the Soviets.

Soviet troubles were very much on the minds of Churchill and Roosevelt when they met at Placentia Bay, Newfoundland, in August. Although the Americans were not yet in the war, the outcome of the Conference made it clear that as the Atlantic Charter—the main product of the meeting—announced, the United States was committed to "the final destruction of Nazi tyranny."[51]

The Atlantic Charter—which seems never to have been signed either by the British or the Americans—was an enunciation of the broad wartime goals of the Western democracies. The negotiations prior to publication of the Charter highlighted the differences between the two great democracies. Britain was still an imperial power of the first magnitude, and its leaders felt uncomfortable with such concepts as free trade and unbridled self-determination. In the fourth point of the Charter, which guaranteed equal access to the raw materials of the world, Churchill demanded the insertion of the modifying phrase "with due respect for [the signatories'] existing obligations." Britain could not lightly abandon "Imperial Preference."

This is not to question Churchill's commitment to the principles of the Charter, which he and Sir Alexander Cadogan had largely drafted, nor to doubt his long-held belief in the centrality of Anglo-American coopera-tion. He was deeply stung by critical accounts of this incident, which he called "tales of my reactionary, Old-World outlook."[52] Nevertheless, Brit-ish and American interests inevitably clashed at times, a fact that was easily forgotten amidst the glow of the meeting at Placentia Bay.

The second point of the Charter, announcing the "desire to see no territorial changes that do not accord with the freely expressed wishes of the peoples concerned," was to cause much friction in Anglo-Soviet rela-tions.[53] It was not clear whether the reference to territorial changes applied to those alterations dating from September 1939, June 1941, or from the date of the Charter. This imprecision, which may have been deliberate, was obviously important, since it could affect the Soviet Union's claim to its territorial acquisitions from the time of the Nazi-Soviet Pact.

The second most important decision stemming from the Roosevelt-Churchill meeting—after the Atlantic Charter—was the decision to send a high-level Anglo-American delegation to Moscow to finish the work Hopkins had begun. On August 12 the president and the prime minister dispatched a joint message to Stalin congratulating him on "the splendid defense that you are putting up against the Nazi attack" and proposing a Moscow supply conference.[54]

Returning to Britain after his meeting with Roosevelt, Churchill began the painful process of allocating resources in advance of conferring with the Soviets. Red Army needs would henceforth receive high priority, as Churchill wrote to Lord Beaverbrook, the minister of supply, on August 30 1941: "It is our duty and our interest to give the utmost possible aid to the Russians, even at serious sacrifices to ourselves. However, no large flow can begin till the middle or end of 1942."[55] Such an attitude on the part of the British prime minister—the note was not written for publication and thus, presumably, reflects Churchill's genuine wishes—makes the repeated Soviet claims that Anglo-American aid was parsimonious seem unfounded.[56]

Sending supplies to the Soviet Union naturally involved stripping British forces of much-needed equipment; Churchill wrote later that "The Service Departments felt it was like flaying off pieces of their skin."[57] Nevertheless, despite the wails and moans from the outraged department heads, reallocation proceded apace. To cite one example: Archibald Sinclair, the air minister, wrote to Eden that he could not comply with Maiskii's request for Merlin aircraft engines. Sinclair wrote: "So serious is the situation that we have had to refuse to supply the Admiralty with Merlins for their motorboats. What I have refused to [A. V.] Alexander [the first lord of the admiralty] on the grounds of the extreme urgency of the RAF requirements I cannot give to Maisky." Eden's terse reply was illustrative of War Cabinet thinking; he wrote Sinclair that "it depends who will use [the engines] better."[58]

In the meantime, pressed hard by the Germans, Moscow cried out for quicker and more massive aid from the West. Even if the Soviet desire to receive supplies immediately was understandable in the circumstances, it took insufficient account of the obstacles blocking swift delivery. The British faced shortages in ship tonnage; the danger of U-boats; inadequate Soviet port facilities; and on the Persian route, the extremely limited capacity of the Basra rail line, which the British eventually had to double. Soviet complaints that Anglo-American supplies did not reach the USSR in mass until after the German Army had ground to a halt in the winter of 1941 must be weighed against the logistical problems confounding Western efforts to deliver as much as they could as fast as they could.

Despite the fact that the British were doing a great deal to help the Soviets, British officials remained sensitive to inferences that they were shirking their duty as allies. On August 27, for instance, Eden engaged Maiskii in what the latter called a "serious conversation." Eden wanted to ascertain the mood of the Soviet people about Britain's supply and military efforts. Given such an opportunity to expound the Soviet view, it is no wonder that Maiskii derided Britain's contribution. He admitted that Britain's aerial bombardment of the Continent was impressive, and for this, Maiskii said, the Soviets were "ready to thank the British government." "But it should be clear to Eden," he continued, "that the bombardment of Germany, for all its undoubted usefulness, cannot have any serious effect on the situation at the eastern front." The British, Maiskii concluded, were more like "spectators" than allies.

As Maiskii prepared to leave, Eden supposedly thanked him for expressing "the genuine mood of the Soviet people." At this, the ambassador decided to impart one more bit of what he called "friendly advice": not only was Moscow upset by Britain's allegedly poor war effort but also with the tone of the Atlantic Charter, which, Maiskii said, read "as if England and the USA imagine themselves as almighty God called upon to judge the rest of the sinful world, including my country."

Somewhat taken aback by the unexpectedly harsh tone of the ambassador's remarks, Eden lied about the origins of the Charter. He said: "In this matter the initiative belongs entirely to the President. When he met the premier, he suddenly took the declaration from his pocket. Churchill, of course, could not object to Roosevelt's proposal." Evidently pleased with his work, having put Eden entirely on the defensive, Maiskii concluded the account of this conversation, which he sent to Moscow, with the smug remark that he hoped that "our reaction to the declaration . . . will serve the British government as a lesson for the future."[59]

One important person was pleased with Maiskii's exposition of Soviet grievances against the British. In one of the few instances from among the published Soviet documents that Stalin actually praised the work of one of his diplomats, on August 30 the dictator wrote to Maiskii:

Your conversation with Eden about England's strategy fully expresses the mood of the Soviet people. I am glad that you so well perceived this mood. The crux of the matter is that the English government helps the Hitlerites by its passive, temporizing policies. The Hitlerites hope to defeat their opponents one at a time—today the Russians, tomorrow the English. . . . Do the English understand this? I think they understand. What do they want? They want, it seems to me, our weakening. If this supposition is true, we must be guarded [ostorozhnyi] in relations with the English.[60]

This telegram, with its repeated rhetorical questions and answers, was cast in the inimitable orthodox seminary style of most of Stalin's writing. Written only two months after the collapse of the Nazi-Soviet partnership, its suspicious tone can only be explained in terms of Stalin's fears that the British would succeed where he had failed, that London, not he, would stand aloof from the Continental fray. Amidst the ruins of all his plans, Stalin projected his own aims on the British leadership. One must doubt that London could have done anything that would have quieted permanently such deep-seated suspicions.

Although the extent of Stalin's mistrust remained unknown to London, the British busied themselves with efforts to speed up delivery of supplies to the Soviet Union. To clear the USSR's supply route from the Persian Gulf, to suppress German influence, and to secure the Mosul oil fields, the British and Soviets collaborated in late August and early September in occupying Iran. After the Shah had refused to accept a joint Anglo-Soviet ultimatum, Iran was invaded from both north and south on August 25. Britain's leaders felt uncomfortable about their role in the invasion. Oliver Harvey wrote in his diary that it was "our first act of 'naked aggression.' A[nthony] E[den] rather ashamed of himself, so too is P. M. But I tell him it is essential for us to get our base and the oilfields secure while the going is good."[61] Both London and Moscow regarded the occupation of Iran as a necessary measure if one of the USSR's few supply lines was to be kept open. Strangely, a "curiously persistent press campaign" accused the Foreign Office of being too lenient with the Shah, whom the British press labeled pro-Nazi.[62] Geoffrey Dawson of *The Times* was the ringleader of the attack. Nevertheless, the ruthlessness of the Persian incident should have convinced observers that the British government was prepared to keep the lines open to the USSR, by force if necessary.

Just as important as keeping the supply lines open, however, was ascertaining just what supplies the Soviets needed most urgently. For this purpose, during their meetings off the Canadian coast, Roosevelt and Churchill decided to send two high-ranking representatives to Moscow to consult with Stalin. Lord Beaverbrook and W. Averell Harriman were chosen to lead the British and American delegations to the Moscow Con-

ference. Harriman, the scion of a wealthy railroad family, replaced the ailing Hopkins as Roosevelt's ambassador-at-large. Beaverbrook, a millionaire Canadian freebooter and owner of the largest newspaper group in Britain, was an unusual character, who loved power for its own sake and courted powerful people, regardless of their political convictions. After Hitler's invasion of the USSR, Beaverbrook became enamored of the Soviet Union and especially Stalin, acting, as Churchill later wrote, as "the champion in the War Cabinet of aid to Russia."[63] There was a distinct element of political calculation in such a stance. The advent of World War II found the Labour party in disarray, and some observers felt that after the war it might split into moderate and radical factions. Beaverbrook had extensive contacts with factory workers, first in his capacity as minister of aircraft production, later as minister of supply. He hoped to ingratiate himself with the moderate Left by posing as the advocate for aid to the USSR, organizing a "tanks for Russia" week and pressing hard for an early second front in Western Europe. In a letter he wrote to Churchill in mid-September, he proposed "a raid of a major nature" in Northern France. He set out his reasons: "This raid would have effects of great importance. It would surprise the enemy and encourage our friends. It would be evidence to the Russians of our good faith and to the world of our growing strength. And it might well force the Germans to withdraw first class troops from the Eastern Front in anticipation of further more extensive operations."[64] What he did not say, of course, was that it would also help advance the cause of Lord Beaverbrook.

Churchill was less inclined to smooth the path for Beaverbrook's political career with the bodies of British soldiers. Remembering Britain's enormous losses in World War I, the prime minister refused to order a hasty and dubious invasion of France.

Beaverbrook's advocacy of a second front was bolstered by two messages Stalin sent to the prime minister in early September. On the third, Stalin requested the British to take some action "that would divert 30–40 German divisions from the Eastern Front" and to increase shipments of supplies. "Without these two kinds of aid," Stalin wrote, "the Soviet Union will be either defeated or weakened to the extent that it will lose the ability to help its Allies by active operations."[65] When Maiskii delivered this note on September 5, Churchill read it "attentively," and Maiskii later informed Stalin that it made "a deep impression" on both the prime minister and Eden. Bolstering his leader's argument, Maiskii declared that the British response to Stalin's appeal "might be a turning point in history." "Everything depends," Maiskii continued, "on the position which the British government takes."

Stalin's note may have made as deep an impression on Churchill as Maiskii claimed, but the prime minister was not about to be persuaded into committing British troops to a premature assault on Europe solely to relieve the Soviets. Although he told Maiskii that he would sacrifice fifty thousand British lives if by doing so he could draw twenty German divisions from the eastern front, Churchill declared a landing in France to be "impossible." "The Channel that prevents the Germans from leaping over to England," he stated, "also prevents the English from jumping over into France." He also said that a landing in the Balkans would be "unrealistic." The British simply did not "have the forces, the aviation, or the tanks," Churchill said. He continued: "I do not want to delude you: until winter we cannot give you any serious help—not by opening a second front, not by securing the wider arms supplies needed by you. All we can give you is a drop in the ocean."[66] The next day, September 6, Churchill repeated much the same arguments in a message to Stalin. He wrote: "Action, however well meant, leading only to costly fiascos would be no help to anyone but Hitler."[67]

Stalin sent the prime minister another note on September 13, once again calling for a British attack on Nazi-occupied Europe. He prefaced the appeal with a remark greatly at variance with his note to Maiskii of August 30. "I have no doubt," he wrote, "that the British Government wants the Soviet Union to win and is searching for ways to attain that goal." He offered his own suggestion: "It seems to me that Britain could safely land 25–30 divisions at Archangel or ship them to the southern areas of the USSR via Iran for military cooperation with the Soviet troops on Soviet soil in the same way as was done in the last war with France."[68] Revisionist historians have accepted Stalin's assertion uncritically, and one of them faults the British for having "no intention of sending their men to die in what appeared to be a losing situation."[69] There is certainly some truth in this claim; the last thing Britain's thinly stretched army needed was another failed expedition on behalf of an ally, duplicating the debacles in France, Norway, and Greece. But reluctance to commit British forces to a dubious military venture was only one of several reasons why Churchill felt unable to promise a British contingent for service in the USSR. What Stalin either did not understand, or pretended to misunderstand, was that British forces were already more overextended in 1941 than they had been during World War I. In that war, for instance, the British had not had to keep a watchful

eye on the Japanese. In 1941 the British Empire was vulnerable at virtually every point, and London simply did not have the manpower that Stalin attributed to her. Also, the Soviets did little to facilitate mutual military planning with Britain. Indeed, Cripps and other British officials tried to extract the military information necessary for planning joint operations with the Soviets from Molotov, who would not release any details either of Soviet or of German dispositions.

Ambassador Cripps delivered Churchill's reply to Stalin on September 19 and had a long talk with the general secretary in the Kremlin. According to Cripps, Stalin appeared "more confident and less worried than he had been at my previous interview." This was probably true. The German offensive into the Ukraine, which had resulted in the surrender of Kiev and the capture of over six hundred thousand Soviet soldiers—the shock of which had no doubt prompted Stalin's September 13 note to Churchill— had been followed by a lull in German activity as Hitler prepared for what he thought would be the final push on Moscow.[70] Stalin might have believed that the German assault had at long last spent itself.

In his note to Stalin, Churchill avoided an outright rejection of the proposal to send a British force to the USSR, deflecting the request with the bland assurance that "all possible theatres in which we might effect military cooperation with you have been examined by the Staffs. The two flanks North and South certainly present the most favourable opportunities." The prime minister refused to be more specific. British reluctance to commit ground forces to the eastern front is understandable, considering the mishandling of the Soviet forces and the capture by the Germans of millions of Soviet soldiers. The prospect of placing several hundred thousand British soldiers under Soviet command must have sent a shudder through Churchill. Nevertheless, Churchill's assurances that the British General Staff was seriously studying the possibilities of sending British troops to the USSR was only half true. The General Staff was, indeed, studying such options, but, as Churchill's later telegraphic exchanges with Cripps demonstrate, the prime minister himself never had any intention of pursuing such a course. Churchill closed his note to Stalin by expressing the hope that Britain and the USSR, by their combined efforts, including promises of British material aid to Ankara, might bring Turkey into the war on the Allied side.[71]

In his discussions with Stalin after he had delivered Churchill's note, Cripps complained of Soviet secretiveness and a lack of cooperation with the British Military Mission. Though admitting that Soviet liaison methods sometimes "lacked order and method," Stalin quickly returned to the attack, claiming that "not all the members of the British Mission conducted themselves as they should." He accused a British officer stationed in Sevastopol, for instance, of "anti-Soviet propaganda" and impugned the reliability of British intelligence, hinting darkly that their errors of inter- pretation might not be accidental. Though professing to be satisfied with Anglo-Soviet cooperation in Iran, Stalin complained that American sup- plies of steel plate were niggardly: "He had asked for 100,000 tons of steel plates, and had been promised only 1,000 tons. He would of course accept that amount, or anything else that might be offered, but in view of the fact that the American output amounted to many millions of tons he considered that the Soviet Union was getting very little." When Cripps countered this by telling Stalin of Beaverbrook's "tanks for Russia week," about which Stalin had not yet heard, this seemed to have the desired effect, because Stalin soothingly replied that "he did not wish Great Britain to go short of war material needed for her own defence, either by sending material manufactured in England or by foregoing what we should otherwise have received from the U.S.A." Sir Stafford understandably felt that the inter- view had gone better than his previous audiences with Stalin.[72]

Cripps was not, however, pleased with his treatment at the hands of Beaverbrook and Harriman after the members of the supply mission ar- rived in Moscow on September 28. Beaverbrook and Harriman decided that Cripps and the American ambassador, Laurence Steinhardt, should be excluded from the meetings with Stalin, since it was felt that the two ambassadors were not in Stalin's good graces. Once again, as so often before, newcomers on the scene felt that the first essential step toward working closely with the Soviets was to gain Stalin's trust and, if possible, his friendship. Beaverbrook had other reasons for excluding Cripps. As Harriman later noted: "He was always ill at ease with teetotalers, he explained to Harriman, particularly Socialist teetotalers who were candi- dates for sainthood."[73] What Harriman does not mention in his account is that Beaverbrook intended the Moscow Conference to be entirely his own show; he did not want that long-time advocate of Anglo-Soviet rapproche- ment, Sir Stafford Cripps, to be able later to claim credit for the good will that would surely flow from Moscow to London once Western supplies were on the way to the USSR.

Some of Beaverbrook's measures to keep Cripps in the dark were petty and ill-judged. For example, Cripps did not even see an account of the Moscow talks until over a month later—and even then only a severely abridged version. Beaverbrook even poked fun at Cripps when conferring with Stalin. The Soviet dictator had asked what the British felt about Ivan Maiskii. Beaverbrook answered and then asked how the Soviets felt about Cripps. According to Beaverbrook's notes: "Stalin gave what I thought was a negative shrug and said: 'Oh, he's all right' without enthusiasm. I said: 'He's a bore?' and Stalin said 'Like Maisky?' I said, 'No, like Mme. Maisky.' Stalin enjoyed the joke immensely."[74] This sort of malicious badinage, combined with Cripps's exclusion, was obviously intended to undercut Sir Stafford's effectiveness and did so.

Before leaving London, Beaverbrook had tried to ensure the success of his mission to Moscow by convincing a reluctant Churchill to authorize offering the Soviets nearly everything they might request within the bounds of reason. Cripps, indulgent toward the Soviets though he was, was tired of the Kremlin's secretiveness and advocated hard bargaining tactics, extracting military information in exchange for aid. It was a good idea, and, when Beaverbrook arrived in Moscow, the ambassador tried to sell this approach, without success. Beaverbrook laid out his reasons for not tying material aid to a loosening of Soviet military information: "The one way to break down the suspicious attitude which had given rise to Russian secrecy was to make clear beyond a doubt the British and American intention to satisfy Russian needs to the utmost in their power, whether the Russians gave anything or not. It was to be a Christmas-tree party, and there must be no excuse for the Russians thinking they were not getting a fair share of the gifts on the tree."[75]

The first meeting with Stalin, on Sunday, September 28, was successful, and the two emmissaries returned to their hotel[76] "well satisfied with the results," as General Ismay, the ranking British military representative, later recorded.[77] Beaverbrook tried to assure Stalin of Britain's intention to send troops to aid the Soviets by indicating that "the British were building up divisions in Persia which might be joined in the Caucasus with the Russians." Stalin was not so easily assured and responded tartly and with some justice: "There is no war in the Caucasus but there is in the Ukraine." Stalin seemed more anxious to get British troops committed to the defense of the USSR than to a second front in France. He pressed for a British force to be sent to Archangel or the Ukraine but said that "he didn't know enough about the situation [in France] but had confidence in Churchill's judgement."

Discussing peace terms, Beaverbrook stressed the importance of American public opinion in forming the postwar world "and urged Stalin to use the American press to build up a better understanding in America of Russia." According to Harriman's notes: "I asked him [Stalin] whether he had any other ideas about peace terms. He turned to Beaverbrook and said 'Are the Eight Points [of the Atlantic Charter] going to satisfy you?' Beaverbrook was non-commital and I asked what Stalin had in mind. Stalin said 'What about getting the Germans to pay for the damage.' Beaverbrook dodged the answer with some generality about 'We must win the war first.' "[78] This is one of the earliest examples of a tendency that was to persist throughout the war: Western leaders were consistently more reluctant than Stalin to discuss the specifics of a postwar settlement. They were more inclined to focus narrowly on the purely military measures needed to win the war.

The Soviets, by contrast, remained unwilling to divulge military information that the British believed they needed to arrange for the smooth delivery of supplies. When asked for details, the Soviets would simply demand even more material. According to General Ismay, who conducted separate meetings of the military staffs, "When we tried to elucidate the basis of their astronomical requirements of equipment, we could get no answer out of [the Russians]. We asked, for example, how many anti-tank guns were alloted to a division, adding that our divisions had seventy-two. The reply was, 'It depends on what sort of division.' When we suggested that an infantry division might be taken as an example, the reply was, 'That depends on where it had to fight.' "[79] Britain's military representatives found such conversations extremely frustrating.

In a peculiarly characteristic Soviet pattern—repeated at almost every meeting between Stalin and his allies—Stalin's second meeting with Beaverbrook at the Kremlin was less congenial than the first. The Anglo-American representatives returned from the talk on September 29 "in the depths of depression."[80] Stalin had been rude and had doggedly claimed that his allies were not doing enough to supply Soviet forces.

On September 30 Stalin proposed for the first time a formal Anglo-Soviet "alliance not only for war but for post-war as well" to build upon the base of July's Joint Agreement. "Stalin remarked that all the Soviet Government officials favoured the proposal," as if that were a serious consideration. Beaverbrook "answered that he personally favoured it" and promised to champion the idea when he returned to Britain.[81]

During the final ceremonies of the Conference, General Ismay had a fascinating ten-minute talk with Stalin about postwar military matters.

Stalin told the British general that "England ought to have a large army." He continued in the same vein, saying:

He quite understood why we could not at the moment establish a Western Front [though he continued to press for a British contingent on the Eastern Front]. He then continued in the following sense: the whole situation in Europe had changed. Never again can England rely on her navy alone. She must have conscription and a large army in time of peace. There will always be "Petains" in France and therefore no reliance can be placed in the future on the French Army or people. Japan finds it possible to maintain a large army in addition to a large navy. So why not England?[82]

This is an important insight into Stalin's strategic thinking. Interesting too is his complete equation of "England," as he called it, with Japan—both bourgeois "island races."

Mounting Disagreements

The negotiation of the treaty that Stalin had proposed, which was to be between Britain and the Soviet Union, excluding the United States, would cause the first major wartime rift between the two Western democracies. The Soviets would exploit the differences between the Americans and British to further their own ends and would come within a hair's breadth of full success.

Returning from Moscow, Beaverbrook touted the conference as a complete success and, given his personal political standards, it probably was. The two Western powers had agreed to supply the USSR with essential war materials—what Ismay called "our life's blood." The terms of the agreement stated that the supplies would "be made available at British and United States centres of production." But, in the end, Anglo-American ships carried 90 percent of the supplies along the treacherous Murmansk route, only to be greeted by Stalin's complaints that his allies were shirking their responsibilities.[83] Nor, as Cripps had feared, did Western largesse prod the Soviets toward greater openness regarding military intelligence.

As if to illustrate how negligible the effect of ever-increasing Western supplies would be on Soviet contrariness, during the Moscow Conference, on September 30, three British naval officers from the Moscow Military

Mission were expelled from the Soviet Union without what the British considered reasonable explanation. Meeting with Molotov to protest the expulsions, Cripps, in Sir Orme Sargent's words, "went off the deep end." Still angry, Cripps fired off a telegram to the Foreign Office: "We should not allow this to pass without a good deal of action on our part . . . the only possible, and almost inevitable, action would have to be the withdrawal of the Naval Mission in Moscow and from the Black Sea on the basis that we would not expose them to further risks of anonymous accusations and consequent action by [the] Soviet Government."[84] On October 2 the War Cabinet decided to turn the other cheek rather than force a showdown with Moscow over such a relatively minor matter. So Eden telegraphed Cripps the next day, telling the ambassador to ignore the expulsions.[85] Throughout the war, the British continued to tolerate churlish behavior on the part of their Soviet ally without retaliation because of their belief, unsupported by any empirical evidence, that, if treated kindly, Moscow would learn to trust the West and would lose its supposed fear of the Western imperialists. His postwar claims notwithstanding, even Churchill at times flattered himself that he could handle Stalin.

General Mason-MacFarlane, head of the British Military Mission in Moscow and generally an advocate of the greatest possible assistance to the Red Army, allowed his frustration with such treatment at the hands of the Soviets to boil over in a telegram to the War Office. "The Russians are not normal," he wrote, "neither do they acknowledge services rendered except on the rarest of occasions."[86] The diplomatic community in Moscow, isolated from the Soviet people, generally kept in the dark, and summoned by their hosts only when a specific service was required, tended toward gloominess. Life in Moscow could be frustrating indeed, and the strain was not eased by the evident reluctance of the London government to respond firmly to provocative Soviet acts.

While London prepared the machinery to convey Western supplies to the USSR, the tenuous equilibrium on the Russian front was shattered on September 30, when the Germans launched their final attack on Moscow, advancing fifty miles on the first day.[87] Soviet losses in men, equipment, and territory were greater than at any previous stage of the war. Some German units actually came within sight of the Kremlin's towers.

The deteriorating military situation had an immediate effect in the diplomatic sphere. A worried Stalin sent Churchill a note praising the success of the Moscow Conference, which, he said, "had a most favourable effect." He then came to the point: "I admit that our present requirements in military supplies, arising from a number of unfavourable circumstances on our front and the resulting evacuation of a further group of enterprises, to say nothing of the fact that a number of issues have been put off until final consideration and settlement in London and Washington transcend the decisions agreed at the conference."[88] Stalin wanted even more than agreed at the conference.

Churchill's reply was poorly thought out. He had already sent Stalin a message that had reached the Kremlin on October 1, in which he warned of trouble in Iran. "There are in Persia," he wrote, "signs of serious disorder among the tribes and of a breakdown of Persian authority." The prime minister felt that if such "disorder" continued it "will mean wasting our divisions in holding down these people."[89] Now, answering Stalin's note, Churchill wrote on October 12 that Britain could best help the USSR by freeing Soviet divisions in Iran for duty on the eastern front:

> About Persia: Our only interests there are; first, as a barrier against German penetration eastwards, and secondly, as a through route for supplies to the Caspian Basin. If you wish to withdraw the five or six Russian divisions for use on the battlefront, we will take over the whole responsibility for keeping order and maintaining and improving the supply route. I pledge the faith of Britain that we will not seek any advantage to ourselves at the expense of any rightful Russian interest during the war or at the end.[90]

Cripps, whose unpleasant duty it was to deliver the prime minister's message, gave the note to Molotov on October 14, telling the Foreign Office afterward, with considerable understatement, "I do not think he liked the suggestion about Persia very much."[91] Molotov told Cripps that Iran and the eastern front were "two different questions." When the ambassador asked how the Soviets proposed to supply British troops if they were to be sent to the Soviet Union, Molotov replied that "until that time [comes when British soldiers arrive] the question has a platonic, abstract character."[92]

In his telegram to the Foreign Office after this meeting, Cripps posed an obvious question: "If, as the Prime Minister's message suggests, we have enough forces to take over the occupation of the whole of Persia, would it not be possible for us to send some into the Caucasus and let the Russians leave a few troops in the North of Persia?"[93]

Churchill did not reply to Cripps until ten days later, but his explanation was reasonable and convincing. He described Stalin's requests for twenty-five to thirty-five British divisions as "a physical absurdity" and proceded to explain the logistical limitations. "It took eight months," Churchill wrote, "to build up ten divisions in France only across the channel when shipping was plentiful and U. boats few. It is only with the greatest difficulty that we have managed to send the 50th division to the Middle East in the last six months . . . all our shipping is fully engaged . . . the margin by which we live and make munitions of war has only narrowly been maintained." Churchill then explained the problems associated with shifting British units north from the Caucasus: "[The] Russians have five divisions in Persia which we are willing to relieve. Surely these divisions should defend their own country before we choke one of the only supply lines with the maintenance of our forces to the northward. To put two fully armed British divisions from here into the Caucasus or north of the Caspian would take at least three months. They would then only be a drop in the bucket."[94] Churchill's argument may have made good logistical sense, but it was poor politics. True, as Churchill said, a British contingent would have been a drop in the bucket, and, arriving as it would after three months, the immediate crisis would by then have passed. But failing to send even a token British force to the eastern front left Churchill open to the not entirely unfounded accusation that he wanted to see Germany and the USSR weaken each other while Britain stood aside.[95]

The Soviets, for their part, did nothing to ease the situation. No matter what force the British might send to the Soviet Union, Moscow would surely have deemed it a pittance. Nor were the Soviets very helpful to the leading British advocates of sending troops. When Cripps, for example, tried his best to be encouraging by asking Mikoian how the Soviets proposed to supply British soldiers once they arrived in the USSR, the latter snapped back that there was no need to discuss such problems since the troops were not yet in the Soviet Union.[96] The Soviets' harshness with Cripps was a tactical mistake, since it is clear that Sir Stafford hoped to get British forces committed to the Caucasus in order later to draw them further north, into the fighting. As he told Molotov on October 22, "In his opinion, if the English troops would enter the Caucasus, then, perhaps, it might be possible to push them further."[97] Cripps had not included these remarks in the account of the conversation he had sent to London; he was clearly hoping that British commitment of troops to Persia would set in train a series of events that would lead to sending British soldiers to fight in the USSR. But clumsy Soviet diplomacy allowed this opportunity to pass; the Soviet policy of treating all foreign ambassadors as committed enemies of the USSR prevented them from using Cripps's genuine good will to further their interests. Also, while pressing hard for the dispatch of British divisions, Stalin at no time lowered his demands for Anglo-American supplies, in fact upping the ante day by day. Stalin wanted both increased supplies and British ground forces. Demanding both made it less likely that he would get either.

On October 15–16 Cripps and the rest of the diplomatic community were evacuated from Moscow as the Germans approached the capital. On the sixteenth, the normally cowed population of Moscow broke into a panic as German units threatened the city, and the NKVD disappeared. Even Stalin reportedly fled Moscow for two days—though this claim has never been substantiated—and the authorities did not restore order by instating martial law until October 19.[98] The evacuation and the rumors that no doubt flew among the diplomatic community understandably impressed upon Cripps the seriousness of the Soviet military predicament, which, he believed, the Foreign Office did not understand—London was not fully alive to the imminence of a Soviet collapse. He felt logistical details were of less importance than the need to make a demonstration of Allied solidarity to bolster Soviet morale.

Having witnessed some of the chaos in the capital, Cripps wrote the Foreign Office on October 25: "I make full allowance for the fact that Molotov and others are stressing this point [about a British force] for reasons of policy, but I am satisfied beyond a doubt that there is a widespread general obsession with this question. Officially I am beginning to be anxious as to [the] result of this on morale during the winter." Despite the logistical obstacles, Cripps reasoned, the urgency of the situation demanded the "immediate dispatch of a force not less than a corps, with an adequate proportion of RAF." The British Military Mission at the embassy agreed with this assessment, Cripps wrote, "but [they] desire that I should stress the fact that these suggestions are only a temporary remedy, and that whatever we send, the Russians will inevitably press for more."[99]

In another telegram the next day, Cripps responded to the prime minister's message of October 24, accepting the military arguments against sending a large British force but urging that, "a drop or two in a bucket or tumbler may make a great deal of difference when a stimulant is urgently needed."[100] Sir Stafford felt that he and General Mason-MacFarlane should return to London to discuss measures to overcome the crisis. In a phrase that stung Churchill, Cripps wrote: "We have never yet explained to them frankly over here our own position. [The Soviets] are now obsessed with the idea that we are prepared to fight to the last drop of Russian blood as the Germans suggest in their propaganda."

Churchill had what he no doubt believed would be the last word in this exchange, and in doing so he showed that more lay behind his reluctance to send British soldiers to the Russian front than concerns about rail and shipping capacity. On October 28 he wrote Cripps that "it would be silly to send two or three divisions into the heart of Russia to be cut to pieces as a symbolic sacrifice." Churchill had neither forgotten nor forgiven Soviet policy between August 1939 and June 1941, and he would not leave Cripps's repetition of Soviet accusations unanswered:

> I fully sympathise with you in your difficult position, and also with Russia in her agony. [But] They certainly have no right to reproach us. They brought their own fate upon themselves when by their pact with Ribbentrop they let Hitler loose on Poland and so started the war. They cut themselves off from an effective second front when they let the French Army be destroyed. If prior to June 22nd they had consulted with us beforehand, many arrangements could have been made to bring the great help we are now sending them in munitions earlier. We did not however know till Hitler attacked them whether they would fight or what side they would be on. We were left on our own for a whole year while every Communist in England, under orders from Moscow, did his best to hamper our war effort. . . . That a government with this record should accuse us of trying to make conquests in Africa or gain advantages in Persia at their expense or being willing to fight to the last Russian soldier leaves me quite cool. If they harbour suspicions of us it is only because of the guilt and self-reproach in their own hearts.

As for Cripps's suggestion that he should return to London, Churchill wrote: "I do not think it would be any use for you and MacFarlane to fly home now. I could only repeat what I have said here, and I hope that I shall never be called upon to argue the case in public."[101]

Churchill, for one, had clearly lost none of his old distaste for Soviet Communism. His recitation of the recent history of Anglo-Soviet relations left Soviet accusations of British parsimony in tatters, and his arguments against sending British soldiers to disappear in the Soviet Union were unimpeachable—as things turned out. But even such a forceful case would have looked petulant and ill-judged had the battle for Moscow not ended in Soviet victory.

Two things are, however, curious about Churchill's note. In the first place, it was relatively easy to answer Cripps's repetition of Soviet charges in a telegram intended for British eyes alone, but the prime minister would seldom answer Soviet accusations directly, nor would any high-ranking British official do so. They would, instead, continue to tolerate the worst sort of innuendo from their Communist allies while maintaining an odd solicitude for Soviet sensibilities. Also, the last line of Churchill's telegram was revealing: he would maintain the public facade of Allied unity while behind the scenes the old differences between London and Moscow would persist. Later, as the Grand Alliance neared victory over Nazi Germany, the prime minister would face a formidable task steering public opinion around to recognize the Soviet threat to the European balance of power. How could a public that had been told that the war was being fought for universal democratic principles also be persuaded that their great eastern ally's war aims were fundamentally incompatible with these principles? The British government's chosen method to deal with this problem was to ignore or deny it.

Even after receiving the prime minister's telegram, Cripps felt that Churchill did not understand the tenuousness of Soviet resistance. On October 29, after what he described as "the fullest consideration," he sent a reply to Churchill, whose arguments he claimed were "of no assistance to me" in answering Soviet accusations and demands. Cripps wrote, "I am not concerned now any more than you are by Russian reproaches from any moral point of view," but, he argued, he was worried about Soviet morale.

The main point of Cripps's telegram was that he, as ambassador, was neither sufficiently informed nor authoritative enough to argue Britain's case. He recalled Eden's visit to the Middle East earlier in the year and contrasted this with the fact that the foreign secretary had not yet visited Moscow. "And yet," he argued, "it could hardly be denied that the Soviets are now more important to us as Allies than the Greeks ever were." Cripps also suggested that General Ismay should return to the USSR for high-level military coordination. (Having been excluded from the Moscow Supply Conference, Cripps could not have known that Lord Beaverbrook had offered to have Ismay discuss strategic matters with his Soviet counterparts, a suggestion that met with no response.) "We seem," Cripps complained with a good deal of force, "to be trying to carry on two relatively unrelated wars to the great benefit of Hitler instead of a single war upon the basis of a combined plan."[102] The telegram was well-reasoned, persuasive, and moderate, and it planted the seed of Eden's eventual visit to Moscow in

December. In a second telegram, Cripps argued that he should attend the lower-level military mission talks already underway in Tiflis, while Eden could handle the larger political questions directly with Stalin.[103]

While the debate between the London government and its embassy in Moscow raged over whether to send British soldiers to the Soviet Union, a British Trade Union Conference (TUC) delegation led by its general secretary, Sir Walter Citrine, visited the USSR to confer with Soviet fellow trade unionists. The visit sheds light on the gradual evolution of British public opinion toward the Soviet Union and its war effort. Citrine was known as a vocal anti-Communist because of the Soviet Union's frequent efforts to infiltrate and subvert the British trade union movement. For this and other reasons, Cripps and Citrine had long been at loggerheads. The USSR's new-found friends also held Citrine's prewar anti-Communism against him, as shown by this extract from Oliver Harvey's diary: "Moscow . . . is menaced with a visit from that bogus booster, Citrine and a T.U.C. party. How Cripps will hate it! Citrine comports himself as a little Führer, ordering Cabinet Ministers [or their secretaries?] about. . . . He hates Soviet Russia and is one of those Labour leaders who are throwing dust in the eyes of Labour. He could easily become an appeaser for fear of Communism."[104]

Harvey's fears were entirely misplaced. Citrine's public reaction to visiting the USSR illustrates the ever-increasing sympathy in Britain for the Soviet Union and the curious schizophrenia of Britain's Labour party to the "Soviet experiment," as it was called. Citrine was indeed a bitter opponent of domestic Communism. In 1964 he wrote of the British Communist party that "here was a body that was determined to use every available means to undermine the faith of trade unionists in their elected officers and to convert that movement into a revolutionary force no matter what distress this might bring to the average worker."[105] But in 1942, in a book describing his visit to the USSR in the Autumn of 1941, Citrine told quite a different story:

> We [of the TUC] had at all times proclaimed the right of the Russian people to work out their own destiny in their own way. . . . It was our deep conviction that the great social and economic achievements of the past twenty years in Russia, were founded on the right principle of collective ownership and control. British Labour believed that the goal of production for use and not for profit, which Russia had striven

to apply, was one which other countries would eventually have to emulate.[106]

The Soviets had merely "chosen" a different road to the same goal. "Russia is ruled by a dictatorship," Citrine conceded, "but it is not a personal dictatorship in the sense of one man ruling the country. It is the dictatorship of a Party."[107] British workers were more advanced—so the underlying assumption ran—and would thus not require the stern tutelage as administered by the Kremlin to their Soviet counterparts.

Upbeat accounts of the Soviet war effort and society such as Citrine's were designed to assure the public that the USSR would stay in the war and that, though admittedly using methods quite unacceptable in Britain, the Soviet leadership shared common long-range goals with the Western democracies. Feeding on such propaganda, and inspired by the Soviet defense of Moscow, British public opinion became increasingly pro-Soviet.[108]

In reality, Anglo-Soviet cooperation was never as smooth as wartime accounts claimed. In contrast with Citrine's glowing public portrayal of the USSR, the major meeting during the TUC delegation's visit (between Cripps, Citrine, and Molotov in Kuibyshev on October 23) had not gone at all well. As Sir Orme Sargent wrote upon reading an account of the talk: "The interview seems to have degenerated into an unseemly wrangle between Molotov and Sir S. Cripps." After brief, perfunctory pleasantries about the common desire for growing cooperation between the two nations' trade unions, Molotov got down to the more serious business of charging the British with evasion of their responsibilities. Molotov said: "The efforts of the Soviet and British armies should be united on one common front or on two fronts and the sooner this was done the better. . . . The ultimate outcome of the war would be decided by the armies and if they fought together victory would come all the sooner." It is difficult to see what the British hoped to gain through meetings such as these between the two countries' trade unions. Molotov was clearly using the opportunity to press an as yet untapped segment of British public opinion for commitment of British troops. But any corresponding British effort to influence Soviet opinion—or even to determine what that opinion truly was—was doomed from the start, given the USSR's obedient, government-controlled unions.

Molotov used the forum to the fullest, complaining that "we have not received any answer, neither a negative one nor a positive one," to Stalin's request for twenty-five to thirty-five British divisions. Cripps denied Molotov's accusation, claiming that Churchill and General Sir John Dill had told Maiskii in London "why we could not accept this proposal [by Stalin]." Molotov replied that, according to Soviet records, there had been no such British response and continued: "Sir Stafford Cripps has spoken very often about sending English troops to the Caucasus but there is no front [there]. There had been a question of sending English troops to fight on the front through Iran, Archangel or through the Caucasus to the second front in the South but we have received no answer." Sir Walter Citrine tried to smooth things over by suggesting that this was no matter for telegrams and that he would personally raise the matter with Churchill once the TUC delegation had returned to London. This suggestion upset Cripps, who evidently saw it as a personal slight, claiming that "the matter had better be dealt with by him." Molotov then put the ambassador on the spot by siding with Citrine, thus humiliating Cripps.[109]

His humiliation was intensified when, on November 1, Cripps at long last received accounts of Beaverbrook's meetings with Stalin. Among other unpleasant news contained in these telegrams, such as the fact that Beaverbrook had offered to leave General Ismay in Moscow for strategic talks, Cripps learned that Molotov had been right on October 23, and that the Soviets had not, in fact, received a clear response to Stalin's request for British divisions. It is hard not to sympathize with Sir Stafford, who on November 5 telegraphed the Foreign Office:

> It must be remembered that Molotov was present at all these discussions [with Beaverbrook and Harriman], but that at Beaverbrook's request, and since the conversations were only to concern the matters which he came out to discuss—which I understood to be questions of supply—I was not present. This has, of course, put me in an entirely false position as regards Molotov and probably explains a phrase which he used to me the other day and to which I did not then attach any significance. When I was pointing out that I had urged upon His Majesty's Government a certain course of action, he remarked that he was afraid that I had no power of persuading them.

Beaverbrook's obtuseness had caused significant confusion in Anglo-Soviet relations. Cripps continued: "In these circumstances I can see no use in my remaining here to act as an occasional post-box." The only thing that could induce him to stay, Cripps wrote, was if the British government should decide to negotiate a full treaty of alliance with the USSR to replace the joint agreement of July, an alliance that Stalin had hinted he wanted during his conversations with Beaverbrook. In such a case, Cripps said, he might still be useful in Moscow. Cripps also argued that since Stalin had raised with Beaverbrook the issue of postwar treatment of Germany and the idea of postwar Anglo-Soviet cooperation, the British should discuss the "whole question of peace objectives and of [the] Atlantic Charter" with the Soviets.[110]

Before answering Cripps, Eden met with Maiskii on November 6 and at long last formally responded to Stalin's request of September for British divisions. Eden told Maiskii that "the Prime Minister had made it plain that it was quite outside our powers to dispatch such a force." Eden continued: "We had offered to relieve Soviet troops in North Persia and send a small force to the Caucasus, but the Soviet Government had not accepted these offers." Eden was only being partially truthful; the British had indeed offered to relieve Soviet troops in Persia and had more than once offered to send a British force into the Caucasus, an offer derided by both Molotov and Stalin, but Churchill had never given Stalin a clear rejection regarding the dispatch of British soldiers to the Russian front. Instead, he made counterproposals and allowed the Soviets to draw their own conclusions. This said, Stalin and Molotov were in no position to complain of British unresponsiveness; the Soviet leaders had frequently given no answer at all to British approaches before June 22.

On November 10, Eden wrote apologetically to Cripps, trying to down-play the importance of the political discussions during the Beaverbrook-Harriman-Stalin meetings. Eden reassured Cripps by stretching the truth, claiming that the talks were almost entirely centered on supply issues, and that Beaverbrook "asks me to assure you that there were no serious diplomatic talks at all."

Turning to Cripps's proposals about setting Anglo-Soviet relations on a firmer basis, Eden wrote that the British had already proposed staff talks with the Soviets but had received no response. As for Cripps's suggestion about a discussion of postwar frontiers, Eden wrote: "At the present stage when it is so impossible to predict what the situation at the end of the war will be, it is really quite impracticable to formulate our peace objectives for discussion with our allies more than is done in the Atlantic Charter." With this comment, Eden was simply repeating the "logically defensible" decision the British reached in August 1940, that "political changes produced during this war ought not to be recognised *de jure* pending a general peace settlement."[111] The British government's overriding interest lay in forming a war-winning coalition, and Britain's leaders were well aware of the fact that this would mean reconciling—at least for the war's duration— widely divergent and often flatly contradictory interests. Excessive concern for such matters as postwar frontiers could disrupt a fragile equilibrium. To cite one example, the Free Poles and the Soviets, the British rightly believed, could scarcely work comfortably in harness if they were squabbling whether to include Vilna in the USSR or Poland. Far better, London felt, to postpone such abrasive issues until a comprehensive postwar peace conference. This decision had drawbacks, however, as the USSR was in a much weaker position vis-à-vis Britain in 1941 than she would be in 1945. Also, since London's decision to place territorial questions in limbo was made without consultation with Moscow, the Soviets did not feel bound by this policy. London's efforts to prevent such problems as a Russo-Polish rift were doomed from the start.

Stalin's Mood

Although unprepared to discuss a comprehensive postwar European order, the British government was prepared to sign a long-term treaty of friendship with the Soviets, Eden told Cripps. This step, which had been judged politically unacceptable in July, would now be all right, a sign of how far British opinion had moved in only four months. Eden identified the purpose of such a treaty: "The important thing is surely that the Russians should know that we are prepared to carry forward our collaboration with them into the peace and beyond. This has been explained to M. Maisky and I shall be grateful if you will emphasise our general attitude in this respect to Stalin or Molotov at any convenient opportunity."[112] In closing, Eden tried to reassure Cripps about his centrality in Anglo-Soviet relations and of the necessity for him to remain in Moscow preparing the groundwork for future talks. In a following telegram Eden wrote: "If opportunity offers, I hope myself at a not too distant date to pay you a visit and join you in this and other work."[113]

Cripps, understandably, felt Eden had given him very little to build upon. As the ambassador had found to his chagrin, the Soviets did not regard him as privy to inside information. And now the foreign secretary was telling him to assure the Soviets of Britain's good will but at the same time explicitly to avoid discussion of a postwar settlement or, indeed, discussion of any detailed problems. These contradictory directives nettled Cripps, who on November 13 wired to Eden: "I find it difficult to know how I am to prepare the ground in a hard frost without any implements." As for the idea of deferring territorial questions until a peace conference, Cripps wrote: "I am not in the least criticising your method of dealing with [this matter] which may well be the best under the circumstances. I merely record the fact that I can do nothing to help." The time had come, Cripps felt, for his return to Britain, since "I came here to do a special job and not as a professional diplomatist, and it was understood that when the job was at an end I should leave."[114]

In the meantime, Churchill intervened, apparently without consulting Cripps, to attempt to minimize the damage done by the muddled and incomplete signals passing between Moscow and London. There were four major outstanding issues: (1) The British were anxious to begin high-level military consultations, whereas the Soviets seemed content with material assistance; (2) Stalin wanted either a second front or a British force in the Soviet Union itself; (3) the Soviets were adamant that Britain should pressure the governments of Finland, Romania, and Hungary, if not actually to declare war on them, whereas Britain was reluctant to do so; (4) Stalin wanted a full discussion of plans for a postwar settlement. In his message to Stalin on November 7, Churchill addressed points one and three, again dodging the question of a second front. The prime minister offered to send General Wavell, the commander in chief in India, Persia, and Iraq, "to meet you [Stalin] in Moscow, Kuibyshev, Tiflis or wherever you will be." Accompanying General Wavell would be General Paget, commander in chief designate for the Far East.

Turning to the matter of Germany's three client states, Romania, Hungary, and Finland, Churchill urged Stalin to "consider whether it is really good business that Great Britain should declare war" on the three; the prime minister added, "My judgement is against it" since "Finland has many friends in the United States." Finland had numerous friends in Britain as well, owing almost entirely, of course, to the resistance she had shown in her short war with the USSR in 1939–40. As for Romania and Hungary, Churchill wrote, "These countries are full of our friends: they have been overpowered by Hitler and used as a cat's paw. But if fortune turns against that Ruffian they might easily come back to our side."[115]

Stalin's reply, dated November 8, was received in London on the eleventh. Stalin echoed his earlier complaints to Cripps that Anglo-Soviet relations were hampered by a "lack of clarity." (How different it must have been to work with the confusing British after his experience with Hitler.) Stalin attributed the friction between the two countries to two factors: "(a) There is no definite understanding between our two countries on war aims and on plans of the post war organisation of peace. (b) There is no agreement between the USSR and Great Britain on mutual military assistance against Hitler in Europe." The rest of Stalin's message was harsh and uncompromising. Referring to Churchill's proposal to send Generals Wavell and Paget to the USSR for consultations, Stalin said he would be willing to meet them if they were prepared to negotiate a treaty based on the two points above: "If, however, the mission of the Generals is confined to the questions of information and to the consideration of secondary matters, it would not be, I think, worth while to intrude upon the Generals. In such a case it would be also very difficult for me to find the time for conversations." Turning to the question of Britain's attitude toward Romania, Hungary, and Finland, Stalin wrote, "It seems to me an intolerable situation has been created in the question of declaration of war by Great Britain." Stalin accused his ally of bad faith and a "negative attitude," asking several rhetorical questions: "Why is all this being done? To demonstrate the lack of unity between the USSR and Great Britain?"[116] This was the same distrustful tone Stalin had used in his telegram to Maiskii in August; now, however, he was airing his dark suspicions.

Stalin's note was further evidence that the problems dogging Anglo-Soviet cooperation since the German invasion of the USSR had neither disappeared nor lessened. The Soviet dictator was still demanding that the British commit themselves on the political plane either to invade the Continent or to send British forces to fight in the east; only after that commitment had been made might the Soviets discuss details and reveal vital military information—though, of course, there was no guarantee that they would be more free with intelligence even in such a case. For their part, the British were unwilling to commit themselves politically to a course for which they had little enthusiasm anyway, when their allies would supply little or none of the military intelligence needed to make such an important decision. If the purpose of Stalin's aggressive note was to compel the British to commit themselves, the effect was more nearly the opposite.

Stalin's tone disturbed the Foreign Office. Meeting with Maiskii the next day, November 12, Eden told the ambassador that the note raised several "very large issues" and that a British response would follow only after a period of consideration. "At the same time," Eden said, "I cannot conceal from you that the Prime Minister and the Cabinet were surprised and pained at the tone and the contents of the message." Reporting his talk with Maiskii to Cripps, Eden laid out the government's course: "M. Stalin's message betrays a mood which we must do our best to transform, but we feel for the moment that any reply, whether argumentative or apologetic, would only make matters worse. A few days for reflection on both sides may be all to the good."[117]

With incomplete Soviet documentation, a definitive explanation of Stalin's note is difficult. There was a certain amount of justice, it would seem, in his demand that his ally declare war on all the nations waging war against the USSR. Churchill's arguments against doing so, however, also made perfect sense: the British might have been able gradually to increase pressure on the three nations and would have more influence over them if relations were maintained—and they could, perhaps, secure their defection from the Nazi side should the military situation turn around. Also, American opinion, which was, Churchill argued, strongly pro-Finnish, was as important to Britain as Stalin's peace of mind, if not more so. Although it is certain that average Soviet citizens would have welcomed even a moderately successful second front in the West, it is difficult to believe that they were clamoring for a British declaration of war on Romania, Hungary, or Finland, as Stalin claimed.

Stalin's note was not only a manifestation of his suspicions of his ally's motives but also a manifestation of his characteristic desire to tie down as many loose ends as possible. The German offensive on Moscow was at its most critical point, but Stalin's demands contained in his letter to Churchill suggest that he had already begun thinking about the postwar settlement. The general secretary was receiving assessments from Maiskii of the British public's mood, which was becoming ever more sympathetic to the Soviet Union's plight, and he may have reasoned that this was an opportune moment to press the British to recognize what Molotov would later call the Soviets' "minimum conditions"; in other words, recognition of the USSR's territorial gains since the Nazi-Soviet Pact.[118] Britain's refusal to declare war on Finland and Romania was an overt indication that London had not yet accepted Stalin's acquisition of Bessarabia, North Bukovina, and the portions of Finland seized in 1940. Having declared war on Romania and Finland, Britain would be in no position diplomatically to defend these nations' territorial claims against the USSR at the peace conference.

The hypothesis that what lay behind Stalin's demands was a desire to force recognition of his earlier territorial gains is supported by the contents of his speech to the Soviet people by radio on November 6. Although paying lip service to the principles of the Atlantic Charter, the Soviet dictator spoke of the need to expel the Nazi invader from Soviet territory, explicitly including Estonia, Latvia, Lithuania, Belorussia, Bessarabia, and North Bukovina. The fate of these territories was clearly on his mind when he dispatched his note to Churchill, though evidently few in London noticed the connection.

Upon reading Stalin's note, Cripps drew quite different conclusions. He believed that Stalin suffered from "the Russian Georgian suspicion of Western European countries" and that the General Secretary "has never had any real contact with Western ways and diplomatic usages." (Apparently Cripps discounted the time since 1929 at least that Stalin had conducted Soviet foreign policy, a longer tenure than any Western head of state.) Cripps argued that Stalin's suspicion was deep rooted and that it remained for the British to assuage him. "Stalin is not convinced," Cripps told the Foreign Office, "that we are in the war with the Russians wholeheartedly and without reservations. He has his own ideas as to tests which will convince him one way or the other or will predispose him to such ultimate conviction." In a telegram that followed immediately, Cripps continued this line of reasoning with a familiar refrain: "I feel that the present is the most critical moment in our relationship [with the Soviet Union] and that action taken now will go far to determine the whole course of those relations during and after the war."[119]

There is no evidence beyond Cripps's own repeated claims, however, that Stalin had devised a "test" of British good will. To be sure, there is abundant evidence that the Soviet dictator harbored suspicions about British intentions, but then suspicion was scarcely a stranger to Stalin and was certainly not confined to doubts about British friendship. There is, however, a second, more serious flaw in Cripps's reasoning: even if one were to accept his premise that Stalin had dreamt up a litmus test of British intentions, there was nothing to prevent him from continually raising his criteria for demonstration of British good will.

Nevertheless, solely to appease the Soviets, on December 6 Britain would declare war on Romania, Hungary, and Finland, even going so far as to launch naval-air raids on Petsamo, the Finnish nickel-mining town. It was ironic that the British should have chosen December 6—the day before Pearl Harbor—to do so, since the Soviets would not declare war on Japan until 1945. Evidently, Stalin was never troubled by the urge to assure his allies of his sterling character and good intentions.

Churchill had had enough of Cripps's demands to do more for the Soviets. Furthermore, the prime minister read Sir Stafford's requests to return to London as a poorly veiled political threat designed to drum up support to pressure the government to pursue a more forthcoming policy toward the USSR. Taking up the challenge, Churchill dictated a telegram to Cripps threatening the ambassador with political oblivion should he argue his pro-Soviet case in public. After assuring Cripps that he had read all his telegrams, Churchill wrote: "All the same I am sure that it would be a mistake from your point of view to leave your post and abandon the Russians and the Soviet cause" while the USSR's affairs were in such a perilous state. Churchill then came to the point:

> Your own friends here would not understand it. I hope you will believe that I give you this advice not from any fear of political opposition which you might raise over here by making out we had not done enough etc. I could face such opposition without any political embarrassment though with much personal regret. The Soviet Government, as you must see upon reflection could never support you in an agitation against us because that would mean that we should be forced to vindicate our action in public which would necessarily be detrimental to Soviet interests and to the common cause. Force of circumstance would compel them to make the best of us. After all, we have wrecked our Air and Tank expansion programmes for their sake, and in our effort to hold German air power in the West we have lost more than double the pilots and machines lost in the Battle of Britain last year. You must not underrate the strength of the case I could deploy in the House of Commons and on the broadcast, though I would be very sorry to do so. The Government itself was never so strong or unchallenged as it is now. Every movement of the United States towards the war adds to that strength. You should weigh all this before engaging in a most unequal struggle which could only injure the interests to which you are attached. I have taken full note of your wish to come home. Indeed you told me about it before you returned last time. You may be sure I will tell you when to come at the right moment for you and for the cause. It may be for some months yet.[120]

This note, which was probably an example of Churchill thinking on paper, was rejected by the Cabinet on November 17, undoubtedly under Eden's influence. It was poorly designed to persuade Cripps, who would most probably have received it as a personal challenge. Also, Cripps's arguments for returning had been based—at least overtly—not on a desire to do combat with Churchill but rather on his belief that he was poorly informed and no longer effective in Moscow. Both arguments had an element of truth, but Churchill, as an old politician, had sensed a political challenge. The prime minister's note is most interesting from a political angle, illustrating as it does the sort of pressure a British prime minister faces. Opposition can coalesce around any issue at any moment. It is equally illuminating that Churchill's note was rejected by his Cabinet colleagues as too harsh and therefore likely to push Cripps in the very direction Churchill did not wish him to go.

The Cabinet's response to Cripps was couched in soothing language and, though the argument was repeated that "it would be difficult for His Majesty's Government at the present time to define at all precisely" just what sort of postwar collaboration there might be between Britain and the Soviet Union, the Cabinet promised Cripps that Eden was prepared to visit Moscow to clear up outstanding problems. The Cabinet's decision to send Eden to Moscow was a direct result of the strident tone of Stalin's most recent telegram. Relations between the two allies had never been cozy, but the general secretary's note seemed to the British to signal Moscow's growing suspicion of the extent and quality of the British war effort. As is clear from the prime minister's telegrams to Cripps, Churchill at least believed that Stalin had very little with which he could reproach his allies, but the fact that he felt compelled repeatedly to counter the arguments of those who belittled Britain's military measures showed that he was sensitive to such attacks, however unfounded he believed them to be.

On December 4 Eden discussed Stalin's note with the American ambassador, John G. Winant, showing how Britain's leaders took Soviet accusations to heart. Eden said: "The terms of this message were such as to leave no doubt that Stalin was in a mood of suspicion and even resentment to a degree that might adversely affect the cooperation of the two Governments in the prosecution of the war."[121] In the reworded message to Cripps, the Cabinet told the ambassador that they hoped the proposed visit of the foreign secretary would reassure Moscow of Great Britain's good intentions.

At a Cabinet meeting on November 17, during which the telegram to Cripps was discussed, Churchill continued to argue against a British declaration of war on Finland, Romania, and Hungary. In his diary, Oliver Harvey wrote of the situation: "P.M. most obstinate. At the same time Maisky continues to insist on profound misgiving which this policy is causing in Russia. A. E. doesn't see how to advance matters now. He has next to no support except from the Beaver."[122] Although the Cabinet refused to specify Britain's postwar aims, or to declare war yet on all those nations fighting the USSR, the decision to send Eden to Moscow was an important step toward acceptance of at least part of Stalin's demands. High-level political missions—at least in democratic countries—have certain peculiar dynamics: they force the participants to agree to something, almost anything, to avoid leaving the meeting empty-handed. Stalin, who was subject to little pressure from public opinion, could afford to be obstinate; Eden could not, even if he had wanted to, which he certainly did not. Eden, as Cripps and Beaverbrook before him, was determined to go down in history as the man who had reconciled Britain with Soviet Russia. Also, by the time the foreign secretary arrived in Moscow, the German assault on Moscow had spent itself, and the Soviet counterattack was dealing Hitler's forces their first major reverse of the war. Pro-Russian sympathy swelled in Great Britain, making a tough British negotiating position less tenable politically.

Far more important than the events around Moscow, so Churchill felt, was the Japanese attack on Pearl Harbor. Almost as soon as he heard the news, the prime minister determined to visit Washington immediately. As he wrote in his memoirs: "I never had any doubt that a complete understanding between Britain and the United States outweighed all else, and that I must go to Washington at once with the strongest team of expert advisors who could be spared."[123] The prime minister left Britain by sea, accompanied by Lord Beaverbrook; Field Marshal Dill, former chief of the Imperial General Staff; Air Marshal Portal, chief of the Air Staff; and Admiral Pound, first sea lord—in all, a weighty delegation.

Eden, who was leaving London for Moscow as the news of Pearl Harbor reached Britain, was strongly opposed to Churchill's trip to Washington. Eden argued that so many leaders should not leave Britain at once, but Churchill was deaf to the foreign secretary's entreaties. Eden had other reasons for wanting Churchill to remain in London. In his diary, Oliver Harvey called Churchill's visit to the United States "lunatic," and on December 12 he wrote: "A. E. very anxious to know whether P. M. had gone or not, fears if he does it will take all the limelight off the Moscow visit."[124]

Like Beaverbrook before him, Eden tried to assure the success of the Moscow Conference before leaving London. The important thing, he felt, was to calm Stalin's suspicions of Britain by being as forthcoming as possible. When he learned that Churchill had ignored his objections and would go to Washington, Eden rushed to secure authorization to reassure Stalin that this was not an anti-Soviet move. As Harvey wrote: "We must work with Stalin on [a] basis of absolute confidence."[125] The foreign secretary pressed the Chiefs of Staff to release a British contingent for service on the Russian front and, when his request was rejected, tried to secure an increase of British material aid to the Soviet Union. He was determined not to appear in Moscow empty-handed.[126]

On his way to Washington, the prime minister telegraphed Eden: "Before you left you asked for views of Chiefs of Staff on the question whether it would be to our advantage for Russia to declare war on Japan, Chiefs of Staff considered views are as follows: Russian declaration of war on Japan would be greatly to our advantage, provided, but only provided, that the Russians are confident that it would not impair their Western front either now or next spring."[127] Churchill wrote that if Stalin volunteered to declare war on Japan, Eden should not discourage him but that the British should not press the Soviets too closely. As it turned out, when they met, Eden was so busy fending off Stalin's demands and accusations that he had no time to broach the subject of Japan.

The war against Imperial Japan was only one of many new problems facing Britain's leaders in December 1941. In a very short span of time, the war had changed course dramatically. After the bombing of Pearl Harbor, the United States had finally become a combatant rather than an interested—albeit deeply involved—neutral. The diplomatic ramifications of America's changed role quickly became apparent. At the same time, in the frozen countryside west of Moscow, the Wehrmacht's seemingly irresistable forward movement had been checked. The USSR's victories, like America's entry into the war, profoundly altered the diplomatic equation. Only five months previously, Britain had stood alone among the great powers in resistance to Hitler's bid for European supremacy. In December 1941 London was alone no longer.

The destinations of Churchill and Eden symbolized Britain's changed status in the war effort. The prime minister was steaming toward Washington and the foreign secretary toward Murmansk. London was now only one of several focal points of the Allied war effort and no longer necessarily the most important. The London government now had to face taxing political questions that previously had lain dormant while more pressing military problems were attended to. From December 1941 onwards, Allied leaders began to pay greater attention to shaping the postwar world. The destinations of Churchill and Eden represented the very different courses open to

British decision makers. The prime minister, by going to Washington as soon as possible after Pearl Harbor, clearly signalled—entirely intentionally—the great value he placed on the transatlantic tie. He had chosen not to go to Moscow, indeed he had not seriously considered doing so. For Churchill, alliance with the United States meant far more than the utilitarian link with the USSR. It was, in his opinion, a union of both power and common values.

For Eden, by contrast, the emotional link that Churchill felt with the other great English-speaking democracy was largely lacking. The foreign secretary would self-consciously distance himself from Churchill's pro-Americanism. Eden felt keenly Britain's position as a European power and hoped to develop a correspondingly European-centered foreign policy. Eden's generation had twice witnessed a German challenge of the European balance of power, and one can therefore understand why, for the foreign secretary, the primary task of British diplomacy appeared to be the prevention of a postwar recurrence of the German menace. With the collapse of French power, Britain had to choose with which other great power to cooperate as a balance against postwar Germany. For Churchill the choice was obvious: he looked west, hoping that shared Anglo-American values would lay the foundation for a lasting alliance. But Eden recalled how the United States had shown such promise as an international actor in 1918–19, subsequently to withdraw into isolation. Eden later reminded his colleagues that, whereas America could afford to isolate herself once again after the war, the Soviet Union was, like Britain, a European power with a vested interest in restraining Germany. Moscow was thus, in Eden's opinion, Britain's natural ally. Focusing narrowly as he did on a possible renewal of the German threat, Eden underestimated the extent to which the USSR might replace Germany as a challenger to European and British security once the Nazi threat no longer bound the Grand Alliance together in common cause.

CHAPTER SIX

A DISMAL

TALE OF CLUMSY

DIPLOMACY

DECEMBER 1941 –

APRIL 1942

Britain's Soviet policy was in disarray when Eden arrived in Moscow. The War Cabinet was not of one mind concerning the desirable degree of cooperation with Soviet Russia. Churchill was inclined to limit the Anglo-Soviet partnership to military matters, leaving aside political and territorial problems until the war's end. The prime minister was concerned primarily with defeating Nazi Germany and, in the process, with forging a strong and lasting Anglo-American alliance—thus, his voyage to Washington almost immediately after Pearl Harbor. Churchill was actuated in part by a desire to strengthen the unity of the English-speaking peoples, but he also hoped that the democratic bloc would act as a counterweight against European dictatorships, Stalin's as well as Hitler's.

Other voices in the Cabinet sounded a markedly different note. Lord Beaverbrook persistently advocated an increase in material aid to the Soviet Union as well as the opening of a second front in Europe, and Anthony Eden believed that Stalin required assurances of Britain's good intentions. On November 29, 1941, Eden presented a memorandum to his Cabinet colleagues in which he argued that the object of his forthcoming trip to Moscow should be to assure Stalin that Britain did not desire an "Anglo-American peace" and that Great Britain intended to fight on until the destruction of German military might. (This latter point was designed to calm Stalin's supposed fears about Britain's reluctance to open a second front.)[1]

Eden's meetings in Moscow with Stalin and their aftermath would decide which strain in British diplomatic thinking would prevail—those favoring closer ties with Moscow, or those hoping for greater Anglo-American political coordination.

It is difficult to pinpoint Eden's motives in pressing for a more forthcoming British attitude toward the USSR. There was, however—at least on the authority of Oliver Harvey—an element of political calculation behind the foreign secretary's position. Eden hoped to dominate the headlines during his trip to Moscow.[2] Churchill had taken an early and commanding role in Anglo-American wartime relations, and it is likely that Eden, as foreign secretary, hoped to concentrate on that sphere of foreign policy in which he could personally play a greater role. The prime minister, though wanting to establish a direct relationship with Stalin, was not nearly as inclined to interfere in the details of Anglo-Soviet relations as he was with the transatlantic connection. Relations with Moscow would be Eden's domain.

The prime minister's trip to America had already somewhat eclipsed Eden's hour in the sun. Therefore, the foreign minister was not inclined to share his moment of glory with any other Briton in Moscow. Remarkably, in light of the troubles ensuing from Beaverbrook's secretiveness in October, Eden almost repeated the former's mistake by excluding Ambassador Cripps from the talks with Stalin. As Oliver Harvey wrote: "Talked to A. E. Thinks it best to have first talk with Stalin entirely alone, without Cripps as Stalin has evinced a strong preference for this. It is difficult to leave Cripps out but the important thing is to get S. to talk freely".[3]

Cripps, it seems, was too vociferous and dogged about pressing the Soviets for military information in exchange for Anglo-American supplies and, perhaps, men. To be sure, Sir Stafford was ready to recognize Soviet territorial acquisitions made prior to June 22, but, he argued, British recognition should come at a price.[4] Stalin, for his part, had already heard everything Cripps had to say, and he evidently found the ambassador's persistance wearying. Sir Alexander Cadogan, the permanent under secretary for foreign affairs, who accompanied Eden and Harvey to Moscow, remembered the troubles caused by the exclusion of Cripps from the Beaverbrook-Harriman-Stalin meetings and persuaded Eden to include the ambassador this time.[5]

During a German air raid on December 16, Cripps and Cadogan combined their talents to produce a British draft agreement to be handed to the Soviets the next day.[6] The main points of the draft were: a promise by Britain and the Soviet Union to "collaborate in every possible way until the German military power has been so broken as to render it incapable of further threatening the peace of the world"; a promise that neither nation would sign secret agreements with third parties dealing with postwar matters; promises of postwar mutual economic assistance; and a commitment to collaborate in the postwar reconstruction of Europe.[7]

Conversations with Stalin

The talks again followed the peculiar Soviet pattern of amicability in the first meeting followed by a harsh second session. The Soviets also produced a draft, not differing markedly from the British document and filled with the same bland generalities, but in the first session of the conference, late on December 17, Stalin made it clear that he intended the Soviet draft primarily for public consumption. What he really wanted was "a secret protocol concerning the map of Europe after the War." Stalin then proceeded to list Soviet desiderata for postwar Europe: Germany, Stalin felt, should be dismembered, Austria reconstituted as an independent nation, and the Sudetenland restored to Czechoslovakia. Italy should lose territory to Yugoslavia, and Hungary should suffer the same fate at the hands of Romania and Czechoslovakia. Turning closer to home, Stalin told Eden: "As to the frontiers of the Soviet Union we should like to see the frontier in Finland and the Baltic Provinces restored to its position in 1941, immediately before the outbreak of war. So far as the frontier with Poland is concerned the Curzon line should form the basis for this with perhaps some slight variation one way or the other." The use of the "Curzon line"[8] would involve a considerable loss of territory for Poland, but she could be compensated, Stalin said, by being given East Prussia and by a cession of German territory up to the River Oder. The Soviet Union, Stalin said, must also have bases in Finland and Romania.

By way of compensation for Soviet gains, Stalin suggested that Britain should receive similar concessions; that is, "on the French coast, some military and naval bases, such as Boulogne and Dunkirk; also Belgium and Holland should be in open military alliance with Great Britain, who should have the right to maintain in those countries naval and air bases." This was the way that Stalin had dealt with Hitler, and he evidently believed that the same rules applied with the British. The public declaration issued by the two sides would consist of uplifting generalities, while the real business was done in the secret protocols.

If this is how Stalin thought the British would be willing to negotiate, he was mistaken. Before Eden left Britain, the American secretary of state Cordell Hull had telegraphed that, in the opinion of Washington, the British should refrain from signing any secret protocols. Even had Hull not telegraphed, the British would not have committed themselves to definite territorial agreements during the Moscow Conference. As we have seen above, the War Cabinet had decided upon such a policy as early as August 1940.

Stalin's detailed comments surprised Eden, who responded, "I must confess that we have not gone so far as to examine this in detail as you have here, and I would not commit my colleagues on such a question without first consulting them." Trying hard to gain Stalin's confidence, Eden said: "I want to be quite frank about this matter. Even before Russia was attacked Mr. Roosevelt sent a message to us asking us not to enter into any secret arrangements as to the post-war reorganisation of Europe without first consulting him. This does not exclude our two countries from discussing a basis for the peace." Eden tried to steer the talks toward a discussion of military questions by asking if Stalin would not like to combine the British and Soviet draft treaties and thereby dispose of political questions for the moment. In an often-quoted response, Stalin said: "I think that what you have submitted is a kind of declaration, whereas ours are two agreements. A declaration I regard as algebra, but an agreement as practical arithmetic. I do not wish to decry algebra, but I prefer practical arithmetic." When Eden hedged, Stalin returned to the point: "What about the attachment of the secret protocol?" Stalin had easily gained the initiative, putting the British foreign secretary on the defensive. Eden answered apologetically: "I am afraid we have a troublesome Constitution, and, apart from the question of America, we have to consult the Dominions, who are helping us in the war and naturally expect to be consulted as to what we arrange as regards national frontiers after the war." Eden was evidently concerned that he had not yet captured Stalin's trust—the central purpose of the conference so far as the foreign secretary was concerned. He interpreted Stalin's demands for restoration of the USSR's frontiers as evidence that the general secretary was uncertain of Britain's determination both to remain in the war and, after the war, to prevent the renewal of German revanchism. So he tried to reassure the general secretary about

Britain's intention to fight Germany to the end: "I can assure you that we are entirely realistic in our determination to stop the Germans from repeating their aggression, and I very much hope that you fully understood that." But Stalin was not discussing Britain's determination to win the war—on this point the British had proven themselves. What he wanted was a redrafting of Europe's frontiers. He told Eden: "My desire is to establish that the war aims of our two countries are identical, as then our alliance will be all the stronger. If our war aims were different then there would be no alliance." A veiled threat, to which Eden responded with an astounding comment: "I agree. I see no reason why our war aims should be different." He hoped simply to "reconcile" the two countries' aims.

After discussing the Japanese attack and various supply problems the Allies faced with the opening of a new theater of operations, Stalin revealed why he now felt in a sufficiently strong position to press the USSR's postwar claims. Blatantly lying, he told the credulous Eden that, "the war policy of the Soviet Union has so far been that of a fighting retreat." In fact, the Soviets' greatest defeats stemmed at least in part from a misguided propensity to launch premature counteroffensives.[9] Confidently predicting ever-widening Soviet attacks now that the German tide had begun to turn, the dictator boasted: "The German Army is not so strong after all. It is [strong] only because it has an enormous reputation." So sanguine was Stalin that in a little noted comment he stated that he would declare war on Japan in 1942. The British minutes record Stalin saying: " 'We can do nothing now, but in the spring we shall be ready, and then will help.' He made it quite clear," Eden recorded, "that the antagonism between Russia and Japan could only be settled by force." The session then ended in a sumptuous feast, which, as the British guests noted, contrasted sharply with average Russian fare.

Harvey judged the first meeting a success, writing that night: "A. E. got back about 11 after 4 hours with Stalin including a champagne supper at the end. I think he has made a most successful start."[10] Eden felt that he had stood up to Stalin's demands for a secret protocol. But, as his telegrams to the Foreign Office show, he was uneasy with the flow of the talks. He felt that his arguments against a treaty dealing with postwar frontiers had been "in vain." Summing up, however, Eden said that the "conversation was most cordial throughout."[11]

On December 19 the War Cabinet reassured Eden that he was correct to refuse Stalin's demands for an immediate comprehensive treaty settling postwar frontiers. They wrote: "If we publicly abandon this principle we shall have no defence against territorial claims put forward by other Allies, such as Poles, Czechs and Greeks. On the other hand, a secret engagement is, as you already told Stalin, out of the question." Moreover, the telegram continued, any treaty to which Britain could be a party must conform to the Atlantic Charter and must also dovetail with American opinion, "but Stalin's present demand might well be held by the United States' Government to infringe the 2nd and 3rd clauses of the Charter, or at any rate to constitute a doubtful interpretation which they would not accept. . . . Recent correspondence with representatives of the Baltic States by the United States' Government, who have publicly refused to recognise the annexation of these States, have clearly implied that they consider the Atlantic Charter applies to their case."

Eden did not answer the Cabinet's telegram until late on December 19, thanking London for its "most helpful" suggestions. By this time Eden had already met twice again with Stalin, finding that the dictator's veneer of cordiality had vanished.

True to the standard Soviet pattern, too frequently repeated to be mere accident, Stalin appeared at the second meeting in a gruff mood. He immediately brushed aside Eden's attempts to discuss drafts of a public agreement with the curt response: "I am more interested in the question of the future frontiers of the USSR." And, true to his word, Stalin doggedly pursued this question throughout the meeting. The dictator candidly revealed why the British had been unable to outbid the Germans in August 1939: "The Soviet Government is very interested in this question [of the European frontiers of the USSR] because during the time of the Chamberlain Government in the earlier negotiations they broke down on this very question of the Baltic countries and Finland, and we want to know what is the position on this matter of the present British Government."[12] Stalin called recognition of the Soviet Union's pre-June 22 frontiers "absolutely axiomatic" and rudely told Eden that this issue should be decided immediately and should not be a matter for discussion by the British Cabinet.

Eden prevaricated, telling Stalin: "The present position [of the British government] is that we do not recognise the independent existence of any of these States. They have no diplomatic status with us." This was simply not true. In fact, the three Baltic States maintained consulates in London (and still do).

Stalin was persistent. Revealing how confident he was about the military situation, he told Eden: "We might reoccupy the Baltic States in the near future, and how are we to know that in that event Great Britain will not deny to us these frontiers?" Using a transparent bargaining device, Stalin feigned indignation when Eden reiterated that he could not independently determine British policy regarding territorial changes. "If you say that," Stalin answered, "you might well say tomorrow that you do not recognise the Ukraine as forming part of the USSR." The British certainly might have. Anti-Soviet activity flourished in the Ukraine, both during and after the war. Questioning Eden about the Baltic States, Stalin was getting the foreign secretary to commit himself at the very least to the restoration of the Ukraine to Soviet control. The notion that Great Britain might seek a partition of a weakened Soviet Union after the war must not have seemed impossible to Stalin, who, after all, could recall Britain's intervention in the Civil War.

Eden was too harried and disconcerted by Stalin's changed mood to sense the implications of the question. He replied: "That is a complete misunderstanding of the position. It is only changes from the pre-war frontiers that we do not recognise. The only change in the Ukraine is its occupation by Germany, so of course we accept the Ukraine as being part of the USSR." This comment gave Stalin part of what he wanted, and he returned to comparing Churchill's government with Chamberlain's, an insult of some significance to Eden, whose own reputation owed a great deal to his supposed opposition to Chamberlain's foreign policies.

Eden tried to be conciliation itself, promising that, "If you wish for it and attach great importance to this point, then I will try and get a favourable answer for you upon it." Eden also pointed out that the analogy to Chamberlain's policy was flawed since the Baltic States were no longer regarded in London "as independent States." But Stalin was better informed than Eden thought him to be and would not allow this remark about nonrecognition to pass unchallenged. He pressed the question: "Where is the evidence of that? You still have their representatives in London." After hearing Eden's jesuitical and embarrassed explanation, Stalin termed Britain's Baltic position "very curious," as indeed it was in Eden's presentation. After a further acrimonious exchange, Stalin said that the question of the Baltic States and the USSR's western frontiers "is really what the whole war is about," later calling the matter "the main question for us in the war." Stalin, taking a page from Eden's book, argued that the Baltic States were included in the Soviet Constitution as an integral part of the USSR, claiming, "We [too] are bound by the provisions of our Constitution."

Eden's reply reflected the British government's decision not to confront the Soviets on delicate issues. He told Stalin: "Of course you are and we have no objection whatever to that, but we are not bound by your Constitution. . . . I didn't hear of these frontiers which you now propose until I came here last night and I cannot agree to them until I have consulted both my own Government and America." This was another prevarication. Eden had, of course, known all about the Soviet territorial claims, as they had been the bone of contention between Great Britain and the Soviet Union since his return to the Foreign Office in December 1940, and indeed before.

After further argument of a similar nature, Stalin threatened not to sign any new treaty. Eden was disappointed and said that British and Dominion opinion would be upset as well, since "nothing in these agreements in any way weakens the claims that you have put forward as regards frontiers." Stalin countered, again clothing his designs in the trappings of democratic language: "We too, have our public opinion here and they would certainly be horrified if they learnt that Great Britain was not prepared to support us on the question of our frontiers in the Baltic States." He accused the British and Americans of wording the Atlantic Charter so as to be "directed against the USSR." He asked: "Why does the restoration of our frontiers come into conflict with the Atlantic Charter?" Eden's reply was poorly thought out. He said: "I never said that it did." He continued to argue that recognition of post–1939 territorial changes would open an exceedingly wriggly can of worms.

But Stalin showed just how reasonable he could be. The question of the Baltic States was a simple matter between Britain and the Soviet Union; no third parties need be involved. On other questions, the dictator assured his guest, the Soviet Union would remain admirably flexible. In a crucial remark, Stalin said: "The Polish frontier remains an open question and I do not insist upon settling that now. What I am most interested in is the position in Finland, the Baltic States and in Roumania." Stalin's success in getting the British to declare war on Romania and Finland might now pay dividends.

From the British point of view, the second meeting had not gone at all well. Stalin had refused to sign the British draft treaty and had persistently bullied Eden. The latter was proud of the fact that he had stood up to Stalin by refusing to recognize Soviet border claims immediately. Much like his resignation from the Foreign Office in 1938, however, Eden had defended form rather than substance. He had simply refused to exceed his powers as foreign secretary, while at the same time assuring Stalin that he would champion the Soviet cause back in London. At no point had he questioned the legitimacy of the Soviets' claims; indeed he implied that he fully sympathized with them. Nor had he countered Stalin's accusations with his own; he did not, for example, mention the Nazi-Soviet Pact when the Soviet leader had taunted him with Chamberlain. In all, Eden had given a feeble performance.

On the next day, December 18, Stalin returned to the attack. But this time his approach was more subtle. He rewrote article four of the British draft agreement—the one guaranteeing postwar cooperation in the political and economic life of Europe—to read: "The two contracting parties undertake to work together for the reconstruction of Europe after the War with full regard to the interests of both parties in their security as well as to *the interests of the USSR in the restoration of the frontiers violated by Hitler's aggression*" [italics added].[13] Eden could not, of course, accept such wording, as it implied an acceptance of the Soviets' gains during the period August 1939–June 1941.

Stalin acted hurt, saying: "I want to emphasise the point that, if you decline to do this [accept the redrafted article], it looks as if you were creating the possibility for a dismemberment of the Soviet Union." Eden rushed to reassure the dictator: "That is not in the least the case." Stalin then employed an extraordinary argument in defense of his redraft: "I must insist that these should be left untouched, because there has been much talk in Europe of our intentions to Bolshevise Europe and to keep other people's territory, &c. so that I would like to have these principles clearly stated to remove all apprehension from people's minds on the point."

Eden argued that if he were to accept the Soviet wording he would, in fact, also be recognizing the pre–June 22 Russo-Polish border. When Stalin played down this idea, saying he "would give a letter to make that quite clear" that the Polish frontier was not part of the agreement, Eden replied, correctly: "Yes, but that is how it will be read throughout the world." The impasse reached between the two sides is shown in the following exchange toward the end of the meeting. Referring to the Soviet draft, Eden said "I am afraid I cannot possibly accept it," to which Stalin replied: "That is very regrettable."

Again, following the familiar Soviet pattern, the final meeting, on December 20, was more cordial. Stalin was reconciliation itself, telling Eden: "I do not think that failure to sign the treaties now should be regarded in too tragic a light. If the treaty is signed in London in two or three weeks time, it will come to much the same thing. Our relations will be based on the July agreement, and they will become closer." After all, Stalin could afford to be friendly. Eden had been so hard pressed protesting his inability immediately to sign the treaty desired by the Soviets that he had done nothing actually to modify the Soviet position.

Reading the British account, one gets the distinct feeling that Eden was greatly relieved by Stalin's changed tone. He said: "I am very glad to hear what you say about Anglo-Soviet relations and your view that these are going to improve. . . . " Telling Stalin what he wanted to hear, Eden continued: "As regards the question of the frontiers, I do not regard this as an obstacle to the development of our future relations. . . . The main point is that these agreements, as drafted, in no way prejudice the Soviet Government's territorial claims; on the contrary, they would help to further them." This last comment could well serve as a fitting epitaph for the Moscow Conference.

Eden's New Soviet Policy

From June 1940 through most of 1941, Britain had refused to recognize de facto Soviet sovereignty over the gains the Soviets had made on their western borders owing to the Nazi-Soviet Pact. Indeed, in 1939 Chamberlain had balked at accepting the Soviet formula for "indirect agression" through the Baltic States—a clause upon which Stalin had insisted. British refusal to sign away the Baltic States had cost her dearly: it was one of the principal reasons why Stalin had signed a pact with the Nazis (who had no such scruples about defending the rights of other nations). In June 1940 the Soviets received their reward for abetting Hitler when they occupied the Baltic States. But, even after the fall of France, the British Foreign Office, in desperate straits to be sure, had ignored Sir Stafford Cripps's repeated appeals to try to buy Soviet friendship—or neutrality—by recognizing Moscow's suzerainty over Estonia, Latvia, and Lithuania. Anthony Eden came close to doing so in April 1941, but manifest Soviet disinterest in better relations with Britain had dissuaded him.

And now Eden was telling Stalin that he would return to London with the intention of convincing his government to recognize Soviet claims. The foreign secretary had abandoned his contention that territorial matters must be left to the peace conference, in direct violation of the instructions he had received from the Cabinet on December 19.

It is notable that during the next few weeks there would be relatively little negotiation between Moscow and London. Having pressed his demands on Eden, Stalin would leave the British alone to debate the relative merits of accepting or rejecting his position. He would sit back and wait for a reply, leaving Maiskii to make the occasional prodding comment. And, rather than debate Soviet demands with the Kremlin, the British would choose instead to argue among themselves, and eventually with the Americans as well. In this great debate, Eden came to supplant Cripps as the most vocal advocate of conciliating Stalin.

Why was Eden prepared to argue a course that Britain had refused to take when that nation had been in much worse circumstances? After all, in December 1941 the United States entered the war, and the Germans had been repulsed at the gates of Moscow. Germany's ultimate defeat had never looked likelier. After his return to London, on January 5 Eden elucidated his reasons for accepting Stalin's demands in a telegram he sent to the prime minister, who was still in the United States. Reflecting the influence of Cripps, Eden wrote: "I am clear that this question is for Stalin [the] acid test of our sincerity and unless we can meet him on it his suspicion of ourselves and the United States Government will persist." Eden listed three reasons "for immediate recognition":

(1) essential need at present time for really close and intimate collaboration and consultation with [the] USSR, which, if we do not meet them on this, will be, I feel sure, limited to matters on which they require our help and that of [the] United States of America. This may make all the difference after the war as well as now.

(2) Fact that nothing we and the United States of America can do or say will effect [*sic*] situation at end of [the] war. If Russians are victorious they will be able to establish these frontiers and we shall certainly not turn them out.

(3) Russians have [a] strong case on ground of security. So far as their claims in Finland and [the] Baltic States are concerned it is in our interest too that they should be in [a] strong position in the Baltic.

I realise, of course, that [the] great difficulty with [the] United States Government must be apparent conflict with [the] Atlantic Charter. (Russians would, of course, contend that there is no conflict with first clause since they were in possession of territory in question when attacked by Germany. In regard to second and third clauses, they claim that as far as Baltic States are concerned these voted themselves into [the] Soviet Union and although this is hard to swallow, it is equally hard to make this point to our allies.) *I think that the Russians having endorsed [the] Atlantic Charter might agree to [a] formula designed to meet [this] difficulty, since they would foresee no obstacle, when time came, in arranging for necessary vote in their favor.* We might try to make this [a] condition of our according recognition they demand.

While I do not for a moment minimise difficulties of persuading [the] United States Government to treat matter on basis of stark realism, I am convinced that [the] attempt should be made, and I hope that you will see your way to make it while you are at Washington [italics added].[14]

Churchill was not as concerned as his foreign secretary about allaying Stalin's supposed fears of an "Anglo-American peace." Indeed, at that very time the prime minister was with President Roosevelt trying to create the basis for just such a peace. The tone of Eden's telegram ran counter to Churchill's mood, which explains the tenor of his response. Like Eden's note, Churchill's telegram deserves to be quoted at some length, representing as it does the opposite pole of British thinking:

Your [telegram] surprises me. . . . We have never recognised the 1941 frontiers of Russia except *de facto*. They were acquired by acts of aggression in shameful collusion with Hitler. The transfer of the peoples of the Baltic States to Soviet Russia against their will would be contrary to all the principles for which we are fighting this war and would dishonour our Cause. This also applies to Bessarabia and to Northern Bukovina and in a lesser degree to Finland which I gather it is not intended wholly to subjugate and absorb.

Churchill admitted that the USSR could successfully press her claims for part of the territories in question "upon strategical grounds," such as with the approaches to Leningrad and certain Baltic islands. The prime minister argued, however:

In all other cases transference of territory must be regulated after the war is over by freely and fairly conducted plebiscites very differently from what is suggested *in your paragraph 3 section 4*. In any case there can be no question of settling frontiers until the Peace Conference. I know President Roosevelt holds this view as strongly as I do and he has several times expressed his pleasure to me at the firm line we took at Moscow. I could not be an advocate for a British Cabinet bent on such a course.

I regard our sincerity to be involved in the maintenance of the principles of the Atlantic Charter to which Stalin has subscribed [italics added].

Turning to Eden's arguments in favor of recognition, Churchill reminded his foreign secretary: "About the effect on Russia of our refusal to prejudice the peace negotiations at this stage in the war, or to depart from the principles of the Atlantic Charter, it must be observed that they entered the war only when attacked by Germany, having previously shown themselves utterly indifferent to our fate, and indeed they added to our burdens in our worst danger." As for Eden's arguments that if the Soviets occupied the disputed territories at the end of the war the Americans and British would be unable to eject them, Churchill showed just how far removed his thinking was from Eden's. The prime minister pointed out that Eden was "making a very large assumption about the conditions which will then prevail. No-one can forsee how the balance of power will lie, or where the winning army may stand," he continued. "It seems probable, however, that the United States and the British Empire, far from being exhausted, will be the most powerfully armed and economic *bloc* the world has ever seen, and that the Soviet Union will need our aid for reconstruction far more than we shall need theirs." Churchill repeated his vow: "But there must be no mistake about the opinion of any British Government of which I am the head; namely, that it adheres to those principles of freedom and democracy set forward in the Atlantic Charter. . . . I conceive, therefore, that our answer [to Stalin] should be that all questions of territorial frontiers must be left to the decision of the Peace Conference."[15]

Evidently, Churchill was not yet a convert to Anthony Eden's "stark realism." Interestingly, however, in his postwar account of this matter, published in 1950, Churchill quoted his telegram extensively but omitted the italicized section ("in your section 3 paragraph 4") without acknowledging that he had done so.[16] Eden was by that time a potential Conservative prime minister, and Churchill evidently did not wish to damage his friend's reputation. The effect of the omission is, of course, to lead the reader to believe that the suggestion for new fraudulent plebiscites in the disputed territories was Stalin's, whereas, in fact, the idea was entirely Eden's.

Once the genie was out of the bottle, however, it could not be returned so easily as Churchill hoped. True to his promises to Stalin, Eden had consulted the Dominions about the Soviet demands. The response of Australian Prime Minister John Curtin is instructive. Australia was paralyzed by fear of a Japanese invasion, and minor European territorial disputes seemed somewhat recondite. On December 24 Curtin telegraphed Churchill: "Attitude we are inclined to recommend is to accede to Stalin's wishes as far as possible providing that he undertakes to commence the war against Japan in the near future. We imagine that the United States attitude would be much the same, i.e. one of complete realism."[17] Curtin would prove as wrong in his estimate of the American response as in his belief that the London government would prove able to draw the Soviets into the war against Japan in exchange for recognition of their territorial demands.

On January 17, when Churchill returned to London from his Washington sojourn, the issue of the Soviet Union's western frontiers immediately became one of the thorniest disputes dividing the War Cabinet. On January 28 Eden submitted a critical six-page memorandum entitled "Policy Towards Russia," in which he elaborated upon the themes of his January 5 telegram to Churchill. The foreign secretary advocated immediate British recognition of Soviet sovereignty over the Baltic States, Bessarabia, and northern Bukovina. The problem of the Russo-Polish border could, Eden believed, be left in limbo for the time being, as Stalin had apparently agreed in Moscow.

In his memoirs, published in 1965, Eden, by then the Earl of Avon, employed a deceptively convincing argument justifying his 1942 position. "We did not want to recognise any Soviet position in the Baltic States," Eden explained, "but it seemed inescapable that, if Hitler were overthrown, Russian forces would end the war much deeper in Europe than they had begun it in 1941. It therefore seemed prudent to tie the Soviet Government to agreements as early as possible."[18] This sounds plausible, and in all probability by 1965 Eden had convinced himself that such reasoning underlay his judgment in 1942. But this is only part of the story. Eden quotes large segments of his January 28 memorandum in his memoirs, but he deletes those parts that do not tend to support his argument. The memorandum begins: "On the assumption that Germany is defeated and German military strength is destroyed, and that France remains, for a long time at least, a weak Power, there will be no counterweight to Russia in Europe." Eden quotes this passage, supporting, as it does, the impression that the primary object of British diplomacy in this case consisted in restraining a rapacious USSR. In 1965 such an argument would appear farsighted. Eden does not, however, quote the sentence immediately following in his memorandum, in which he enumerated his reasons for accepting Stalin's territorial demands: "But it may yet be necessary to maintain co-operation with Russia (a) because she might otherwise be tempted to collaborate with Germany in view of the historical tendency to, and economic urge for, those two Powers to work together; (b) in order to recreate in our own interest the balance of power in Europe against the possibility of a revived Germany, which balance has been destroyed by the collapse of France; (c) in order that, militarily speaking, Germany should be encircled." Further on in the memorandum, in another passage he did not choose to include in his postwar account, Eden pursued the idea of facilitating the growth of Soviet power: "Looked at purely from the strategic point of view it may well be in the British interest that Russia should be established once again on the Baltic, so as to be able better to dispute with Germany the naval command of that sea than she was able to do during the period since 1918, when her access to the Baltic was limited to Kronstadt."

From the full memorandum, it is clear that Eden was urging acceptance of Stalin's demands not solely to restrain future Soviet demands, as his postwar account would lead one to believe, but rather to augment the Soviet strategic position as a balance against a possibly renascent Germany. To be sure, Eden noted that the Soviet Union might present a threat to the European balance of power. If the Soviets were to defeat Germany "before the war potential of Great Britain and America is fully developed," Eden argued, "Russia's position on the European continent will be unassailable." The victorious Soviet government might set about erecting Communist governments in the areas liberated from the Germans. Eden continued rather hopefully: "But this possible development is in itself a reason for establishing close relations with the Soviet Union now while their policy is still in a fluid state, in order to exercise as much influence as possible on the moulding of their future course of action." Eden believed that if Britain could ingratiate herself with the USSR now, then after the war she could draw upon a well of Soviet good will. The foreign secretary acknowledged his intellectual debt to Sir Stafford Cripps:

> Our acquiescence or refusal cannot affect Russia's post-war frontiers one way or the other: if she is in occupation of the territory involved at the end of the war, neither we nor America will turn her out. Probably, however, M. Stalin's demand is intended as an acid test to find out

how far His Majesty's Government are prepared to make unpalatable concessions in order to obtain the post-war co-operation of the Soviet Union: in other words, to see what value we attach to that co-operation and what sacrifice of principle we are prepared to make in order to achieve it. If this is really M. Stalin's object, he is not likely to be prepared to accept any smaller or alternative concession in its place. Sir S. Cripps, whom I have consulted since his return from Russia, holds that this is a case of all or nothing, and that our refusal to satisfy M. Stalin will be the end of any prospect of fruitful co-operation with the Soviet Governmment in our mutual interests, and that Soviet policy will revert to the pursuit of purely selfish aims.

Accepting Stalin's demands would not be a simple matter, Eden admitted:

There is bound to be difficulty in practice in harmonising day to day Anglo-Russian co-operation with Anglo-American co-operation. Soviet policy is amoral; United States policy is exaggeratedly moral, at least where non-American interests are concerned. In America there is still a widely-spread feeling of distrust and dislike of Russia, which the pact with Hitler and Russia's attack on Finland greatly augmented. As United States opinion, however, becomes more realistically minded under the stress of war, this feeling may be gradually modified.

Continuing in the same vein, Eden wrote: "The question of the Baltic States is the first example of this conflict of principle between the United States and the Soviet Government. The Soviet Government have endorsed the Atlantic Charter, but at once seek leave to by-pass one of its principles, while the United States Government, for the present at least, regard them as sacred." [The second sentence of this passage was also omitted from Eden's postwar account.]

Having decided to surrender on this point of principle, Eden maintained that concessions must now be extracted from Stalin in exchange for British acquiescence. Employing curious and somewhat racist logic, the foreign secretary wrote: "It would not do to make this, or, indeed, any concession to M. Stalin without requiring a suitable *quid pro quo*. He would, in his oriental mind, interpret such an omission as a sign of weakness." Stalin, Eden was saying, must be treated as a village bazaar trader made good. The "suitable" counterclaims for which Britain should press, he thought, should be recognition by Moscow of the need for a defensive federation of the Balkan States; a guarantee of postwar Anglo-Soviet cooperation; and Soviet support for the establishment of British bases on the European coast, in keeping with Stalin's suggestions at the Moscow Conference.

One remarkable thing about these British counterdemands is that they were formed hastily as an afterthought, rather than as an integral part, of genuine negotiations with the Soviets. That is, presented with Stalin's demands, Eden cast about for various British desiderata that he could point to later as a sort of compensation for London's flexibility, should anybody accuse him of having played Stalin's fool.

Significantly, Eden did not include in his list a demand, or even a request, that the USSR commit itself to declare war against Japan by a certain date or after the defeat of Hitler, a particularly serious omission in view of the high diplomatic price paid later in the war for such a Soviet pledge. Nor did the foreign secretary even mention the American desire for emergency landing rights in Siberia. Instead, Eden seemed satisfied that "our answer to M. Stalin's demand might well, in certain circumstances, affect the Russian decision to make war on Japan or to refrain from doing so." In other words, once Soviet confidence had been won, and if the war against Hitler was going well, Stalin might of his own volition declare war on Japan to assist his allies. How different was Eden's reasoning from that prompting Stalin's demand the previous autumn that Great Britain declare war on Finland, Romania, and Hungary.[19]

Most surprising, however, coming from a man with Eden's experience in diplomacy, were the contradictions and fuzzy logic contained in this pivotal memorandum. On the one hand, the foreign secretary faulted the Americans for what he saw as their cumbersome and hypocritical morality and for their inability to deal with an "amoral" Soviet foreign policy. On the other hand, however, Eden evidently believed that Stalin was demanding a "sacrifice of principle" from his allies as the "acid test" of Western friendship toward the USSR. If Britain failed this peculiar test, Eden reasoned, Stalin would revert "to the pursuit of purely selfish aims," and Britain would lose the opportunity to capitalize on Soviet good will after the war. Eden did not explain why, however, if Stalinist diplomacy was amoral, the Soviets would ever feel compelled to repay British largesse. Nor did Eden entertain the notion that British generosity over the Baltic States might easily whet Stalin's appetite for territorial expansion rather than sate it.

One historian has argued that the British hoped to reconstruct "not . . . the balance of power, but . . . the Concert of Europe."[20] In other words, by recognizing an expanding Soviet sphere of influence in Eastern Europe—about which Britain could do very little anyway—Eden wanted to create a stable European order based on consensus among the victorious, satisfied powers, duplicating the reasonably durable order of 1815.

Such reasoning may have been the basis of Eden's memorandum, but if so, his historical thinking was flawed, as was his understanding of Soviet Russia. In 1815, the great powers had just defeated Napoleon, and they agreed among themselves about the need to prevent the domination of the Continent by any single great power. In the 1940s, however, Stalin's USSR was more akin to Bonaparte's France than to any of the status quo powers of 1815 Europe. Unless one dismisses as so much sound and fury Soviet claims to being a revolutionary power, there was little reason to believe in 1942 that the Soviet Union had abandoned its intentions to disrupt and, if circumstances were favorable, supplant the old European order. Indeed, Britain's experiences with Soviet policy during the period of the Nazi-Soviet Pact should have dictated a policy of caution toward Soviet aims. With one exception, it is difficult to distinguish any difference between Eden's misguided efforts to transform Stalinist Russia into a satiated power and the better-known appeasement of Hitler before the war: by 1942, the prewar antiappeasers had become wartime appeasers of Stalin.

The British Debate

To understand why Eden's arguments were not met with hoots of derision, one must look at the military situation in early 1942. The Grand Alliance's long-term prospects for victory looked very good, since the combined might of the USSR, Great Britain, and the United States was potentially overwhelming. But it would take time to bring that power to bear, and in the meantime, the Western Allies had suffered a long string of military fiascos. In the Far East, British military prestige was at a low ebb after the loss of two of her greatest capital ships, the *Prince of Wales* and the *Repulse*, both sunk on December 10. Singapore, the so-called "Gibraltar of the East," fell two months later. Nor did Britain fare better in the West. On February 12, Sir Alexander Cadogan vented his frustrations in his diary, reflecting on Britain's malaise:

The blackest day, yet, of the war. Singapore evidently only a drawn-out agony. Burma threatened. . . . So China will go out of the war when Burma collapses. Meanwhile, "Scharnhorst," "Gneisenau" and "Prinz Eugen" cockily steamed out of Brest this morning and up the *Channel* in broad daylight, and so far I have been unable to hear that we have been able to knock any paint off them. We are nothing but failure and inefficiency everywhere and the Japs are murdering our men and raping our women in Hong Kong. . . . I am running out of whisky and can get no more drink of any kind. But if things go on as they're going, that won't matter.[21]

The Americans were also suffering their reverses.

Only the USSR, it seemed, was able to take the wind out of the Axis sails. Soviet winter counteroffensives, limited at first, threatened to deal the German army its first decisive defeat as panic spread among Hitler's men. British sympathy for the Soviet Union, which had climbed steadily throughout 1941, soared in the new year. American ambassador John G. Winant mentioned the new British mood in a dispatch to Washington on January 13. "There has been growing popular appreciation here because of Russian war efforts," he wrote. "I do not feel that this is based on communistic ideology but respect for a power that had been underrated and was meeting the test of stopping the German war machine."[22]

Britain's new-found enthusiasm for things Soviet bolstered the reputation of one familiar figure. After Eden left Moscow, Sir Stafford Cripps finally got his wish and returned to Britain on January 23, 1942, after eighteen months in the USSR. And he was, as one historian of British wartime politics has noted, "acclaimed as though sent by providence to set the world right."[23] The conservative *Northern Daily Mail* noted, a touch ironically, that "The emotional hopes encouraged on Sir Stafford Cripps' return to [?from] Russia, the great and hopeful spirit that he breathed into his speeches somehow led people to believe that here was the man that was going to put a fresh crusading spirit into the War Cabinet and set it building a new heaven and new earth whose door would be flung open on the first day of peace."[24] The fact that Cripps had been singularly ineffective as ambassador and had been virtually ignored in the end by his hosts was not widely known and did not prevent him benefiting from Soviet prestige. The popular imagination envisioned him as virtually responsible for bringing the USSR into the war on the Allied side.

In reality, Cripps had left the USSR under a cloud; indeed, the Soviets had not even arranged a farewell ceremony for him. The various times during the previous autumn when the Kremlin had deduced that Sir Stafford was not kept completely informed of his government's position may have convinced the Soviets that he was a cipher. Or perhaps Stalin was signaling his displeasure that his territorial demands had not been met immediately. Back in London, however, Cripps would continue to advocate conciliation of the USSR in spite of his ill treatment, hoping that this would one day open the USSR to outside influences. Whatever the reason for Soviet coolness toward Cripps's departure, his mission ended as it had begun—with exaggerated hopes and meager results.

Cripps did little to dispel public misconceptions about his role in Anglo-Soviet relations. Quite the contrary, he identified himself completely with the war effort of the USSR. On Sunday, February 8, he addressed the nation over the radio, painting an image of the new world supposedly desired by all the Allies:

> We are anxiously reaching out to that time, when the new world for which the peoples are longing, and for which almost every man and woman is daily hoping, begins to show itself in clear outline on our horizon. Not the New Order of brutalised domination with which Hitler has sought to delude the people, but a world of new values, cleansed of the old evils and offering a full and free manhood to the people of every class, religion, nation, and colour—that practical ideal for which we equally as the people of Russia and of the occupied countries of Europe are in reality fighting, that hope which makes all our sacrifices seem worth while, that positive achievement which we are determined shall issue from this ghastly war, itself the brutal negation of every teaching of our Christian civilisation.

Cripps then suggested that in Great Britain both government and people were not giving their all for the war effort, which contrasted markedly, in his opinion, with the heroic feats of their Soviet allies. He asked his listeners "some simple questions":

> Can you do more than you are doing now to help the common cause? Are your hardships and sacrifices comparable to those of the Soviet citizens who are fighting your battle just as you are fighting their battle? Are you making a 100 per cent effort?
>
> I have felt in this country since my return a lack of urgency; I may be wrong but I feel in it the atmosphere in contrast to what I felt in Russia, I feel that we are not "all out" in our effort and determination.[25]

It is easy to see from this speech why Sir Stafford would later be known as "austerity Cripps." But in February 1942 his earnestness evidently struck the right chord among the British public, many of whom were disillusioned with their government's performance. "Mass Observation," a British opinion poll, noted that Cripps's speech sparked a "sensational effect" among the unusually high number of listeners.[26]

Responding to Cripps's new-found popularity, Churchill offered him the Ministry of Supply, without a seat in the War Cabinet. But Cripps, who was not oblivious to his changed political position, refused to accept this largely administrative job, which would have given him little say in policy-making. Cripps remained aloof from the government, criticizing its conduct of the war without being saddled with personal responsibility.

These tactics worked, and on February 23, Cripps entered the War Cabinet as lord privy seal and leader of the House. Cripps, whose left-wing credentials were impeccable, easily eclipsed Lord Beaverbrook as the darling of the pro-Soviets and continued advocating accession to Soviet demands. The party system remained in its wartime flux, and Cripps must have entertained hopes of leading a new party in the future—as had Beaverbrook before. Cripps told a correspondent from the newspaper of his constituency, "I don't propose, so long as I remain a member of this Government, to ally myself with any party or creed."[27]

Anthony Eden, whose political antennae were better developed than his diplomatic abilities, was also sensitive to the shifting political wind and wanted to "dish the Whigs," as it were. Eden's support came from the Left of the Conservative party, and he knew that considerable political advantage would accrue to the man seen as linking East and West. Now was the moment to strike. His memorandum to the Cabinet must be seen in this light. Eden also participated in a group called the "Anglo-Soviet public relations committee," "in order," as one Foreign Office memorandum said, "that there should be a responsible body dealing with the public aspects of Anglo-Soviet relations and that they should, if possible, steal the thunder of irresponsible left-wing bodies." But the experiment was unsuccessful, since, as the memorandum continued, "This the committee has . . . conspicuously failed to do."[28] Nevertheless, Eden remained undaunted by this setback; he was intellectually and politically committed to transforming Anglo-Soviet relations.

This is not to claim that the foreign secretary was an unrelievedly cynical opportunist, willing to sacrifice his principles and other people's independence and territory for temporary personal political gain. On the contrary, he had been convinced by Cripps, and by his talks with Stalin, that intimate Anglo-Soviet cooperation was possible if and only if the issue of the disputed territories could be settled beforehand. As with most people, Eden was able to convince himself that personal, political, and national advantage laid at the end of the same path. For Eden, domestic political realities simply made Cripps's arguments all the more compelling than they would have been had the mood in Britain been more hostile to the Soviet Union.

At a critical meeting on February 6, the War Cabinet considered the Soviet demands. On the previous day, they had decided to limit discussion to one question: how the Soviet position should be presented to President Roosevelt. In the end, the discussion ranged over the pros and cons of accepting the Soviet demands. Beaverbrook opened the talk with a strongly worded argument for acceptance. "Relations with Russia were deteriorating," he said, and something had to be done to check the slide. Also, he told his colleagues, "It was worth remembering that so far Russia had contributed far more to the war effort than the United States to whom we had made such frequent concessions." Therefore, excessive—in Beaverbrook's opinion—deference should not be paid to American scruples.

Eden agreed, using arguments he had employed frequently already. He asked his colleagues to look at "Anglo-Russian relations in their wider sense": "In this matter our part should be to reconcile the divergent points of view of Russia and the United States . . . such reconciliation was by no means out of the question. One way of doing it would be to accept M. Stalin's demand as it stood; subject, of course, to success in obtaining the acquiescence of the United States."

Clement Attlee, the lord privy seal and future Labour prime minister, evinced his distaste for the whole matter, saying that he "thought that the proposal outlined by the Foreign Secretary was dangerous and might, indeed, stultify the causes for which we were fighting." He said the whole question of territorial demands was "too reminiscent of what had been done in the last war" and that acceptance of Stalin's demands was "both wrong and inexpedient."

On this occasion, Churchill was able to convince most of his colleagues that Stalin's demands should be conveyed to Roosevelt, accompanied by a "balanced statement" from the British, pointing out both the pros and cons of acceptance. His own preference, he repeated, was "that all these matters should be settled at the Peace Conference." But he would agree, as a compromise measure, to submit the matter to Roosevelt.[29]

The prime minister, knowing perhaps that his views were not shared by a majority of the Cabinet, had deferred judgment and had promised to abide by the American president's decision, hoping that Roosevelt would side with him against accepting the Soviet demands. On the other hand, Eden had sensed victory and felt that the supposedly self-evident expediency of accepting Stalin's demands would convince the recalcitrant Roosevelt. Confident of success, he agreed to submit the matter to Washington.

One member of the War Cabinet was not at all pleased. Lord Beaverbrook wrote a sulky memorandum the day after the Cabinet meeting, attacking the decision to refer the problem to the United States. "This, in my judgement was a mistake—flinching from our clear responsibility," he wrote. He explained his opposition to the Cabinet's decision: "At the moment we entered into alliance with Russia, the past was all forgotten. No basis for a confident collaboration was possible, except that which recognised Russian territories as they stood at the moment when the German onslaught made the Russians our allies. The Baltic States are the Ireland of Russia. Their strategic control by Moscow is as essential to the Russians as the possession of the Irish bases would be valuable to us."[30]

Beaverbrook was sufficiently agitated over the matter to threaten the prime minister with a press campaign attacking Churchill's unwillingness to recognize Russia's 1941 frontiers. Attlee and Ernest Bevin, the minister of labour, were infuriated by Beaverbrook's high-handedness; the former even threatened to resign if Britain were to recognize the Soviets' territorial gains. In a paper he wrote in March, Beaverbrook later recalled the incident and presented a dubious and rather self-pitying justification for his February 18 resignation: "Attlee's resignation when in the wrong would have been more important than mine when in the right. For Attlee has a party, I have none. Attlee had political friends, I stand alone."[31]

In spite of the disgruntled Beaverbrook, Eden pressed ahead with the Cabinet's plans. On February 10, he dispatched a telegram to Lord Halifax, now Britain's ambassador in Washington, summing up Stalin's demands and asking Halifax to speak with the president. Eden confessed to being still a bit troubled by the proposed course: How could he assent to Stalin "without doing violence to the Atlantic Charter?" He continued: "If we cannot [accede to Stalin's claims], is it wise to offer Stalin a part, only, of what he wants? I am advised by Sir S. Cripps (and our experience of 1939, as you will remember, would tend to confirm this) that any appearance of haggling may only increase his suspicions. But I am apprehensive of the effect of a flat negative."[32]

Eden posited two alternative compromise formulas should the Americans find recognition of the USSR's frontiers unpalatable, either the Soviets might be granted the right to have bases in the Baltic States or they might be given a promise from the prime minister to support Soviet claims at the Peace Conference. Again showing signs of Cripps's influence, Eden wrote: "These two offers are based . . . on requirements of Russian 'security,' for which [the] Soviet Union have [sic] been striving ever since [the] 1917 Revolution in order that [the] Soviet Government may be enabled to complete [the] unfinished social and economic experiment within Russia without danger of foreign intervention or war." That a Conservative foreign minister could advance such an argument is evidence of a radical transformation of British opinion toward the USSR. The previous June Eden had argued that "politically Russia was as bad as Germany and half the country would object to being associated with her too closely."[33] By February he had become an almost complete convert to Cripps's views about Soviet Russia. Eden closed his telegram with the suggestion that President Roosevelt might want to join with Britain in extracting his own counterconcessions from Stalin in return for his sanction of Soviet territorial demands.[34] The foreign secretary sounded confident that President Roosevelt would yet see the light and cease being "exaggeratedly moral."

Eden's hopes proved premature. On February 17, Halifax met with President Roosevelt and then with Sumner Welles, the under secretary of state, and found the results disappointing. The president refused to be cornered, saying that he "thought that it was largely a question of interpretation but that it would be undesirable to get into too much detail at this stage which would involve us both in a secret treaty, [the] difficulties of which were obvious." This was discouraging, but Halifax cautioned that "the President was really thinking aloud and too much importance should not be attached to his indications of opinion at this stage." It looked as if Churchill's gamble had paid off: Roosevelt's initial inclination had been similar to the prime minister's own views.

Welles was even less inclined than the president to accept Stalin's demands outright. Halifax presented Eden's case faithfully, but the American appeared unmoved:

Welles said he must have time for reflection. He thought that it was [the] most important question of policy that had arisen and was fully alive to its urgency. . . . His first reaction was not to like either of your [Eden's] alternative suggestions—and he spoke about the necessity of building a new world on principle—if it was not again to crash sooner or later let us stick to the Atlantic Charter. If we gave away principles now, what would prevent an indefinite sequence of further Russian blackmail later? If we once started subordinating peoples to a regime they repudiated, we were sowing the seeds of trouble.

Referring to Stalin's argument that Soviet occupation of the Baltic States was a necessary buffer against a revanchist Germany, Welles continued: "He [Welles] sometimes looked forward to a divided Germany, which might minimise all these future dangers for which we were now being pressed to make [a] sacrifice of principle of doubtful expediency."[35] Halifax ended his account with a warning to Eden: "Neither he [Welles] nor the President was expressing anything but first reactions. . . . I think on this sort of thing Welles' advice, whatever it is, will finally prevail."

Having given Welles and the president time to ponder the problem, Halifax met with the two American leaders again on February 20. Clearly Welles's first reaction had prevailed, as Halifax told Eden: "After full consideration the President did not like either of your suggestions. He felt that both were difficult to reconcile with the Atlantic Charter, and that it was premature to attempt detailed treatment of the problem." The president proposed to talk with Maksim Litvinov, former Soviet commissar for foreign affairs, now ambassador to Washington, hoping that he might be able to reach some compromise solution with the Soviets.

Halifax, who knew the difficulties of dealing with the Soviets, suggested that Roosevelt might be underestimating the obstacles. He also pointed out that, if the president were to involve himself, this might put Eden in a bad light, since, as Halifax said, "It was with us and not with [the Americans] that Stalin wished to sign a treaty, although Stalin said that he understood the necessity of . . . referring to the Americans and would be glad to have their assent."[36]

After receiving this telegram, Eden met with Sir Alexander Cadogan and other Foreign Office officials to discuss what to do next. The foreign secretary was upset at being thwarted by President Roosevelt and vented his feelings at the meeting. Cadogan recorded the incident in his diary:

Meeting. . . . about Stalin's frontier demand. Americans are sticky about it—quite rightly. How funny A. [Eden] is! Because it fits in with his trip [to Moscow], he is quite prepared to throw to the winds all principles (Atlantic Charter) which he has not drafted. This amoral realpolitik line was never his. We shall make a mistake if we press the Americans to depart from principles, and a howler if we do it without them. But P.M. can be trusted to see to that![37]

On February 25, the War Cabinet discussed Halifax's telegram, and once again the familiar divisions surfaced. Churchill argued that Roosevelt's willingness to deal directly with the Soviets was "of advantage to us," because the president would undoubtedly urge a Soviet declaration of war on Japan. The deliberately vague Cabinet notes do not identify who responded to this remark, but the transcript notes that "the view was expressed" that "it would be particularly unfortunate if the United States tried to bargain agreement on this matter for a Russian declaration of war on Japan." The speaker was, most probably, Eden; at any rate, the foreign secretary argued that the president was "not aware of the difficulties" involved in dealing with the Kremlin.

In the end, despite Churchill's objections, the Cabinet authorized Eden to draft a note to Winant, the American ambassador.[38] He did so, and later the same evening he delivered the message to the Americans in which he argued that Roosevelt was "unduly optimistic." He warned that Stalin "will not be willing to discuss the rights and wrongs of the situation"—though how Eden knew this must be a matter of conjecture, since the record does not indicate that he ever tried such an approach during the Moscow talks.

As early as November, Eden had told the War Cabinet that Stalin must be given no grounds to fear an Anglo-American condominium. In the note he now handed to Winant, Eden claimed disingenuously that he hoped for a successful result from the Roosevelt-Litvinov talk. (In fact, had Roosevelt been successful, Eden's diplomacy would have looked inept.) But, he continued: "We fear that if the President were to argue this matter alone with M. Stalin, the latter might suspect that we had agreed to this procedure in order that the United States Government might bring pressure to bear upon him, and he might resent it accordingly."[39]

Eden's willingness to oppose Churchill openly over policy toward the USSR may have owed as much to personal reasons as to political conviction. Although Churchill was, and would remain, the British public's first choice as wartime prime minister,[40] many M.P.s thought that Churchill was slipping, and that holding the offices of prime minister, leader of the House of Commons, and minister of defence as he did, he was carrying too great a burden. Parliamentary discontent was given sharper focus when, on February 18, Beaverbrook resigned his War Cabinet post. The reasons for his resignation are unclear. As we have already seen, he later explained his actions as being prompted by dissatisfaction over the government's Soviet policies. Beaverbrook may have been trying to capitalize on Churchill's political embarrassment, making his own bid for the premiership.

If that was Beaverbrook's aim, his resignation was an unmitigated disaster. It forced Churchill to reshuffle his Cabinet, but Sir Stafford Cripps, not Lord Beaverbrook, was the beneficiary. The prime minister bowed to public opinion, resigning one of his own posts, leadership of the House, to Cripps, who thereby gained a seat in the War Cabinet.

According to Oliver Harvey, this move miffed Eden, who had been "rather bitten . . . with leading H. of C. as a stepping stone to being P.M. later. He [Eden] doesn't want Cripps to groom himself for P.M."[41] The foreign secretary must certainly have thought that the role of peacemaker between the Soviet Union and Great Britain would provide the exposure denied him by the Cabinet reshuffle.

For a while, Cripps was whispered about as a possible replacement for Churchill.[42] But an American observer astutely noted a flaw in Cripps's personality that would cripple his chances, in spite of his apparent popularity. Assessing the potential opposition to Churchill, Harriman wrote to President Roosevelt on March 6: "Cripps wears a hair shirt and wants everyone else to do the same. The British are prepared to make any sacrifice to get on with the war but are not interested in sacrifice for its own sake."[43] Although Cripps did not represent a long-term threat to Churchill's leadership, the prime minister had little cause for complacency. Unlike Roosevelt, who was secure in office between elections, Churchill faced the possibility of challenge to his authority throughout the war.

On February 26 Eden wrote Halifax that in order to prevent future Allied disagreements "all big political questions arising out of the war shall be dealt with by means of tripartite discussions." Eden continued, "The ideal forum for such tripartite discussions would be informal meetings between Mr. Winant, M. Maisky and Myself."[44] This would have been handy indeed. As foreign secretary, Eden would have carried more weight than the two ambassadors. He was determined both to dominate relations with Moscow and to exclude the meddlesome American president as far as possible.

In the meantime, Maiskii had been pestering the British for an answer to Stalin's demands. The continued successes of the Red Army contrasted unflatteringly with the poor performance of Britain's armed forces and seemed to many in Britain to entitle the USSR to her territorial claims, though why this should have been so is not entirely clear. It was at this time, on February 23, Stalin addressed the Red Army, speaking of the need to eject the Nazi invader from the Socialist homeland but not mentioning Anglo-American assistance and, when speaking of Germany, differentiating once again between the "Hitler clique" and the German people.[45] This last note sounded ominous in London. The Foreign Office considered, then rejected as unfounded, the notion that Stalin was preparing the groundwork for a separate peace. Alexander Cadogan pointed out, however, that "one must be uneasy with Stalin as an ally. He is always reinsuring."[46]

Stalin had in fact said nothing in his speech to the Red Army that he had not already said before. As early as July 1941 he had distinguished between the Nazis and the German people, and in his agreement with Britain of that month he had promised to sign no separate peace with "Hitlerite Germany." But Eden seized on the Soviet dictator's speech of February 23 to bolster his case for recognition of Soviet demands. In a telegram to Halifax, the foreign secretary warned that Stalin's tone might be signaling a "switchover to propaganda preparatory for separate peace with Germany, if so desired."[47] Eden was using the threat of a separate Russo-German peace to make his point, but he did not regard such a possibility as even remotely likely, as he admitted later.

The pressure was mounting on Churchill to accede to Stalin's demands. Because of the discouraging course of the war and his supposed reluctance to do more to help the Soviets, Churchill sensed he was facing an imminent revolt in his government. Cadogan noted that Churchill was "losing his grip," writing on March 4: "Poor old P. M. in a sour mood and in a bad way. I don't think he's well and I fear he's played out."[48]

Eden kept the heat on, writing a personal message to Churchill on March 6 to urge him to send a message to the president advocating strategic talks with Stalin. "But for such exchanges to take place with any chance of success," Eden wrote, "it is indispensable that we should first clear this frontier question out of the way. Otherwise Stalin will neither talk nor listen."

Churchill's defenses were exhausted, and on March 7 he gave in, dispatching a dispirited and curiously disjoint letter to Roosevelt:

> The increasing gravity of the war has led me to feel that the principles of the Atlantic Charter ought not to be construed so as to deny to Russia the frontiers she occupied when Germany attacked her. This

was the basis on which Russia acceded to the Charter, and I suspect that a severe process of liquidating hostile elements in the Baltic States, etc., was employed by the Russians when they took these regions at the beginning of the war. I hope therefore that you will be able to give us a free hand to sign the treaty which Stalin desires as soon as possible. Everything portends an immense renewal of the German invasion of Russia in the Spring and there is very little we can do to help the only country that is heavily engaged with the German armies.[49]

This was obviously a crucial telegram. Almost exactly two months previously, on January 8, Churchill had threatened resignation rather than accept Stalin's demands. In his postwar account Churchill is evasive about the reasons for his about-face. He claimed he was still opposed to acceptance, "but . . . under pressure of events, I did not feel that this moral position could be physically maintained. In a deadly struggle it is not right to assume more burdens than those who are fighting for a great cause can bear. My opinions about the Baltic States were, and are, unaltered, but I felt that I could not carry them forward at this time."[50] Writing in the postwar glow, Churchill was following his own famous advice by practicing "magnanimity."[51] Earlier in his book, however, Churchill acknowledges growing doubt among some M.P.s about his ability to remain in charge of Britain's war effort with undiminished authority. Churchill claims that such pressure came from those below ministerial rank and continues: "There was no whisper of intrigue or dissidence, either in the War Cabinet or in the much larger number of Ministers of Cabinet rank."[52]

If Churchill's account is accurate, then he must certainly have been anxious to retain the support of his ministerial colleagues. In the War Cabinet, however, only Clement Attlee and Ernest Bevin unreservedly sided with Churchill in strongly opposing Soviet demands. The others were, like Archibald Sinclair, either lukewarm to the idea of crossing the Soviets, or, like Eden and Cripps, adamantly in favor of placating Stalin. Churchill must have reasoned that, in the end, personal preferences must go by the boards, and that this was not an issue worthy of risking the breakup of his coalition government.

Another factor may have influenced Churchill's decision. As he said in the last line of his note to Roosevelt, the prime minister had information pointing to a renewed German assault against the Soviets in the spring, and this would bring with it further pressure to open a second front immediately. By bowing to Stalin's demands now, Churchill may have reasoned, he would in the future be able to resist American pressure to commit British forces in what he judged to be a premature assault on Nazi-occupied Europe. Churchill was walking a tricky tightrope: his moral sense opposed giving Stalin what he wanted, and yet at the same time he had to balance the interests of his allies against his personal inclinations. As one historian has commented, "At this juncture [Churchill] wanted neither to discourage his ally Stalin . . . nor to thwart his friend Roosevelt, who might give in to popular clamor to concentrate in the Pacific and abandon Atlantic First."[53] The clamor to emphasize the Pacific theater would have increased had the American public sensed British unwillingness to get on with the war against Hitler. Even though Churchill had excellent reasons for his reticence to open a second front, his arguments for delay would have carried little weight with an impatient American public thirsting for quick moves to win the war. By accepting Soviet political demands, indeed by going further in this respect than Washington was prepared to go, Churchill was trying to preempt American calls to do more for the Soviets. Such a policy, though hardly ideal, might at least have the benefit of avoiding what Churchill feared most, another Paschendaele.

Transatlantic Quarrel

Churchill was overly optimistic in his attempt to defer American demands for the opening of a second front in Europe. On March 9, influenced by General Marshall, Roosevelt sent his first suggestion for the opening of a second front during the summer of 1942 to his friend, the "Former Naval Person": "I am becoming more and more interested in the establishment of a new front this Summer on the European continent," the president wrote, "certainly for air and raids. . . . And even though losses will doubtless be great, such losses will be compensated by at least equal German losses and by compelling Germans to divert large forces of all kinds from Russian fronts."[54]

Roosevelt's talk of a second front may have been meant as a partial alternative to accepting Stalin's demands, which he opposed. Delivering the prime minister's note on March 8, Halifax spoke with the president who, as the ambassador later told the Foreign Office, "professed [the] strong conviction that we need not be afraid of Russia quitting the war on

this. He stressed the difficulty of [the] United States concurring in action
that you [Churchill] desire to take and the danger of our proceding alone—
a fact which would surely come out." But Roosevelt's was not the princi-
pled opposition of Sumner Welles:

> [The President's] mind is already (?moving) along the only remaining
> line, i.e. of saying to Stalin that we all recognise his need for security,
> that to put anything on paper now is impossible and would lead to
> dangerous explosive opinion here [in the United States], that [the]
> future of [the] Baltic States clearly depends upon Russian military
> progress, and that if during or after the war the Russians re-occupy the
> Baltic States, neither [the] United States nor Great Britain would or
> could turn them out. Why then should Stalin worry?[55]

Foreign Office reactions to Roosevelt's attitude were divided. Sir Orme
Sargent wrote that the president had misunderstood British reasoning;
London was not worried about the possibility that Stalin might sign a
separate peace. The "main point" behind giving in to the Soviets was "to
get into real contact with the Russians on the conduct of the war." Beaverbrook had tried to gain the same elusive Soviet trust back in October 1941
by holding a "Christmas tree party," handing out Anglo-American goodies
to Stalin. That angle had not worked, Sargent and those who agreed with
him reasoned, so Stalin's paranoia must be deeper than first thought. If
material aid could not do the trick, perhaps a gift of little nations would.

Sir Alexander Cadogan opposed this drift in British thinking. On March
10, he wrote:

> If we *knew* that compliance with Stalin's demands wd. make an
> essential difference to his conduct of the war, would ensure his loyal
> and intimate consultation and cooperation with us and would not
> merely lead to further demands, I should say that we could risk
> trouble in America. But, personally, I feel little assurance on any of
> these points, and I shd. be very much afraid of getting the worst of
> both worlds. Rightly or wrongly we decided to consult the U.S. (I
> don't see how we could have avoided it), and I shd. take it as
> axiomatic that we can only go ahead on lines agreed with them.[56]

Cadogan was swimming against the tide. The foreign secretary had long
ago vanquished any doubts he might have felt about acceding to Stalin's
demands. On March 9 Eden sent Halifax a telegram asking him, if possible, to dissuade Roosevelt from his intention to speak directly with Litvi-

nov, and the next day the foreign secretary followed this with another telegram written after he had read Halifax's communication of the eighth, which had recounted the president's latest attitude toward the Baltic question. This message is interesting, showing as it does Eden's true reasons for wanting to accept Stalin's demands. Addressing Halifax, the foreign secretary wrote:

> You have reported that [the] President holds [the] firm conviction that Russia would not quit the war on this matter. This leads us to fear that [the] President does not grasp the real reason for the importance which we attach to giving Stalin [a] satisfactory answer. . . . We regard it of highest importance at this stage of the war to leave nothing undone which would enable us to get into real contact with Stalin, to exchange ideas with him freely on all subjects connected with the conduct of the war and thus give ourselves maximum chance of securing that [the] Soviet Government should pay some attention to our views and those of [the] United States Government. To take one example alone, we cannot conceive that Stalin will enter the war against Japan, or would pay the slightest attention to suggestions from us that he should consider doing so, until his demands are out of the way.

Eden did not, however, make acceptance of Stalin's demands contingent upon a Soviet declaration of war against Japan by a certain date, as we have already seen, nor would he do so at any time. Eden called the present lack of consultation with Stalin "deplorable" and thought it the "height of unwisdom" to "deprive ourselves of establishing such contacts by refusing to admit Stalin's claims to the Baltic States." Eden was nettled by Roosevelt's arguments against acceptance. After all, the president had never met Stalin, whereas he, Eden, had done so and could claim greater knowledge of the man. The foreign secretary continued:

> [The] President's reply amounts to saying that we rather hope Russia will not regain the Baltic States but recognise that we could not do anything about it if she did. This will surely appear to Stalin so uncollaborative a state of mind as to confirm his suspicion that he can expect no real consideration for Russian interests from ourselves or the United States; that we wish Russia to continue fighting purely for British and American ends; and that we would not mind seeing Russia and Germany mutually exhaust each other. This would confirm [the]

natural Russian inclination to have no regard for anything but Russia's own interests and would make impossible any fruitful collaboration with Russia at this critical juncture.[57]

In the meantime, as Eden was telling Halifax how to instruct the president, Churchill, off his own bat, dispatched an extraordinary note to Stalin on March 9. As well as assuring the general secretary that British supplies would continue in undiminished volume and that the British air campaign against Germany would be renewed with increased ferocity as the spring weather improved, Churchill made an astonishing gaffe. He wrote: "I have sent a message to President Roosevelt urging him to approve our signing the agreement with you about the frontiers of Russia at the end of the war."[58] Cadogan was aghast: Churchill's note would appear in Washington as an attempt to force the president's hand. Hitherto, the debate over Soviet demands had been a closed affair between the two democracies. Now Churchill was informing Stalin that only Roosevelt blocked British recognition of the Soviets' claims. Eden had known of Churchill's intention to send the note but had failed to inform Cadogan, an omission for which the foreign secretary later felt compelled to apologize.[59] Eden did not want the president's intervention to derail his policy.

But if Roosevelt was actually upset by Churchill's note to Stalin, he kept his objections to himself. There is no evidence to suggest that the president took any notice. He was, however, angered by the activity of another member of the War Cabinet. Sir Stafford Cripps gave an interview to the *Daily Mail* on March 7 and had allowed publication in *Life* magazine in the United States. Cripps told readers that the Baltic States had once belonged to Tsarist Russia and had been snatched away from the Bolsheviks "expressly . . . to weaken that country strategically." He did not mention anything about national self-determination or about Soviet recognition of these independent countries in the interwar years. Cripps, whose inclination to argue the Soviet cause seemed actually to increase in proportion to his distance from Moscow, continued: "To protect Leningrad it is essential that the Russians should control the Gulf of Finland and the Baltic coast; it is also necessary that there should not exist small States close to the vital points of Soviet industry which can be made use of by hostile powers as a base for attack." Cripps assured *Life*'s readers that "The Soviet Government has no intention, and of this I am certain, to demand anything more in the way of territorial aggrandisement." Sir Stafford prophesied that "The Russians would not . . . attempt to impose any specific economic system upon the Germans provided they give up their allegiance to Hitler. . . . This I can say with certainty . . . that the Russians do not want to interfere with the internal affairs of other countries." Showing that his stint in Moscow had done little to dull his left-wing edge, Sir Stafford denied that the inefficiencies of Communist organization or the chaos caused by Stalin's terror had hampered the Soviet war effort. Quite the contrary, according to Cripps: "In fact, the war has shown that [the Soviets] are the only people of Europe who have been able to meet the blitz tactics of Hitler with success." Surely, Cripps argued, this was a resounding affirmation of the need for planned economies.[60]

Meeting with Halifax on March 12, Roosevelt objected to the tone of Cripps's interview. Welles, who was present, complained that "this . . . looked rather like trying to force the hand of the United States Government." But once Cripps's interview was published, there was little the Americans could do, and the discussion turned to other matters. In spite of Halifax's protestations that if Roosevelt were to speak directly with the Soviets this would be "in the highest degree embarrassing" for Eden, the president persisted in his original intention of meeting with Litvinov. Speaking with Halifax after the meeting, Welles made no secret of his intention to oppose Stalin's demands to the end. In Halifax's account, "[Welles] is strongly opposed to the President using the argument to Litvinov about Stalin being able to hold the Baltic States after the war if he gets them whatever the United States or we may feel, and he will do his best to prevent the President following this line when he sees him early tomorrow."[61] Welles's appeal to the president to take a stand against the Soviet demands on principle won the under secretary few friends in London. Dredging up the worst epithet he could imagine, Harvey wrote that Welles "is another Wilson only 20 years out of date."[62]

Welles's arguments evidently had the desired effect on the president who, when he met Litvinov later on March 12, did not hint that a Soviet fait accompli at the end of the war would get Stalin what he wanted. Instead, Roosevelt "made it clear that he was somewhat put out by the fact that Stalin had not approached him directly. . . ." The president said that, "under no conditions would he subscribe to any secret treaty. Nor could he subscribe to any open public treaty with regard to definite frontiers until the war had been won." The president assured Litvinov that Stalin had no reason to fear that the United States would support a postwar settlement leaving the USSR vulnerable to renewed German attack "ten or fifteen years after the war." The U.S. government would, the president stated, support any "legitimate steps" designed to protect Soviet security, "solely provided that these steps were in reality based on the legitimate needs of the Russian people for their security." The president frequently used the term "legitimate," leaving the Soviets to guess what he meant.[63]

The Foreign Office reacted rabidly to the news of this meeting. The author of one memorandum called Roosevelt's approach "pitifully inadequate" and opined that "it is very unfortunate that Mr. Welles should have restrained the president from mentioning the only sensible idea which he seems to have had in his head." Sir Orme Sargent chimed in, writing that Roosevelt

> intends that we shall have no independent policy in Europe if he can prevent it and that when he applies his veto he intends that it shall be obeyed. Unless therefore Stalin saves the situation by withdrawing his demand, we shall find ourselves forced to decide whether we will use this as an occasion for asserting our independence or whether by submitting to the President's wishes [*sic*] ruling we will abandon our liberty of action in regard to our future relations with the Soviet Government.

Anthony Eden added his own opinion in this peculiar outburst of hyperbole. He called Roosevelt's performance "a dismal tale of clumsy diplomacy."[64]

Some insight into the reasons for this extraordinary reaction (the language was much more immoderate than that used to discuss quarrels with the Soviet Union) is provided by an entry in Harvey's diary, where he wrote: "Whilst F. D. R. can legitimately claim that we should decide nothing without consultation with him, he cannot properly claim that he can over-rule our foreign policy or deny us a foreign policy at all. Russia and we were allies before USA came in. We are both Europeans and nearer the German menace."[65] The British wanted things both ways: they were pleased to elicit American opinions, but only so long as Washington accepted British faits accomplis.

Britain had stood alone against Nazi Germany for a year, and, although their prospects for ultimate victory had been slimmer during this time than they were in 1942, there had been a certain freedom of action in being alone. American entry into the war made the British cause much stronger, but British diplomats resented the fact that their new transatlantic allies would not accept junior status. Why such resentment was never leveled at the Soviets—who, after all, were far more demanding and less approachable than the Americans—is one of the curious aspects of wartime diplomacy. Later in the war, the Americans would reciprocate this attitude, often being more suspicious of the British than the Soviets. It was as if the ease with which the two democracies generally cooperated bred contempt, whereas the inaccessibility of the Soviets somehow made them more enigmatic and therefore attractive.

Churchill, for his part, felt uneasy with the decision to accept Stalin's demands, which he nevertheless felt must be met, and he understood Roosevelt's hesitations more easily than did the Foreign Office. To try to overcome the president's doubts, the prime minister asked his friend Lord Beaverbrook, a true believer, to go to Washington to present the best possible British case. Beaverbrook left Britain by sea on March 20.

The Soviets were apparently far less agitated by Roosevelt's meeting with Litvinov than were the British. When Eden spoke to Maiskii on March 17, in Eden's words Maiskii "seemed resolved not to take a tragic view of the President's attitude."[66] Stalin could use the occasion of the Anglo-American tiff to drive a wedge between his two allies. In his reply to Roosevelt, Stalin simply said that the Soviet government "had taken note of [the president's] communication." And, as Maiskii told Eden when the two met again on March 23, the Soviet government had not solicited the American opinion, only wishing to consult with London in this matter. Churchill's airing of the Anglo-American rift was bearing bitter fruit;[67] his note to Stalin had confirmed for the Soviets the Anglo-American difference of opinion. The Kremlin could afford to ignore Roosevelt's objections, secure in the knowledge that the prime minister was not only prepared to accept Soviet frontier claims but also that Churchill had urged Roosevelt to concur.

In the meantime, as the Foreign Office fumed, President Roosevelt evidently had enjoyed his foray into relations with the Soviet Union. The president became the next in the long, monotonous line of Western statesmen who thought they alone possessed the secret for managing Stalin. On March 18 Roosevelt wrote a particularly fatuous note to Churchill: "I know you will not mind my being brutally frank when I tell you that I think I can personally handle Stalin better than your Foreign Office or my State Department. Stalin hates the guts of all your top people. He thinks he likes me better and I hope he will continue to do so."[68] This was the beginning of Roosevelt's disastrous courtship of the Soviet dictator. The situation was not, however, without its comic aspect: while the Foreign Office was busily denouncing Roosevelt for his allegedly Neanderthal attitude to the

Soviet "experiment," across the ocean, the president was confidently writing that the Foreign Office was out of touch with Moscow's mood.

While Roosevelt was dreaming of the possibilities of single-handedly reversing Soviet foreign policy, Stalin responded to Churchill's note of March 9. On March 14 Stalin wrote: "As to paragraph one of your message—concerning the frontiers of the USSR—I think we shall have to exchange views on the text of an appropriate treaty, if it is approved for signing by both parties."[69] The draft agreement worked out between the British and Soviets in Moscow might need more work, Stalin was saying. The British had accepted in principle Soviet absorption of the Baltic States; now Stalin was reserving his options to press for more.

Soviet willingness to play the two democratic allies off against each other left the British with a knotty problem. As Cadogan recorded in his diary on March 23: "Maisky told A.[Eden] of Soviet reaction to U.S. communication about Stalin's demands. It amounts to 'Thank you very much for the information' and a renewal of the demand to us! Just what I feared. A. will want to go ahead. I shall have to resist."[70] A Foreign Office meeting the next day was all Cadogan had feared. He wrote: "Meeting with A. and others about Russia. I had to go into opposition. I'm sure its all wrong in view of President's attitude, to give Stalin all he asks. A. evidently annoyed, but I can't help that."[71] The general direction of Foreign Office thinking can be seen from this entry.

The War Cabinet meeting the next day, March 25, was decisive. Eden argued that "he thought the best course was to explain our difficulties to the United States Government and say that we felt bound to go ahead with the negotiations [with Russia]." The foreign secretary felt that "delay was dangerous." His arguments won the day, and the War Cabinet concluded that they "had taken all possible steps to consult the United States Government on this matter" and just hoped that, after the British proceded to sign an agreement with Stalin, Roosevelt "would not take any step that indicated a marked divergence of view."[72] The British resented the fact that Roosevelt tried to block their recognition of Soviet conquests—even though they had sought the president's opinion—and now the War Cabinet decided to forge ahead without American support, all the while hoping that Roosevelt would not air Anglo-American differences in public.

The next day, Eden transmitted the Cabinet's decision to Lord Halifax in Washington. Eden wrote that, since Stalin's answer to Roosevelt had left the British with a choice, they had decided to proceed along the course begun during the Moscow Conference. He continued:

I fully realise that the President will not like it if we now tell Stalin that we are prepared to go ahead with our treaty negotiations on the basis of his frontier claims, and that in doing so we shall be creating trouble for him with his public opinion. Had circumstances been more favourable I should have naturally wished to spare him this embarrassment, but things being as they are I cannot take the risk of keeping Anglo-Russian relations in a state of suspended animation any longer.

In a second telegram, Eden justified the British course:

This country, as a European Power for whom collaboration with a victorious U.S.S.R. after the war will be essential, cannot afford to neglect any opportunity of establishing intimate relations of confidence with Stalin. Fact is that at present time there is no frank discussion with Russians at all on major questions concerning conduct of the war. However unreasonably, Russians take the attitude that [the] question of Stalin's demand must be cleared out of way before such frank relations can exist.

Eden asked Halifax to speak with the president, to ask him to "abstain from any overt action which would indicate that there is any divergence of opinion between us." At any rate, Eden argued, this was not a matter for a major rift, since "looked at from the practical point of view the concession which we are called upon to make does not involve us in any onerous commitment."[73] Eden took an irreversible step two days later, when he told Maiskii of the British intention to press ahead without American support, "to conclude with [the Soviets] a treaty on the lines discussed between M. Stalin and myself in Moscow."[74]

The Americans learned of the War Cabinet's decision on March 30, three days after Eden spoke with Maiskii. Halifax, meeting with Welles, presented Eden's arguments faithfully but made an odd admission when he confessed to a hint of doubt: "For my own part I recognised, as I had no doubt did the Cabinet, the difficulty of understanding Stalin's insistence on any purely logical grounds." Referring to the Soviet Union's alleged years of paranoia, supposedly the result of capitalist encirclement, Halifax drew on a dubious source, former American Ambassador Joseph Davies's *Mission to Moscow*, to support his argument that the USSR must be assured of security and equality among the great powers if it were ever to rejoin the family of nations.[75] Welles accepted the unwelcome news quietly.

By this time Beaverbrook had arrived in Washington. Halifax told the

Foreign Office that he had met with Beaverbrook "and put him wise" about the Cabinet's decisions made while he was at sea, so that Beaverbrook would be well informed to meet the president later that day. Halifax also told Eden that he had been less than candid when he spoke with Welles the day before. He had not told the American about Eden's talk with Maiskii, since "I think he, and probably the President will be surprised at your having said so much to Maisky before hearing the President's reactions."[76] Hearing this, Eden hurried to ask Halifax not to tell the Americans the details of his meetings with Maiskii, instead asking the ambassador simply to say that the Soviets had been informed of the British position.

When Beaverbrook met the president, he did not belabor the Baltic issue. Beaverbrook's biographer mistakenly attributes this to the fact that he took up the question of a second front as being a larger and more attractive cause with which to captivate Britain's shop stewards. Although there may be some truth in this, surely the main reason Beaverbrook did not press the president about accession to Soviet demands is that the War Cabinet had already decided to act unilaterally. What was left to discuss?[77] According to Beaverbrook's standard procedure, the Foreign Office was left guessing about the content of his talks with the president—Beaverbrook sent them no record.

Halifax met with Sumner Welles the next afternoon, April 1, recording that the "general atmosphere was sorrowful, but much less resentful than I had feared." Roosevelt had not changed his mind, though he would make no public display of opposition, Welles said. But, he told Halifax, "[Roosevelt] could certainly indicate no approval, and it must be expected that this silence would be construed as disapproval." The president felt that the whole scheme was ill-advised and that surrendering to Stalin's claim to the Baltic States "would only encourage further demands." The president had instructed Welles to insist on one condition in return for American quiescence: "It would be helpful from the point of view of the Atlantic Charter and United States public opinion," Halifax summarized Welles's remarks, "if you could get some stipulation inserted, whereby, when Russia was again able to take over these countries, Stalin would agree that any people who wished to emigrate could be entitled to do so with their property. This should also apply to the parts of Finland and East Poland that might be concerned." On the Foreign Office copy of this telegram, Churchill penned "Surely this is right!" next to the passage above. Evidently, he still felt uneasy with the whole matter.

In conversation with Welles, Halifax correctly predicted that the Soviets would object to such a condition being attached to the treaty. He told Welles: "I anticipated that Stalin would think that acceptance of it would be destructive of his main case." How could the Soviets admit that people wanted to leave the Soviet Union—much less removing their personal property—without revealing how bogus the Baltic States' plebiscites, voting to enter the USSR, had been?[78]

Now that the decision had been made to press on without the Americans, the Foreign Office concentrated on two points: what the treaty with the USSR should actually contain and how best to sell Soviet occupation of the territories in question to the American public.

On April Fool's Day, a weighty group of Foreign Office officials met to discuss the second problem. (It was only the first of many such meetings; the Foreign Office file dealing with how Britain should present her case in America is over an inch thick.) All present knew that Britain's recognition of the USSR's 1941 boundaries would not set well with the American public, whose opinion was considered vital, however backward and unreasoningly anti-Communist it seemed. The British hoped to present the War Cabinet's decision to sign the treaty with the Soviets in such a light that it would not appear to violate America's war aims as enunciated in the Atlantic Charter—a prodigious feat. With this in mind, the Foreign Office group agreed that "the less said about the Atlantic Charter the better, and in particular no play should be made with the plebiscites which had been held in the Baltic States." The group felt that six main points should be stressed to the American public: (1) Soviet demands were "essentially modest compared with what they might have asked"; (2) Soviet domination of the Baltic was preferable to German; (3) "the Baltic States were bound to fall under the domination of any victorious great power in Eastern Europe"; (4) "the Soviet treatment of national minorities had been excellent in the cultural field. Stalin had personally been responsible for this policy, and it would now be applied to the Baltic States"; (5) Anglo-Soviet wartime cooperation was "vital," and this treaty would facilitate friendly relations; (6) "the Communist bogey was far more dangerous if the Russian demands were not met than if they were."

The group had discussed only propaganda dealing with Soviet gains in Finland and with the annexation of the Baltic States. As for Soviet conquests in the southwest, "it was felt that nobody was particularly interested in Bessarabia, and that point could be more or less ignored."

A decision had been made that the American public must be hoodwinked. American voters were not as sophisticated as the assembly of realists in the Foreign Office; consequently, the Soviet Union must be made to look a legitimate and worthy ally if Nebraskan doubts were to be overcome. The American public could not, it was felt, digest the complex workings of wartime diplomacy. It would not be enough to claim simply that British power was limited and that the Soviet Union was a necessary, if distasteful, partner in the Grand Alliance. Instead, the public would be told that things were not as bad in the Soviet Union as many had thought before the war. No need to worry about Soviet conquests, the Foreign Office was claiming; after all, Stalin had personally guaranteed cultural autonomy for each and every nationality within the USSR. The prewar distrust of Soviet aggressiveness had been merely a "bogey"—once, that is, Stalin's demands were met.

Toward the end of the war, and indeed after May 1945, as it became clear to the Foreign Office that Stalin's conception of the postwar world was radically different from Britain's, public opinion would not easily be turned around. Lying to the public—or at least twisting the truth out of shape—was a mistake of the first magnitude.

One must remember, when reading these proposals, that the British Left had long seen the Foreign Office as the main stumbling block in the path of Anglo-Soviet cooperation. Indeed, in November 1940 Cripps had told the American ambassador in Moscow, Laurence Steinhardt, that the Foreign Office "were so hostile to the Soviet Union that they would prefer to risk the Empire rather than permit a rapprochement to take place."[79] When Cripps had made this remark, there had been some truth in the accusation, as an entry in Cadogan's diary shows. Referring to Eden's return to the Foreign Office in late 1940, Cadogan wrote, "Glad to find A[nthony Eden] not 'ideological' [about the USSR] and quite alive to the uselessness of expecting anything from these cynical, blood-stained murderers."[80] By April 1942 Cadogan had become no less skeptical about the prospects of general cooperation with Moscow. He was, however, only a civil servant, not an elected official. Nine months of alliance with the Soviet Union had seen a change of opinion where it counted most: the foreign secretary returned from his visit to Moscow convinced that Britain must do everything in its power to win Soviet trust. Others had failed in working with the Kremlin, Eden reasoned, because they had been "exaggeratedly moral." In the future, no one would be able to fault him with that.

On April 5 Eden submitted a draft treaty to the War Cabinet, which included the statement that the British government took "full regard" of "the desire of the U.S.S.R. for the restoration of its frontiers violated by the Hitlerite aggression." This was much the same wording upon which Stalin had insisted in December. For the time being—also as agreed in Moscow—the treaty draft left the Russo-Polish border dispute in abeyance, a simmering problem. Eden also suggested that, since Molotov had accepted an invitation to the United States, the foreign commissar should be prevailed upon to visit London en route, to sign the proposed Anglo-Soviet treaty.[81] On April 8 the War Cabinet discussed and approved the foreign secretary's proposals.[82]

In four short months the British government had reversed the position it had held since June 1940: a tenacious refusal to recognize Moscow's gains made, in Churchill's words, "in shameful collusion with Hitler." From shortly after Cripps's arrival in Moscow until March 1942, the disputed territories—especially the Baltic States—had been one of the central questions of dispute in Anglo-Soviet relations. Now the British government, owing to the determined efforts of Eden, had accepted Stalin's arguments and reversed its position. And, in doing so, they sided with the Soviets against their American allies.

In fact, there was more than a little contempt among the British for the supposedly unsophisticated attitude of the Americans. On April 11 Halifax wrote an assessment of the likely impact in the United States of an Anglo-Soviet agreement including recognition of Russia's territorial gains. The ambassador wrote that the proposed treaty would be attacked by "the great mass of the people who are strongly sentimental and vaguely idealistic" and by "isolationists and professional anti-Britishers." Liberals "who, though they may profess to admire Russia, are even more attached to the Wilsonian ideals of self-determination," might also not bow unquestioningly to the force of the British case.[83]

Nor were all members of the Foreign Office inclined to accept Roosevelt's proviso that all those wishing to emigrate from the territories in question be allowed to do so. In a memorandum written on April 11, Mr. Warner reminded his colleagues that such measures were unnecessary since "under the Soviet Constitution of 1936 the constituent republics enjoy a considerable degree of local autonomy, cultural and otherwise." To be fair, such sentiments—though not specifically contradicted—represented the minority opinion. The majority view is best reflected in the sheepish comment by the author of one memorandum who wrote that, when it came to selling the treaty to the public, "the more window dressing we had the better."[84] Evidently, even archrealists have their moments of doubt.

CHAPTER SEVEN

TRIUMPH OF

ACCOMMODATION?

APRIL–JUNE 1942

In the spring of 1942, the British, and more exactly Anthony Eden, were about to confront a vexing problem. The attempt to buy Stalin's friendship by recognizing the legitimacy of his territorial demands was doomed to failure from the start. The Soviets and the British were at cross purposes, as would become clear by the time Molotov arrived in London on May 21.

Eden hoped to achieve three positive results by acquiescing to Stalin. First, he wished to prevent a separate Russo-German peace. The Foreign Office did not regard such a peace as likely, but, as Sir Alexander Cadogan warned, one could never be sanguine with an ally like Stalin. Second, he hoped that recognizing Soviet sovereignty over the disputed territories would limit the future Soviet appetite for conquest while inclining the Kremlin toward making counterconcessions to the British. Eden had developed this theme in his memorandum of January 28 to the War Cabinet:

> Superficially this demand [for recognition of his 1941 boundaries] is very reasonable when we recall how much M. Stalin might have asked for. . . . It may, of course, be argued that we have no right to suppose that M. Stalin's present demand is final, and that it will be followed in due course by others. But, even so, the fact that we had granted this demand would not prevent us from resisting further demands which he might subsequently make. Indeed it would strengthen our position for doing so.[1]

Eden's third and most important reason for accommodating Stalin was, as he stated at the time but failed to mention in his memoirs, to gain Stalin's trust. Acknowledging the influence of Sir Stafford Cripps, the foreign secretary wrote in his January memorandum that Stalin regarded the frontier issue as "the acid test" for judging the sincerity of Britain's friendship. Two months later, in a telegram to Halifax on March 10, Eden wrote that the object of gaining Stalin's confidence was "the real reason for the importance which we attach to giving Stalin [a] satisfactory answer."[2] In the same telegram the foreign secretary specifically denied that British motives were primarily to prevent a separate Russo-German peace.

British goals were grand enough, but the outcome would depend upon what Stalin made of this display of British good will. For the London government, recognizing Soviet sovereignty over the disputed territories was a genuine concession. Although some in the Foreign Office were enamored of the Soviet Union, and were therefore enthusiastic about extending recognition, most British leaders, certainly Churchill, felt that under more favorable circumstances it would be best to deny the Baltic States to the Soviet Union. The misconception underlying British policy— and on this point Eden had completely fooled himself, as had Churchill to a lesser extent—was that the Soviets would see British acquiescence in the same light as they saw it themselves, that is, as a sacrifice of principle. The Soviets would not. During his visit to London in late May, Molotov would claim that it was his government, not the British, that had made "a great concession on their part" by leaving the Russo-Polish border question open for the moment.

By recognizing the *legitimacy* of Stalin's claims and by refusing to question the spuriousness of the Soviet-run plebiscites in Estonia, Latvia, and Lithuania, the British had not bolstered their bargaining position, as Eden had confidently predicted, but had actually undercut it. Having decided to avoid an unseemly and possibly damaging wrangle with their ally over the legitimacy of Communist goals, the British could not easily turn around and claim compensation for a concession of principle. Furthermore, in his future dealings with his Anglo-American Allies, Stalin would now feel free to cloak his distinctly undemocratic designs in the trappings of democratic phrasing, without fear of contradiction.

Eden should have anticipated future difficulties when he presented the two draft treaties to Maiskii on April 13. (There were two separate drafts, one military and one political.) The Soviet ambassador was noncommittal and unenthusiastic about the British documents. He immediately pounced on the wording of article 1 in the political draft. It read that the two parties "Undertake that, in the settlement of post war questions connected with the organisation of peace and security in Europe, they will act by mutual agreement and in concert with the other States concerned."[3] The Soviet

Union would surely not want the Balkan States nor Poland to interfere in such important matters as the organization of security in postwar Europe. Besides, did this talk of "the other States concerned" include the defunct governments of Estonia, Latvia, and Lithuania? Maiskii sensed a trick. Eden rushed to assure his guest that the reference to other states was intended to include only the United States.

The British drafts also included two other points the impact of which Eden tried to soften. The first concerned the frontiers of Poland. In his draft, Eden had diluted the wording that Stalin had proposed on December 18. Instead of merely referring to both parties' desire for security, and for the restoration of the USSR's "frontiers violated by Hitler's aggression," Eden included the phrase "in accordance with the two principles of not seeking territorial aggrandisement for themselves and of non-interference in the internal affairs of other nations." Also, the foreign secretary had added, "It is understood that the reference to the frontiers of the Union of Soviet Socialist Republics . . . does not affect the frontier with Poland." Eden told Maiskii, rather apologetically, that this was the best method for handling the tricky Polish problem, since "while all Poles might not be reasonable people, I was most anxious not to make any difficulties with General Sikorski and Count Raczyinski."

The second point Eden felt he had to explain was article 4, included upon President Roosevelt's insistence, stating that after the war people, along with their "movable property," should be allowed to leave those territories that had, or would, change hands dating from "1st January, 1938." Eden told the ambassador that he "hoped very much" that the Soviet government would accept this provision as it would help soothe American public opinion.[4] The foreign secretary was evidently oblivious to the fact that, by making this article appear solely as a sop to the Americans, he was not facilitating its acceptance by Moscow.

The talk had not been as cordial as Eden might have hoped, especially as the British were giving the Soviets most of their demands. But then Maiskii had no real authority, and his captiousness could be dismissed as a healthy unwillingness to put his neck on the line. One had to be cautious as a Soviet diplomat, since Moscow could find grounds for objection in even the most apparently favorable treaty.

Three days later, Maiskii returned with further objections about wording. Although he assured Eden that he had not yet received an official response from Moscow, Maiskii nevertheless, in Eden's words, "put me through a catechism on the draft texts of our treaties." The ambassador's objections were similar to those he had raised on April 13, but naturally more refined, since he had now had time to study the documents. He added one more point: Why should there be a confederation of states in Central, Eastern, and South-Eastern Europe while there was no corresponding arrangement in Western Europe or Scandinavia?

Eden could hardly voice the real reason, that these confederations were needed to offset Soviet power in Eastern Europe. At any rate, Maiskii surely knew this. The foreign secretary dodged an answer, saying "I hardly thought that confederation in the West was as likely." Eden then did a rather curious thing. Apparently without prompting from Maiskii, judging from Eden's own record of the talk, he told the ambassador, "I would like to put his Excellency unofficially a suggestion which had occurred to me." He referred to the article in the draft political treaty guaranteeing the right of emigration for those who did not wish to remain under Soviet rule after the war. "While I understood that the Soviet Government might be reluctant to embody any such a declaration in the treaty itself," Eden said, "they might not have the same objection to making it simultaneously but separately, more especially since I understood that such a declaration would be consistent with the terms of the Soviet Constitution itself." Eden suggested that Maiskii's "Government might feel able, at the time of the signature of the treaty, to make [this] declaration either in the form of a letter from the Ambassador to me or by some other method."[5]

This was very strange. So far in the two talks Maiskii had not questioned this particular article, though he had objected to much else. In both conversations Eden had raised the issue himself, thereby implying that he did not feel comfortable with Roosevelt's proviso. The foreign secretary's motives are hard to fathom. Perhaps anticipating a hostile reception in the Kremlin, he was simply suggesting an alternative in advance. Eden's extraordinary behavior was, however, probably prompted by nothing more than wounded amour propre, a reluctance to follow Washington's lead. He had resented what he felt to be Roosevelt's "intrusion" into Anglo-Soviet relations. Eden's memoirs shed further light on this attitude: "I accepted the fact that the United States must in time become the dominant partner in Anglo-American councils. In 1942 this was not so. . . . I had to judge how far in meeting [the problems of Anglo-Russian relations] I could, at the Foreign Office, insist on my point of view, how far be unreservedly for Mr. Churchill in his sentiment for his transatlantic allies."[6] Eden also refused to be sentimental about the travails of the Baltic States' inhabitants. His object was to gain Stalin's trust, and embarrassing articles foisted upon him by Washington implying that the Soviet Union was a rapacious power would certainly not help.

American opinion was a persistent problem for the Foreign Office, though it was felt that the ill effects that signature of the proposed treaty might create in America could be assuaged by proper presentation and lively propaganda. On April 19 Eden telegraphed Halifax saying that, in his opinion, extensive publicity of the Anglo-Soviet treaty would be harmful; but in all events, when the story finally came out, as come out it must, it should be fed first to the press in Britain, "in order," as Eden wrote, "that it may be sent from here by American correspondents and radio commentators in this country after they have received guidance." In a second telegram to the British Embassy in Washington, Eden outlined the nature of the tutelage that lay in store for London's press corps. He wrote, "We propose to adopt the policy of justification of our action rather than apologetic excuse." The main thrust of the two-page note was that Soviet domination of the Baltic was in every way preferable to German and that control of the Baltic States was one of the USSR's "vital interests." "It is obvious from experience," the note continued, "that Leningrad and the adjacent region can never be secure against a major aggressor unless Russia is established in the Baltic States." The treaty, Eden argued, must be portrayed as restricting the USSR, not as letting her loose on Europe: "We are not, as enemy propaganda has put out, selling Eastern Europe to Russia. The terms of the treaty show that her demands have been limited to safeguarding her frontiers. The interests of Poland and other Eastern European countries are safeguarded and Russia admits British interest in the post-war settlement in Eastern Europe."[7]

It is clear from these two telegrams that Eden still felt that Soviet aims were both limited and defensive, and that he had composed the best possible formula both to guarantee Soviet security and to safeguard the independence of other Eastern European nations. The foreign secretary should perhaps have waited, however, before indulging in such optimism: he had not yet received Stalin's response to the British drafts.

Unsophisticated American opinion was not alone in believing the direction of Britain's Soviet policy to be both unsound and immoral. As the entry of April 22 in Oliver Harvey's diary shows, there were many malcontents closer to home:

Victor Cazalet [M.P.] is flapping about the H. of C. stirring up opposition to our Soviet Treaty because of the Baltic States. This is part of the Polish offensive [the Poles were understandably upset by the prospect of any treaty moving the USSR westwards] but it threatens to assume serious proportions. There is only too much anti-Soviet feeling about in influential quarters on both sides of the House to make trouble easy. The Chief Whip is by nature on that side, the Cabinet itself is lukewarm, even or especially the Labour members. But Cripps is now back, thank goodness, and I hope Stalin doesn't make matters difficult by haggling.[8]

Clearly, many of Britain's leaders remained untouched by the wave of pro-Soviet sympathy sweeping the country. Eden was staking a great deal on his confident prediction that Stalin would prove reasonable. The trouble with advocating a more accommodating line toward Moscow, as the foreign secretary would discover, was that while one could expect to be roundly denounced by the British Right for "softness" to Communism, Stalin would never seem to be grateful. If nine-tenths of the Soviet demands were met, the Kremlin would inquire suspiciously about the missing tenth, meanwhile raising yet higher standards for passing the test of friendship. The whole process could be excruciatingly vexing.

The foreign secretary's hopes were dashed when Stalin's reply arrived on May 1. In a telegram addressed to the prime minister, the Soviet dictator said the British draft

differed in some material respects from the text of the agreements which were under discussion while Mr. Eden was in Moscow. In view of the fact that these drafts reveal fresh divergencies of opinion which it would be difficult to solve by correspondence, the Soviet Government have decided, despite all obstacles, to send M. Molotov to London in order, by means of personal discussion, to dispose of all the matters which stand in the way of the signing of the agreements.[9]

This seemed reasonable enough, but the British received the Soviet redraft of the treaty, which Maiskii delivered to Eden, like a blow to the solar plexus. The military segment of the treaty was essentially unchanged, but the Soviets had altered the political portion beyond recognition. Perhaps predictably, the article guaranteeing the right of emigration was axed. "The Ambassador," Eden later reported, "said that the Soviet Government wished to omit altogether our proposal which would allow the inhabitants of such territories who may wish to do so the right to leave such territories without hindrance and to carry their movable property with them. [Maiskii] said that, so far as the Baltic States were concerned, this matter had already been dealt with and plebiscites had already been held." Eden remonstrated that the Soviet position took insufficient account of "American suceptibilities." But the ambassador was unmoved. As for the suggested guarantee of autonomy for the Baltic States, Maiskii stated coolly that he "had no instructions from his Government." Moscow would continue to ignore this particular British point.

Most disconcertingly, however, Stalin had now increased his demands. Eden's memorandum of his talk with Maiskii continues:

> [The Soviets] wish to sign a secret protocol with us in which we would make plain the desire of both parties for their joint security. To give effect to this His Majesty's Government would declare its willingness to agree to a pact of mutual assistance between Russia and Finland and Roumania under a guarantee of the independence of these latter two States and at the same time the Soviet Government would agree to a similar pact of mutual assistance between ourselves and Belgium and Holland.[10]

This new Soviet demand for a secret protocol was both disquieting and ironic. Oliver Harvey noted, "This makes me laugh. It was the Bolsheviks who in 1917 published all the secret treaties of the last war and put the democracies to shame. So much so that H.M.G. at last learned their lesson and will never have another secret treaty, not even to please Stalin."[11] Maiskii was told that Britain could not possibly sign a secret protocol.

The harshness of Stalin's response came as no surprise to at least one person. Sir Alexander Cadogan felt that his warnings about the futility of appeasing Moscow had been vindicated. On May 3 he wrote in his diary:

> Maisky has given Soviet reply to our draft Treaties. Pretty bad: they cut out all we had put in to save the Polish case and American susceptibilities. It is curious that A.[nthony Eden], of all people, should have hopes of "appeasement"!! Much better say to the Russians "We can't discuss post-war frontiers: we want to work with you now and later: let's have a mutual guarantee. Frontiers can easily be agreed upon later. . . ." I believe, still, it would be better not to crawl to the Russians over the dead bodies of *all* our principles.[12]

A chastened Eden presented the Soviet drafts to the War Cabinet on May 4. The foreign secretary pointed out that the Soviet documents differed from the British draft on four critical points (excluding Maiskii's proposal for a secret protocol, which had not been submitted to the British in writing): first, there was no provision for emmigration; second, "the Russians had tightened up the provisions in regard to the Baltic States, and now asked for a more definite statement of our position," (i.e., Stalin would no longer accept a simple reference in the treaty to the Soviet frontiers "violated by the Hitlerite aggression"); third, the Soviet drafts made no mention of the inclusion of Great Britain in future negotiations concerning the Russo-Polish frontier; and fourth, there was no mention of the British desire for a Balkan Confederation. In other words, all the counterconcessions for which Eden had confidently argued Britain must press had been either rejected or ignored by Stalin.

The War Cabinet, which as a body had been from the start considerably less enthusiastic about accommodating Stalin than had Eden, dug in its heels at this latest Soviet line. His talk with Maiskii had even had a cathartic effect on Eden, who, as Cadogan wrote, "realises we can at least go no further, and no use haggling." Only one War Cabinet member still felt that Stalin had not gone too far. Cadogan continued: "All members of the Cabinet [are] sound (except perhaps Cripps, who didn't know what he was talking about, as he hadn't read the drafts of the Treaties.)"[13] The British leaders were particularly appalled by Maiskii's suggestion that Britain sign a secret protocol, creating mutual assistance pacts between the Soviet Union on the one hand and Finland and Romania on the other, a proposal that the Cabinet viewed as a thinly veiled framework for Soviet domination of these countries. Eden was authorized to draft a response, which, as the minutes record, "should not state, in terms, that we were not prepared to make any further concessions; but it should set out in detail the reasons why we felt unable to make concessions beyond the position set out in the draft treaty."[14]

Eden strove valiantly to tone down the Soviet demands when he met Maiskii the following day. But the ambassador was adamant as ever, alleging that his country "had to bear virtually the whole burden" of the war, and that this had "created a measure of resentment, even bitterness, in Moscow." Maiskii then delivered a long soliloquy, stressing the enormous sacrifices made by the USSR, belittling the British war effort, and ending with a crass attempt at extortion. "If [the British] were unable, for whatever reason, to give Russia help on the military side," he told Eden, "then it seemed more than ever desirable to help her politically. That was why [Maiskii's] Government had hoped that we would be willing to agree to their draft of the treaty." Maiskii would not budge on any point. He refused to admit the necessity, or even desirability, of mollifying American public opinion by including the article granting the right of emigration, saying that "he thought it quite likely that American opinion would not like the treaty. But would Article 4 really help with the United States? He thought not."

Eden complained that the Soviet draft contained no provision for British participation in delineation of the Russo-Polish border, and that the Soviets had eliminated the passage, which the British draft had contained, specifically exempting the Polish border from London's promise to recognize the USSR's 1941 frontiers. Eden told the ambassador that, with the exception of the Baltic States, Bessarabia, and Bukovina, His Majesty's Government "were not prepared at this stage to commit themselves on questions affecting the peace settlement, particularly questions of frontiers, considering that these should be left for settlement at the end of the war." The Soviet draft, if accepted, would have been a de facto recognition by Britain of Stalin's gains in Poland from the days of the Nazi-Soviet Pact and would have been a betrayal of the Poles. Stalin had seemingly accepted British reluctance to decide the Polish issue during Eden's visit to Moscow, but now that the question of the Baltic States appeared settled, the Soviet dictator evidently felt free to renew old claims.

Eden was surprised by the resurrection of this demand and "made it quite clear" to Maiskii "that unless we could be met in respect of Poland, we could not be expected to sign the treaty." When the ambassador said that agreement on frontiers need not be public, Eden once again reminded his guest that Britain could not be a party to secret treaties dividing up Europe. Maiskii persisted: If Britain could not guarantee Soviet security in a secret protocol, then it became "essential that [British] approval of [the] proposed pacts between Russia and Finland and Roumania should be embodied in the [public] treaty or in some other declaration at the same time." This was too much for the exasperated Eden, who rather pathetically "pointed out to the ambassador that this demand had never been made in Moscow. It was despairing," Eden recorded, "to try to negotiate with the Soviet Government when they invariably raised their price at every meeting." Indeed it must have been.

Getting nowhere on this point, Eden tried to get Maiskii to relent to the idea of a Balkan confederation—the "*quid pro quo*" for which Stalin's "oriental mind" was supposedly geared. Maiskii "then embarked on a long and somewhat involved explanation, the general effect of which was that, while the Soviet Government were not at all opposed to confederation, they were unwilling to declare here and now that it was the right solution for this part of Europe. To do this would be to encourage the exiled Governments here [in London] in all sorts of political exercises, some of which might not be very helpful."[15] This was rather amusing: in December Stalin had dismissed a similar British argument, that territorial questions be left for the Peace Conference. Maiskii was unwittingly negating his Leader's argument.

Clearly an impasse had been reached. The British, or at least those who had advocated accommodation with Stalin, had seen themselves as being admirably flexible. They were nonplussed by the Soviet response, having expected some hint of gratitude from Moscow. What they got instead was a slap in the face accompanied by a demand for more concessions. Eden found himself in a bind and scrambled to find some formula that would assuage the Soviets without doing further violence to British interests. In a talk with Oliver Harvey, who was also a committed advocate of a pro-Soviet foreign policy, Eden decided that, as a form of insurance, another treaty draft should be prepared, one that "would have no mention of frontiers, would avoid that issue and it could be offered as an alternative to the other treaty if the Russians won't have it."[16] Alexander Cadogan had suggested such a course in late April.[17]

On May 7 the full Cabinet discussed, and decisively rejected, accepting the Soviet draft. Only Cripps, who once again arrived late for the session, argued in favor of acceptance. Ernest Bevin, the minister of labour and Britain's most influential trade unionist, was adamant that Roosevelt's proviso about emigration be included in any treaty. Clement Attlee was equally dogged about the need for a Balkan Confederation. With this newly heightened mood against accommodating the Soviets among his Cabinet members, Churchill felt free to vent his spleen at Moscow. Cadogan records the prime minister saying: "We must remember that this [recognition of the USSR's 1941 frontiers] is a *bad* thing. We oughtn't to do it, and I shan't be sorry if we don't."[18] If this comment reflected the prime minister's feelings about the proposed treaty, however, then his thinking had undergone a change since he had spoken to Winant on May 4. According to the American's account of the talk,

My conversation with the Prime Minister on this subject was very brief. I feel that he reluctantly came to the conclusion that acceptance of the Russian position was necessary. Both the Prime Minister and Eden feel that Stalin has made the Baltic States–Finnish issue the basis of trust in Britain as a friendly ally. They believe that if mutual confidence could be established it would mean a great deal in the prosecution of the war and in building the future peace. They do not believe that failure to meet Stalin's wishes would lead to a Russian-German arrangement.[19]

Churchill, however, had never been as comfortable with the proposed treaty as Eden was. The first signs of Soviet obtuseness had galvanized his latent suspicions of the Soviet Union.

After the Cabinet meeting, a quick telephone call to Maiskii convinced Eden that, for the moment at least, the Soviets would not budge. The foreign secretary asked whether Maiskii's government had sent a reply to the questions he had raised in the conversations of May 1 and 5. "M. Maisky said that he had none so far, and that he was hoping for a further communication from [Eden]."[20] Obviously, nothing could be expected from Maiskii, since his role in such an important affair was merely that of a glorified postman. Stalin had promised to send Molotov to London to iron out the outstanding differences; the British would have to wait until his arrival before any real progress could be made.

The Molotov Mission

For two weeks the British anxiously awaited Molotov's visit. An aura of mystery surrounded his plans: the Soviets refused to specify the time the foreign commissar intended to arrive in Britain, merely asking the Foreign Office for general permission to land a four-engined plane in Scotland. As if to heighten the sense of intrigue, Maiskii insisted that Molotov, after landing in Britain, should be transported from Scotland to London by train rather than by air. Evidently, the Soviets wanted to forestall an arranged "accident" aboard an R.A.F. airplane. For fear of possible assassination attempts, or perhaps from uncertainty about the receptiveness of the British public, Molotov also requested that news of his visit to London, and afterwards to Washington, be witheld from the press until his return to Moscow. Indeed, Molotov seemed genuinely frightened traveling to London, the nexus of the world's greatest imperial power. After his arrival, when staying at Chequers, the prime minister's country residence, Molotov demanded that his hosts provide him with the room keys for the entire mansion and had his bed sheets arranged in such a fashion that he could leap up instantly and grab a revolver placed on his night stand. One developed odd habits residing in Stalin's Kremlin.[21]

As the British waited for Molotov to descend from the skies, Oliver Harvey became impatient with the delay. The enemies of accommodation with the USSR were afoot and using this interlude to rally the opposition. On May 15 Harvey wrote in his diary: "Still no Molotov. This delay is tiresome because uninformed and obstructive opinion against the negotiations is taking shape. The Foreign Affairs Committee of the House of Commons is working itself up. The egregious Simon [Lord Chancellor] has written to the P.M. about it on the high moral tone: Duff [Cooper, M.P.] too is anti. So the sooner we get it over the better."[22] Eden had his own explanation for Molotov's tardiness. He told the American ambassador on May 7 "that his [Eden's] insistence on the inclusion of the clause suggested by [the Americans] to permit the evacuation of dissenting inhabitants, with other changes in the Soviet text, was responsible for Molotov's postponement."[23] The foreign secretary still did not feel comfortable with the American clause and blamed it for heightening Soviet suspicions.

At long last, on May 20 Molotov arrived in Scotland. The next day he met with Churchill, Eden, and Attlee at Number 10 Downing Street. The foreign commissar wasted no time on pleasantries, getting down to business at once. He told his hosts that "he was authorised to conduct negotiations in London concerning two questions." He continued, reading a prepared statement: "The first question raised several points arising out of the discussions which took place in December last. There were two draft treaties, the protocol proposed by the Soviet Government and the draft letter from M. Stalin on the subject of Poland. The second question concerned the opening of a second front in Europe." Molotov told his listeners that, although the draft treaties were vital, the Soviet government "considered the [second front] as on the whole more important." He implied that the opening of such a front would be in the best interests not only of the Soviet Union, but also of Great Britain and the United States.

It was a carefully worded statement in which Molotov had discreetly pressed certain points, while at the same time camouflaging Soviet weaknesses. Stalin must have determined that the Polish border issue should be on the agenda, though significantly Molotov had not mentioned the Baltic States. The Soviets had already won that round; from now on they would pretend to assume that the futures of Estonia, Latvia, and Lithuania had been settled. And they would expend their energies on other, more hotly disputed topics.

Most interesting of all, perhaps, was the way in which Molotov had mentioned the second front. While he admitted this question was of paramount importance, he carefully argued that the opening of such a front would be in his allies' own interests, that a landing by Great Britain and the United States on the coast of Europe would not be seen in Moscow as a favor to be given or witheld by the Western democracies. The Soviets were determined to avoid paying a heavy political price for their allies' military cooperation, though they were not above demanding the reverse—political favors for their own military achievements.

After a short discussion about the need to maintain the secrecy enshrouding Molotov's visit, the foreign commissar reverted to the purpose of his visit: he asked for a clear exposition of British objections to the Soviet draft treaties. But Churchill, who did not want the conversation to degenerate into an academic debate, avoided specifics, saying that the Soviet draft was "not at all free from certain grave difficulties as far as this country was concerned. It could be argued that it contravened the spirit of the Atlantic Charter. At the same time it was quite clear that President Roosevelt would not favourably endorse the Treaty, either in the British or in the Soviet form, and that very sharp criticism would arise in the United States which would be reflected in England and which would certainly lead to serious controversy detrimental to our common effort." In spite of these drawbacks, Churchill said, the British were prepared to sign their own draft as proof of their genuine friendship toward the USSR.

Molotov, who was not the type to be swayed by Churchillian oratory, replied that "so also the opinion of his own country must be considered." The Soviet government, he claimed, faced constraints similar to those confronting the British: "The Soviet draft stated the minimum conditions acceptable to the Soviet Government and public opinion, and it would be difficult—perhaps, indeed, impossible—to make any further concessions." He did not say just what concessions his government had already made.

If Soviet public opinion imposed its constraints upon the kind of treaty that Molotov was prepared to sign, he at least faced no restrictions—as Churchill had—in addressing specific points of the proposed treaty. Molotov was not afraid of offending his hosts. He continued:

When he spoke of "minimum conditions," he meant that his Government insisted on recovering the territory violated by Hitler, and they could make no concessions in this respect. Further, it was not sufficient simply to restore what existed before the war: the Soviet Government must secure their territory on their north-western and south-western frontiers. Without some guarantees in this respect [he was referring to the proposed pacts of mutual assistance], no one in the Soviet Union would approve the Treaty. If within these limits it should prove possible to find an agreed draft, that would be very good. If, however, it was not found possible to come to terms with His Majesty's Government on this basis it might be better to postpone the whole matter.[24]

To this Churchill replied that winning the war was the first priority, and that any appearance of discord between the three Allies must be squelched lest it give comfort to the Nazis. Then the prime minister outlined some of the problems faced by the Anglo-Americans in preparing a cross-channel invasion, an exposition Molotov took in good part. After this the meeting adjourned until later in the day.

Churchill was not present at the second meeting, which was held at 3:30 P.M. The discussion was much more detailed than it had been in the morning, with the two sides ploughing through the Soviet draft, article by article. Eden's attempt to raise the issue of emigration was cut short by Molotov, who said "he would like to deal first with the points which had already been discussed in Moscow, and then with others that had been raised since."

The Polish question soon emerged as the central issue of dispute. The British draft political treaty had included a clause specifically exempting the Russo-Polish border from British recognition of the Soviet Union's 1941 frontiers, an exemption Stalin had explicitly accepted in December. Molotov denied this, saying that "his Government had been somewhat surprised at the British draft. M. Stalin and he himself had the impression that it was agreed that the Soviet Government and the Polish Government would reach direct agreement as between allies." The Soviet Union was prepared, Molotov said, to leave the question open until a later date, but the matter should be settled between Moscow and the Poles. Molotov stated that his government "was prepared to give a letter to the Polish Government [promising to settle the exact boundary later], which should not, however, be mentioned in the treaty."

Eden replied that "he saw no objection to dealing with the matter outside the Treaty by means of an exchange of letters." Indeed, although he did not mention it, this is the method the foreign secretary had suggested to Stalin in December. What his government did object to, Eden continued, was that the Soviet draft letter, which Molotov proposed to substitute for the disputed article in the treaty, did not include a reference to a possible British role in the delineation of the Russo-Polish border.

Molotov replied that he would readily sign an agreement based on the Curzon Line, evidently intending to suggest that, since that line had been drawn by a British minister, His Majesty's Government had already had their say in the matter. Molotov continued that "this remained the Soviet aim, in view of the great sacrifices made by the USSR." But Molotov "added that certain minor alterations would have to be made in the Curzon Line in favour of the Soviet Government." The foreign commissar did not elaborate upon what these "minor alterations" would be.

Eden was clearly disconcerted. Molotov was taking no notice of the considerable distance the British government had already traveled toward meeting Soviet demands. The foreign secretary reminded his guest of this important fact: "[Eden] recalled that when he was in Moscow he had no authority to agree on the Soviet proposals concerning the Baltic States. Now on that point His Majesty's Government were prepared to agree; they had made this concession . . . the only thing they wished to do was to safeguard their position with Poland."

Molotov seemingly ignored this allusion to the Baltic States, replying instead that Poland had no reason to worry about losing territory to the USSR, since she could easily be compensated by the gift of East Prussia after Germany's defeat. The Soviet government was being admirably flexible, Molotov continued, since they were prepared either to settle the Polish frontier issue at once, on the basis of the Curzon Line, or to postpone the whole issue for the time being. Countering Eden's allusion to British concessions, Molotov said: "In proposing to leave the Soviet-Polish frontier open to further discussion, his Government were leaving undecided the greater part of their Western frontier. This was a great concession on their part and he asked what concession His Majesty's Government were prepared to make. The concession he asked of His Majesty's Government was that the latter should not maintain their support of the Polish cause." This was nothing if not forthright. Eden had felt abashed about alluding directly to the appropriateness of Soviet counterconcessions; his counterpart suffered from no such qualms about demanding the reverse. Molotov was asking the British to desert the cause for which they had ostensibly entered the war. In the face of this astonishing request, Eden tried to respond in a conciliatory manner. He said he concurred with the proposal to hand East

Prussia to the Poles, calling the idea "very wise," but he disputed Molotov's contention that the British were siding with Poland against the USSR.

Molotov persisted, saying that in exchange for a note from Stalin delaying the settlement of the Polish question, he wanted the British to agree to the pre-June 1941 frontier. He said that "M. Stalin in his recent Order of the Day had claimed the restoration of all the frontiers violated by Hitler, and this point could not be abandoned."

As Eden well knew, Molotov's proposal amounted to no "concession" at all; it merely masked a promise to accept Soviet demands in their entirety. All Molotov was offering in return was that British acceptance would not be made public during the war. Eden tried yet again to evoke a glimmer of recognition from Molotov of the concession that Britain had already made.

> He recalled that in Moscow the Soviet Government had already made plain that they would leave open the question of the Soviet-Polish frontier. But they then asked His Majesty's Government to recognise their claim to certain other frontiers [that is, the Baltic States]. To that His Majesty's Government now agreed and he was therefore somewhat surprised that the Soviet Government seemed to think that they were entitled to ask some further concession of His Majesty's Government.

Abandoning his earlier reticence about pressing for counterconcessions, Eden asked Molotov if the latter had an objection to inserting into the treaty a reference to the need for a Balkan Confederation. "M. Molotov agreed that this question had been discussed in Moscow. The Soviet Government had certain information to show that some federations might be directed against the Soviet Union. The question was for the future and he thought that it might be better to deal with it when it was raised in definite form." Eden might have taken a page from Molotov's book by touting postponement of this matter as a serious concession by Britain; but instead he hurriedly assured his Soviet guest that Britain "would never, of course, be [a party] to any scheme directed against the Soviet Union." On this bitter note the meeting broke up for the day.[25]

Quite a day it had been. The whole tone of the talks had come as an eye-opener to Anthony Eden. After the foreign secretary met with Cadogan the next day, the latter noted: "Don't think A. has got many illusions left."[26] Molotov's attitude toward the Polish problem had been particularly disquieting. He had tried to drive a wedge between the Poles and Great Britain, and Eden knew that without British diplomatic support—perhaps even with it—the Poles would find themselves locked in an unequal struggle negotiating with the Soviet colossus.

Curiously, Eden had readily assented to Molotov's suggestion that Poland be given East Prussia after the war. He did so before giving much thought to the ominous implications of such an important proposal. What if the USSR were to sign a compromise peace with Germany before occupying East Prussia? After all, Stalin was only pledged to fighting "Hitlerite Germany." Poland would receive little compensation in this case. Even more disquieting was the motive underlying this example of Soviet largesse. The westward transportation of Poland, at Germany's expense, was intended, as one scholar and diplomat has pointed out, to transform Poland into a vassal state, a state that would forever be dependent on the Soviet Union for protection against German revanchism.[27]

The talks resumed inauspiciously the next afternoon with a renewal of the squabble over Poland. Molotov repeatedly accused Eden of wanting to restore Poland's pre–1939 frontiers. The latter parried each of Molotov's thrusts, denying that an agreement to leave the matter in abeyance for the time being would prejudice Soviet interests. Molotov was not mollified. Finally, trying to lay the matter to rest, Eden resorted to a lie, saying "that the Anglo-Polish treaty did not recognise Poland's old frontiers, nor did it recognise the frontiers of 1939. It neither recognised the original frontiers nor the changes that had been subsequently made in them." This was too much for one anonymous figure in the Foreign Office who penned a large question mark next to his minister's comment. Britain had indeed recognized Poland's old frontiers.

The rest of the meeting was equally unproductive: Eden inquired as to why the Soviets had omitted any reference to the right of people to emigrate from lands that might change hands during the war. The foreign minister used a disingenuous hypothetical example: "If it was agreed to transfer E. Prussia to Poland, it would certainly be desirable that arrangements be made enabling the German population to be removed." Molotov was not so easily fooled. He replied: "That he quite agreed that this principle should be applied in the case of E. Prussia, but he did not indicate that he would accept this article in the treaty. He said that it introduced a new and complicated question, and to include it in the treaty would encourage all kinds of propaganda on the part of dissatisfied elements." To allow free emigration from any of the Soviet Republics would have posed an unacceptable risk for the rulers in the Kremlin, since it would open the floodgates and advertise to the world the failure of the Soviet "experiment." It would require more than a polite suggestion from Eden to make the Soviets accept this disputed clause. The British minutes note laconically that "it was consequently agreed to leave this article for further discussion."

Turning to the next point, Molotov inquired about the British attitude toward the secret protocol that Maiskii had suggested earlier in the month, the protocol creating mutual assistance pacts between the USSR on the one hand and Finland and Romania on the other. Without committing himself, Eden asked what the nature of the proposed pact would be. Why were the Soviets so anxious to obtain British participation when the matter clearly involved only the nations concerned? Molotov answered evasively, saying that Romania and Finland had both broken their treaty obligations by participating in the German attack on Russia. What he was proposing, Molotov said, was nothing more than a return to the status quo ante.

This explanation did not satisfy Eden, who replied that he still did not understand the need for British participation in the proposed pacts. If Romania and Finland were to retain their independence, as Molotov assured him they would, then the foreign secretary thought that the matter should be handled with those countries' representatives after the war. Eden brushed aside Molotov's assurances that the Soviet government was prepared to accept similar pacts between Britain on the one hand and Holland and Belgium on the other. Eden said that the British government "for their part were not contemplating pacts" of this nature.

Molotov then explained the need for the proposed secret protocol:

The Soviet Government considered it necessary to insist on the restoration of the previously existing treaties in order to prevent the recurrence of events which took place in 1941. If the conclusion of treaties with Belgium and Holland did not interest His Majesty's Government, that of course was the affair of the latter. He agreed that it might be possible to submit a draft of the Protocol, [as Eden had requested] but what interested him was [Eden's] attitude to the question, and he would like this explained more fully. He recalled that the question was raised in December last, when it was discussed on broader lines. He asked, finally, whether the idea was accepted in principle.

Molotov was persistent as ever: he wanted Eden to commit himself there and then. But Eden protested that he must first see a Soviet draft before he could give an informed answer. On this inconclusive note the third meeting broke up.[28]

Molotov's reasons behind pressing for British acceptance of a secret protocol are as clear now as they must have been to Eden at the time. That the protocol was to be secret belied Molotov's assurances that Romania and Finland would retain their independence. The two countries were still at war with the USSR: a strange sort of independence this that would enable the USSR to determine their postwar foreign policies. By getting Britain's blessing on the proposed secret pacts, Stalin would be creating a form of insurance. Should Soviet troops at some time in the future march into either Romania or Finland, in response to threats real or imagined, Stalin could point to Britain's imprimatur. There might be howls from London, certainly, but publication of the secret protocols would divide British opinion.

Eden had wisely resisted Molotov's pressure to assent immediately to the protocols. Indeed, the foreign secretary was not in a mood to accommodate the Soviets at all. Eden had subscribed wholeheartedly to Sir Stafford Cripps's theory that once the Baltic States issue had been laid to rest the Soviets would be transformed into cooperative and genuine allies, but now he was thoroughly disillusioned. Molotov, rather than moderating his demands in response to gestures of British friendship, continually raised new ones.

Eden's policy lay in ruins; he now faced the task of devising a new approach. Should it prove impossible to reach agreement on the thorny questions raised by the existing draft treaty, Eden felt that perhaps it would be better to submit for Soviet consideration the alternative, and less comprehensive, treaty drafted by Sir Alexander Cadogan. This was the document that Eden had authorized Cadogan to prepare earlier in the month, after his discouraging meetings with Maiskii. This new draft treaty now seemed to offer the only way out of the Anglo-Soviet deadlock.

Cadogan's draft contained little that could be regarded as controversial. The first section was a restatement of the July 1941 Anglo-Soviet Agreement, announcing an alliance and ruling out any separate peace by either party "with the Hitlerite Government or any other Government in Germany that does not clearly renounce all aggressive intentions." Only the second part of Cadogan's draft contained anything new. In this section, the two parties pledged themselves to an alliance against Germany and German revanchism. Both governments promised to cooperate "to render impossible a repetition of aggression and violation of the peace by Germany" and to assist one another in the postwar reconstruction of Europe. Most importantly, the draft included no reference to frontiers.[29]

Eden and Churchill first showed the document to Molotov during an informal meeting on the night of May 22. The next day, when talks resumed, Eden asked his guest what he thought of the new draft. The Soviets had clearly not studied the document—not a good sign—so to give them time to do so the British delegation left the room.

After the British returned, Eden explained that his motive for submitting the new draft had been to circumvent the impasse over the Polish question and also over the emigration clause. The new document was not intended as a substitute for a full treaty, Eden explained, but rather as an interim agreement. When Molotov asked what the main differences between the new and the old drafts were, Eden continued:

> The new draft introduced the idea of a 20-year pact of mutual assistance which could only be ended if a general system of security was set up with which both Governments were satisfied. At the same time he felt confident (though he had not consulted them) that the American administration would have no objection to the present draft, which would carry British co-operation with the Soviet Union into the after-war period. . . . Though the treaty admittedly did not deal with vexed questions such as frontiers, it was obvious that if we were to have a 20 year pact, it must be our desire that Russia, as our ally, be strong and secure.

Molotov responded coolly to the new British draft. He most probably could not have accepted it immediately, even had he wanted to, without Stalin's approval. Despite his prominence in the Soviet hierarchy, he had been sent to London with what must have been explicit instructions from his boss. Molotov said that the draft, "with certain additions, could certainly be considered . . . [but] he thought it would be impossible to discuss it with his Government from here by telegraph." He then said that there were a number of questions still unresolved in the old draft and that "he would prefer to finish the discussion of these while leaving open the question of this new alternative treaty."

An inconclusive discussion ensued in which Eden resolutely countered Molotov's advocacy of a secret protocol. The two also clashed over the emigration clause. Molotov said that his government had no objection to "national minorities," such as Poles in Lithuania, being allowed to emigrate. But he felt that if, for example, Lithuanians were allowed to leave Lithuania itself, this "would inevitably incite the inhabitants of the territories in question to make claims against the Soviet Government."

Eden continued his tepid defense of the clause, pointing out "that the British draft was not very far-reaching. It only recognised the desirability of making appropriate provision in the eventual peace settlement. *It therefore hardly amounted to much more than a pious hope*" [italics added].[30] As Eden saw it, the emigration clause would be no more than a sop to Western, particularly American, public opinion. He had evidently not yet completely abandoned his belief that he could patch together a deal with the Soviets that would have the outward appearance of defending individual rights.

Certainly Cadogan still had his doubts about the firmness of the foreign secretary's attachment to principle. His uncertainty was compounded by the fact that Eden's private secretary, Oliver Harvey, was still urging a pro-Soviet line à la Cripps. On the evening of May 23, Cadogan recorded his worries in his diary: "Must keep A. firm on Polish question. I *think* he'll be all right. But he is subject to temptation and that ass Harvey's advice."[31] Cadogan need not have worried. Eden had already been stung once by the Soviets. He was in no mood to bend further.

When the talks resumed at 4 P.M. the next day, it soon became obvious that neither side had moved on any of the fundamental disputes. Molotov would still not consider the British draft, insisting that discussions center on the Soviet document. Eden argued on the other hand that the new British draft contained little except clauses upon which agreement had already been reached. The only major addition had been the proposed twenty-year mutual assistance guarantee, and that, Eden said, represented "a bigger offer than His Majesty's Government had ever made in the course of history." His eloquence was wasted on Molotov, however, who felt that the Soviet draft was more appropriate and argued that "as regards American opinion . . . he believed that there was no foundation for saying that this treaty would be disapproved there. There were friendly elements in America who would certainly not raise any objections to it."

The rest of the meeting was consumed by caviling over semantics. The Soviets did drop their insistence on a secret protocol, but this was only a cosmetic change, since they then demanded that all the protocol's provisions now be embodied in the treaty proper.[32]

It now seemed to the British that there would be no agreement. The Soviets would not accept the British alternative draft, which was a thoroughly innocuous document, and the British themselves could not ratify the Soviet treaty. So far, the only clear result of all the negotiations since the December Moscow Conference had been the British promise to recog-

nize Soviet sovereignty over the Baltic States, Bessarabia, Northern Bukovina, and those parts of Finland captured by the USSR in the Russo-
Finnish War. Britain had received nothing in return.

Sir Alexander Cadogan was pleased that the Soviets would at least get
no more out of the British. On the evening of May 24 he wrote of that day's
meeting between Molotov and Eden:

> [Eden] had wisely come to the conclusion [that] he should press our
> alternative mutual assistance treaty on the Russians. . . . [The Sovi-
> ets] still won't look at our alternative Treaty, so we went through the
> drafts of the others and agreed to put the points to the Cabinet
> tomorrow. [The Russians] *are* extraordinary people to deal with—
> they wear their suspicions on their sleeve! A. now longing to get out
> of his promise about frontiers (Winant has been twisting his tail.) But
> it's a bit late for that now![33]

There seems to have been another meeting during the evening of May
24, though no record of the talks seems to exist in the Foreign Office files,
nor does the British official historian mention it. However, both Harvey
and Cadogan refer to the occasion in their diaries. The Soviets evidently
modified their position on the Polish border issue "to the extent," Harvey
wrote, "which even Alec Cadogan says would be difficult for us to refuse."[34] For once Cadogan and Harvey agreed, since the former moaned in
his diary: "Unfortunately [the Soviets] had come a long way on the Polish
frontier question, and it will be difficult to break on that!"[35]

Some insight into Eden's thinking, and also into the kind of influence
Oliver Harvey was able to exert on the foreign secretary, is provided by the
continuation of the private secretary's diary entry of May 24:

> A. E. getting hesitant about the treaty because of . . . American
> opposition coupled with that of elements in the H. of C. Even Cardi-
> nal Hinsley [Archbishop of Westminster] has written to express ab-
> horrence of it. A. E. now obviously eager to get away from the old
> treaty and on to the new. I tell him it is no use listening to the
> Catholics, they are on the side of darkness anyway. As for the H. of
> C. opposition it is of the worst and wettest elements. And in assess-
> ing American criticisms we must bear in mind the unlikelihood of
> America cooperating in policing Europe after the war. Russia and
> ourselves are part of Europe and we must contrive to work together or
> be prepared to fight each other. We should be very careful, after the

Russians have come so far, not to break with them lightheartedly. They will snap back into a dangerous isolationism.[36]

But Harvey was losing the battle for Eden's soul. The foreign secretary had advocated accommodation of the Soviets in order to convert them into genuine allies, and also so that he could reap the rewards as the great conciliator. It was now becoming quite clear that, not only were the Soviets no friendlier but also that the political risks, and costs, of accommodating Moscow were growing daily.

Eden was not the same diplomat he had been at the Moscow Conference. Then he had been very much in the glare of world attention; to have returned from Moscow empty-handed would have broadcast failure. But news of Molotov's visit was being kept from the public, and there were not the same pressures bearing down on the foreign secretary. Besides that, Eden was now on his home turf, backed by Cabinet colleagues who were less pro-Soviet than the general British public. Eden was not anxious to reach agreement with the Soviets whatever the cost, as he had been in Moscow.

Molotov had evidently sensed a stiffening of the British position and was pulling back. This would account for the moderation of his Polish demands. In this more compliant mood, the foreign commissar and Maiskii received Winant at the Soviet Embassy at 10 P.M. on May 24. Molotov inquired about the American attitude toward opening a second front in Europe during the summer of 1942. Following the account Winant sent to Roosevelt, "I explained to [the Soviets] that we were trying to cooperate with them, that we [the United States and Great Britain] were both interested in a second front. . . . I also told them very frankly that I did the best I could to present the Russian point of view to [President Roosevelt] and to Mr. Hull, but that [they] were both definitely opposed to a British-Russian treaty containing agreements on frontiers." This comment evidently had the desired effect on Molotov, who said that the President's opinion was "a matter for their serious consideration." This was quite a change from April when the Soviets had merely "taken note" of the president's objections to the course of the Anglo-Soviet talks.

Molotov asked if Winant had seen Eden's draft treaty, which did not mention frontiers. The American answered that he had not only seen it but had in fact collaborated with the foreign secretary over the wording of certain sections (the day before, Eden had told the Soviet delegation that he had not consulted the Americans about the new draft). Winant then records: "[Molotov] told me that he would reconsider the draft treaty and perhaps refrain from making any decision until after he had talked with the President." Winant ended his telegram to Roosevelt with his analysis of the reasons for the change in the Soviet position. "The Russians," he wrote, "are deeply interested in establishing a second front. They feel that both the Prime Minister and Eden have great sympathy for their point of view, but that [General Sir Alan Francis] Brooke [chief of the Imperial General Staff] is reluctant to move and that they could get no definite commitments on action this year."[37]

This had clearly been a critical meeting. Before Winant's visit to the Soviet Embassy, the Anglo-Soviet talks had been stalled. To be sure, Molotov had modified his position on Poland somewhat, but he had still refused to consider the new British draft treaty. The impasse had been summed up in one adjective by Harvey: "worrying."[38]

But Winant's intervention had broken the logjam, much to the ambassador's surprise. He wrote: "I had just gotten back to our Embassy when I got a call from Eden, saying that Molotov had called him in the interim asking for an appointment tomorrow morning to discuss the [new] draft treaty."[39]

Writing in 1965 about this episode, Eden evidently no longer remembered what had convinced the Soviets to assent to his new treaty. He wrote:

> The Russian motive in accepting this new text, which contained no mention of frontiers, after battling so long and so obdurately for our recognition of their "minimum conditions," is obscure. The chief purpose in the Soviet Government's negotiation was to secure a second front in Europe as soon as possible. At some stage in our talks Molotov probably became convinced he could not get his way over frontiers and decided that more was to be gained in the military field by accepting our new terms, and going to Washington with the Treaty signed, than by failure to agree.[40]

Eden's account is accurate as far as it goes, but it gives little credit to American intervention, and to the persistent American refusal, owing largely to Sumner Welles, to give their approval to British recognition of wartime territorial changes. Nevertheless, Eden's tenacious refusal to succumb to Molotov's hammering on the Polish question certainly played its part. Molotov apparently thought he was facing a solid Anglo-American bloc; had he only known how shaky this united front was, he might not have agreed to the new text.

The talks resumed the next day in an altogether more cordial atmosphere. Molotov said that he had informed his government that the Americans would prefer the new draft treaty and that he had therefore been authorized to discuss the terms of the new document. "He had not yet had final instructions concerning the new treaty, but he hoped that he might receive these either to-night or to-morrow morning." A few minor semantic changes were agreed to by both sides before the meeting broke up.[41] Signing of the Treaty was scheduled for the next day, subject to Moscow's approval.

The Americans, and most of the British, were delighted that the Soviets had accepted a treaty containing no reference to frontiers. Sumner Welles told Lord Halifax that he thought the outcome of the negotiations had been "a miracle" and that "it was certainly a great load off his mind."[42] But at least one Briton was disgruntled. Oliver Harvey had seen his advice ignored and wrote that night in his diary: "I'm not sure I like this treaty as much as the old because of this extension into the post-war period. The old treaty would have fixed the frontiers of Russia and nothing much more. As to the future our hands were not tied. If I were America [*sic*], I would be more shocked by this new treaty than by the other. However we have Winant's word for it."[43]

But Harvey's was a lone voice crying in the wilderness. The mood of the War Cabinet was jubilant, and great praise was heaped on Anthony Eden. All agreed that the new treaty was "greatly to be preferred" over the Soviet draft—and even for that matter over the older British draft. The prime minister said that "the War Cabinet were greatly indebted to the Foreign Secretary for his skillful handling of the negotiations and for the very satisfactory result which has been achieved."[44] Explaining to his colleagues what he felt were the reasons for Molotov's abrupt reversal, Eden said "that he was now convinced that M. Molotov was anxious to cooperate with us after the war. It was also quite evident that M. Litvinoff [Soviet ambassador to the United States] had not kept the USSR authorities informed of opinion in the USA."[45] Eden's explanation of Soviet behavior became generally accepted. Even Sumner Welles offered a similar explanation to Lord Halifax when the two met on June 2: "[Welles] thought that M. Molotov, when he got to London had realised how strong the revulsion of feeling in the [United States] would be against the earlier draft treaty."[46]

On May 26 Molotov, evidently receiving the required permission from his boss, signed the treaty amid scenes of general rejoicing. Harvey wrote that Churchill was "beside himself with pleasure at A. E.'s new treaty which saves him from the old."[47] Cadogan, who knew the background of the whole story, found the acclamation of Eden's work a trifle ironic. He wrote: "Winston relieved and delighted, and bouquets were heaped on A.!"[48]

The Treaty signed, Molotov was whisked off to Washington for talks with President Roosevelt. During his visit to America, as Sumner Welles wrote eight years later, Molotov "made no demand that the American [*sic*] and British reconsider their refusal to recognize Russia's frontiers prior to June 1941."[49] To many people at the time, at least to those who did not know the whole story, the Eden-Cripps approach to dealing with the Soviet Union seemed to have been a resounding success. Molotov had shelved Soviet aspirations in deference to Western public opinion, and Britain and Russia had pledged themselves to twenty years of friendship and alliance.

CONCLUSION

> To this day I have never been able to understand why, when people choose to use the term Cold War to describe our relations with the Soviet Union, they begin with the end of World War II, as though there were some sharp difference between what went on after that time and what had gone before it. Indeed, one gains the impression that many people are only imperfectly aware that the Soviet Union existed prior to the Second World War.
>
> —George F. Kennan, 1982[1]

An overarching theme runs throughout Soviet-British relations during the initial years of World War II. As early as 1939, Stalin showed that he had reasonably clear war aims. He wanted to annex territory on the western border of the USSR—the Baltic States, Eastern Poland, some or all of Finland, and Bessarabia and Bukovina. Given the sharp vicissitudes of the international situation between 1939 and 1942, the most remarkable thing about Soviet policy is how little these aims changed. Whether his partners were the Germans or the British, Stalin would advance roughly the same territorial demands. The force and stridency with which he advocated his interests would vary with the fortunes of the Red Army and the strength of his partners and opponents, but his goals remained relatively stable when contrasted with those of other wartime leaders.

This is not to accept the claims of the Stalin legend, which hold that the Great Leader understood the direction of history and foresaw each twist and turn in the international arena. Stalin's aims would change as the war progressed; his appetite would grow as new opportunities for the expansion of Soviet power presented themselves, although he would moderate his demands when faced with firm resistance. In this he was very different from Hitler. But throughout the war, even during the most bitter and dangerous periods of fighting—as when Eden was in Moscow—Stalin would display an overriding interest in shaping the postwar world to fit his pattern.

Stalin's approach differed greatly from the British attitude toward the war. To be sure, the British government was not completely oblivious to its interests, nor was it uniformly altruistic, but at times London allowed the towering goal of defeating Hitler to dominate the political horizon. Reversing Clausewitz's dictum that war is the continuation of politics by other means, in 1941–42 Britain subordinated inter-Allied political disputes to the largely military goal of beating the Germans. Throughout the period examined here, London placed the preservation of Allied unity, which it deemed necessary to defeat Hitler, above the advancement of its plans for postwar Europe. At any rate, these plans were as yet inchoate, as Eden's meetings with Stalin had revealed. Later in the war, the British would become more concerned about the impending postwar order, but by then the changing correlation of forces, to adopt a useful Soviet term, had reduced the importance of the British voice while correspondingly increasing Soviet influence.

It must be stressed here that the British were justified in placing great value on inter-Allied harmony. The defeat of Germany was both a military and a political goal. But British leaders at times seemed to forget that there was no reason why they had to be cast perennially in the role of mediator. After June 1941 theirs was not the most dangerous strategic position, and the Soviets needed Allied unity as much as London did, if not more. Britain's position required a delicate balance between the needs of wartime and those of the postwar, and this balance was askew in British foreign policy during this period. It was not enough simply to rid Europe of Hitler; the peace also had to be won.

The numerous British efforts to woo Moscow examined in these pages suffered from an underlying misunderstanding of Soviet foreign policy in particular and the nature of the Soviet system in general. Whereas the British aimed to smooth over differences between allies and to reach a long-term understanding with Moscow, typified by the twenty-year pledge of alliance in the Anglo-Soviet Treaty, the Soviets continued to treat London not only as an ally but also as a competitor and a potential opponent. Ironically, in this respect the Soviets were being more faithful than the London government to the British foreign policy tradition, which had wisely shunned vague long-term settlements in favor of opportunism and flexibility.

The Anglo-Soviet Treaty of May 1942 marked the culmination of a two-year quest by the British government to build a closer relationship with the Soviet Union. That quest had begun in May 1940, when London decided to dispatch Sir Stafford Cripps to Moscow in an effort to convince Stalin to reverse his policy of cooperation with Hitler. Despite his obvious enthusiasm for the task and his great expectations, Cripps had been singularly ineffective. Stalin had not been interested in what the British had to offer.

Even the outbreak of the Russo-German War had not brought Britain and the Soviet Union together in the manner envisioned by Cripps and those who shared his views; although the two nations were allied, it was a peculiar, frigid, and suspicious partnership. Now, with the signing of the new treaty, one more attempt was being made to put relations between the two countries on a new footing. Although the treaty was the work of Eden, its inspiration had come from Cripps; one need only look at the proposals drafted by Sir Stafford in October 1940, as well as his steady stream of telegrams to the Foreign Office during his time as ambassador, to discover the origin of Eden's ideas about accommodating Stalin. By 1942 the British government had finally decided to follow Sir Stafford's advice and accept most of Stalin's territorial claims, in a desperate hope that they would thereby win Soviet trust. May 1942 thus witnessed the pinnacle of British attempts to appease Moscow.

Churchill and Eden both learned from this fruitless effort to win Soviet confidence, and after the war they would construct a hardy myth, claiming that from the start they had foreseen the emerging Soviet threat to the European balance of power and had striven in vain to warn their credulous American allies. The background to the Anglo-Soviet Treaty, however, belies this somewhat self-serving version of events.

The debate over who first understood that the USSR was an expansionist power would arise only after the war. In June 1942 most opinion in the West held that the new Anglo-Soviet Treaty was a success. In Britain the *Daily Express* and the *Manchester Guardian* both praised the treaty; the *Times* congratulated Eden, calling the treaty "the outstanding achievement of his career." Other Allied opinion was equally effusive: South African Field Marshal Smuts said that the treaty was "a stabilising factor in this war," and Australian Prime Minister John Curtin hailed it as "an indication to the world that these two great countries have been thinking ahead."[2] The Polish and Baltic States' exile governments were understandably relieved that the treaty had not mentioned territorial changes, and they thanked the American government for—in Alfred Bilmanis's words—their "magnanimous and righteous support."[3] Even the Swedes professed to be pleased; the American ambassador in Stockholm told the State Department that "certain apprehensions held by [the] Swedish Government with regard to the Atlantic Charter have been somewhat allayed."[4]

The British remained hopeful that, as Sir Orme Sargent told Winant, the warmth of Molotov's reception in the West "must prove helpful in dissipating Russia's anti-foreign complex," which had been caused by Moscow's "ignorance with regard to the outside world and of course to the ostracism to which they had been subjected for some twenty years."[5] This was a telling sign of how far the Foreign Office had come to accept Cripps's arguments about the USSR; Sargent had been among those most skeptical of Sir Stafford's claims in 1940 and 1941.

As for the Soviets, although press comment in Moscow was "unusually generous" about the treaty, the American representative there noted that "a good deal more seems to be made of Soviet-American relations than of Anglo-Soviet relations."[6] This should have come as no surprise; whereas the new treaty was filled with uplifting generalities about Anglo-Soviet friendship, the price of Soviet postponement of their territorial demands had been President Roosevelt's promise of a second front. Molotov confirmed that, from the Soviet point of view, the most important result of his journey was not the Anglo-Soviet Treaty but Roosevelt's pledge. In a speech to the Supreme Soviet on June 19, he stated that "complete accord had been reached with respect to urgent questions concerning the formation of a second front in Europe in 1942."[7]

In an account of inter-Allied diplomacy, two British historians have expressed the prevailing view of the Anglo-Soviet Treaty, calling it "a major diplomatic achievement" and "a personal triumph for Mr. Eden." They argue that the foreign secretary "had achieved the apparent marvel of reconciling Russian acquisitiveness with American sensibilities, while maintaining the amiability of both parties."[8] But beyond pointing out that the treaty maintained the outward appearances of Allied unity, the two authors are at a loss to show just why it was a diplomatic triumph.

How well had the British served their interests by signing the long-awaited Anglo-Soviet Treaty? Was it as great a triumph as those involved in the negotiations believed it to be at the time? Although the mood among Britain's leaders, especially Churchill, was buoyant, what had Britain actually gained by evading the Soviet draft treaty? In order to answer these questions it is first necessary to understand what considerations impelled Molotov to execute his about-face, why he dropped his insistence that the British immediately accept his government's "minimum conditions." The key to this understanding lies in the Soviet approach to war and in the military situation of late May 1942.

As a result of their ideology, Soviet Communists had a greater feel for the interrelation of politics, strategy, and military power than did most of their Western counterparts. When Pierre Laval once asked Stalin to encourage Catholicism in the USSR as a sop to the Pope, the dictator replied: "The Pope! How many divisions has *he* got?"[9] This was more than an offhand comment; it reflected the way the Soviets looked at the world. Stalin was inclined to view the world in terms of military, economic, and political power, and to discount moral and intellectual factors.

The father of the USSR, Lenin, had exhibited a deep interest in military affairs, annotating Clausewitz's works, and writing of the latter's famous saying that warfare was an extension of politics: "The Marxists have always considered this axiom as the theoretical foundation for the meaning of every war."[10] Indeed, the history of the Soviet Union from 1917 through Stalin's reign suggests that the line separating peace and war in that nation was exceedingly thin at times, the "class war" being pursued vigorously enough to prompt one Western historian to term Stalin's collectivization drive "the war against the nation."[11]

If Stalin regarded the war against the kulaks as necessary, he considered competition and conflict between the USSR and its capitalist neighbors inevitable, as he avowed repeatedly. All those who did not uncritically accept the political line of the vanguard of the proletariat—that is, the program of the Communist party of the Soviet Union—might serve as temporary allies of the Kremlin, but to Moscow's way of thinking such allies remained potential mortal enemies of the Worker's State, in spite of their temporary complicity. Thus, when the Soviets negotiated with the British, they were not only conferring with an ally but also with a latent enemy. To Moscow, the outside world remained unrelievedly hostile to the USSR.

In 1928, at the Sixth World Congress of the Communist International, one of the theses adopted stated: "The overthrow of capitalism is impossible without violence, i.e., without armed uprisings and wars against the bourgeoisie. In our era of imperialistic wars and world revolution, revolutionary civil wars of the proletarian dictatorship against the bourgeoisie, wars of the proletariat against the bourgeois states and world capitalism, as well as national revolutionary wars of oppressed peoples against imperialism are unavoidable as has been shown by Lenin."[12] The distinctions between revolutions, civil wars, and international wars were considerably blurred in the minds of the Communist leadership. War of one sort or another occupied such a prominent place in their mentality, and in their political outlook, that to discuss political and military considerations of the Kremlin as though the two could be separated into watertight compartments is to misunderstand profoundly the Soviet approach to world affairs.

Molotov's behavior in London quickly revealed how he regarded political and military matters as two parts of the same equation. This was in sharp contrast to the Western Allies, who at times acted as though military plans were somehow divorced from political matters. In his first meeting with Churchill, Molotov said that he had come to Britain to discuss two questions, the political treaty and the issue of the second front, and that of the two questions the latter was by far the most important. When Churchill suggested that the foreign commissar discuss the practicability of the second front with the chief of the Imperial General Staff, Molotov "expressed a preference for a discussion in the first place on the political plane."[13] Molotov's assertion, repeated throughout his visit to the West, that he believed the decision to open a second front to be a political, rather than a military question was more than a bargaining ploy designed to force his allies' hand; it was an unquestioned assumption. In the Soviet Union, unlike the West, no division existed between political and military authority, and political interests outweighed military considerations as a matter of course. His allies' protestations that an invasion of France would depend primarily upon military factors, such as the availability of landing craft or Allied air superiority, must have struck Molotov as prevarication.

The Soviet leaders' perception of the indivisible link between politics and warfare meant that, to a far greater degree than the Western Allies, the Soviets based their political demands upon a cold-blooded analysis of comparative military advantage. Thus, in December 1941, as the USSR's armies were repulsing the Nazis from the gates of Moscow and it seemed that German strength was less formidable than previously imagined, Stalin bombarded Eden with a numbing list of territorial demands.

But in late May 1942 the Soviet military position changed dramatically. Just before the Soviet offensive in the Ukraine, on May 1 Stalin had announced to the Soviet public, "The Red Army has attained the turning point in the course of the war and gone over from active defense to successful offensive against the enemy troops." "The period of the liberation of Soviet lands from Hitlerite scum [*nechisti*]" had now begun, Stalin declared. And, lest anyone misunderstand which Soviet lands were to be liberated, Stalin continued: "Comrades! We are conducting a war that is patriotic and . . . just. We have no aims to sieze someone else's country, to subjugate someone else's peoples. Our goal is noble. We want to liberate our Soviet land from the German-fascist scoundrels. We want to liberate our brother Ukrainians, Moldavians [Bessarabians], Belorussians, Lithuanians, Latvians, Estonians, Karelians [Soviet Finns] from that shame and degradation to which the German-fascist scoundrels have subjected them."[14] Stalin was clearly optimistic about the prospects of rolling the Germans back and adding to the gains already made during the Soviet winter offensives. The dictator's optimism had also been evident in his conversations with Eden.

But Stalin pressed his temporary advantage too far by continuing his offensive operations into the spring, when the warmer weather and drier roads enabled the Germans once again to turn their greater mobility and superior tactical organization to advantage. The Soviet offensive from the Izium salient into the Ukraine was cut to ribbons by well-executed and timely German counterattacks, and more than 200,000 Red Army soldiers were captured by the Germans in this battle of encirclement, which raged from May 20 to 30.[15] Soviet military disasters multiplied with alarming rapidity when the tenuous equilibrium in the Crimea dissolved—as it had in the Ukraine—and the Germans, encouraged by their successes, launched their summer offensive toward Stalingrad and the Caucasus oil fields.

Molotov began his meetings with the British on May 21, that is, just as Soviet martial fortunes began to wane. Day by day, Stalin confronted disquieting fresh evidence that, although the Germans had suffered reverses during the winter, the USSR would nevertheless face a formidable challenge to its existence in a second successive summer of ferocious German attacks. The general secretary no longer confidently predicted victory in 1942 as he had done repeatedly earlier in the year. The gloomy outlook at the front was reflected in the changing Soviet diplomatic position. When Molotov departed for London, the Ukraine battle was still hanging in the balance; the foreign commissar's instructions had been to press for full British acceptance of the Soviet draft treaty.[16] By May 24, however, the German pincers had closed, and Molotov had evidently been told by telegram that his first priority should be to secure a commitment by the British and Americans for opening a second front, to relieve the intensified pressure on the Red Army.

As far as one can tell, given the gaps in Soviet documentation, Molotov had sensed that the British, and even more importantly the Americans, were refusing to commit themselves to opening a second front, in part because of their objections to Soviet territorial demands. This was, however, a misperception; British reluctance to land in France owed more to memories of Ypres and the Somme than to any anxiety for Polish independence. Nevertheless, it appears that the Kremlin interpreted the situation differently: if acceptance of the harmless British draft treaty and the temporary suspension of frontier discussions would incline the Western democracies more favorably toward an early invasion of France, then it was a price Stalin would gladly pay. Molotov's meeting with Winant on the night of May 24 had apparently convinced the foreign commissar that Soviet acceptance of Eden's draft treaty would put the Americans in a more compliant mood, which would in turn prod the British. On May 25 Eden told the Cabinet that he felt the Kremlin had been kept poorly informed about American objections to the Soviet draft treaty by Ambassador Litvinov, and that Molotov's sudden change of heart could be explained by his learning for the first time about the intensity of these objections. This explanation is not convincing, however, because Litvinov had sent the Kremlin an account of his talk with Roosevelt in April, when the president had dwelt at some length on American reservations to the Soviet proposals.[17] The Soviets had not suddenly learned of American protests during Molotov's journey; rather, Stalin now had his reasons for listening to Washington.

Washington must also have seemed to Molotov to be the best place to press for a second front. Churchill and his generals were hesitant to rush into an invasion of Europe; while Molotov was in London, he got almost no encouragement regarding an early invasion. But the Americans were more willing to commit themselves. The foreign commissar's impressions in this respect were confirmed when, during his visit to Washington, he extracted from President Roosevelt a promise that the United States would invade Europe in 1942. On June 11, after Molotov left Washington, the United States and the Soviets issued a joint press release stating that "full understanding had been reached with regard to the urgent tasks of creating a second front in Europe."[18]

As for the Anglo-Soviet Treaty itself, it contained nothing objectionable to the Soviets. Indeed, in at least one respect Stalin had gained his objective before the treaty was even signed. The British had more than once promised to accept Soviet sovereignty over the Baltic States, even though they had not done so in the formal treaty. This promise was something the British did not always later care to remember. Writing in 1950, Churchill said, "There was no doubt . . . where the right lay. The Baltic States should be sovereign and independent peoples." He lamented Soviet domination of these nations and proudly claimed that Britain had refused to do more than recognize de facto this particular manifestation of Soviet imperialism. Stretching the point, Churchill wrote: "Juridically this is how the matter stands now."[19]

This may indeed have been the juridical position of the British government, as Churchill claimed, but Stalin could always recall that London had at one time vowed to extend de jure recognition. Knowing this, he undoubtedly felt that British objections to Soviet occupation of the Baltic States after the war were merely pro forma, designed for public consumption. In the postwar world, had Britain even bothered to oppose the Soviet takeover of these republics, it would most probably have been a futile gesture; by 1945 the British had far more to object to in Soviet conduct than their annexation of Estonia, Latvia, and Lithuania.

So even though the Soviets had been forced to execute a diplomatic retreat by their need to secure some relief from German attacks, they had not lost sight of their permanent objectives. Their conciliatory behavior toward their Western Allies had in no way compromised their overall goals. Stalin had postponed advocacy of his territorial aims; he had not renounced them.

If Soviet political and military efforts were well coordinated, the British, and the Americans as well, showed a marked inability to unify these two aspects of their war effort. In a comment to Fitzroy Maclean, a former foreign service officer and commando who was preparing to act as British liaison with Tito's partisan movement in Yugoslavia, Churchill shed some light on his own attitude toward the political-military balance. Maclean had inquired about the wisdom of sending British material aid to Communist partisans: "So long, [Churchill] said, as the whole of Western civilisation was threatened by the Nazi menace, we could not afford to let our attention be diverted from the immediate issue by considerations of long-term policy. We were as loyal to our Soviet Allies as we hoped they were to us. [Maclean's] task was simply to find out who was killing the most Germans and suggest means by which we could help them to kill more. Politics must be a secondary consideration."[20] To be sure, as pointed out above, the British decision to prosecute the war against Germany, even if it meant sacrificing other desiderata, was itself a political decision. And this decision might in fact have been unavoidable. The inflexibility of Britain's will to crush Nazism completely, the constancy of her goal, was one of the dynamics of a democracy at war. The Anglo-American crusade against Nazism—to borrow Eisenhower's term—was in many ways more "ideological" than was the Soviet war effort, rhetorical excesses notwithstanding. At no point, for example, would the Western democracies angle for a separate peace with Germany, as the Soviets evidently did in 1943.[21]

J. F. C. Fuller, the conservative British historian and military theoretician, has attributed this inflexibility of democracies at war to a "tribal morality." "The motive force of democracy is not love of others," Fuller wrote, "it is the hate of all those outside the tribe, faction, party or nation. The 'general will' predicates total war, and hate is the most puissant of recruiters."[22] This is somewhat overdrawn, if perhaps understandable coming from one who experienced two world wars. Fuller's comment is, however, perceptive. Democracies seem to face difficulties mustering the political will to fight limited wars involving less than a conflict between absolute principles. The moral differences between the democratic side and that of its opponents must be drawn in the most stark fashion if a war effort is to be sustained for long. Concepts such as national interest and political advantage are very often deemed unworthy reasons for sacrificing human lives. A vivid example of this attitude was a comment made by General Marshall in 1945, when the British advocated the occupation of Czechoslovakia by Western forces before the Soviets could get there; Marshall wrote indignantly to Eisenhower saying, "Personally, and aside from all logistic, tactical or strategical implications I would be loath to hazard American lives for purely political purposes."[23]

Marshall's concern for the lives of his troops was laudable, and his reasoning would be immediately comprehensible to most Western readers. One could hardly hope, however, for a clearer illustration of the way in which the Western attitude toward the military-political balance differed from the Soviet view. On April 1, 1945, for example, Stalin asked his General Staff, "Well, who is going to take Berlin, we or the Allies?" Marshal I. S. Konev replied that they would and that they "would take it before the Allies did."[24] The irony in Marshall's reluctance to sacrifice lives for political gain was, of course, that the war against Germany was being fought precisely for "political purposes." Ignoble or not, war always is.

Fortunately, during World War II, when so much was at stake, in the mind of the British public Hitler's Germany did indeed approximate absolute evil. As a result, there was broad agreement among the electorate of the need for unity to defeat Germany. Unlike the United States, Britain formally suspended party politics during the war—though of course political activity flourished and there were numerous Cabinet reshuffles. No General Election was called between 1935 and 1945, the idea being that all domestic political quarrels paled into insignificance in the face of the Nazi threat. It was the duty of all men of good will, so the reasoning went, to cooperate in furthering the cause.

But with unity came restrictions. Churchill was certainly unable single-handedly to formulate British foreign policy. His was a coalition government, and the goals of that coalition were to defeat first Hitler and then Japan. Beyond these two broad aims, Churchill had no clear mandate. The Soviet Union was fighting on the side of the angels. And not everyone accepted the Moscow link with the same reservations so eloquently expressed by the prime minister in his famous speech of June 22, 1941, when he announced that he would unsay nothing he had said about the USSR in the previous twenty years, even though the Soviet Union was now an ally.

Some British politicians, such as Cripps and Eden, felt that differences in the Grand Alliance could be suppressed for the sake of unity as easily as the truce had been declared in domestic British politics. This was certainly the idea behind the British government's decision to postpone consideration of territorial questions until after the war. So, for the sake of Alliance unity, the British refused to wield some of the political weapons that were in their arsenal during the early years of the war that would slip away by 1945. In 1941 and 1942 the Soviets without doubt needed British help more than the reverse, at least in the short term. At no time, however, did London outline a firm policy toward the Soviet Union, nor did the British ever attach a price tag to the aid they gave the USSR.

It is highly doubtful that a united Anglo-American diplomatic hedgehog defense could have prevented the Soviets from absorbing the Baltic States, but it is not beyond the bounds of possibility. Moscow might at least have settled for domination as opposed to outright annexation. Certainly, the Soviets later proved responsive to Western pressure in such places as Iran, Greece, and Austria. The best example of the ways that a judicious use of Western pressure might have altered Soviet policy was Finland, where Allied sympathy for the Finns unwittingly caused Stalin to hold back. Milovan Djilas, a Yugoslav Communist leader when he met with Stalin in 1947, writes that Stalin lamented his "mistake" in failing to occupy Finland. "We were too concerned about the Americans," Stalin said, "and they wouldn't have lifted a finger."[25] Maksim Litvinov also later suggested that had the West made their objections to Soviet demands more forcefully than they did, Moscow might have hesitated before securing its dominance over all of Eastern Europe. In an interview with the left-wing journalist Edgar Snow in October 1944, the former foreign commissar was uncommonly frank when reflecting upon the causes of growing East-West tension. Snow quoted him as saying, "Diplomacy might have been able to avoid [the growing rift] if we [in the West] had made clear the limits of our needs, but now it is too late, suspicions are rife on both sides."[26] Litvinov might have added that by 1944 Anglo-American leverage was no longer what it had once been.

In the spring of 1942 Sumner Welles studied the record of the Versailles Conference hoping to discover lessons to apply in World War II. Looking back in 1950, he wrote: "The more I read about the negotiations of 1919, the more I was convinced that our wisest course would be to try to work out with our allies now, before V-day, as detailed an agreement as possible. Our armed strength, the moral authority of President Roosevelt [and, he might have added, of Winston Churchill] and, even more perhaps, our allies' need of us, would give us infinitely greater leverage now than we would have after victory was won."[27] This judgment, made by a perceptive observer intimately involved in the course of events, is difficult to dispute. The Anglo-American allies allowed a promising opportunity to slip past for exercising greater influence over the postwar world than they would be able to exert later in the war.

Instead of setting clear limits upon what they considered to be legitimate Soviet demands, the British at times were more anxious to avoid the appearance of an Anglo-American condominium. To be sure, during the London talks with Molotov, Eden stubbornly refused to accept Soviet demands regarding Poland; however, rather than telling the Soviets what Russo-Polish boundary Britain would find acceptable, Eden remained deliberately vague. He even resorted to a lie about British obligations to Poland, simply to avoid quarreling with Molotov.

Rather than engaging the Soviets in frank negotiations and facing the fact that such an approach would entail some unpleasant confrontations, the British leaders, one after another in dismal succession, persisted in their misguided attempts to build a genuine and lasting friendship with Moscow. Such a friendship remained a chimera, and one can only wonder why anyone ever thought otherwise. The question is frequently posed why the Soviets were such effective diplomats during the war. One answer is that, unlike many Western diplomats, the Soviets accepted the hostility of every other state as a fact of international life and considered any alliance with a foreign power to be a passing phenomenon. Stalin and Molotov were able to press for full acceptance of their demands untroubled by the compulsion to find a reasonable compromise with their allies of the moment. Indeed, as pointed out above, the remarkable thing about Soviet foreign policy during the volatile period 1939–42 is its constancy; although the USSR's allies changed, Soviet demands remained much the same. Stalin's demands of the Allies bore a striking resemblance to his demands of Hitler, a fact that suggests that the Kremlin cared less about the good will of its partners than it did about concrete territorial gain.

Nevertheless, the British continued to believe that they must first win Stalin's trust before they could hope to build a smoothly functioning alliance. Each British effort to win Soviet confidence failed in turn. Sir Stafford Cripps had been confident in 1940 that the Anglo-Soviet rift had been caused by a colossal misunderstanding for which inept Conservative diplomacy was to blame. He found, to his chagrin, that Stalin was no more inclined to befriend a Socialist ambassador than a Nazi. Indeed, during the first year of Cripps's stay in Moscow, the German ambassador, Schulenburg, could always gain the ear of the Kremlin more easily than could Sir Stafford. And toward the end of Cripps's term as ambassador, the Soviets virtually ignored him, believing—as a partial result of the antics of Lord Beaverbrook—that he had lost the trust of his government.

Beaverbrook, too, had believed that he could win Soviet trust, but he had a different approach than the more austere Cripps. Whereas Cripps felt he could win Soviet hearts by demonstrating his sincerity and his fidelity to Socialist principles, Beaverbrook characteristically felt he could buy Stalin by holding a "Christmas tree party," handing out military supplies like Christmas crackers. His approach was ultimately no more successful than Cripps's.

Underlying these various British attempts to buy Soviet trust and friendship, as though they were commodities for sale in an exotic oriental bazaar, was a certain unstated condescension toward and contempt for the Soviets themselves. In the Foreign Office records, one reads ad nauseam that Stalin possessed an "oriental" or "Asian" mind, and that he was unused to and confused by Western diplomatic ways—in spite of the fact that he had directed Soviet foreign policy far longer than any Western head of state had been in office. While the Foreign Office flattered itself by treating Stalin as a tyro in diplomacy, however, the Soviet dictator was handily outmaneuvering London.

British diplomats also convinced themselves that Soviet foreign policy was not guided primarily by the Kremlin's assessment of Soviet interests; London interpreted Stalin's demand for recognition of the Soviet Union's western frontiers less as a demand for territory than as a "test" of British willingness to make "unpalatable sacrifices" needed to convince Moscow that Britain had at long last mended its anti-Soviet ways. This argument was advanced in spite of at least two things known to the Foreign Office at the time that cast doubt on its validity. First, Soviet territorial demands antedated Anglo-Soviet cooperation; so, unless one accepts that Stalin had devised an identical test of Hitler's good will in 1939, there is little reason to assume that he did so for the British in 1941–42. Second, Stalin himself never explicitly couched his demands in the form of a test. To be sure, in December Stalin had claimed that London's refusal to accept Soviet conquests was unfriendly, but he had not said anything about a test. That idea was the product of British minds alone, especially that of Sir Stafford Cripps.

The most tragic, or perhaps pathetic, attempt during this period to buy Soviet friendship was certainly the British decision to sanction Soviet absorption of the Baltic States. Even Churchill was not entirely free from the pull of this extraordinary delusion. Talking to General Sikorski in April 1942, the prime minister had defended his country's course, saying that "in spite of the opposition in Great Britain on the part of Parliament, the Anglican clergy, not to mention the Catholics, the conservative aides, etc., and in spite of the objections raised by the United States Government, a political treaty with Russia will be concluded. It is not an ideal one. It might cause some deception; nevertheless, this attempt has to be made."[28]

British appeasement of the Soviets might have made sense had the Foreign Office, or the Cabinet, developed clear counterdemands prior to recognizing Stalin's territorial claims, but they did not. Three arguments were advanced to support British accession to Soviet demands. First, the British public, and to some extent Parliament, had been impressed by the Red Army's performance against the Wehrmacht, especially when contrasted with the lackluster accomplishments of Britain's own armed forces at this stage of the war. Opinions of this sort may have been the crucial consideration for Churchill. The evidence regarding his opinions about recognition of Soviet claims is contradictory: in January he told Eden that he would resign rather than head a government that would be a party to an agreement recognizing Soviet claims, but by March he had changed his mind and was asking Roosevelt to acquiesce to British recognition. It seems clear that, for Churchill at least, the primary consideration in accepting Stalin's demands was the need he felt to quiet those who were clamoring, ever more loudly, for some Allied effort to ease the pressure on the Red Army. Churchill was deeply convinced that a premature invasion of Europe would be a fiasco that would not help the Red Army and would perhaps permanently cripple British strength; at the very least it would incur enormous casualties. Churchill decided that, given the choice between thousands, perhaps hundreds of thousands, of British dead and recognition of Soviet sovereignty over the Baltic States, the second was the better option. But, as we have seen, even in late May the prime minister expressed doubts to the Cabinet about the wisdom and ethics of such a course.

The second, and superficially more compelling, reason advanced in favor of recognizing Stalin's demands was a concern lest the Soviet dictator sign a separate peace with Hitler. The Red Army was an invaluable asset to the Allied cause: at no point in the war after June 1941 did the Western Allies face more than one quarter of the Wehrmacht. Should Stalin have decided to come to terms with Hitler, the damage to Allied chances for victory would have been incalculable. Surely, one might argue, prevention of a separate peace was sufficient cause to appease Stalin.

Close examination of this second argument shows it to be largely hollow. Had Stalin decided to approach Hitler, it is highly doubtful that he would have been restrained from doing so by reflecting upon British largesse over the Baltic States. Stalin had not allied the Soviet Union with the West because it was the better side; he had become Britain's ally only when forced. It is a colossal overestimation of the importance to Stalin of British friendship to assume that he would have been deterred from approaching Hitler by displays of London's flexibility. Also, it should be remembered, Hitler himself had already once given his imprimatur to Soviet sovereignty over the disputed states, and he would most probably have done so again as part of any armistice acceptable to Moscow. At any rate, in the spring of 1942 there were no hints in the West of a Russo-German rapprochement, and the British did not take this threat seriously.

This brings us to the third reason, the Cripps-Eden motivation for accepting Stalin's demands. On several separate occasions, Eden wrote that, though he did not fear a separate Russo-German peace, he felt that Stalin was demanding a British sacrifice of principle to overcome all the suspicions clouding Anglo-Soviet relations since 1917, a sacrifice that would provide the basis for a new and genuine Anglo-Soviet friendship.

British appeasement did not lead to the creation of such a lasting friendship; instead, the immediate result of British flexibility over the Baltic States was—much to Eden's consternation—increased Soviet pressure over the Russo-Polish border dispute. Molotov maintained that the British had not made any sacrifice of principle but had simply acceded to legitimate Soviet demands. There would be no counterconcessions from Moscow. Most importantly, the divisions separating the Soviet Union from "capitalist" Britain did not magically disappear thanks to British accommodation.

By May 1942 the British found themselves in a bind. They had the worst of both worlds: they had sacrificed a principle and had received nothing in return. Only haphazard American intervention and Soviet reverses on the Eastern Front saved Churchill's government from recognizing by treaty Soviet sovereignty over the disputed territories. It is tempting to draw a parallel between the British experience in the spring of 1942 and the much better known, and far more serious, experience of appeasement before the war. In neither case was the British government able to moderate the appetite of its negotiating partner. Evidently, however, the prewar lesson had gone unlearned.

What the British government did not realize was that the Soviets were *already* cooperating more closely with America and Britain than they had done with any other nations since 1917. The highly xenophobic and suspicious nature of Stalin's Soviet Union precluded a more intimate alliance. Opening the USSR to the outside world after Stalin had taken such great pains to quarantine his empire from foreign influences would have required a fundamental change in Soviet government and society, a change much greater than British diplomacy alone could effect. Stalin had become Britain's ally overnight when the "objective circumstances," that is the German attack, had forced him to do so. He would have renounced the alliance equally quickly had it ceased to serve his interests. British flexibility over the Baltic States would do nothing to change this.

In June 1946 Maksim Litvinov granted an interview in the Kremlin with another American journalist, Richard C. Hottelet. Litvinov, who was soon dismissed from the Soviet government—an event perhaps not entirely unrelated to this extraordinary interview—made some remarks that shed light on the futility of British attempts to appease Moscow. He told the American that the "root cause" of the growing cold war was "the ideological conception prevailing here [in the USSR] that conflict between Communist and capitalist worlds is inevitable. . . . There has been a return to the outmoded concept of security in terms of territory—the more you've got the safer you are." Hottelet then asked a crucial question: "Suppose the West were suddenly to give in and grant all Moscow's demands . . . ? Would that lead to good will and easing of the present tension?" "It would lead," Litvinov answered, "to the West's being faced after a more or less short time, with the next series of demands."[29] Clearly, appeasement of such a government was bound to be an exercise in futility.

Had the British government chosen not to appease Stalin in 1942, it bears repeating, this would most probably not have secured the independence of the Baltic States or Eastern Europe. Stalin later told Djilas that "everyone imposes his own system as far as his army can reach. It cannot be otherwise."[30] And it was the Red Army, not American or British forces, that drove the Germans from Eastern Europe, giving the Soviets the opportunity to establish their domination there. But Stalin's comment was made in 1947, after the wartime allies had already fallen out. As such, it was more an explanation of Soviet policy as executed than a statement of what Stalin had intended to do from the start of the war. Nobody can say with certainty whether timely Allied pressures might have been able to limit Soviet gains. Perhaps the frequent British lament that nothing could be done to prevent Soviet control over the Baltic States became a self-fulfilling prophecy.

What one can say with certainty, however, is that British methods of dealing with Moscow over the question of the Baltic States were woefully inept. As Eden admitted later in the war, his position on this matter had weakened his ability to resist further Soviet claims.[31] By refusing to approve of Soviet gains, Britain might not have been able to prevent Soviet expansion, but at least it would not have been a party to it. It is interesting to recall General Charles De Gaulle's refusal in 1944 to sanction the consolidation of Soviet control over Poland, even though France was too weak to alter Soviet policy. De Gaulle wrote in his memoirs: "However little weight France's attitude might have at the moment, it could later be important that she had adopted it at that particular moment. The future lasts a long time. All things are possible, even the fact that an action in accord with honor and honesty ultimately appears to be a prudent political investment."[32]

This is not to say that no agreement with the Soviet Union was possible, or that the Soviets were devils with whom the West could not talk without becoming defiled. Cooperation with the USSR was possible, desirable, and necessary on certain issues. But the experience of Britain's relations with the Soviet Union from 1940 to 1942 surely teaches some lessons: that cooperation with the Kremlin was most successful when limited to those questions upon which the Soviets felt agreement was in their own interests, and that, above all else, relations were best when conducted in as unsentimental and calm a manner as possible (one is reminded of Talleyrand's famous warning against zeal in foreign affairs). One thing is absolutely clear: unilateral gestures by the West designed to win Soviet confidence by sacrificing Western interests or principles were hopelessly naive. There is no evidence to suggest that actions of this sort had the desired effect. Quite the contrary, if Moscow took any public notice of such gestures—which they rarely did—then the Western sacrifices were ascribed to weakness, or to the irresistible pressures of public opinion. The Soviets did not expect goodwill gestures, they discounted Western sincerity, and, most importantly, they did not respond in a like manner. British experience with the question of the Baltic States graphically illustrates the futility of such one-sided friendship offerings. Unfortunately, given the fact that political pressures to reach accommodation with Moscow were generally very strong, and that those who called loudest for such accommodation were frequently those least well informed about the difficulties involved in working with the Soviets, emotionally detached conduct of relations with Moscow was more often than not impossible. The results were particularly unfortunate for Western diplomacy, for Eastern Europe, and for the postwar European balance of power.

NOTES

Abbreviations

DGFP   U.S. Department of State. *Documents on German Foreign Policy,*
         1918–1945. Series D. Washington, D.C., 1957.
FO   British Foreign Office.
FRUS   U.S. Department of State. *Foreign Relations of the United States.*
         Washington, D.C., 1953– .
N   Northern Department of the British Foreign Office.
NA   U.S. National Archives, Washington, D.C.
NKID   People's Commissariat of Foreign Affairs.
NSR   *Nazi-Soviet Relations, 1939–1941: Documents from the Archives of the Ger-*
         man Foreign Office. Edited by Raymond J. Sontag and James Stuart Beddie.
         Washington, D.C., 1948. Reprint, Westport, Conn., 1976.
PRO   British Public Record Office, Kew.
SAO   USSR, Ministry of Foreign Affairs. *Sovetsko-angliiskie otnosheniia vo*
         vremia velikoi Otechestvennoi voiny, 1941–1945. 2 vols. Moscow, 1984.
SAmO   USSR, Ministry of Foreign Affairs. *Sovetsko-amerikanskie otnosheniia vo*
         vremia velikoi Otechestvennoi voiny, 1941–1945. 2 vols. Moscow, 1984.

Introduction

1. The best study of Soviet wartime diplomacy scarcely touches on the period 1940–
   42: Vojtech Mastny, *Russia's Road to the Cold War: Diplomacy, Warfare, and the
   Politics of Communism, 1941–1945* (New York, 1979). There are many excellent
   studies of wartime Anglo-Soviet relations, all of which deal in passing with the
   period covered by this work. See, for example, the two fine studies by Elisabeth
   Barker, *British Policy in South-East Europe in the Second World War* (London,
   1976) and *Churchill and Eden at War* (London, 1978) and Victor Rothwell, *Britain and the Cold War, 1941–1947* (London, 1982). The only book to examine
   Anglo-Soviet relations in detail for the period 1940–42 is Gabriel Gorodetsky,
   Stafford Cripps' Mission to Moscow, 1940–42 (Cambridge, 1984). Readers looking for a very different view about this period are advised to read Gorodetsky's
   erudite book. Gorodetsky finds more to admire in Stafford Cripps's diplomacy
   than I do, and he describes his account of Soviet-British relations as "revisionist."
   Gorodetsky limits his study to the Cripps mission, whereas the present work continues the story until the Anglo-Soviet Treaty of May 1942.
2. One outstanding exception to the tendency to focus on the later years of the war is
   Sarah Meiklejohn Terry, *Poland's Place in Europe: General Sikorski and the Ori-*

gin of the Oder-Neisse Line, 1939–1943 (Princeton, 1983). Terry has many useful insights into the part Poland played in Anglo-Soviet relations at this time.

3. From 1939 on, the lost provinces would form the basis of Stalin's territorial claims; indeed in May 1942, Molotov would call Soviet sovereignty over these areas the Soviets' "minimum conditions." See Chapter 7.

4. Barbara Jelavich, *St. Petersburg and Moscow: Tsarist and Soviet Foreign Policy, 1814–1974* (Bloomington, Ind., 1974), p. 314.

5. For an interesting insider's account of the stormy German-Soviet partnership, see Gustav Hilger and Alfred G. Meyer, *The Incompatible Allies: A Memoir-History of German-Soviet Relations, 1918–1941* (New York, 1953). Another memoir history, this one showing the activities of the Communist party in Germany during the years of formal German-Soviet cooperation, is Ruth Fischer, *Stalin and German Communism: A Study in the Origins of the State Party* (Cambridge, 1948). For an excellent analysis of Stalin's "German orientation," or preference for working with Germany, see Robert C. Tucker, "The Emergence of Stalin's Foreign Policy," *Slavic Review* 4 (1977).

6. Extracts from Stalin's speech to the Fourteenth Congress of the Communist Party of the Soviet Union, December 1925, in Jane Degras, ed., *Soviet Documents on Foreign Policy* (Oxford, 1952), 2:69–76.

7. Hilger and Meyer, *The Incompatible Allies*, p. 130.

8. The testimony of Soviet defectors is almost unanimous in claiming that Stalin secretly sought an agreement with Hitler while allowing Litvinov to publically advocate collective security. See Ismail Akhmedov, *In and Out of Stalin's GRU: A Tatar's Escape from Red Army Intelligence* (Frederick, Md., 1984), p. 86, and Walter G. Krivitsky, *In Stalin's Secret Service: An Exposé of Russia's Secret Policies by the Former Chief of the Soviet Intelligence in Western Europe* (New York, 1939). A fascinating samizdat account by the former director of the Foreign Commissariat's Press Department is Evgenii Gnedin, *Iz istorii otnoshenii mezhdu SSSR i fashistkoi Germaniei: Dokumenty i sovremennye kommentarii* (New York, 1977). For an excellent recent scholarly synthesis arguing that Stalin continually sought a deal with Hitler during the 1930s, see Bianka Pietrow, *Stalinismus, Sicherheit, Offensive: Das "Dritte Reich" in der Konzeption der sowjetischen Aussenpolitik, 1933–1941* (Melsungen, 1983).

For an assessment of Maxim Litvinov's advocacy of collective security, see Henry L. Roberts, "Maxim Litvinov," in *The Thirties*, vol. 2 of *The Diplomats, 1919–1939*, ed. Gordon Craig and Felix Gilbert (New York, 1953), p. 363. A less reliable account is Arthur Upham Pope, *Maxim Litvinoff* (New York, 1943).

9. For two recent scholarly histories of the failure of collective security, see Jonathan Haslam, *The Soviet Union and the Struggle for Collective Security in Europe, 1933–39* (New York, 1984), and Jiri Hochman, *The Soviet Union and the Failure of Collective Security, 1934–1938* (Ithaca, N.Y., 1984).

10. Winston S. Churchill, *History of the Second World War* (Boston, 1948–54), 1:354.

11. Ibid., 347.

12. All citations from the Butler-Helfand talk of September 13, 1940, are taken from PRO, N6758/30/38.

13. Nikolai V. Sivachev and Nikolai N. Yakovlev, *Russia and the United States,* trans. Olga Adler Titelbaum (Chicago, 1979), pp. 144 and 148. For similar arguments see B. N. Ponomaryov and A. A. Gromyko, eds., *History of Soviet Foreign Policy* (Moscow, 1969), and Ivan M. Maisky, *Memoirs of a Soviet Ambassador,* trans. Andrew Rothstein (New York, 1967).

14. Soviet historical accounts of this period, which suffer from a tedious uniformity, stress how the Western Allies remained on the defensive while the Germans crushed Poland. Because this interpretation is constantly repeated, one may infer that the point is to suggest that had the USSR allied itself with the West, it too would have borne the brunt of the fighting against Hitler. This essentially reasonable argument is weakened somewhat by the role the USSR played in crushing Polish resistance—a story that never figures in Soviet histories. For one of the most recent Soviet accounts of diplomacy before 1941, see Pavel Sevastyanov, *Before the Nazi Invasion: Soviet Diplomacy in September 1939–June 1941,* trans. David Skvirsky (Moscow, 1981). An earlier but more interesting account (because of the author's role as a representative in Britain, 1932–43) is Ivan M. Maisky, *Kto pomogal Gitleru* (Moscow, 1962). For a good account of the role the Japanese threat played in Soviet policy during the late 1930s, see Jonathan Haslam, "Soviet Aid to China and Japan's Place in Moscow's Foreign Policy," in *Some Aspects of Soviet-Japanese Relations in the 1930s,* ed. Ian Nish (London, 1982), pp. 35–58.

15. J. V. Stalin, *Works* (Moscow, 1954), 7:13–14.

16. Nikolai Bukharin first formulated the Soviet theory that revolutions are "absolutely inevitable" in war. As with his other victims, once he had defeated and executed Bukharin, Stalin adopted his ideas. See Stephen F. Cohen, *Bukharin and the Bolshevik Revolution: A Political Biography, 1888–1938* (London: 1974), pp. 256–58.

17. Memorandum of conversation between Cripps and Stalin, July 1, 1940, PRO, N6526/30/38.

18. In November 1940 Molotov told Hitler that "the focal point of the aspirations of the Soviet Union [was] south of Batum and Baku in the general direction of the Persian Gulf." Stalin also hoped to expand Soviet control of the Black Sea and to gain bases on the Turkish Straits. Schulenburg to the German Foreign Office, November 26, 1940, *NSR,* pp. 258–59. Stalin's designs are discussed in greater depth in Chapter 4.

19. F. S. Northedge and Audrey Wells, *Britain and Soviet Communism* (London, 1982), p. 76.

20. For an account of Eden's talks with Stalin in December 1941, see Chapter 6.

21. Sumner Welles memorandum of conversation with Lord Halifax, February 18, 1942, *FRUS 1942,* 3:519.

22. Quoted in Barker, *Churchill and Eden at War,* p. 244.

23. Welles to Berle, April 4, 1942, *FRUS 1942,* 3:542.

24. Such was the opinion of President Roosevelt, at least, who, in December 1942, told Henry Wallace that during the spring of that year "he had stepped in and prevented the British and Russians from arriving at an accord that would give the Russians [the Baltic States, Bessarabia, and Eastern Poland]." Henry A. Wallace,

The Price of Vision: The Diary of Henry A. Wallace, 1942–1946, ed. John Morton Blum (Boston, 1973), pp. 159–60. In fact, American resistance to Soviet claims owed more to Roosevelt's advisors than to the president's own efforts. For a recent restatement of the view that British wartime diplomacy was more astute than American, see Michael Howard, *War and the Liberal Conscience: The George Macaulay Trevelyan Lectures in the University of Cambridge* (Oxford, 1981), pp. 115–19. Howard claims that "it is perfectly true that the British Government did not share the sanguine expectations of American liberals about the nature of the post-war world: it had a more lively and realistic insight into the political and above all the economic difficulties [of the postwar period]." In Chapters 6 and 7 I argue that in the spring of 1942, at least, American liberals better understood the unfolding problems of working with the USSR than did their British counterparts.

25. Quoted in Martin Gilbert, *Winston S. Churchill* (London, 1975), 4:385.

Chapter 1

1. Molotov to the fifth extraordinary session of the Supreme Soviet, October 31, 1939, General Sikorski Historical Institute, *Documents on Polish-Soviet Relations, 1939–1945* (London, 1961), 1:65–69. For a good account of Allied strategic dithering, see Martin Gilbert, *Winston S. Churchill* (London, 1983), 6:chaps. 1–16.
2. Sir William Seeds to FO, January 1, 1940, PRO, N40/40/38.
3. Winston S. Churchill, *History of the Second World War* (Boston, 1948–54), 1:543.
4. Seeds to FO, January 2, 1940, PRO, N71/71/38.
5. J. R. M. Butler, *Grand Strategy September 1939–June 1941* (London, 1957), 2:71–79.
6. "Memorandum by the Chairman of the German Economic Delegation to the Soviet Union [Schnurre]," February 26, 1940, *DGFP*, 8:814–17.
7. "Report from the Yugoslav Minister in London," December 23, 1939, PRO, N504/30/38.
8. War Cabinet, "Review of Military Policy in the Middle East," January 10, 1940. Also Fitzroy Maclean memorandum, February 12, 1940.
9. Maclean memorandum, ibid.
10. Maclean memorandum, January 17, 1940, PRO, N1147/283/38.
11. Maclean memorandum, February 2, 1940, PRO, N2736/1310/38.
12. Quoted in E. Llewellyn Woodward, *British Foreign Policy in the Second World War* (London, 1970), 1:64.
13. Ibid., 71.
14. Maclean memorandum, January 13, 1940, PRO, N1013/71/38.
15. John Le Rougetel to FO, January 22, 1940, PRO, N1424/1310/38.
16. See for example, Sir Orme Sargent to Hughe Knatchbull-Hugessen, January 4, 1940, PRO, N1752/40/38.
17. Sargent to Knatchbull-Hugessen, February 15, 1940, PRO, N103/30/38.

18. Knatchbull-Hugessen to FO, February 2, 1940, PRO, N1566/96/38.
19. R. M. A. Hankey minute, February 21, 1940, PRO, N2574/40/38.
20. Sir R. Hoare to Lord Halifax, February 23, 1940, ibid.
21. "Contacts with M. Gugushvili of Caucasian Separatist Movement in Paris," April 18, 1940, March 4, 1940, October 23, 1940, PRO, N5043, 2671, 6931/40/38.
22. Minutes by William Strang, February 20, 1940, and Maclean memorandum, undated, PRO, N2209/40/38.
23. Secretary of State for India to FO, February 21, 1940, PRO, N2270/40/38. General Sir A. P. Wavell also warned the FO of the threat, Wavell to War Office, February 12, 1940, PRO, N1752/40/38.
24. Knatchbull-Hugessen to FO, February 26, 1940, PRO, N2634/40/38.
25. Knatchbull-Hugessen to FO, February 29, 1940, PRO, N2714/40/38.
26. Woodward, *British Foreign Policy*, 1:110–12. For an account of French strategic plans to attack the USSR in 1940, see C. O. Richardson, "French Plans for Allied Attacks on the Caucasus Oil Fields, January–April, 1940," *French Historical Studies* 8 (1973). Unfortunately, Richardson neglects the British role in these plans.
27. Le Rougetel to Laurence Collier, January 11, 1940, PRO, N1068/96/38.
28. R. A. Butler memorandum, February 8, 1940, PRO, N1390/30/38. Woodward says the meeting took place on January 30, but the document is dated February 8. Woodward, *British Foreign Policy*, 1:107.
29. War Cabinet memorandum, Chiefs of Staff, March 8, 1940, PRO, N3313/40/38.
30. Ivan Maisky, *Memoirs of a Soviet Ambassador: The War, 1939–1943* (New York, 1967), p. 49.
31. Nichols minutes of talk with Greek Minister, March 2, 1940, PRO, N2749/30/38.
32. Le Rougetel to FO, March 3, 1940, PRO, N2723/40/38.
33. Le Rougetel to FO, March 5, 1940, PRO, N2806/30/38.
34. Knatchbull-Hugessen to FO, February 29, 1940, PRO, N2604/30/38.
35. French police raided the Soviet Trade Delegation in Paris on February 5. The French Communist party opposed the war against Germany during the period of the Nazi-Soviet Pact, as did other Western Communist parties.
36. Next to this passage of the telegram, Maclean wrote "blackmail."
37. Sir Archibald Clark Kerr to FO, March 4, r940, PRO, N2779/40/38.
38. Sir Stafford Cripps [in Chunking] to FO, March 4, 1940, PRO, N2780/40/38, and Cripps to Butler, March 4, 1940, PRO, N2781/40/38. For an account of Cripps's unsuccessful efforts to arrange a visit to Moscow in September 1939, see Gabriel Gorodetsky, *Stafford Cripps' Mission to Moscow, 1940–42* (Cambridge, 1984), pp. 7–9.
39. Maclean comments about Cripps's telegrams, March 8, 1940, PRO, N2779/40/38.
40. Alexander Cadogan, *The Diaries of Sir Alexander Cadogan, 1938–1945*, ed. David Dilks (New York, 1972), p. 262.
41. War Cabinet record, March 12, 1940, PRO, N3208/40/38.
42. Woodward, *British Foreign Policy*, 1:109.
43. War Cabinet record, March 12, 1940, PRO, N3208/40/38.
44. Maclean memorandum, undated but after March 23, 1940, PRO, N3698/40/38.

45. Knatchbull-Hugessen to Sargent, March 15, 1940, PRO, N3492/40/38.
46. Cadogan memorandum, March 23, 1940, PRO, N3698/40/38.
47. Sargent memorandum, March 24, 1940, and Cadogan memorandum, March 26, 1940, PRO, N3363/30/38.
48. FO to Knatchbull-Hugessen, March 25, 1940, PRO, N3588/40/38.
49. Morgan to FO, March 27, 1940, PRO, N3619/40/38.
50. Cadogan, *Diaries*, p. 265.
51. Halifax to Le Rougetel, March 28, 1940, PRO, N3706/5/38.
52. Peake minutes of conversation with M. Korj, March 29, 1940, PRO, N4233/5/38.
53. Woodward, *British Foreign Policy*, 1:110–12.
54. Ibid.
55. Seeds to Sargent, March 29, 1940, PRO, N3706/5/38.
56. War Cabinet conclusions, March 29, 1940, PRO, N3738/40/38.
57. The text of Molotov's speech is in Jane Degras, ed., *Soviet Documents on Foreign Policy*, (London, 1953), 3:436–49.
58. Le Rougetel to Halifax, April 23, 1940, PRO, N4905/30/38.
59. Gladwyn Jebb memorandum for Cadogan, March 30, 1940, PRO, N3921/5/38.
60. Joint Intelligence Committee report on the Caucasus, April 2, 1940, PRO, N5087/40/38.
61. Sir Frederick Leith-Ross to Sargent, April 5, 1940, PRO, N4003/5/38.
62. Sir A. Faulkner to Sargent, April 4, 1940, PRO, N4004/5/38, and Faulkner to Sargent, April 6, 1940, PRO, 4005/5/38.
63. Maclean memorandum, April 4, 1940, PRO, N4155/5/38.
64. Marquess of Lothian to FO, April 8, 1940, PRO, N4114/5/38.
65. Butler minute, April 11, 1940, ibid.
66. "Ambassador Schulenburg to State Secretary Weizsäcker," April 11, 1940, *DGFP*, 9:134–36. It is interesting to contrast Schulenburg's opinion that the Soviet government was always well informed with the notion, frequently expressed in Britain, that the Soviets in general, and Stalin in particular, did not understand the world outside the Soviet Union.
67. War Cabinet conclusions, April 15, 1940, PRO, N4511/40/38.
68. War Cabinet conclusions, April 19, 1940, PRO, N4767/5/38.
69. Halifax to Le Rougetel, April 19, 1940, PRO, N4749/5/38.
70. Maclean memorandum, April 22, 1940, PRO, N5298/5/38.
71. Butler memorandum, April 23, 1940, PRO, N5062/30/38.
72. Halifax to Le Rougetel, April 29, 1940, PRO, N5273/5/38.
73. Peake memorandum, April 30, 1940, PRO, N5496/5496/38.
74. War Cabinet record, April 30, 1940, PRO, N5341/5/38.
75. Maclean and Steel memorandum, May 1, 1940, PRO, N5449/5/38.
76. Cadogan, *Diaries*, p. 277.
77. War Cabinet record, May 6, 1940, PRO, N5499/5/38.
78. Halifax minute, May 8, 1940, PRO, N5524/5/38.
79. Vansittart to Halifax, May 9, 1940, PRO, N5554/5/38.
80. *New Statesman*, May 11, 1940.
81. The British were also hopeful that by dealing with the Soviets they might deter

the Italians from aligning with the Germans. The Foreign Office learned that the French ambassador in Rome had been told that "the Italian Government have been impressed by the prospect of commercial negotiations between H.M.G. and the Soviet Government . . . the Soviet Government may be preparing some surprise for the German Government." Strang minute, May 11, 1940, PRO, N5589/5/38.

82. War Cabinet, May 14 and 15, 1940, PRO, N5499/5/38.

83. Butler minutes and Soviet protest note, May 16, 1940, PRO, N5799/5/38.

84. Butler to Halifax, undated but possibly May 18, 1940, PRO, N5799/5/38.

85. Hugh Dalton Papers, Dalton Diary, British Library of Economic and Political Science, 17.5.40, 4/1; War Cabinet, May 18, 1940, PRO 5499/5/38.

86. War Cabinet, May 18, 1940, PRO, 5499/5/38.

87. "Brief for Sir Stafford Cripps on the Far East," May 22, 1940, PRO, N5648/40/38.

88. "Brief for Sir Stafford Cripps on the Balkans," May 23, 1940, ibid.

89. "Brief for Sir Stafford Cripps on Turkey," May 22, 1940, ibid.

90. Maclean wrote the briefing on May 21. The Germans broke through the Allied lines on May 13 and 14 and reached the Channel coast at Abbéville on May 20.

91. "Brief for Sir Stafford Cripps on Soviet Policy," May 21, 1940, PRO, N5648/40/38. Over a year later, the counselor of the Yugoslav Legation in Moscow echoed Maclean's opinions, telling the American ambassador that Stalin had "a deep seated hatred of Britain" because of "the historic frustration by the British of Soviet territorial ambitions." He said that "Stalin desires and is seeking to bring about the dissolution of the British Empire in anticipation of territorial gains." Stalin was only working with Germany in hopes that Hitler's conflict with Britain would weaken Germany "as to no longer constitute a serious threat to the Soviet Union." Such a view, Steinhardt added, "is shared by some of the best informed diplomats in Moscow." Steinhardt to Secretary of State, May 31, 1941, Confidential File, NA 740.001 European War 1939/11527.

92. Maclean minute, May 22, 1940, PRO, N5661/5/38.

93. Maisky, *Memoirs*, p. 137.

94. *Daily Worker*, May 27, 1940.

95. Maisky, *Memoirs*, p. 136.

96. Butler minute, May 23, 1940, PRO, N5298/5/38.

97. There is some reason to believe that Maiskii, as a Litvinov appointee, was an advocate of Soviet alignment with the West rather than with Nazi Germany. This, at least, is the contention of Leon Helfand, who defected from the Soviet embassy in Rome in the summer of 1940, PRO, N6758/30/38. For Maiskii's alleged sympathy for the West, see also A. Nekrich, "The Arrest and Trial of I. M. Maisky," *Survey* 22 (1976). Nekrich was a graduate student under Maiskii during the 1950s.

98. Dalton minute, May 25, 1940, PRO, N5661/5/38. Also see Dalton Diary, 25.5.40, 4/1.

99. Halifax to Le Rougetel, May 27, 1940, PRO, N5661/5/38.

100. H. Hanak, "Sir Stafford Cripps as British Ambassador in Moscow, May 1940 to June 1941," *English Historical Review* 370 (1979): 57.

101. Dalton Diary, 27.5.40, 4/1.
102. War Cabinet, May 31, 1940, PRO, N5689/40/38.
103. Le Rougetel to FO, June 1, 1940, PRO, N5732/5/38.
104. Memorandums by Sargent, Cadogan, and Halifax, June 2 and 3, 1940, PRO, N5689/40/38.
105. Earle to Secretary of State, June 10, 1940, NA, 740.0011 European War 1939/3643.
106. Gilbert, *Winston S. Churchill*, 6:358. Even Gorodetsky, whose treatment of this episode is extremely detailed, plays down the possibility of an Allied attack on the USSR and the fact that Cripps's mission was conceived as an alternative to such an attack. He argues that the initiative for Cripps's appointment came from the Soviets, who saw in Cripps a sympathetic figure. He writes, "The appointment had been literally forced by the Russians on an indifferent Cabinet." Whereas it is true that the Soviets insisted on Cripps being named ambassador, the initiative to send him to Moscow was entirely British. Gorodetsky, *Stafford Cripps*, p. 38.
107. H. Hanak, "Cripps, 1940–41."
108. Douhet quoted in Edward Warner, "Douhet, Mitchell, Seversky: Theories of Air Warfare," in *Makers of Modern Strategy*, ed. Edward Mead Earle (Princeton, 1943), p. 491.
109. Dalton, Diary, 28.6.39, vol. 20.
110. Ibid.
111. Quoted in Michael Howard, *The Continental Commitment*, (London, 1974), p. 129.
112. John Erickson, "Threat Identification and Strategic Appraisal by the Soviet Union, 1930–1941," in *Knowing One's Enemies: Intelligence Assessment before the Two World Wars*, ed. Ernest R. May (Princeton, 1984), p. 412.
113. John Colville, *The Fringes of Power: 10 Downing Street Diaries, 1939–1955* (New York, 1986), p. 83.
114. "Attempts by the OGPU to enlist the services of British subjects," October 22, 1940, PRO, N6930/6930/38.
115. Cripps's Papers, Nuffield College, Oxford, Draft Article for the *Tribune*, p. 566.
116. Colville, *Fringes of Power*, p. 92.

Chapter 2

1. Quoted in Patricia Strauss, *Cripps—Advocate and Rebel* (London, 1943), p. 23.
2. Quoted in Colin Cooke, *The Life of Richard Stafford Cripps* (London, 1957), p. 64.
3. Cripps's Diary, quoted in Eric Estorick, *Stafford Cripps: Master Statesman* (London, 1949), p. 64.
4. Stafford Cripps, "Can Socialism Come by Constitutional Methods?," in *Problems of a Socialist Government*, ed. Christopher Addison (London, 1933), p. 63.
5. Cripps Papers, Speech Notes 540, Nuffield College, Oxford.

6. Cooke, *Cripps*, p. 93.
7. Morrison to Cripps, April 19, 1929, Cripps Papers, 590, and Cooke, *Cripps*, p. 104.
8. Election Pamphlet, 1930, Cripps Papers, 604.
9. K. Harris, *Attlee* (London, 1982), p. 97.
10. Stafford Cripps, "Can Socialism Come?," in *Democracy Up To Date* (London, 1939), and *Where Stands Socialism To-day?* (London, 1933).
11. Stafford Cripps, *Towards Christian Democracy* (London, 1946), p. 12. This is a collection of Cripps's speeches and lectures from the war years.
12. Stafford Cripps, *The Struggle for Peace* (London, 1936), p. 65.
13. Socialist League membership card including a copy of the league constitution, Cripps Papers, 687. Cripps was one of the leading lights of the League until its dissolution in 1937 when, because of its members' participation in the Unity Campaign, the Labour party's National Executive ruled membership in the League to be incompatible with membership in the party. The best account of the League, and of Cripps's role in it, is Ben Pimlott, "The Socialist League: Intellectuals and the Labour Left in the 1930s," *Journal of Contemporary History* 6 (1971).
14. Cripps, *Towards Christian Democracy*, p. 54.
15. Washington speech notes, 1934, Cripps Papers, 558.
16. Cripps, *Democracy Up To Date*, p. 21.
17. Ibid.
18. Ibid., p. 23.
19. Ibid., p. 101.
20. Cripps, "Can Socialism Come by Constitutional Methods?" p. 66
21. Cripps, *Where Stands Socialism?* p. 37.
22. Cooke, *Cripps*, p. 164.
23. Ibid.
24. Beatrice Webb, *Beatrice Webb's Diaries 1924–32*, ed. Margaret Cole (London, 1956), pp. 303–4.
25. Cripps, "Can Socialism Come by Constitutional Methods?" p. 39
26. Cripps to Lennox-Boyd, October 1937, Cripps Papers, 551.
27. Labour Party Policy Memorandum No. 102 by C. R. Attlee and Stafford Cripps, January, 1933, Dalton Papers, 2/1, British Library of Political and Economic Science.
28. *Report of the Thirty-Third Annual Conference of the Labour Party, Hastings, 1933* (London, 1933), p. 135.
29. Cripps, *Problems of a Socialist Government*, p. 8.
30. Cripps, *The Struggle for Peace*, p. 34.
31. Cripps to supporter, Cripps Papers, 616.
32. Ibid., 104.
33. Quoted in Estorick, *Cripps*, pp. 124–25.
34. Aberdeen speech notes, March 13, 1938, Cripps Papers, 501.
35. Cripps denied the charge that he was funding his own campaign, claiming that his total monetary contribution was limited to the £25 it had cost him to mail a memorandum to Labour supporters advocating a United Front of the Left to oust

Chamberlain. However, this claim was deceptive, as a letter Cripps wrote to Montague Burton on January 25, 1939, shows. Cripps was asking for a contribution toward the operation of the "Tribune," "which," Cripps wrote, "is very largely focusing the support for [the Unity Campaign] at the present time. . . . The circulation at the moment I believe to be about 30,000 and it is doing invaluable work. I am carrying most of the expense of it myself to the tune of nearly £1,000 a month and I am anxious if possible to get some help so that we may be able to maintain its utility at this specially critical time." Cripps Papers, 508.

36. Richard Cripps to Sir Stafford Cripps, March 1939, Cripps Papers, 567.
37. Ivan Maisky, *Memoirs of a Soviet Ambassador: The War, 1939–1943* (New York, 1967), p. 37.
38. Unpublished article for the "Tribune," Cripps Papers, 566.
39. Winston Churchill, *History of the Second World War* (Boston, 1948–1954), 2:134.
40. Diary entry, 23.1.39, Dalton Papers, II 3/1, British Library of Economic and Political Science.
41. Cripps to FO, October 10, 1940, PRO, N7323/40/38.
42. Cripps to FO, December 23, 1940, PRO, N7526/40/38.
43. Max Beloff, *The Foreign Policy of Soviet Russia, 1929–1941* (Oxford, 1949), 2:320.
44. Adam Ulam, *Expansion and Coexistence* (New York, 1974), p. 297.
45. Nikita Khrushchev, *Khrushchev Remembers* (Boston, 1970), p. 134.
46. "The Ambassador in the Soviet Union to the Foreign Ministry," May 29, 1940, *DGFP*, 9:470–71.
47. Cripps to FO, June 12, 1940, PRO, N5808/30/38.
48. Halifax to Cripps, June 13, 1940, ibid.
49. Cripps's briefings in May had warned of Soviet aggression as well as German. See Chapter 1, n. 88.
50. Cripps to FO, June 14, 1940, PRO, N5840/5/38.
51. This theme is explored in depth in the following chapters.
52. Beloff, *Foreign Policy of Soviet Russia*, p. 327; and Ulam, *Expansion and Coexistence*, p. 296.
53. "The State Secretary in the German Foreign Office to the German Ambassador in the Soviet Union," June 14, 1940, *NSR*, p. 147.
54. Cripps to FO, June 15, 1940, PRO, N5729/93/38.
55. Cripps to FO, June 17, 1940, PRO, N5840/5/38.
56. Cripps to FO, June 17, 1940, PRO, N5808/30/38.
57. Ibid.
58. Cripps to FO, June 17, 1940, PRO, N5840/5/38.
59. Molotov to Halifax, June 17, 1940, PRO, N5788/93/38.
60. Ivan Maisky, *Memoirs*, pp. 138–39.
61. Ridsdale memorandum, June 18, 1940, PRO, N5863/30/38.
62. "Secret Supplementary Protocol," to the "German-Soviet Boundary and Friendship Treaty," September 28, 1939, *NSR*, p. 107.
63. Cadogan memorandum, December 13, 1940, PRO, N7448/5/38.
64. Cripps to FO, June 21, 1940, PRO, N5729/93/38.

65. Butler memorandum, June 21, 1940, PRO, N5788/93/38.
66. Soviet broadcast quoted in German telegram, *NSR*, p. 156.
67. Cripps to FO, June 23, 1940, PRO, N5863/30/38.
68. Memorandums by Collier, June 26; Sargent, June 28; and Butler, June 28, 1940, ibid.
69. "The German Ambassador in the Soviet Union to the German Foreign Office," June 23, 1940, *NSR*, p. 155.
70. "The German Ambassador in the Soviet Union to the German Foreign Office," June 26, 1940, *NSR*, p. 159.
71. Ibid.
72. Sargent to Halifax, June 24, 1940, PRO, N5863/30/38.
73. Sargent to Cripps, June 24, 1940, ibid.
74. Ibid.
75. Molotov told the Supreme Soviet that "the Soviet Union has never recognised" Romania's "seizure" of Bessarabia. Extracts of the speech are published in *Soviet Documents on Foreign Policy*, ed. Jane Degras (Oxford, 1953), 3:447.
76. Halifax to Dalton, June 26, 1940, PRO, N5863/30/38.
77. Undated FO memoranda, PRO, N5888/30/38.
78. Cripps to FO, June 27, 1940, ibid.
79. See Introduction, at n. 18.
80. Cripps to FO, July 1, 1940, PRO, N5937/30/38.
81. Stalin quoted in Vojtech Mastny, *Russia's Road to the Cold War: Diplomacy, Warfare, and the Politics of Communism, 1941–1945* (New York, 1979), p. 18.
82. Degras, *Soviet Documents on Foreign Policy*, p. 201.
83. These citations are taken from Cripps's longer, thirteen-page account, which did not reach the Foreign Office until September. Record of Cripps's Meeting with Stalin, July 1, 1940, PRO, N6526/30/38.
84. Cripps to FO, July 1, 1940, PRO, N5937/30/38.
85. Svetlana Alliluyeva, *Only One Year* (New York, 1969), p. 392.
86. This was the phrase used in the Soviet account given to the Germans of the Cripps-Stalin conversation, as Molotov put it, "on instructions from Stalin," "The Ambassador in the Soviet Union to the German Foreign Office," July 13, 1940, *DGFP*, 10:207–8.
87. Mastny, *Russia's Road to the Cold War*, p. 29.
88. See n. 50.
89. FO comments on Cripps to FO, July 1, 1940, PRO, 5937/40/38.
90. Maisky, *Memoirs*, p. 98.
91. A. M. Samsonov, *Vtoraia mirovaia voina, 1939–1945: Ocherk vazhneishikh sobytii* (Moscow, 1985), p. 60
92. Alexandr Nekrich, *June 22, 1941* (Columbia, S.C., 1968), p. 46. The Soviet academic establishment later pilloried Nekrich for his alleged ideological apostasy in this book. For the first shot in this attack, see G. A. Deborin and B. S. Tel'pukhovskii, "V ideinom plenu u fal'sifikatorov istorii," *Voprosy istorii* 9, 1967: 127–40.
93. "The Ambassador in the Soviet Union to the German Foreign Office," July 13, 1940, *DGFP* 10:207–8.

Chapter 3

1. See Chapter 2, n. 89.
2. Dalton Diary 23:319, Dalton Papers II, British Library of Political and Economic Science.
3. Alexander Cadogan *The Diaries of Sir Alexander Cadogan 1938–1945*, ed. David Dilks (New York, 1972), p. 319.
4. FO to Cripps, June 17, 1940, PRO, N5855/40/38.
5. Cripps to FO, June 18, 1940, ibid.
6. "The Ambassador in the Soviet Union to the German Foreign Office," July 13, 1940, *DGFP* 10:207–8.
7. Butler memorandum, July 11, 1940, War Cabinet, July 16, 1940, PRO, N6005/6005/38.
8. Butler to Halifax, July 19, 1940, ibid.
9. Harry Pollitt had been the leader of the British Communist party.
10. Cripps to FO, July 27 and 30, 1940, PRO, N6072/30/38.
11. Cripps to FO, July 27, 1940, ibid.
12. *Soviet Documents on Foreign Policy*, ed. Jane Degras (London, 1953), 3:461–69.
13. "The Ambassador in the Soviet Union to the German Foreign Office," June 26, *NSR*, p. 162.
14. Halifax to Alexander, August 19, 1940, PRO, N6105/40/38.
15. Cripps to FO, August 8, 1940, ibid.
16. E. Llewellyn Woodward and Rohan Butler, eds., *British Documents on Foreign Policy*, ser. 3 (London, 1953) 5:711.
17. Cripps to FO, August 8, 1940, PRO, N6105/40/38.
18. Ibid.
19. Vansittart to Halifax, August 9, 1940; Maclean memorandum August 9, 1940, ibid.
20. FO to Cripps, August 13, 1940, ibid.; also General Sikorski Historical Institute, *Documents on Polish-Soviet Relations, 1939–1945* (London, 1961), 1:97.
21. Cadogan, *Diaries*, p. 321.
22. FO to Cripps, August 20, 1940, PRO, N6263/40/38.
23. Cripps to FO, August 22, 1940, PRO, N6372/5/38.
24. FO to Cripps, September 19, 1940, ibid.
25. See Chapter 2, n. 68. In a memorandum written on September 28, Dr. Karl Schnurre, head of the Eastern European and Baltic section of the Commercial Policy Division of the German Foreign Office, testified once again to the utility of the Soviet economic connection: "The supplies from the Russians have heretofore been a very substantial prop to the Germany [*sic*] war economy," "Foreign Office Memorandum," September 28, 1940 *NSR*, p. 201.
26. Butler memorandum, September 4, 1940, PRO, N6559/30/38.
27. D. N. Pritt, "Open Letter to Sir Stafford Cripps," *New Statesman and Nation*, September 14, 1940.
28. Telegrams from Lothian, PRO, N6454/2039/59.
29. Cripps to FO, September 21, 1940, PRO, N6681/5/38.
30. Ibid.

31. Alexander to Cadogan, September 17, 1940, PRO, N6630/30/38.
32. Butler memorandum, October 7, 1940, PRO, N6814/30/38.
33. Ibid.
34. Cripps to FO, October 8, 1940, PRO, N6808/30/38.
35. Cadogan, *Diaries*, p. 330.
36. Ibid.
37. E. Llewellyn Woodward, *British Foreign Policy in the Second World War* (London, 1970), 1:488–89.
38. Cripps to FO, October 13, 1940, PRO, N6875/30/38. Cripps had already been warned that strict secrecy might prove impossible to maintain.
39. War Cabinet Conclusions 271 (40), October 15, 1940.
40. FO to Cripps, October 15, 1940, PRO, N6875/30/38.
41. Ibid.
42. *DGFP*, 10:207.
43. Cripps to FO, October 16, 1940, PRO, N6874/5/38.
44. Cripps to FO, October 18, 1940, PRO, N6926/5/38.
45. "Soviet-Iranian Relations," October 20, 1940, PRO, N6868/1424/38.
46. Cripps to FO, October 22, 1940, PRO, N6875/5/38.
47. Cripps to FO, October 22, 1940, PRO, N6927/5/38.
48. Collier memorandum, October 24, 1940, PRO, N6875/5/38.
49. Halifax to Churchill, October 26, 1940, ibid.
50. Butler memorandum, October 29, 1940, PRO, N7063/40/38.
51. Marcus Wheeler, *The Oxford Russian Dictionary* (Oxford, 1972), p. 71.
52. Cripps to FO, October 31, 1940, PRO, N7046/5/38.
53. Maclean memorandum, November 3, 1940, ibid.
54. Cripps to FO, November 1, 1940, PRO, N7106/5/38.
55. Postan to Maclean, November 8, 1940, PRO, N7154/5/38.
56. Dalton to Halifax, November 9, 1940, PRO, N7243/5/38.
57. Rendel to FO, October 26, 1940, PRO, N7046/1310/38.
58. Maclean memorandum, November 8, 1940, PRO, N7148/5/38.
59. "Letter from the Reich Foreign Minister to Stalin," October 13 1940, *NSR*, pp. 212–13.
60. Cripps to FO, November 11, 1940, PRO, N7165/40/38.
61. Cripps to FO, November 11, 1940, PRO, N7173/40/38.
62. Cripps to FO, November 11, 1940, PRO, N7165/40/38.
63. Cripps to FO, November 11, 1940, PRO, N7166/40/38.
64. Ibid.
65. Cripps to FO, November 20, 1940, PRO, N7238/40/38.
66. Maclean memorandum, December 3, 1940, PRO, N7366/40/38.
67. Dalton memorandum, November 8, 1940, PRO, N7356/40/38.

Chapter 4

1. "Memorandum of the Conversation" between Hitler and Molotov, November 13, 1940, *NSR*, p. 243.

2. "Memorandum of the Conversation" between Hitler and Molotov, November 12, 1940, ibid., p. 229.
3. George F. Kennan, *Russia and the West under Lenin and Stalin* (New York, 1960), p. 322.
4. Barry A. Leach, *German Strategy against Russia, 1939–1941* (Oxford, 1973), p. 77.
5. For the best explication of Hitler's long-range plans and how they would have affected the USSR, see Gerhard L. Weinberg, *The Foreign Policy of Hitler's Germany: Diplomatic Revolution in Europe, 1933–36* (Chicago, 1970), 1:74–82.
6. "Memorandum of the Conversation" between Hitler and Molotov, November 13, 1940, *NSR*, p. 243.
7. Ibid., p. 232.
8. Ibid., p. 240.
9. Ibid., p. 252.
10. This argument is developed in Gerhard L. Weinberg, *World in the Balance: Behind the Scenes of World War II* (Hanover, 1981), pp. 14–15.
11. "The German Ambassador in the Soviet Union to the German Foreign Office," November 25, 1940, *NSR*, pp. 258–59.
12. E. Llewellyn Woodward, *British Foreign Policy in the Second World War* (London, 1970), 1:399.
13. Cripps to FO, November 19, 1940, PRO, N7233/40/38.
14. Cripps to FO, November 16, 1940, PRO, N7200/40/38.
15. Steinhardt to Secretary of State, November 27, 1940, NA, 741.61/90.
16. Steinhardt to Secretary of State, December 16, 1940, Confidential File, NA, 741.61/915.
17. Steinhardt to Secretary of State, February 8, 1941, NA, 741.61/920.
18. Ibid.
19. Maclean memorandum, November 21, 1940, PRO, N7233/40/38.
20. Cripps to FO, November 20, 1940, PRO, N7238/40/38.
21. Cripps to FO, December 19, 1940, ibid.
22. FO to Cripps, December 2, 1940, PRO, N7233/40/38.
23. FO to Cripps, December 2, 1940, PRO, N7354/40/38.
24. Cripps to FO, December 3, 1940, PRO, N7366/40/38.
25. Cripps to FO, December 8, 1940, and Maclean memorandum, undated, PRO, N7387/40/38.
26. Cripps to FO, December 16, 1940, ibid.
27. FO to Cripps, December 18, 1940, ibid., and Cripps to FO, December 19, 1940, PRO, N7500/40/38.
28. Cripps to FO, December 23, 1940, PRO, N7526/40/38.
29. Sir Stafford Cripps, *The Struggle for Peace* (London, 1936), p. 83.
30. John Colville, *The Fringes of Power: 10 Downing Street Diaries, 1939–1955* (New York, 1986), p. 309.
31. Winston S. Churchill, *History of the Second World War* (Boston, 1948–54), 2:570.
32. Eden to Cripps, December 28, 1940, PRO, N7500/40/38.
33. Eden to Cripps, January 17, 1941, PRO, N290/290/38.

34. Cripps to FO, December 29, 1940, PRO, N7500/40/38.
35. Eden memorandum, December 27, 1940, PRO, N7548/40/38.
36. Cripps to FO, December 29, 1940, ibid.
37. Maclean memorandum, January 1, 1941, and Collier memorandum, January 1, 1941, ibid.
38. Eugene Lyons, *Assignment in Utopia* (New York, 1937), p. 631.
39. Cripps to Halifax, October 10, 1940, PRO, N7323/40/38.
40. Erik Estorick, *Stafford Cripps: Master Statesman* (London, 1949), p. 218.
41. Eden to Cripps, December 29, 1940, PRO, N7558/40/38.
42. Woodward, *British Foreign Policy*, 1:596–97.
43. Maclean memorandum, January 1, 1941, PRO, N54/3/38.
44. "The German Ambassador in the Soviet Union to the German Foreign Office," January 17, 1941, *NSR*, pp. 270–71.
45. Maclean memorandum, January 21, 1941, PRO, N7403/1056/38.
46. Eden to Cripps, January 29, 1941, PRO, N382/3/38.
47. "Record of an Interview between His Majesty's Ambassador and M. Molotov on February 1st, 1941," PRO, N829/3/38.
48. Cripps to FO, February 1, 1941, PRO, N402/3/38, and Cripps to FO, February 2, 1941, PRO, N411/3/38.
49. Cripps to FO, February 2, 1941, PRO, N411/3/38.
50. Cripps to FO, February 8, 1941, PRO, N476/3/38.
51. Cripps to FO, February 16, 1941, PRO, N697/22/38.
52. Butler memorandum, February 15, 1941, PRO, N639/3/38.
53. Cripps to FO, February 20, 1941, PRO, N759/22/38.
54. Cripps to Mikoian, February 21, 1941, PRO, N830/22/38.
55. Cripps to FO, February 22, 1941, PRO, N675/3/38.
56. Eden (in Cairo) to Cripps, February 24, 1941, PRO, N733/3/38.
57. Moscow Embassy to FO, February 27, 1941, PRO, N752/290/38.
58. David Carlton, *Anthony Eden: A Biography* (London, 1981), p. 184.
59. "The Ambassador in the Soviet Union to the Foreign Ministry," March 1, 1941, *DGFP*, 12:277–78.
60. Quoted in Max Beloff, *The Foreign Policy of Soviet Russia, 1929–1941* (Oxford, 1949), 2:363.
61. Woodward, *British Foreign Policy*, 1:602.
62. Ibid.
63. Cripps to FO, March 24, 1941, PRO, N1229/3/38.
64. FO to Cripps, March 26, 1941, PRO, N1257/3/38.
65. "Memorandum by the Ambassador to the Soviet Union, at the Time in Germany," *DGFP*, 12:666–69.
66. "The Ambassador in Turkey to the Foreign Ministry," May 24, 1941, ibid., 873.
67. Prince Paul's information was only accurate in part. At the time, Hitler was still intending to invade the USSR in May. Belgrade Embassy to FO, March 30, 1941, PRO, N1316/78/38.
68. Churchill to Stalin, April 3, 1941, PRO, N1366/78/38.
69. Cripps to FO, April 5, 1941, and FO to Cripps, April 7, 1941, PRO, N1397/78/38.

70. Cripps to FO, April 6, 1941, and Cripps to FO, April 8, 1941, PRO, N1429/78/38.
71. Cadogan to Churchill, April 9, 1941, PRO, N1510/78/38.
72. Ibid.
73. Churchill, *History*, 3:357.
74. Albert Seaton, *The Russo-German War, 1941–1945* (New York, 1970), p. 16. Also see Barton Whaley, *Codeword Barbarossa* (Cambridge, Mass., 1973), pp. 62–63.
75. Ronald Lewin, *Ultra Goes to War: The Secret Story* (London, 1978), pp. 108–9. Also see F. W. Winterbotham, *The Ultra Secret* (London, 1974), p. 70.
76. Gorodetsky rightly places a great deal of the blame for this bungled affair on Eden, who accepted much of Cripps's reasoning but did not keep Churchill informed that he had done so. Nevertheless, it is difficult to agree with Gorodetsky's complete exoneration of Cripps, whose refusal to deliver Churchill's note and subsequent decision to hand Vyshinskii a memorandum containing his "personal views" was eccentric, to say the least. Gabriel Gorodetsky, *Stafford Cripps' Mission to Moscow, 1940–42* (Cambridge, 1984), pp. 122–24.
77. Cripps to Vyshinskii, April 11, 1941, PRO, N1848/78/38.
78. Cripps to FO, April 12, 1941, PRO, N1573/78/38.
79. Eden to Churchill, April 15, 1941, and Martin (quoting Churchill) to Eden, April 16, 1941, ibid.
80. Churchill, *History*, 3:361.
81. Whaley, *Codeword Barbarossa*, p. 63. Also Churchill, *History*, 4:493.
82. V. A. Anfilov, *Nachalo velikoi Otechestvennoi voiny* (Moscow, 1962), p. 23. By 1971 the intellectual fashion in Moscow had changed, and Anfilov moderated his criticisms of Stalin; what had once been Stalin's vice was now a Soviet virtue. "The Soviet government made attempts by diplomatic means to hamper an attack against the Soviet Union or to postpone its date," Anfilov writes. "It demanded of military leaders that they not give the Fascist high command any pretext for provocation." Nevertheless, he continues: "at the same time [the Soviet government] did not weaken their attention to the question of defense of the country." V. A. Anfilov, *Bessmertnyi podvig* (Moscow, 1971), pp. 178–79.
83. John Erikson, *The Road to Stalingrad* (London, 1975), p. 83.
84. Ibid., p. 95.
85. Jack Scott (*News Chronicle*) relayed by Moscow Chancery, April 18, 1941, PRO, N1829/78/38.
86. Joseph Paul Goebbels, *The Goebbels Diaries, 1939–1941*, ed. and trans. Fred Taylor (New York, 1983), p. 315.
87. G. K. Zhukov, *Reminiscences and Reflections* (Moscow, 1985), 1:273.
88. Ibid., 276.
89. Erikson, *Road to Stalingrad*, p. 80.
90. Jane Degras, ed., *Soviet Documents on Foreign Policy* (Oxford, 1953), 3:489.
91. Maisky, *Memoirs of a Soviet Ambassador: The War, 1939–1943* (New York, 1967), p. 150.
92. Anfilov, *Bessmertnyi podvig*, p. 179.

93. Petro Grigorenko, *Memoirs*, trans. Thomas P. Whitney (New York, 1982), p. 115.

94. Ibid., pp. 116–21.

95. Goebbels, *Diaries*, pp. 356–57.

96. Ibid., p. 328.

97. Cripps to FO, April 3, 1941, PRO, N1386/3/38, and Cripps to FO, April 17, 1941, PRO, N1667/3/38.

98. Eden to Cripps, April 18, 1941, PRO, N1781/3/38.

99. Eden to Cripps, April 16, 1941, PRO, N1386/3/38.

100. Collier memorandum, April 19, 1941, PRO, N1902/3/38.

101. Cripps to FO, April 18, 1941, PRO, N1828/3/38.

102. Cripps to FO, April 18, 1941, PRO, N1692/3/38.

103. Cripps to FO, April 19, 1941, and Collier memorandum, April 22, 1941, PRO N1725/3/38.

104. Churchill memorandum, April 22, 1941, PRO, M461/1.

105. Butler memorandum, April 25, 1941, PRO, N1801/3/38.

106. Quoted in J. B. Hutton, *Hess: The Man and His Mission* (New York, 1970), p. 167.

107. Churchill to Roosevelt, May 17, 1941, in *Churchill and Roosevelt: The Complete Correspondence*, ed. Warren F. Kimball (Princeton, 1984), 1:187–88.

108. Quoted in Hutton, *Hess*, p. 181.

109. F. D. Volkov, "Neudavshiisia pryzhok Rudol'f Gessa," *Novaia i noveishaia istoria* 6 (1968).

110. Churchill, *History*, 3:55.

111. Volkov, "Neudavshiisia pryzhok Rudol'f Gessa."

112. Gorodetsky, *Stafford Cripps' Mission to Moscow*, p. 135.

113. On March 31, 1941, Rashid Ali, the Prime Minister of Iraq, led a pro-Fascist coup. The British refused to recognize the new government and eventually organized a military expedition that cooperated with local forces to dispose of Ali. By June 1 the former government of Iraq had been reestablished. Soviet recognition of Ali's regime was more an irritant that anything else. Moscow was in no position to extend material support to the rebels; however, Soviet behavior in this matter is a vivid illustration of how little Stalin valued a closer relationship with Britain.

114. Eden memorandum, June 2, 1941, PRO, N2570/3/38.

115. Maisky, *Memoirs*, p. 149.

116. No record of Maiskii's talk with Cadogan exists in the Foreign Office records, nor does Cadogan mention the meeting in his diary. Maiskii may have been confused about either the date or the person who relayed the military intelligence to him. Be that as it may, Maiskii did receive such warnings, and his reaction to the news, as described in his memoirs, is no doubt genuine.

117. Degras, ed., *Soviet Documents on Foreign Policy*, 3:489.

118. FO to Cripps, June 2, 1941, PRO, N2800/290/38.

119. FO to Stockholm Embassy, June 6, 1941, ibid., and PRO, N2669/290/38.

120. John Cameron memorandum, June 9, 1941, PRO, N26741/3/38.

121. General Sikorski Historical Institute, *Documents on Polish-Soviet Relations, 1939–1945* (London, 1961), 1:105. Contempt for the Red Army's abilities was widespread in the West. See, for example, Sir Basil Liddell Hart, *Memoirs* (London, 1965), 2:291.

122. Molotov speech to the Supreme Soviet, October 31, 1939, in Degras, ed., *Soviet Documents on Foreign Policy*, 3:389–90.

123. Cripps Papers, 592, Nuffield College Library, Oxford.

124. Churchill, *History*, 3:371–73.

125. Cripps quoted in the *Sheffield Telegraph*, Cripps Papers, A6.

126. F. S. Northedge and Audrey Wells, *Britain and Soviet Communism: The Impact of a Revolution* (London, 1982), p. 77.

127. *NSR*, p. 244.

128. See Chapter 3.

129. Charles Gati, "The Stalinist Legacy in Soviet Foreign Policy," in *The Soviet Union since Stalin*, ed. Stephen F. Cohen and Alexander Rabinowitch (Indiana, 1980), p. 280.

130. Quoted in E. H. Carr, *The Bolshevik Revolution, 1917–1923* (London, 1953), 3:70.

131. Robert C. Tucker, "The Emergence of Stalin's Foreign Policy," *Slavic Review* 4 (1977): 584.

132. Ibid., p. 571.

133. *NSR*, p. 212.

134. This is the central thesis of Barton Whaley's *Codeword Barbarossa*.

135. Oliver Harvey, *The War Diaries of Oliver Harvey 1941–1945*, ed. John Harvey (London, 1978), p. 29.

Chapter 5

1. The analogy to Napoleon, though easily and frequently made, can be misleading. In World War II the Germans had a closer historical parallel to draw upon, their defeat of tsarist Russia in 1917.

2. Jane Degras, ed., *Soviet Documents on Foreign Policy* (Oxford, 1953), 3:492. One of the more interesting aspects of Stalin's speech was the way he drew on Russian national historical example to cast his leadership in a nationalist, rather than Communist, light. The non-ideological tone of the speech was immediately apparent, and many Soviet citizens still remember being surprised by Stalin's opening remark: "Comrades! Citizens! Brothers and Sisters!" A full text of the speech is in "Radio Address by J. V. Stalin, Chairman of the Council of People's Commissars of the U.S.S.R., Chairman of the National Defense Committee," July 3, 1941, NA, 740.0011 European War 1939/13174.

3. Degras, ed., *Soviet Documents on Foreign Policy*, 3:490.

4. John Erickson, *The Road to Stalingrad* (London, 1975), p. 125.

5. Degras, ed., *Soviet Documents on Foreign Policy*, 3:491.

6. During Hitler's rise to power, Stalin had ordered the German Communist party not to cooperate with the Social Democrats. The resulting split in his opposition

eased Hitler's task. For Stalin's reasoning in this matter, see Robert C. Tucker, "The Emergence of Stalin's Foreign Policy," *Slavic Review* 4 (1977). For more on Stalin's role in the tactics of the German Communist party, see Ruth Fischer, *Stalin and German Communism: A Study in the Origins of the State Party* (Cambridge, Mass., 1948), esp. pp. 655–56.

7. Strobe Talbot, ed., *Khrushchev Remembers* (Boston, 1970), p. 170.

8. Quoted in Vojtech Mastny, *Russia's Road to the Cold War: Diplomacy, Warfare, and the Politics of Communism, 1941–1945* (New York, 1979), p. 38.

9. Maiskii to NKID, June 22, 1941, *SAO*, 1:45–47.

10. NKID to Maiskii, June 22, 1941, *SAO*, 1:47.

11. Cripps to FO, June 28, 1941, PRO, N3250/3/38.

12. Cripps to FO, June 27, 1941, PRO, N3231/3/38.

13. "Record of a Conversation of the People's Commissar of Foreign Affairs of the USSR with the British Ambassador," June 27, 1941, *SAO*, 1:47–52.

14. Ibid.

15. Cripps to FO, June 27, 1941, PRO, N3231/3/38.

16. "Radio Address by Mr. M. M. Litvinov, Member of the Supreme Soviet of the U.S.S.R., Former People's Commissar of Foreign Affairs of the U.S.S.R.," July 8, 1941, NA, 740.0011 European War 1939/13173.

17. Arthur Upham Pope, whose biography of Litvinov contains numerous indulgent comments about Soviet foreign policy, claims that "the local radio was off at the time" that Litvinov's address was broadcast. It is reasonable to assume that this was more than mere coincidence. Pope, *Maxim Litvinoff* (New York, 1943), p. 461; also see Alexander Werth, *Russia at War, 1941–1945* (New York, 1964), p. 181, and Louis Fischer, *The Great Challenge* (New York, 1946), pp. 46–47.

18. Molotov inquired anxiously about the Hess mission on June 27. "Record of Conversations of the People's Commissar of Foreign Affairs with the British Ambassador," June 27, 1941, *SAO*, 1:47–52.

19. Cripps to FO, June 29, 1941, PRO, N3239/3/38.

20. Cripps to FO, June 29, 1941, PRO, N3302/3/38.

21. Eden memorandum, June 30, 1941, PRO, N3304/3/38.

22. Ibid. Maiskii was referring to the British diplomatic team, under the leadership of William Strang, which had been sent to Moscow in the summer of 1939 to negotiate a defensive pact with the Soviets. The Strang mission was a failure since the Soviets decided to cast their lot with Hitler—signing the Nazi-Soviet Pact—rather than with the Western democracies. The Soviet contention, at least since Hitler turned on his Soviet allies, has always been that Britain and France did not sincerely desire an alliance with the USSR. As proof of this allegation, the Soviets point to the fact that Strang traveled to the USSR on a slow boat, rather than by airplane, as they say he surely would have done had London been anxious for an alliance.

23. Soviet historians naturally stress how wrong Western military opinion was about the powers of Soviet resistance. One recent history, for example, states that "English and American staffs held the opinion that the defeat of the Soviet Union was inevitable in a very short time—from one to three months after the start of the Soviet-German war." A. M. Samsonov, *Vtoraia mirovaia voina, 1939–1945:*

Ocherk vazhneishikh sobytii (Moscow, 1985), p. 155. Although true, this explanation ignores the fact that Westerners believed that the purges, which are almost never mentioned in post–Khrushchev-era literature, had permanently crippled the Red Army—an understandable misjudgment.

24. Maiskii to NKID, June 30, 1941, *SAO*, 1:55–56.
25. FO to Cripps, July 8, 1941, and FO to Moscow Embassy, July 7, 1941, PRO, N3539/78/38.
26. Cripps to FO, July 8, 1941, PRO, N3528/3/38.
27. "Record of a Conversation of the President of the Soviet of People's Commissars [Stalin] with the British Ambassador," July 8, 1941, *SAO*, 1:69–73.
28. Ibid.
29. This comment does not appear in the British record, which Cripps sent to the Foreign Office. Although it is impossible to verify, the remark would not have been out of character for Sir Stafford, nor would it be a surprise that he decided not to include it in his transcript.
30. Record of Cripps-Stalin conversation, July 8, 1948, *SAO*, 1:69–73.
31. Cripps to FO, July 8, 1941, PRO, N3529/3/38.
32. Later in the war, after their military prospects had improved, the Soviets evidently once again tried to establish contact with the Germans. But during 1941 and 1942 the Germans regarded their own military victory to be too certain to bother parleying with the Soviets. There is a further discussion of this question in the conclusion.
33. Sargent memorandum, July 9, 1941, PRO, N3561/3/38.
34. Ibid. H. Hanak cites this meeting with Winant as the crucial factor in the rejection of Churchill's draft, but it was not. In fact, in the Cabinet discussion late on July 9, American opinion was not mentioned—at least judging from the written record. Hanak, "Sir Stafford Cripps as Ambassador in Moscow, June 1941–January 1942," *English Historical Review* 383 (1982).
35. Churchill to Eden, July 9, 1941, PRO, N3607/3/38.
36. Eden to Churchill, July 9, 1941, ibid.
37. War Cabinet, July 9, 1941, PRO, N3614/3/38.
38. FO to Cripps, July 9, 1941, PRO, N3561/3/38.
39. Cripps to FO, July 10, 1941, PRO, N3565/3/38.
40. Cripps to FO, July 14, 1941, PRO, N3709/3/38.
41. Text of Anglo-Soviet Agreement, Cripps to FO, July 13, 1941, PRO, N3660/3/38.
42. Stalin to Churchill, July 19, 1941, PRO, N3933/78/38.
43. Churchill to Stalin, July 20, 1941, ibid.
44. Maiskii to NKID, June 28, 1941, *SAO*, 1:52–53.
45. "Record of a Conversation of the People's Commissar of Foreign Affairs of the USSR with the members of the Military and Economic Mission of Great Britain," June 30, 1941, *SAO*, 1:56–59.
46. "Record of a Conversation of the People's Commissar of Foreign Affairs of the USSR with the Ambassador of Great Britain," July 2, 1941, *SAO*, 1:60–62.
47. Ibid.
48. Churchill to Stalin, July 28, 1941, PRO, N4107/3084/38.

49. W. Averell Harriman and Elie Abel, *Special Envoy to Churchill and Stalin, 1941–1946* (New York, 1975), p. 75.

50. Figures from Albert Seaton, *The Russo-German War, 1941–1945* (New York, 1970), p. 130.

51. E. Llewellyn Woodward, *British Foreign Policy in the Second World War* (London, 1971), 2:202.

52. Winston Churchill, *History of the Second World War* (Boston, 1948–54), 3:434.

53. Woodward, *British Foreign Policy*, 2:202.

54. Churchill, *History*, 3:444.

55. Quoted in A. J. P. Taylor, *Beaverbrook* (London, 1972), p. 482.

56. For such an argument see Nikolai Sivachev and Nikolai Yakovlev, *Russia and the United States* (Chicago, 1979), p. 165; for a more sustained attack, see P. A. Zhilin, et al., *Kritika osnovnykh kontseptsii burzhuaznoi istoriografii vtoroi mirovoi voiny* (Moscow, 1983), pp. 123–36. Zhilin argues that Western military supplies did not reach the USSR in large quantities until after the German tide had turned. Also, he repeats an old claim first made by Voznesenskii, that Lend-Lease never amounted to more than 4 percent of Soviet domestic wartime production.

57. Churchill, *History*, 3:452–53.

58. Sinclair to Eden, August 23, 1941, PRO, N4902/3804/38.

59. Maiskii to NKID, August 27, 1941, *SAO*, 1:105–09. Although one cannot verify Maiskii's account, which is no doubt exaggerated, both Eden and Maiskii's remarks as recorded in this document seem to be in character.

60. Stalin to Maiskii, August 30, 1941, *SAO*, 1:109.

61. Oliver Harvey, *The War Diaries of Oliver Harvey, 1941–1945*, ed. John Harvey (London, 1978), p. 36.

62. Ibid., p. 43.

63. Churchill, *History*, 3:452.

64. Taylor, *Beaverbrook*, p. 483.

65. A. A. Gromyko, ed., *Correspondence between the Chairman of the Council of Ministers of the USSR and the Presidents of the USA and the Prime Ministers of Great Britain during the Great Patriotic War of 1941–1945* (Moscow, 1957), 2:28.

66. Maiskii to NKID, September 5, 1941, *SAO*, 1:113–16.

67. Gromyko, ed., *Correspondence*, 2:29.

68. Ibid., 31. For a record of the conversation when Maiskii delivered Stalin's note to Churchill, see Maiskii to NKID, September 15, 1941, *SAO*, 1:119–122.

69. Gabriel Kolko, *The Politics of War* (New York, 1968), p. 17.

70. John Erickson, *The Road to Stalingrad*, pp. 211–13.

71. Gromyko, ed., *Correspondence*, 2:32–33.

72. Cripps to FO, September 20, 1941, PRO, N5585/3/38.

73. Harriman and Abel, *Special Envoy*, p. 85.

74. Taylor, *Beaverbrook*, p. 490.

75. Quoted in ibid., p. 487.

76. As part of his efforts to distance himself from Cripps, Beaverbrook had decided not to stay in the British Embassy during his stay in Moscow.

77. Lord Ismay, *Memoirs of General the Lord Ismay* (London, 1960), p. 230.
78. FO to Cripps, November 1, 1941, PRO, N6312/3/38. This document is Beaverbrook's abbreviated account, which he eventually sent to Cripps; it was based on Harriman's notes.
79. Ismay, *Memoirs*, p. 230.
80. Ibid.
81. FO to Cripps, November 1, 1941, PRO, N6312/3/38.
82. PRO, CAB 66/19. Curiously, Ismay does not mention this interesting conversation in his *Memoirs*.
83. Ismay, *Memoirs*, pp. 232–33.
84. Cripps to FO, September 30, 1941, and Sargent Memorandum, October 1, 1941, PRO, N5679/78/38.
85. Eden to Cripps, October 3, 1941, PRO, WM (41) 98th Conclusions, October 2, 1941.
86. Mason-MacFarlane to Chief of the Imperial General Staff, October 2, 1941, PRO, N5585/3/38.
87. Seaton, *Russo-German War*, p. 180.
88. Gromyko, ed., *Correspondence*, 2:35–36.
89. Ibid., 35.
90. Churchill to Stalin, October 12, 1941, PRO, N6026/78/38.
91. Cripps to FO, October 14, 1941, PRO, N6132/78/38.
92. "Record of a Conversation of the People's Commissar of Foreign Affairs with the Ambassador of Great Britain," October 13, 1941, *SAO*, 1:152–54.
93. Cripps to FO, October 14, 1941, PRO, N6132/78/38.
94. Churchill to Cripps, October 25, 1941, PRO, CAB 66/19.
95. Nevertheless, those imputing ulterior motives to Churchill should recall Pershing's problems during World War I. Pershing was adamant that American forces be under American command, not French or British, yet few would accuse the American General of being either a poor ally or being unwilling to fight.
96. Cripps to FO, October 24, 1941, PRO, N6208/78/38.
97. "Record of a Conversation of the People's Commissar of Foreign Affairs with the Ambassadors of Great Britain and the USA," October 22, 1941, *SAO*, 1:156–57.
98. Adam Ulam, *Stalin: The Man and His Era* (London, 1974), pp. 553–54.
99. Cripps to FO, October 25, 1941, PRO, CAB 66/19.
100. Cripps to FO, October 26, 1941, ibid.
101. Cripps to FO, October 26, 1941, and FO to Cripps, October 28, 1941, PRO, N6583/3/38.
102. Cripps to Churchill, October 29, 1941, PRO, N6584/3/38.
103. Cripps to FO, October 28, 1941, PRO, N6224/78/38.
104. Harvey, *War Diaries*, p. 43. This comment shows how many in Britain, like Harvey, never believed that appeasement could be pro-Soviet just as easily as pro-Nazi.
105. Sir Walter Citrine, *Men at Work* (London, 1964), p. 253.
106. Sir Walter Citrine, *In Russia Now* (London, 1942), p. 10.
107. Ibid., p. 88.
108. Ibid., p. 140.

109. Cripps to FO, October 23, 1941, PRO, N6548/3/38.
110. Cripps to FO, November 5, 1941, PRO, CAB 66/19.
111. Eden to Cripps, November 10, 1941, PRO, N6105/40/38.
112. PRO, CAB 66/19.
113. Ibid.
114. Cripps to Eden, November 13, 1941, PRO, CAB 66/99.
115. Gromyko, ed., *Correspondence*, 2:38.
116. Stalin to Churchill, November 8, 1941, PRO, N6540/3/38.
117. Eden to Cripps, November 13, 1941, PRO, CAB 66/19.
118. Molotov raised the question of Soviet "minimum conditions" during his visit to London in May 1942. See Chapter 7.
119. Cripps to Eden, November 15, 1941, PRO, CAB 66/19.
120. Churchill to Cripps, November 15, 1941, PRO, N6575/3/38.
121. *FRUS 1941*, 1:193.
122. Harvey, *War Diaries*, p. 64.
123. Churchill, *History*, 3:625.
124. Harvey, *War Diaries*, pp. 70, 72.
125. Ibid., p. 72.
126. Ibid., p. 68.
127. Churchill, *History*, 3:627.

Chapter 6

1. Eden memorandum, November 29, 1941, PRO, WP(41) 288.
2. Oliver Harvey, *The War Diaries of Oliver Harvey, 1941–1945*, ed. John Harvey (London, 1978), p. 72.
3. Ibid., p. 73.
4. Such at least was Cripps's line of argument after November 1940. See Chapters 3 and 4.
5. See Chapter 5.
6. Alexander Cadogan, *The Diaries of Sir Alexander Cadogan, 1938–1945*, ed. David Dilks (New York, 1972), p. 421.
7. PRO, WP(42) 8. This document contains the complete text of the Stalin-Eden talks. The Soviet version is much less complete; see *SAO*, 1:184–98.
8. The Curzon Line was named after Britain's foreign secretary, Lord Curzon, who tried to delineate the Russo-Polish border along ethnic lines during the Versailles Conference in 1919–20. The Poles, emerging victorious from their war with the Soviets, forced a line considerably eastwards in the Treaty of Riga of 1921. This boundary stood until 1939, when it was forcibly altered by the Soviets according to the terms of the secret protocol of the Nazi-Soviet Pact. After the defeat of Poland in September 1939, what has been called the "fourth partition of Poland" took place, and Molotov exulted to the Supreme Soviet that "nothing was left of this ugly offspring of the Versailles treaty." General Sikorski Historical Institute, *Documents on Polish-Soviet Relations, 1939–1945* (London, 1961), 1:65.
The territory between the Curzon Line and the 1941 frontier was an ethnic

jumble. But, as E. Llewellyn Woodward has written, "After the outbreak of war in 1939 deportations, first by the Russians and then by the Germans, and other changes had the effect of markedly diminishing the Polish population in the areas east of the Curzon Line." Woodward, *British Foreign Policy in the Second World War* (London, 1971), 3:657–62. Stalin's insistence on the Curzon Line was thus an attempt to consolidate his gains from the Nazi-Soviet Pact.

9. After Soviet reverses of summer–autumn 1941 had passed into history, Stalin liked to claim that he had adopted "Kutusov tactics," that is, a strategic retreat akin to Russian strategy during Napoleon's 1812 invasion. The truth was, however, somewhat different. On the night of June 22, 1941, Stalin had ordered his forces to change over to the offensive with the aim of delivering a decisive blow to the invader "and transferring military activities to his territory." Soviet major general Korkodinov has written of Stalin's orders to press offensives in the face of overwhelming German military superiority: "In the northernmost forests [around Belostok] these attacks actually worsened the situation of our troops . . . waiting for the result of these counterblows . . . delayed the start of the withdrawal of the Belostok groups for several days. And during this time the striking forces of the invader were developing an attack from Suvalki and Brest towards Minsk, deeply enveloping the flanks [of the Soviet counterattackers]." Korkodinov, "Fakti i mysli o nachalom periode velikoi Otechestvennoi voiny," in *Voenno-istoricheskii zhurnal* 10 (1965). There were many other examples of misguided Soviet counterattacks.

10. Harvey, *Diaries*, p. 74.

11. Eden to Sargent, December 17, 1941, PRO, N7483/3/38.

12. Stalin's comment is revealing. The current Soviet explanation of the collapse of the Anglo-Franco-Soviet talks of summer 1939—espoused even by the dissident Soviet historian Roy Medvedev—is that the Western Allies "were playing a dangerous political game: they were still hoping for an agreement with Hitler and were trying to direct German aggression eastward." Medvedev, *Let History Judge* (New York, 1972), p. 441. Judging from Stalin's comment, it would seem that the Soviets were more upset by the Anglo-French refusal to sanction Soviet conquest of the Baltic States, eastern Poland, Finland, and Bessarabia than by fear of Western collusion with the Nazis. For the current Soviet official line, see Institut Marksizma-Leninizma pri TsK KPSS, *Velikaia Otechestvennaia voina Sovetskogo Soiuza 1941–1945: Kratkaia istoriia*, 3d ed., (Moscow, 1984), esp. p. 24.

13. All citations from "War Cabinet: Mr. Eden's Visit to Moscow," January 5, 1942, PRO, WP(42) 8.

14. In this telegram, Eden was fulfilling the promise he made to Stalin before leaving Moscow. He gave the Soviet dictator a note in which he said: "I for my part assure You [*sic*] that I will set forth fully to my government the explanation, which You gave me in relation to the position of Your government, and that I will support the initiative of the organization of detailed negotiations of the three countries [Britain, the USSR, and the U.S.] a soon as possible in the near future when it will be convenient for the participants." The questions to be discussed, Eden wrote, would be "the western borders of the USSR," and the three powers should meet "with the goal to arrive at agreement on these and other questions relating to

the organization of Europe after the war." "Enclosure: Letter of the Minister of Foreign Affairs of Great Britain to the President of the Soviet of People's Commissars of the USSR," December 18, 1941, *SAO*, 1:197–98.

Stalin's persistence had paid off; Eden had singlehandedly decided to advocate reversal of the British government's position on territorial matters. Eden to Churchill, January 5, 1942, PRO, N108/5/38.

15. Churchill to Eden, January 28, 1942, PRO, N108/5/38.
16. Winston S. Churchill, *History of the Second World War* (Boston, 1948–54), 3:695. Many historians have relied on Churchill's published version and have thus missed his deletion. See, for example, Sarah Meiklejohn Terry, *Poland's Place in Europe: General Sikorski and the Origin of the Oder-Neisse Line, 1939–1943* (Princeton, 1983), p. 285.
17. Curtin to Churchill, December 24, 1942, PRO, N171/5/38.
18. Anthony Eden, *The Reckoning* (London, 1965), p. 370.
19. "War Cabinet: Policy Towards Russia; Memorandum by the Secretary of State for Foreign Affairs," January 28, 1942, PRO, WP (42) 48.
20. Michael Howard, *War and the Liberal Conscience* (Oxford, 1978), p. 118.
21. Cadogan, *Diaries*, p. 433.
22. *FRUS 1942*, 3:494.
23. Paul Addison, *The Road to 1945: British Politics and the Second World War* (London, 1975), p. 190.
24. Clipping from the *Northern Daily Mail*, November 27, 1942, Cripps Papers, A6, Nuffield College Library, Oxford.
25. The text of Cripps's radio address of February 8, 1942, is contained in Patricia Strauss, *Cripps: Advocate Extraordinary* (New York, 1942), pp. 357–63.
26. Ibid., p. 290.
27. Clipping from the *Bristol Evening Post*, April 21, 1943, Cripps Papers, A6.
28. Warner memorandum, February 3, 1942, PRO, N712/5/38.
29. War Cabinet Record, February 6, 1942, PRO, WM(42), CAB 65/29.
30. Beaverbrook memorandum, February 7, 1942, PRO, CAB 66/22 [WP (42) 71].
31. Beaverbrook quoted in A. J. P. Taylor, *Beaverbrook* (London, 1972), p. 511.
32. Eden to Halifax, February 10, 1942, PRO, N7981/5/38.
33. John Colville, *The Fringes of Power: 10 Downing Street Diaries, 1939–1955* (New York, 1986), pp. 405–6.
34. Eden to Halifax, February 10, 1942, PRO, N7981/5/38.
35. Halifax to FO, February 19, 1942, PRO, N1024/5/38.
36. Halifax to FO, February 20, 1942, PRO, N1025/5/38.
37. Cadogan, *Diaries*, p. 437.
38. War Cabinet Record, February 25, 1942, PRO, WM(42) 24th Conclusions, CAB 65/29.
39. Eden memorandum and enclosure, February 25, 1942, PRO, N1104/5/38.
40. See Addison, *Road to 1945*, p. 195. Addison cites poll figures showing that the percentage of the British electorate supporting Churchill's premiership never fell below 78 percent.
41. Harvey, *Diaries*, p. 98.
42. See Addison, *Road to 1945*, pp. 190–210.

43. W. Averell Harriman and Elie Abel, *Special Envoy to Churchill and Stalin, 1941–1946* (New York, 1975), p. 127.
44. Eden to Halifax, February 26, 1942, PRO, N1113/5/38.
45. Woodward, *British Foreign Policy*, 2:238.
46. Cadogan comment, March 4, 1942, PRO, N1156/5/38.
47. Eden to Halifax, March 7, 1942, PRO, N1174/5/38.
48. Cadogan, *Diaries*, p. 440.
49. Churchill to Roosevelt, March 7, 1942, PRO N1174/5/38.
50. Churchill, *History*, 4:89.
51. This is, of course, part of Churchill's famous "Moral of the Work" from his six-volume *History*. The full "Moral" is: "In War: Resolution, In Defeat: Defiance, In Victory: Magnanimity, In Peace: Good Will."
52. Churchill, *History*, 4:89.
53. George MacGregor Burns, *Roosevelt: The Soldier of Freedom* (New York, 1970), p. 231.
54. Churchill, *History*, 4:198–99.
55. Halifax to FO, March 8, 1942, PRO, N1279/5/38.
56. Sargent memorandum, March 9, 1941, and Cadogan memorandum, March 10, 1942, ibid.
57. Eden to Halifax, March 10, 1942, ibid.
58. Churchill to Stalin, March 9, 1942, PRO, N1300/5/38.
59. Eden memorandum, March 10, 1942, ibid.
60. *Daily Mail*, March 7, 1942.
61. Halifax to FO, March 11, 1942, PRO, N1439/5/38.
62. Harvey, *Diaries*, p. 109.
63. Halifax to FO, March 13, 1942, PRO, N1364/5/38. The Soviet account of this conversation, which Litvinov sent to Moscow, is very different. According to Litvinov's version, Roosevelt hinted that he could accept an Anglo-Soviet agreement about the Baltic States so long as he was not involved; American opinion, he said, was "not prepared" for such deals. The President twice told Litvinov that he would like to meet Stalin, since they were "both realists" and spoke "the same language [na odnom iazyke]." Litvinov to Molotov, March 12, 1942, *SAmO*, 1:155–57. Either Litvinov misunderstood the President—who spoke vaguely on purpose, for fear that too harsh a rejection of Soviet demands would offend Stalin—or else Roosevelt was not being entirely straightforward about his opposition to the impending Anglo-Soviet Treaty; his opposition may only have been for public consumption. Unlike Sumner Welles and Cordell Hull, who clearly opposed the treaty on grounds of principle, Roosevelt's motives in this matter remain murky. He did, however, later boast to his vice president, Henry A. Wallace, that only his intervention had prevented the British from recognizing the Soviet conquest of the Baltic States. Henry A. Wallace, *The Price of Vision: The Diary of Henry A. Wallace, 1942–1946*, ed. John Morton Blum (Boston, 1973), p. 160.
64. Dew memorandum, March 14, 1941, and Sargent memorandum, March 14, 1942, PRO, N1364/5/38.
65. Harvey, *Diaries*, p. 109.

66. Eden memorandum, March 17, 1942, PRO, N1413/5/38.
67. Eden memorandum, March 23, 1942, PRO, N1526/5/38. Maiskii later told Eden that Roosevelt's objections gave him "the impression of political 'reinsurance' " in case of an attack from his "political opponents." Maiskii did "not attribute any serious significance to it." Maiskii to NKID, March 27, 1942, *SAO*, 1:212.
68. Roosevelt to Churchill, March 18, 1942, in *Churchill and Roosevelt: The Complete Correspondence*, ed. Warren F. Kimball (Princeton, 1984), 1:421.
69. Stalin to Churchill, March 14, 1942, in *Correspondence between the Chairman of the Council of Ministers of the USSR and the Presidents of the USA and the Prime Ministers of Great Britain during the Great Patriotic War of 1941–1945*, ed. A. A. Gromyko (Moscow, 1957), 1:47.
70. Cadogan, *Diaries*, p. 442.
71. Ibid., p. 443.
72. War Cabinet Record, March 25, 1942, PRO, CAB 65/29 WM(42) 37th Conclusions.
73. Eden to Halifax, March 26, 1942, PRO, WP(42) 144.
74. Eden to Halifax, March 27, 1942, PRO, N1670/5/38.
75. Halifax to FO, March 30, 1942, PRO, N1701/5/38. Reference to Joseph E. Davies, *Mission to Moscow* (New York, 1941).
76. Halifax to FO, March 31, 1942, PRO, N1711/5/38.
77. Taylor, *Beaverbrook*, pp. 525–26.
78. Halifax to Eden, April 1, 1942, PRO, N1737/5/38.
79. Addison, *Road to 1945*, p. 195.
80. Cadogan, *Diaries*, p. 347.
81. PRO, WP(42) 144. Molotov was not coming to the West solely to sign the treaty. He also hoped to secure an Anglo-American commitment to open a second front in Europe that summer. Although Soviet documentation does not allow a final judgment about Stalin's motives in sending Molotov to London and Washington, it is reasonable to assume in light of subsequent events that the question of the second front took precedence over territorial matters, at least in the short term. In this case, the impetus for Molotov's journey may have come from two telegrams, one from Roosevelt directly to Stalin, and another that Litvinov sent after meeting with the president. See Roosevelt to Stalin, April 11, 1942, in *Correspondence*, ed. Gromyko, 1:18–19, and Litvinov to Molotov, April 14, 1942, *SAmO*, 1:162–63. In both these messages, the President held out the prospect of a second front in Europe in 1942.
82. War Cabinet Record, April 8, 1942, PRO, WP(42) 144.
83. Halifax to FO, April 11, 1942, PRO, N1921/5/38.
84. Warner memorandum, April 11, 1942, PRO, N1939/5/38.

Chapter 7

1. War Cabinet memorandum, January 28, 1942, "Policy Towards Russia," PRO, WP (42) 48.
2. FO to Halifax, March 10, 1942, PRO, N1279/5/38.

3. War Cabinet memorandum, April 10, 1942, "Anglo-Soviet Treaties," PRO, WP (42) 156.
4. Eden memorandum, April 13, 1942, PRO, N1944/5/38.
5. Eden memorandum, April 16, 1942, PRO, N1993/86/38, and Eden memorandum, April 16, 1942, PRO, N1939/5/38.
6. Anthony Eden, *The Reckoning* (London, 1965), pp. 367–68.
7. FO to Halifax, April 17, 1942, PRO, N2056/5/38.
8. Oliver Harvey, *The War Diaries of Oliver Harvey, 1941–1945*, ed. John Harvey (London, 1978), p. 118.
9. E. Llewellyn Woodward, *British Foreign Policy in the Second World War* (London, 1971), 2:246.
10. Eden memorandum, May 1, 1942, PRO, N2336/5/38.
11. Harvey, *War Diaries*, p. 120.
12. Alexander Cadogan, *The Diaries of Sir Alexander Cadogan, 1938–1945*, ed. David Dilks (New York, 1972), p. 449.
13. Ibid., pp. 449–50.
14. War Cabinet, May 4, 1942, PRO, CAB 65/30.
15. Eden memorandum, May 5, 1942, PRO, N2385/5/38.
16. Harvey, *War Diaries*, p. 121.
17. Earl of Avon, *Reckoning*, p. 379.
18. Cadogan, *Diaries*, p. 450.
19. *FRUS 1942*, 3:552.
20. Eden memorandum, May 7, 1942, PRO, N2422/5/38.
21. Winston S. Churchill, *History of the Second World War* (Boston, 1948–54), 4:337.
22. Harvey, *War Diaries*, p. 124.
23. *FRUS 1942*, 3:556.
24. The first meeting between Molotov and the British on May 21, 1942 is recorded in PRO, N2902/5/38. The Soviet record of the negotiations has many gaps; see *SAO*, 1:221–42.
25. The second meeting, also on May 21st, 1942, is in PRO, N2902/5/38.
26. Cadogan, *Diaries*, p. 453.
27. George F. Kennan, *Memoirs, 1925–1950* (Boston, 1967), p. 215. See also Sarah Meiklejohn Terry, *Poland's Place in Europe: General Sikorski and the Origin of the Oder-Neisse Line, 1939–1943* (Princeton, 1983), pp. 284–98. In this excellent book, Terry focuses on the early years of the war, and her account of Polish concerns about Britain's willingness to accommodate Soviet demands is very useful. She hints, however, that the negotiations leading up to the Anglo-Soviet Treaty of 1942 showed that Britain's leaders were willing to accept the essential justice of the Soviet claim to the Curzon Line. In fact, however, British leaders convinced themselves that if they were to accept the Soviet position regarding the Baltic States then Moscow would compromise on the Polish border question and allow Britain a say in the final delineation of the new line. These were, it is argued here, vain hopes. Terry also points out that the Oder-Neisse Line was first suggested by the Poles themselves, though they did not at first, of course, envision it as compensation for the loss of eastern Polish territory.

28. The third meeting with Molotov, held on May 22, is in PRO, N2903/5/38.
29. The full text of the Treaty, based on Cadogan's draft, is printed in Woodward, *British Foreign Policy*, 2:663–65. The Russian-language version is in *SAO*, 1:237–40.
30. The fourth meeting with Molotov, on May 23, is in PRO, N2904/5/38.
31. Cadogan, *Diaries*, p. 454.
32. The fifth meeting with Molotov, on May 24, is in PRO, N2905/5/38.
33. Cadogan, *Diaries*, p. 454.
34. Harvey, *War Diaries*, p. 128.
35. Cadogan, *Diaries*, p. 454.
36. Harvey, *War Diaries*, p. 138.
37. *FRUS 1942*, 3:560.
38. Harvey, *War Diaries*, p. 128.
39. *FRUS 1942*, 3:560.
40. Eden, *The Reckoning*, p. 382.
41. The sixth meeting with Molotov, on May 25, is in PRO, N2906/5/38.
42. Halifax to Eden, June 2, 1942, PRO, N2861/5/38.
43. Harvey, *War Diaries*, p. 129.
44. War Cabinet, May 26, 1942, PRO, CAB 66/30; and WM (42) 67th Conclusions.
45. Ibid. In fact, Litvinov had informed Moscow of Roosevelt's objections. See Litvinov to NKID, March 12, 1942, *SAmO*, 1:155–57.
46. Halifax to FO, June 2, 1942, PRO, N2861/5/38.
47. Harvey, *War Diaries*, p. 129.
48. Cadogan, *Diaries*, p. 455.
49. Sumner Welles, *Seven Decisions That Shaped History* (New York, 1950), p. 130.

Conclusion

1. George F. Kennan, "The View from Russia," in Thomas T. Hammond, ed., *Witnesses to the Origins of the Cold War* (Seattle Wash., 1982), p. 28.
2. Winant to Secretary of State, June 13, 1942, NA, 741.6111/20; also see 741.6111/24 and 741.6111/38.
3. Loy Henderson memorandum, NA, FW 741.6111/39.
4. Johnson to Secretary of State, June 17, 1942, NA, 741.6111/23.
5. Winant to Secretary of State, June 23, 1941, NA, 741.6111/29 Confidential File.
6. Thurston to Secretary of State, June 20, 1942, NA, 741.6111/28.
7. Thurston to Secretary of State, June 19, 1942, NA, 741.6111/27.
8. John W. Wheeler-Bennet and Anthony Nicholls, *The Semblance of Peace* (New York, 1974), p. 50.
9. There are many sources for this comment, one being *The Concise Oxford Dictionary of Quotations* (Oxford, 1981), p. 245.
10. Lenin quoted in Edward Meade Earle, "Lenin, Trotsky, Stalin: Soviet Concepts of War," in *Makers of Modern Strategy*, ed. Edward Meade Earle (Princeton, 1943), p. 323.
11. Adam Ulam, *Stalin: The Man and His Era* (London, 1974), p. 289.

12. Quoted in Earle, "Soviet Concepts of War," p. 334.
13. "First Meeting with the Soviet Delegation, May 21, 1942," PRO, N2901/5/38.
14. J. V. Stalin, "Order of the People's Commissar of Defense," *Sochineniia* 2(15):46–56.
15. John Erickson, *The Road to Stalingrad* (London, 1975), p. 347.
16. Molotov to Stalin, May 21, 1942, *SAO*, 1:221–23.
17. Litvinov to NKID, March 12, 1942, *SAmO*, 1:155–57.
18. "Press Release Issued by the White House, June 11, 1942," *FRUS 1942*, 3:594.
19. Winston S. Churchill, *History of the Second World War* (Boston, 1948–54), 3:695–96.
20. Quoted in Fitzroy Maclean, *Eastern Approaches* (London, 1949), p. 287.
21. The contention that Stalin was seeking a separate peace with Hitler in the summer of 1943 is convincingly made in Vojtech Mastny, *Russia's Road to the Cold War: Diplomacy, Warfare, and the Politics of Communism, 1941–1945* (New York, 1979), pp. 73–87.
22. J. F. C. Fuller, *The Conduct of War 1789–1961* (London, 1961), p. 41.
23. Cited in Dwight D. Eisenhower, *The Papers of Dwight David Eisenhower*, ed. Alfred D. Chandler, Jr. (Baltimore, 1970), 4:2462.
24. Marshal I. S. Konev, "Strike from the South," in *Stalin and His Generals: Soviet Military Memoirs of World War II*, ed. Seweryn Bialer (1969; reprint, Boulder, Colo., 1984), pp. 516–17.
25. Milovan Djilas, *Rise and Fall* (New York, 1985), p. 155.
26. Quoted in Mastny, *Russia's Road*, p. 222.
27. Sumner Welles, *Seven Decisions That Shaped History* (New York, 1950), p. 125.
28. General Sikorski Historical Instutute, *Documents on Polish-Soviet Relations 1939–1943* (London, 1961), pp. 336–38.
29. Richard C. Hottelet ran a five-part interview with Litvinov, January 21–26, 1951, in the *Washington Post*.
30. Milovan Djilas, *Conversations with Stalin* (New York, 1962), p. 114.
31. See Eden's comment cited in the Introduction, n. 23.
32. Charles De Gaulle, *The Complete War Memoirs of Charles De Gaulle* trans. Jonathan Griffin (1959; reprint, New York, 1967), p. 750.

BIBLIOGRAPHY

Documents

Eisenhower, Dwight D. *The Papers of Dwight David Eisenhower*. Edited by Alfred D. Chandler. Vol. 4., Baltimore, 1970.

U.S. Department of State. *Documents on German Foreign Policy, 1918–1945*. Series D. Washington, D.C., 1957.

Foreign Relations of the United States. Washington, D.C., 1953–.

General Sikorski Historical Institute. *Documents on Polish-Soviet Relations, 1939–1945*. Vol. 1, *1939–1943*. London, 1961.

Kimball, Warren F., ed. *Churchill and Roosevelt: The Complete Correspondence*. 3 vol. Princeton, 1984.

Loewenheim, F. L., *et al.*, ed. *Roosevelt and Churchill: Their Secret Wartime Correspondence*. New York; 1975.

Nicholas, H. G., ed. *Washington Despatches, 1941–1945: Weekly Political Reports from the British Embassy*. London, 1981.

Ross, Graham. *The Foreign Office and the Kremlin*. Cambridge, 1984.

Memoirs and Diaries

Akhmedov, Ismail. *In and Out of Stalin's GRU: A Tatar's Escape from Red Army Intelligence*. Frederick, Md.

Barman, T. *Diplomatic Correspondent*. London, 1968.

Berezhkov, Valentin. *Gody diplomaticheskoi sluzhby*. London, 1972.

————. *History in the Making: Memoirs of World War II Diplomacy*. Translated by Dudley Hagen and Barry Jones. Moscow, 1983.

Bilainkin, G. *Diary of a Political Correspondent*. London, 1942.

————. *Maisky: Ten Years' Ambassador*. London, 1944.

Birse, A. H. *Memoirs of an Interpreter*. London, 1967.

Bohlen, Charles. *Witness to History, 1929–1963*. New York, 1973.

Bourke-White, Margaret. *Shooting the Russian War*. New York, 1942.

Butler, Lord. *The Art of the Possible*. London, 1971.

Cadogan, Alexander. *The Diaries of Sir Alexander Cadogan, 1938–45*. Edited by David Dilks. New York, 1972.

Cassidy, H. C. *Moscow Dateline, 1941–1943*. London, 1943.

Channon, Henry. *Chips: The Diaries of Sir Henry Channon*. Edited by Robert Rhodes James. London, 1967.

Churchill, Winston S. *History of the Second World War*. 6 vols. Boston, 1948–54.

Citrine, Walter. *In Russia Now*. London, 1942.

————. *Men at Work.* London, 1964.

————. *Two Careers.* London, 1967.

Colville, John. *The Fringes of Power: 10 Downing Street Diaries, 1939–1955.* New York, 1986.

Cripps, F. H. *Life's a Gamble.* London, 1957.

Crozier, W. P. *Off the Record: Political Interviews, 1932–44.* Edited by A. J. P. Taylor. London, 1973.

Dalton, Hugh. *The Fateful Years: Memoirs, 1931–1945.* 2 vols. London, 1953–57.

De Gaulle, Charles. *The Complete War Memoirs of Charles De Gaulle.* Translated by Jonathan Griffin. New York, 1967.

Duranty, Walter. *The Kremlin and the People.* New York, 1942.

Eden, Anthony. *The Reckoning.* London, 1965.

Ehrenburg, Ilia. *Eve of the War, 1933–1941.* London, 1963.

Elvin, H. *A Cockney in Moscow.* London, 1958.

Fischer, Louis. *Men and Politics: An Autobiography.* London, 1941.

Gafencu, Grigore. *Prelude to the Russian Campaign.* London, 1945.

Gnedin, Evgenii. *Iz istorii otnoshenii mezhdu SSSR i fashistkoi Germaniei: Dokumenty i sovremennye kommentarii.* New York, 1977.

Grigorenko, Petro G. *Memoirs.* Translated by Thomas P. Whitney. New York, 1982.

Haldane, C. *Russian Newsreel: An Eye-Witness Account of the Soviet Union at War.* London, 1942.

Halifax, Earl of. *Fulness of Day.* London, 1957.

Hammond, Thomas T., ed. *Witnesses to the Origins of the Cold War.* Seattle, Wash., 1982

Harriman, W. Averell, and Elie Abel. *Special Envoy to Churchill and Stalin, 1941–1946.* New York, 1975.

Harvey, Oliver. *The Diplomatic Diaries of Oliver Harvey 1937–1940.* Edited by John Harvey. London, 1970.

————. *The War Diaries of Oliver Harvey, 1941–1945.* Edited by John Harvey. London, 1978.

Hilger, Gustav, and A. G. Meyer. *The Incompatible Allies: A Memoir-History of German-Soviet Relations, 1918–1941.* New York, 1953.

Hull, Cordell. *The Memoirs of Cordell Hull.* 2 vols. New York, 1948.

Ickes, Harold L. *The Secret Diary of Harold L. Ickes.* 3 vols. New York, 1953–54.

Ismay, Lord. *The Memoirs of General the Lord Ismay.* London, 1960.

Jordan, P. *Russian Glory.* London, 1942.

Kharlamov, N. *Difficult Mission: War Memoirs.* Translated by Nadezhda Burova. Moscow, 1983.

Kot, S. *Conversations in the Kremlin and Dispatches from Russia.* London, 1963.

Krivitsky, Walter G. *In Stalin's Secret Service: An Exposé of Russia's Secret Policies by the Former Chief of the Soviet Intelligence in Western Europe.* New York, 1939.

Macmillan, Harold. *The Blast of War, 1939–1945.* London, 1967.

Maisky, Ivan M. *Memoirs of a Soviet Ambassador: The War, 1939–1943.* Translated by Andrew Rothstein. New York, 1967.

Nicolson, Harold. *Diaries and Letters, 1939–1945.* London, 1967.

Pritt, David Noel. *The Autobiography of D. N. Pritt.* 2 vols. London, 1965–66.

Rendel, G. W. *The Sword and the Olive: Recollections of Diplomacy and the Foreign Service*. London, 1957.

Shtemenko, S. M. *The Soviet General Staff at War, 1941–1945*. Translated by Robert Daglish. Moscow, 1981.

Standley, W. H., and A. A. Ageton. *Admiral Ambassador to Russia*. Chicago, 1955.

Warlimont, W. *Inside Hitler's Headquarters, 1939–45*. London, 1964.

Werth, Alexander. *Moscow '41*. London, 1942.

——. *Russia at War*. New York, 1964.

Winant, John G. *A Letter from Grosvenor Square: An Account of a Stewardship*. London, 1947.

Zhukov, G. K. *Reminiscences and Reflections*. Moscow, 1985.

Secondary Works

Addison, Paul. *The Road to 1945: British Politics and the Second World War*. London, 1975.

Anfilov, V. A. *Bessmertnyi podvig*. Moscow, 1971.

——. *Nachalo velikoi Otechestvennoi voiny*. Moscow, 1962.

Aster, Sidney. *Anthony Eden*. London, 1976.

——. "Ivan Maisky and Parliamentary Anti-Appeasement." In *Lloyd George*, edited by A. J. P. Taylor. London, 1971.

Barker, Elisabeth. *British Policy in South-East Europe in the Second World War*. London, 1976.

——. *Churchill and Eden at War*. London, 1978.

Bartlett, C. J. "Inter-Allied Relations in the Second World War." *History* 63 (1950).

——. "A Question of Diplomacy: British Military Mission, 1941–1945." *Journal of the Royal United Services Institute for Defence Studies* 118 (1973).

——. "Great Britain and the Rights of Neutral Countries: The case of Iran, 1941." *Journal of Contemporary History* 16 (1981).

Beaumont, J. *Comrades in Arms: British Aid to Russia, 1941–1945*. London, 1980.

Beitzell, R. *The Uneasy Alliance: America, Britain, and Russia, 1941–1943*. New York, 1972.

Beloff, Max. *The Foreign Policy of Soviet Russia, 1929–1941*. 2 vols. Oxford: 1947–49.

Bialer, Seweryn, ed. *Stalin and His Generals: Soviet Military Memoirs of World War II*. New York, 1969. Reprint. Boulder, Colo., 1984.

Birkenhead, Earl of. *Halifax: The Life of Lord Halifax*. London, 1965.

Burridge, T. D. *British Labour and Hitler's War*. London, 1976.

Butler, E. *Mason-Mac: The Life of Lieutenant-General Sir Noel Mason-MacFarlane*. London, 1972.

Butler, J. R. M. *Grand Strategy: September 1939–June 1941*. London, 1957.

Carlton, David. *Anthony Eden: A Biography*. London, 1981.

Cecil, R. *Hitler's Decision to Invade Russia, 1941*. London, 1975.

Colvin, I. *Chamberlain's Cabinet*. London, 1971.

Cooke, Colin. *The Life of Richard Stafford Cripps*. London, 1957.

Creveld, Martin van. *Hitler's Strategy, 1940–41: The Balkan Clue*. Cambridge, 1973.

Dallin, David J. *Soviet Russia's Foreign Policy, 1939–1942*. New Haven, 1942.

Dawson, R. H. *The Decision to Aid Russia, 1941: Foreign Policy and Domestic Politics*. Chapel Hill, N.C., 1959.

Deakin, F. W. and G. R. Storry. *The Case of Richard Sorge*. New York, 1966.

Degras, Jane, ed. *Soviet Documents on Foreign Policy*. Volumes 2 and 3. Oxford: 1952, 1953.

Douglas, R. *The Advent of War, 1939–1940*. London, 1979.

Douglas-Hamilton, J. *Motive for a Mission: The Story behind Hess's Flight to Britain*. New York, 1941.

Erickson, John. *The Road to Stalingrad*. London, 1975.

Estorick, Erik. *Stafford Cripps: Master Statesman*. London, 1949.

Feis, Herbert. *Churchill, Roosevelt, Stalin: The War They Waged and the Peace They Sought*. Princeton, 1957.

Foot, Michael. *Aneurin Bevan*. 2 vols. London, 1962–73.

Gilbert, Martin. *Winston S. Churchill*. Vol. 5, *1922–1939* (London, 1976). Vol. 6, *Finest Hour, 1939–1941* (London, 1983). Vol. 7, *Road to Victory, 1941–1945* (London, 1986).

Gorodetsky, Gabriel. *Stafford Cripps' Mission to Moscow, 1940–42*. Cambridge, 1984.

Gus, M. " 'Taina' missiia Gessa." *Voenno-istoricheskii zhurnal* 9 (1960).

Gwyer, J. M. A. and J. R. M. Butler. *Grand Strategy: June 1941–August 1942*. London, 1964.

Hanak, H. "Sir Stafford Cripps as Ambassador in Moscow, May 1940 to June 1941." *English Historical Review* 370 (1979).

———. "Sir Stafford Cripps as Ambassador in Moscow, June 1941–January 1942." *English Historical Review* 383 (1982).

Harris, K. *Attlee*. London, 1982.

Herring, G. C. *Aid to Russia, 1940–1946: Strategy, Diplomacy, the Origins of the Cold War*. New York, 1973.

Higgins, T. *Hitler and Russia: The Third Reich in a Two-Front War, 1937–1943*. New York, 1966.

Hinsley, F. H. *British Intelligence in the Second World War*. 2 vols. London, 1979–81.

Hutton, J. B. *Hess: The Man and His Mission*. New York, 1970.

Institut Marksizma-Leninizma pri TsK KPSS. *Velikaia Otechestvennaia voina Sovetskogo Soiuza 1941–1945: Kratkaia istoriia*. 3d ed. Moscow, 1984.

Istoriia vtoroi mirovoi voiny, 1939–1945. 12 vols. Moscow, 1974–79.

Ivashin, I. F. *Nachalo vtoroi mirovoi voiny i vneshniaia politika SSSR*. Moscow, 1951.

James, Robert Rhodes. *Victor Cazalet: A Portrait*. London, 1976.

Jelavich, Barbara. *St. Petersburg and Moscow: Tsarist and Soviet Foreign Policy, 1814–1974*. Bloomington, Ind., 1974.

Jones, W. D. *The Russian Complex: The British Labour Party and the Soviet Union*. Manchester, 1977.

King, F. P. *The New Internationalism: Allied Policy and the European Peace, 1939–1945*. Newton Abbot, 1973.

Korkodinov, P. "Fakty i mysli o nachalom periode velikoi Otechestvennoi voiny," *Voenno-istoricheskii zhurnal* 10 (1965).

Lammers, D. "Fascism, Communism and the Foreign Office, 1937–39." *Journal of Contemporary History* 6 (1971).

Langer, J. D. "The Harriman-Beaverbrook Mission and the Debate over Unconditional Aid for the Soviet Union, 1941." In *The Second World War*, edited by Walter Laqueur. London, 1982.

Lash, Joseph P. *Roosevelt and Churchill, 1939–1941: The Partnership That Saved the World*. New York, 1976.

Leach, Barry. *German Strategy against Russia, 1939–1941*. Oxford, 1973.

Leasor, T. J. *War at the Top*. London, 1961.

———. *Rudolf Hess: The Uninvited Envoy*. London, 1962.

Lewin, R. *Ultra Goes to War: The Secret Story*. London, 1961.

Manne, R. "The Foreign Office and the Failure of Anglo-Soviet Rapprochement." *Journal of Contemporary History* 16 (1981).

Manville, Roger, and Heinrich Fraenkel. *Hess: A Biography*. London, 1971.

Martell, Leon. *Lend-Lease, Loans, and the Coming of the Cold War: A Study in the Implementation of Foreign Policy*. Boulder, Colo., 1979.

Mastny, Vojtech. *Russia's Road to the Cold War: Diplomacy, Warfare, and the Politics of Communism, 1941–1945*. New York, 1979.

May, Ernest R., ed. *Knowing One's Enemies: Intelligence Assessment before the Two World Wars*. Princeton, 1984.

Moore, R. J. *Churchill, Cripps and India, 1939–1945*. Oxford, 1979.

Nekrich, Aleksandr. "Arrest and Trial of I. M. Maisky." *Survey* 22 (1978).

———. "Biografiia akademiki I. Maiskogo." *Voprosy istorii* 2 (1964).

———. *June 22, 1941*. New York, 1968.

———. "Politika Anglii v period 'strannoi voiny.' " *Novaia i noveshaia istoriia* 3 (1960).

———. "Politika angliiskogo pravitel'stva na severo-zapade Evropy (sentiabr' 1939 g.–aprel' 1940 g.)." *Novaia i noveishaia istoriia* 5 (1962).

———. *Vneshniaia politika Anglii, 1939–1941 gg*. Moscow, 1963.

Niedhardt, G. *Grossbritanien und die Sowjetunion, 1939–1943*. Munich, 1972.

Northedge, F. S., and Audrey Wells. *Britain and Soviet Communism: The Impact of a Revolution*. London, 1982.

Petrov, V., ed. *"June 22, 1941": Soviet Historians and the German Invasion*. Chapel Hill, N.C., 1968.

Pietrow, Bianka. *Stalinismus, Sicherheit, Offensive: Das "Dritte Reich" in der Konzeption der sowjetischen Aussenpolitik, 1933–1941*. Melsungen: 1983.

Pimlott, Ben. *Labour and the Left in the 1930s*. Cambridge, 1977.

Pope, Arthur Upham. *Maxim Litvinoff*. New York, 1943.

Richardson, C. O. "French Plans for Allied Attacks on the Caucasus Oil Fields, January–April 1940." *French Historical Studies* 8 (1973).

Roberts, Henry L. "Maxim Litvinov." In *The Diplomats, 1919–1939*, edited by Gordon Craig and Felix Gilbert. Vol. 2, *The Thirties*. New York: 1953.

Ross, Graham. "Allied Diplomacy in the Second World War." *British Journal of International Studies* 1 (1975).

———. "Foreign Office Attitudes to the Soviet Union 1941–1945." *Journal of Contemporary History* 16 (1981).

———. "Operation Bracelet: Churchill in Moscow, 1942." In *Retreat from Power*, edited by David Dilks. 2 vols. London, 1981.

Rothwell, Victor. *Britain and the Cold War, 1941–1947*. London, 1982.

Samsonov, A. M. "Moskva v oktiabre 1941 goda." *Istoriia SSSR* 5 (1981).

———. *Vtoraia mirovaia voina, 1939–1945: Ocherk vazhneishikh sobytii* Moscow, 1985.

Seaton, Albert. *The Russo-German War, 1941–45*. New York, 1970.

Sella, A. " 'Barbarossa': Surprise Attack and Communication." *Journal of Contemporary History* 13 (1978).

Sherwood, R. E. *Roosevelt and Hopkins: An Intimate History*. New York, 1950.

Spring, D. W. "The Soviet Decision for War against Finland, 30 November 1939." *Soviet Studies* 2 (1986).

Stafford, D. A. "SOE and British Involvement in the Belgrade Coup d'Etat of March 1941." *Slavic Review* 3 (1977).

Strauss, Patricia. *Cripps—Advocate and Rebel*. London, 1943.

Taylor, A. J. P. *Beaverbrook*. London, 1972.

———. *English History 1914–1945*. London, 1979.

Terry, Sarah Meiklejohn. *Poland's Place in Europe: General Sikorski and the Origin of the Oder-Neisse Line, 1939–1943*. Princeton, 1983.

Trukhanovskii, V. G. *Antoni Iden*. Moscow, 1974.

———. *Uinston Cherchil'*. Moscow, 1968.

———. *Vneshniaia politika Anglii v period vtoroi mirovoi voiny 1939–1945*. Moscow, 1965.

Tucker, Robert C. "The Emergence of Stalin's Foreign Policy." *Slavic Review* 4 (1977).

Volkov, F. D. "Neudavshiisia pryzhok Rudol'f Gessa." *Novaia i noveishaia istoriia* 6 (1968).

———. *SSSR-Angliia 1929–1945 gg.: Anglo-Sovetskie otnosheniia nakanune i v period vtoroi mirovoi voiny*. Moscow, 1964.

Weber, Frank G. *The Evasive Neutral: Germany, Britain, and the Quest for a Turkish Alliance in the Second World War*. Columbia, Mo., 1979.

Weinberg, Gerhard L. *The Foreign Policy of Hitler's Germany: Diplomatic Revolution in Europe, 1933–36*. 2 vols. Chicago, 1970–80.

———. *Germany and the Soviet Union, 1939–1941*. Leiden, 1972.

Werth, Alexander. *Russia at War, 1941–1945*. New York, 1964.

Whaley, Barton. *Codeword Barbarossa*. Cambridge, Mass., 1973.

Wilson, T. A. *The First Summit: Roosevelt and Churchill at Placentia Bay, 1941*. Boston, 1969.

Winterbotham, F. W. *The Ultra Secret*. London, 1974.

Woodward, E. Llewellyn. *British Foreign Policy in the Second World War*. Vols. 1 and 2. London, 1970–71.

Zhilin, P. A. *Kak fashistkoi Germaniia gotovila napadenie na Sovetskii Soiuz*. Moscow, 1966.

Zhilin, P. A., et al. *Kritika osnovnykh kontseptsii burzhuaznoi istoriografii vtoroi mirovoi voiny*. Moscow, 1983.

INDEX

Afghanistan, 17, 18, 24
Aga Khan, 91
Albania, 28
Albert Canal, 64
Alexander, A. V., 86, 154
Allies: negotiations with Soviet Union
  (1939), 4, 28, 79, 146; aid to Soviet
  Union, 152, 154, 155, 158, 161, 162,
  163, 165, 166, 167, 168, 184, 211,
  214. *See also* Grand Alliance
Alliluyeva, Svetlana, 70
Anfilov, V. A., 125
Anglo-Soviet Agreement (July 1941),
  149, 150, 173, 193, 244
Anglo-Soviet Public Relations Commit-
  tee, 204
Anglo-Soviet Treaty (May 1942): nego-
  tiations for, 1, 225, 230, 236–51,
  253, 254, 255, 259
Anglo-Soviet ultimatum to Iran (1941),
  156
Archangel, 158, 161, 172
Ardennes, 59
Asia, 38, 88, 89
Atlantic Charter, 173, 189, 222, 255;
  drafting of, 153; Soviet reaction to,
  155, 162, 178, 191, 199; conflicts
  with Soviet aims, 194–95, 196, 199,
  206, 208, 223, 238; Churchill decides
  to override, 211–12
Atlantic First strategy, 213
Attlee, Clement, 35, 50, 235, 237; op-
  poses Soviet demands, 205, 212
Australia, 149, 197
Austria, 186, 262
Axis, 12, 28, 88, 92, 103, 105, 123, 202

Baku, 21, 88, 100; pipeline, 17; British

consider attack on, 17, 19, 25, 26, 27,
  28, 29, 37
Balkans, 1, 37, 42, 60, 68, 69, 71, 87,
  94, 103, 112, 116, 119, 120, 128,
  137, 158, 200, 227, 233, 235, 241
Baltic Sea, 198, 216
Baltic States, 1, 2, 6, 8, 27, 45, 61, 63,
  66, 74, 77, 109, 110, 111, 190, 194,
  195, 206, 207, 211, 225, 229, 234,
  235, 237, 240, 241, 244, 252, 260,
  265, 268, 269; Soviet occupation of,
  64, 79, 186, 208, 262; assets of, 77,
  78, 80, 82, 89, 100, 105, 108, 110;
  Anglo-Soviet dispute over, 83, 84, 85,
  86, 87, 92, 113, 114, 115, 117, 127,
  129, 148, 189, 191, 193, 199, 215,
  216, 217, 222, 227, 232; Britain accepts Soviet sovereignty over, 220,
  230, 247, 259, 266, 267, 268; bogus
  plebiscites in, 223, 232
"Barbarossa," 98–99, 121
Basra, 86; railway, 87, 91, 94, 95, 154
Batum, 25, 100; pipeline, 17
Beaverbrook, Lord, 7, 151, 154, 172,
  173, 181, 184, 185, 204, 214, 264;
  mission to Moscow, 156–57, 160–62,
  169; favors Soviet demands, 206; re-
  signs, 209, 210; in Washington, 219,
  221–22
Belgium, 186, 232, 243
Belgrade, 95
Belorussia, 2, 79, 178, 258
Berlin, 64, 98, 100, 139
Bessarabia, 2, 8, 42, 61, 99, 223; Soviet
  claim to, 1, 28, 66, 67, 68, 77, 78,
  178, 252, 258; Soviets seize, 6, 83;
  British attitude toward Soviet claim to,
  88, 177, 195, 234, 247